THE FOOD ADVENTURERS

THE FOOD ADVENTURERS

HOW AROUND-THE-WORLD TRAVEL CHANGED THE WAY WE EAT

DANIEL E. BENDER

REAKTION BOOKS

For Jo and Piya

Published by
Reaktion Books Ltd
Unit 32, Waterside
44–48 Wharf Road
London N1 7UX, UK
www.reaktionbooks.co.uk

First published 2023
Copyright © Daniel E. Bender 2023

Printed and bound in Great Britain by TJ Books Ltd, Padstow, Cornwall

A catalogue record for this book is available from the British Library

ISBN 978 1 78914 757 5

CONTENTS

Introduction: Eating Apart

It's November 2021. I'm home in Toronto, two years into the COVID-19 pandemic, and I'm planning a trip around the world.

In 2020, at the height of the pandemic, global travel plummeted by one-third, from 1.5 billion tourists a year to around 400 million. The downturn prompted discussion about the pros and cons of staying put: the decline in greenhouse gas emissions from cars, aeroplanes and cruise ships seemed like good news for the environment, but with an estimated one in ten jobs around the world being connected to travel and tourism, economies were in trouble.[1] Tourism's boosters suggested that the losses were more than financial: food tourism, the United Nations World Tourism Organization had already declared, preserves and supports 'local traditions and diversity'.[2]

However, travellers have already begun to pack their bags again. Thanks in part to what we've come to call 'vaccine passports', an estimated 2 billion tourists are soon expected to travel annually, and I'm charting my itinerary for an eating trip around the world.[3] Even the flight planner for Star Alliance, an agglomeration of airlines that together span the globe, offers an around-the-world ticket specially designed for foodies.[4] 'Travel the world to appreciate its cultural diversity and savour its many flavours,' Star Alliance advertises. Try kebabs in Istanbul or galbi in Seoul – or tweak the itinerary 'to seek out restaurants and food stalls where locals eat'.

As I plan my journey, I decide to follow the route of the *Franconia*, a 'super Cruise Ship' launched by the massive steamship line Cunard in 1922. Between the world wars, this all-first-class ship hosted the 'supreme travel-adventure', an annual around-the-world cruise organized by the travel agency Thomas Cook. The *Franconia*, like all around-the-world cruises during the golden age of steam, skipped Europe's capitals and instead hurried across the Mediterranean to Egypt and through the Suez Canal to European colonies in Asia. Cruises sailed to the British colony in South Asia – today's India, Pakistan, Bangladesh and Sri Lanka. Then they moved on to Singapore, the British bastion at the crossroads of trade routes from South, Southeast and East Asia. Ships to the French colony in Indochina, today's Vietnam, Cambodia and Laos, also called here. So did British ships en route to Australia and New Zealand and Dutch ships sailing to today's Indonesia. In the 1920s Jakarta was called Batavia, the biggest city in Java and the capital of the Dutch East Indies. From Java, some cruises continued to British dominions in Australia and New Zealand with a detour to the French colony at Tahiti – the other island that European travellers had long understood as an earthly paradise. Other ships, like the *Franconia*, sailed to the American colony in the Philippines. The cruise ship routes met again at British Hong Kong before continuing on to China, Japan and Hawai'i.

I open a handsome booklet advertising the *Franconia*'s 1929 cruise. I log onto the around-the-world ticket planner for Star Alliance.[5] I can't follow the ship perfectly: I'm only permitted sixteen stops, and the geopolitical picture has changed. Damascus, an optional excursion for *Franconia* passengers, is now a war zone, and Star Alliance won't permit stops in communist Cuba, once a tourist mecca. But I can do my best, going from New York to Cairo, and onwards to Mumbai, Delhi, Singapore, Shanghai, Tokyo and Honolulu.

I count the hours in the air, and I'm dismayed. I'm interested in the destinations, not the journey itself. During the Cold War, airlines such as Pan American World Airways (Pan Am), which introduced its signature around-the-world flight in 1947, promised luxury service on the most glamorous aeroplane flight possible. No one expects great food and flowing drinks on the plane anymore and, as I click 'economy' on the reservation screen, I resign myself to cramped seats, with soft drinks served in flimsy plastic glasses.

Passengers on the *Franconia* had a very different experience. According to the Thomas Cook booklet, they could enjoy a swimming pool, squash courts and a 'quaint' English smoking room. The 'Punkah Louvre' system of fans would keep their staterooms cool, even during tropical heat. And two dining saloons would feed them 'with the distinction characteristic of Cunard Service'.[6] They could choose among 10,000 bottles of wine and champagne packed in the hold. On this 'most marvellous of all human experiences', Thomas Cook encouraged tourists to luxuriate in the sights and smells they encountered, such as the spices and fruits in Ceylon, Java and Hawai'i, but to remain vigilant. The on-board doctor condensed into pithy warnings the findings from the new field of tropical medicine: don't

The RMS *Franconia's* brochure in 1929 advertised the curious sight of the Egyptian water carrier, but warned passengers against drinking anything but bottled, filtered water.

drink the water; avoid local foods. Stick with the reliable fare on board. Tourists should snap pictures or buy postcards of the curious sight of the water carriers but avoid their water. In its booklet, Thomas Cook even included a photo of an Egyptian water carrier.

When it sailed from London, the *Franconia* carried thousands of bottles of effervescent drinking water and, at sea, somewhere between Egypt and Tokyo, the ship's passengers dined on 'Caviar de Beluga', baked Virginia ham, hominy fritters and 'Glace Francaise [*sic*]'. Still, the booklet promised, the *Franconia's* passengers were adventurers. 'To tour the world, to encircle the globe is one of the most cherished ambitions,' and those who fulfil it, Thomas Cook promised, were the true descendants of Magellan.

Around-the-world holidays have long evoked the age of exploration, yet their changing nature throws into relief how much tourism, over the last 150 years, has become a form of mass culture. In the 1840s, when this book begins, circumnavigation meant an intrepid series of voyages on sailing ship, but by the 1970s around-the-world holidays on cruise ships or jet planes had become accessible to many. Along the way, a new cuisine emerged: tourist food.

Travellers once would have had to rely on whatever locals ate. As the journey became faster and easier and the hotels more lavish and available, tourists kept to continental menus and regarded local food as a measure of difference. To tourists like those on the *Franconia*, local eats seemed strange, maybe disgusting, and likely contaminated with germs. Food became an adventure and, by the time Pan Am planes replaced the *Franconia* as the signature around-the-world tour, tourists showed a renewed, if tentative, desire to sample a few local specialities. Hotels and a handful of restaurants catering to tourists began offering the most approachable, least frightening examples. However, the under-seasoned dishes ultimately tasted more familiar to tourists than to the locals who actually did the cooking and the serving. Today, many still follow advice like Thomas Cook's. Wary of local restaurants, street food and drinking water, they stick with what they know. A few search for adventurous culinary experiences, eating like and with the locals. They hope, perhaps, to eat their way to intercultural understanding.

By 1959, when Pan Am began flying jets around the world, the ticket cost $1,356.60, or $12,894.18 in today's money. In 1967, when Pan Am celebrated its 10,000th flight around the world, it took just 39 hours, 55 minutes of flying time in a Boeing 707 jet.[7]

My 2021 itinerary – were I able to follow it – would cost $7,107. When I press the Star Alliance 'itinerary' button, I receive an error message: COVID-19 quarantine rules mean that I can't follow the *Franconia*'s route from Singapore to Jakarta. I cannot, after all, travel around the world. But at least, as a historian, I can trace the routes of those who did.

This book tells the story of food adventure around the world through six travellers, two fruits, two hotel chains, one meal and a glass of water. Ida Pfeiffer, our first traveller, was an obscure Austrian middle-class widow who circled the globe from 1846 to 1848, a time when few undertook such journeys for pleasure. Her published account transformed her into an international celebrity, as readers devoured her tales of uncomfortable sailing ships and, on dry land, bandits who prowled the roads. When she arrived at her destinations, there weren't hotels with restaurants that guaranteed sanitary European foods, so she ate what her hosts, Europeans or locals, offered. She used her meals everywhere from Brazil to Sumatra not only to prove her bravery as an explorer but to measure the racial status of those she encountered. The more exotic, crude and repulsive the food to her palate, the more savage the cooks, she decided.

Just two decades later, when the French noble the Comte de Beauvoir travelled around the world by both sail and steam, he was often surprised at the good quality of the hotels and clubs where he lodged, relaxed and dined. He found European foods in most places and only occasionally sampled what the locals ate, but not because he worried about sanitary conditions. He travelled in an era of imperial expansion, and his culinary decisions were bound up with his perceptions of what separated the colonized from the colonizers: Europeans and their meals, he wrote, smelled refined, but Indigenous Australians and their hunted game smelled savage. The Chinese and their meals smelled differently still. Through his revulsion, Beauvoir expressed his fear that the Chinese might overwhelm European colonies. The racism that underpinned the European imperial zeal had its own taste and smell.

As Karl Marx declared in the late 1850s, society was witnessing the 'annihilation of space by time'. Marx's primary concern was the expansion of

R.M.S. "FRANCONIA."　　　SUNDAY, SEPTEMBER 2, 1934

Menu

Caviar de Beluga　　　　　　Cantaloupe glace
Hors d'Œuvre—varie

Tortue Claire aux Xeres　　　　Creme d'Asperges
Cold Consomme

Boiled Salmon—Cucumber—Sauce Hollandaise
Fried Fillets of Whiting—Lemon

Noisette of Mutton—Nicoise
Mousse de Volaille en Aspic
Rissoles de Foie Gras—Perigourdine

Prime Sirloin & Ribs of Beef—Horseradish Cream
Baked Virginia Ham—Succotash
Roast Long Island Duckling—Savoury—Apple Sauce
Vegetable Marrow—Cream Sauce　　　　French Beans
Creamed Spinach　　　　　　　　Hominy Fritters
Boiled, Roast, Mashed & Brioche Potatoes

Sorbet a l'Orange

Roast Guinea Chicken—Game Chips—Bread Sauce
Salads—Lettuce & Tomatoes　　Waldorf　　Beatrice

FROM THE GRILL :
Tournedos—Choron

Plum Pudding—Hard & Brandy Sauce　　Gelee au Vin
Apricot Conde　　　　　　　　Loganberry Coup
Patisserie　　　　　　　　　　Glace Francaise

Croute Diana

Dessert　　　　　　Coffee

Passengers on Special Diet are especially invited to make
known their requirements to the Head Waiter

Menu on the
RMS *Franconia*,
2 September 1934.

markets to 'conquer the whole earth'. Ever faster ships, the icons of modernity, linked far-flung colonies to European metropoles. Marx was critical; tourism's boosters, like imperialists, were enthusiastic. At around the same time in London, magazines described with excitement the fast journeys between 'England and her dominions in India': this was 'the modern annihilation of space'. About a half century later, in 1907, as steamships raced across the oceans, the magazines again marvelled: 'every day brings some new story of successful achievement in the annihilation of space.'[8]

As Thomas Cook put it, 'The tourist sighs for more worlds to conquer.' Cook had begun his business with a short railway excursion from his English hometown, but in 1872, he guided his first packaged tour around the world. His travel agency expanded globally with the British Empire. By the 1890s, for £355, Thomas Cook featured annual around-the-world tours with first-class travel and lodging, European foods and local servants. Beer, wine and spirits cost extra.[9] Soon, a variety of travel agencies on both sides of the Atlantic competed to organize tours around the world.[10]

For most tourists in the late nineteenth century, the cost remained prohibitive, but for those with time to spare and money to spend, 'a tour around the world is now a matter of easy accomplishment,' declared *Travel*, a monthly American magazine. 'On the great round-the-world highway we find cosmopolitan hotels,' promised the H. W. Dunning travel agency.[11]

The annihilation of space by time represented the notable feat of the modern age of empire. Jules Verne's sensational novel *Around the World in Eighty Days*, written just a year after Thomas Cook's first guided around-the-world tour, offered adventure through speed, not exploration. In 1889 the real-life journalist Nellie Bly, with backing from the mass-circulation *New York World*, promised to outpace Jules Verne's fictional hero Phileas Fogg. Beginning her journey with a symbolic pilgrimage to visit Verne at his home in France, Bly traced the routes of imperial steamship lines and followed the standard itinerary of around-the-world tourists, including nights at grand colonial hotels. Upon her triumphal return home to New York in just 72 days, she boasted of dining on 'India curry, on Chinese chow and Japanese eel and rice'.[12] In fact, the curry she sampled at the Grand Oriental hotel in Colombo disagreed with her digestion. Its spices 'threatened to give me palpitations of the heart', she admitted. The next morning, a local Sinhalese servant brought her coffee and toast in bed.[13]

More ordinary passengers than Bly also published accounts of their holidays. Around-the-world travelogues became popular literature, an opportunity for the less well-off to travel virtually. Other travellers kept diaries or saved their letters. I immersed myself in dozens of these accounts, both public and private, while researching this book. Soon, I could predict tourists' itineraries, their activities and their meals. I knew that, in Port Suez and Aden, they would toss coins from ships to watch local men and boys dive to retrieve them. In Malaya, they would sniff durian fruits. In Java, they tasted mangosteens in local markets, and dined on rijsttafel in Batavia's grand hotels.

Women and men both travelled and wrote travel accounts, yet they described different sights, tastes, sounds and smells while abroad. When men published their travelogues, they often assumed the role of tour guide, explaining the sites with potted histories. Women, typically on holiday from domestic responsibilities, proved more attentive to taste and smell, and were likelier than men to record the foods they encountered – including those they sampled and those they avoided. Women were more curious, as well, about the private spheres of life in the colonies and sympathetic to female colonial residents, who ran segregated households dependent on the labour and knowledge of local servants and cooks. Their sympathy rarely extended to the local servants and cooks, however.

By the dawn of the new century, as tourism became easier and more luxurious, more tourists worried about the perils that seemed to flow directly from what locals consumed and how they lived. In the early nineteenth century, there were few hotels catering to Euro-American travels in Asia, Africa or South America, so these travellers had to eat locally, and they came to describe their encounters with local foods as the stuff of adventure. Yet, within a few decades, tourists were no longer dependent on local eats. They could reproduce the same narrow tourist path all the way around while eating from European menus.

Consider the holiday itinerary. The packed around-the-world tour, enabled by modern technology, capital and imperial infrastructure, promised reproducibility: trip after trip with the same sights, menus, hotels and speed. Thomas Cook even advertised 'the same voyage made possible to every one [*sic*] by modern methods of travel, by far-flung organization', calling it the 'scientific travel of to-day'. The 'world-traveller' could enjoy the 'spices of Java' without having to dine alongside locals. Mass tourism around the world paradoxically advertised the tastes of home, so that 'comfort' meant distance from locals and their foods.[14]

'A vast amount of capital has been invested not only for the needs of commerce but also that European and Americans may have the comforts of home when travelling in the Orient,' reassured the American travel agency

Temple Tours. The train, ship and hotel meals were 'more occidental than oriental'. Temple Tours advertised its 1925–6 itineraries with a depiction of a typical tourist, tempted to travel around the world – 'It sounds most alluring,' the figure in the ad says – but worried about what to eat along the way: 'I am sure I do not wish to leave a comfortable home and stop at some native inn or apology for a hotel and eat raw fish or octopus and shark's fins, bird's nest soup and a lot of other such things.' The agency reassured customers that such forced meals 'may exist off the beaten line of travel', but that for those taking Temple Tours, the 'struggling mass of humanity' were merely part of the exotic scenery, not dining companions. The agency reprinted menus from tours the year before that suggested high-class, European cuisine. The veal cutlets were 'à la Macedoine' and the spaghetti was 'à la Venitienne'. The roast goose arrived with dressing, cranberry sauce, boiled potatoes and spinach. 'Consommé Celestine' offered the only hint of the East.[15]

By the late nineteenth century, tourists tended to be picky eaters. When tourists could dine exclusively on board or in hotels and when their ships were large enough to carry most of their ingredients in cold storage all the way around, local food became both a curiosity and a gauge of difference. Travellers believed that local food and drinks contained intimidating spices and dangerous germs that, while suitable for locals, were unsafe or otherwise repulsive to Europeans and Americans. Consider, for example, the durian, a large, spiky fruit with a custardy texture. As early as the fifteenth century, Europeans who encountered the fruit recognized that locals loved it, and so they sampled it. Many deemed the taste alone worth the long journey to Asia. By the late nineteenth century, however, tourists who sniffed the durian in Malaya and Java recorded their revulsion in hyperbolic terms: they were reminded of sewer gas, rotting onions, corpses. Tourists learned never to bring the local fruit into the colonial hotel. This was a local delicacy that demanded segregation.

Simply put, by the later decades of the nineteenth century, tourists were sensing local food in new ways, as something that confirmed exoticism and difference. The food Euro-American tourists encountered abroad became something to experience from a safe distance, through sight and smell. Tourists were more likely to snap pictures of local foods, fruits and vendors than to taste. 'We gaze at what we encounter,' wrote the tourism studies scholar John Urry. Tourists gazed but, by the last decades of the nineteenth century, most refused to taste.[16]

Harry Franck, who set out on his around-the-world journey in 1904, tried to gain notoriety as a travel writer by stepping off the beaten path of set itineraries and packaged tours. It wasn't simply that Franck managed to travel all the way around without a penny; he did it while eating the curious local bread in Syria and curries in India. He boasted about eating lizard in Burma.

For the food philosopher Lisa Heldke, the food adventure is an 'expedition into the unknown, a pursuit of the strange. They – *we* – are the food adventurers.'[17] The idea of food as adventure has colonial roots and routes. Food colonialism, notes Heldke, involves the 'appropriation' of local cuisines – and, I add, ingredients and raw materials – for the pleasure and profit of the food adventurer. The experience of around-the-world travel suggests that ingredients and cuisine are not synonyms and not all food adventures were deliberately sought. As Euro-American empires expanded, tourists grew ever more hostile to local cuisines, that is, the production of ingredients into food as informed by a set of cultural traditions and techniques. Yet tourists remained fascinated by local ingredients, especially fruits. They visited markets and street stalls but scoffed at the way locals cooked and ate. When Edith James, an upper-class British woman, sailed on the *Franconia* in 1926, she wanted to see the world's oddities and to smell its strange foods – but she rarely talked to locals or tasted their foods. As mass tourism, travel alienated tourists from immediate societies and cultures.[18] James perceived the world from the segregated space of first class, experiencing empire from the shelter of ships, hotels and dining rooms, and judging cultures based on her interactions with those who served her.

Despite her fears of illness and her scorn for anything locals ate, James did sample mangosteens. Unlike the durian, mangosteens tempted tourists. The mangosteen's hard rind offered reassuring distance from local hands and germs (though it was sometimes so hard for confused tourists to open that they depended upon help from a local servant). Tourists tasted its sweet flavours, imagined that this was how Eden's apple tasted and schemed about how to commercialize it. More than any other food, the mangosteen came to represent for tourists the untapped abundance of the colonized tropics, and they crowned it the 'queen of fruits'. Soon, a myth emerged that the queen of England – in other versions, the Dutch queen – offered a reward to anyone who could bring her a mangosteen. In some accounts, she promised a knighthood. Alongside souvenir postcards, tourists often spirited away mangosteen seeds, even saplings. En route tourists crossed paths with another type of around-the-world traveller: botanical explorers who traversed the tropics in search of the next profitable plant to cultivate in colonial plantations.

Against the backdrop of segregated travel, Juanita Harrison's excursion across the globe, beginning in 1927, involved curiosity and pleasure bound up with a commitment to thwart colonial racial segregation. Harrison, who traced her mixed-race roots to African American slaves and had worked since childhood as a domestic servant and cook, deliberately travelled third class, eager to mix and eat with locals. In the United States most would have recognized Harrison as Black but, during her travels, her light skin tone helped her to blend in wherever she went. She established trust through sharing food. It took Harrison eight years to circle the globe on an erratic itinerary punctuated by breaks for paid work. Over shared meals, while travelling for pleasure, Juanita came to sympathize with independence struggles.

First-class travel, however, encouraged affinity with empire and dangled the alluring opportunity for tourists from the United States and Europe to briefly enjoy the privileges of imperial residents. Tourists flocked to Batavia to sample the famous rijsttafel, a vast feast of many dishes eaten with rice that had emerged in the later decades of the nineteenth century as the characteristic meal of the Dutch colonial household. When local cooks prepared food for colonial residents, they blended local ingredients and recipes from the Indonesian archipelago with Dutch staples. By the turn of the twentieth century, rijsttafel moved into the hotel, an edible example of Dutch colonial power that became a draw for around-the-world tourists. The leg of the itinerary to Batavia represented a departure from the usual routine. For many tourists, it was their one approved opportunity to taste spicy foods. Tourists rarely asked about the recipes, but they did count the number of local men who served them at their rijsttafel, experiencing the thrill of the power of Dutch imperialists.

Independence struggles and the Cold War transformed travel in the second half of the twentieth century, as Euro-American empires contracted, and aeroplanes replaced steamships. At least for those in the Global North, travelling overseas came with the rhetoric of democratization. 'Vacations are a very necessary part of modern life,' declared Pan Am. 'You owe it to your job, your health and your home life to take a vacation.'[19] Holidays abroad were also politicized. Tourism's many boosters argued that travels outside of the continent were a way to share the economic and cultural benefits of American dollars.

Around-the-world travelogues mostly disappeared from bookshops during this era. Why read about someone else's holiday when you had a chance to take one yourself? Guidebooks, however, took off. When Pan

Am first published its around-the-world guidebook in 1951, it encouraged tourists to sample the local foods of now independent nations. Alongside the usual details on climate and sightseeing, the airline listed a few dishes to sample in each destination. In Delhi, for example, try the tandoori chicken but avoid the tap-water.[20] Guidebooks, once indifferent to the foods local people bought and sold, now reviewed a handful of restaurants where the spicing was mild, the water bottled and the dishes approachable.

When Myra Waldo began working as the food consultant for Pan Am and its hotel chain subsidiary InterContinental, the around-the-world journey had become sufficiently attainable that she had forgotten how many times she had made her way all the way around – eighteen, she guessed. For Pan Am, Waldo collected recipes from the airline's employees across the globe and compiled them into her bestselling *The Complete Round-the-World Cookbook* of 1954, which launched her career as a food celebrity and sparked a new genre of cookbook. She criticized the timid tourist who ate only American steak and potatoes in the middle of the tropics. Dinner-table liberalism – that is, the sampling of local food as a deliberate engagement with local culture – promised to overcome the segregations once imposed by colonialism. Over the next two decades, Waldo became the United States' leading popularizer of non-Western foods for tourists and home cooks. After the war, the domestic dinner table offered around-the-world food adventures and the diner became a tourist, foraying into exotic feasting as a sign of cultural sophistication. Such dining was a dash around the world, grabbing a few flavours as if they were souvenirs.

As the critic bell hooks has written, within mass culture, 'Otherness' functions as 'a new delight, more intense, more satisfying than normal ways of doing and feeling'. Eating the other 'becomes spice, seasoning that can liven up the dull dish that is mainstream white culture'.[21] hooks employed 'spice' mostly for its metaphorical meanings, but her point has been literally true as well: when InterContinental advertised the local specialities in its restaurants all around the world, the chain offered spice as an attraction for those visiting newly independent countries. It marketed local food as a desirable adventure and, in the process, it divided the world into those who ate and travelled, and those who served (which is to say, those who must have found the hotel's transformations of local recipes foreign to their own sensibilities). The Cold War promise of spicy foods demanded labour and plenty of it. The lure of tourism during the Cold War wasn't simply the adventure of spice but the fantasy of hospitality, freely given in a capitalist, independent nation, rather than demanded through colonial domination.

'Tourism', notes gender studies scholar Cynthia Enloe, 'creates affections, desires, resentments, admiration, friendship, and contempt.'[22] Friendship was the least likely. Wary tourists were unlikely to interact with anyone other than those who served them within the confines of the hotel.

InterContinental and its rival hotel chain, Hilton International, led the post-war explosion of the tourist industry, chasing each other around the world to open branches. In the economic confidence of a world built on American dollars and cheap oil, both chains believed that regardless of where they built hotels, tourists would follow. Their menus, though, diverged. If InterContinental promised understanding through cautious sampling of local foods, Hilton advertised boozy drinks and tropical Polynesian cuisine, evoking exotic themes, lush with tropical fruits and resplendent with service. Hilton opened branches of Trader Vic's restaurants across the chain. Rather than genuine tastes of gastronomy from the Pacific Islands, the Polynesian foods advertised at the Hilton and Trader Vic's repackaged familiar Chinese American foods as exotic global dishes. The brands grew together, and massive tiki heads guarded the towering, white modernist facades of Hilton hotels everywhere from London to Havana.

The arch Cold Warrior and the chain's founder Conrad Hilton promised that the local prosperity brought by the tourist party would keep communist expansion at bay. In reality the chain's anti-communist promises of 'world peace through travel' clashed with tourists' endless demands for service and their engrained suspicion of local peoples and their foods. There was a lot at stake: a muttered insult or a cockroach in an otherwise immaculate snack bar could shatter the fantasies of racial reconciliation promoted by post-war mass tourism. I read plenty of letters, even directly to Conrad himself, complaining about the service. Both Hilton and InterContinental realized that the idea of hospitality as a mutual benefit was impossible to maintain. Behind the party, tourist hotels were also sites of labour organizing, even open revolution. Conrad built the Hilton in Havana, most notably, for tourists; it became the first capital of Cuba's revolutionaries.

By the end of the Jet Age, anywhere around the world, the roads might still have been bumpy, and the asphalt pitted, but they were well mapped. Food began to seem like the last real exploration: how to get it, how to eat it, learning to get by on it and maybe even liking it. In our new century, when the famed chef and food adventurer Anthony Bourdain swallowed a cobra heart in his television series *A Cook's Tour* in 2013, he proclaimed food as a worthwhile adventure. Try everything, at least once, he recommended.

Bourdain encouraged a fresh generation of new tourists to eat the most daunting of local meals and snap pictures of the feat. Today's Instagram feeds have their culinary histories.

As travel itself became ordinary, eating was the adventure. When food from afar became an adventure, it changed the way we all eat. Despite this long history of fear and aversion, culinary tourism, travel for pleasure with the express intention of eating local, has emerged in the twenty-first century as one of the very fastest growing segments of the global tourism industry. When one set of food traditions becomes exotic and another cuisine, we annihilate space and substitute taste as the measure of distance and difference. Tourism has a lot to do with the way we, as a society, order the world's eating into cuisine or adventure.

Note on Place and Food Names

The names of places and key foods have changed, especially in the process of independence and decolonization. In general, I have used the words as written in the original texts. Older place names differ from contemporary iterations and, where needed to locate readers, I have signalled the newer name in text. As well, I have on occasion signalled the contemporary names of foods and ingredients. Otherwise, I have reproduced the names as tourists recorded them. Throughout, I have tried to balance an acknowledgement of the cultural and political importance of how we name places and foods with attention to the language of particular historical moments.

PART I:
FROM SAIL TO STEAM,
1840–1900

Ida Pfeiffer, 1856, photograph by Franz Hanfstaengl.

1

Ida Pfeiffer

Ida Pfeiffer had her head examined in 1855. She was in New York, nearing the end of her second voyage around the world, when she visited the offices of the *American Phrenological Journal*. Phrenology, then considered a science, measured the shape of heads to gauge character and intelligence and, in Ida's case, to figure out what made some humans into explorers. Someone at the journal measured her skull, its shape and its bumps, to understand the nature and source of her wanderlust. The journal printed the results for the world to read.

Ida was born in 1797 in Vienna, the landlocked capital of the Habsburg empire. She had felt trapped in her loveless marriage to a disgraced doctor, a civil servant who ran afoul of government officials and struggled to find work. She led a humdrum, middle-class life in urban Austria, caring for her two children. She longed to be elsewhere, going places no one – which is to say, no white explorer – had gone before. When her children were grown and her husband dead, she set off to circumnavigate the world.

Ida fashioned herself as an explorer, but she was in fact a tourist, travelling for pleasure. Emerging networks of global travel made her two trips around the world possible, but the paucity of infrastructure such as hotels or restaurants meant she would face danger and discomfort. She pieced her trips together unaided by canals, travel agencies or, for the most part, steam. There was no tourist trail for her to step away from; if anything, she helped to blaze it. She wrote about her journeys in bestselling books. Her son wrote the preface to her last volume, published after her death. Newspapers and magazines printed her arrival in their city and some, like the *American Phrenological Journal*, tried to explain why a middle-class woman craved travel. She even became a member of the Geographical Society of Berlin.[1]

Her journeys, as she made sure her readers knew, took courage. Without hotels or railroads, she had to eat whatever was locally available: a strong stomach helped. So too, according to the phrenologists, did having the right shape of head. 'Your phrenology is, for the most part, evenly developed,' the journal told Ida. 'You have great force and character, power of endurance, fortitude, and ability to execute whatever designs you may have.' They also noted that she was 'quite sensitive as to character and reputation', befitting a woman who wrote about her journeys among cannibal tribes in Sumatra or traversing bandit-ridden roads unguarded between Delhi and Bombay. The journal responded in kind, writing that she 'has astonished the world by her travels', as 'decidedly a marked character' who 'may be regarded as the most wonderful woman of the age'.[2]

During the years in which Ida travelled, the British, French, Portuguese and Dutch empires were all struggling to govern lands over which they had claimed sovereignty. She travelled in those grey areas of empire, first during an around-the-world trip from 1846 to 1848, on the eve of European revolutions that challenged monarchies, including her native Austria-Hungary, and later in 1851–5 during the violent consolidation of European power, especially in Asia. The balance of power was changing forever. Empires that controlled territory only in Europe, like Austria-Hungary, were declining. Europe's key imperial and economic powers, such as England, France and the Netherlands, claimed far-flung colonies, which Ida longed to visit.

On her around-the-world journey, Ida arrived in today's Indonesia as the Dutch, having crushed a rebellion by several allied kingdoms between 1825 and 1839, were militarily extending their rule to other islands in the archipelago and into the interior of Java, Sumatra and Sarawak. Ida reached Tahiti in 1847, the same year that Queen Pōmare IV, who had rebelled against a French protectorate in 1843 – the French had responded with violent annexation – returned from exile to a humiliating settlement. In 1856, the French had sent warships to threaten the Vietnamese emperor Tự Đức. British power in India was also expanding even as Ida visited. By 1857, the last full year of Ida's life, sepoys – Indian soldiers serving under British command – mutinied, beginning an unsuccessful rebellion that would eventually lead to direct control by the British crown. The last Mughal emperor of India left for exile in Burma. By 1859, for those Indian nobles and potentates who remained, their power was largely symbolic. On her last journey to the tropics, Ida lent her hand to the rush for empire; she was a key co-conspirator in a failed plot to extend French influence in Madagascar.

Like many travellers who imagined themselves as explorers, she felt compelled to build a natural history collection, and she gathered insect specimens on her travels. But her real interest was the local humans, whom she regarded as another form of specimen. The more 'savage', the less affected by empire, the better. She did not conduct phrenological measurements of their heads, but she gazed at them with an interest in physiognomy, recording signs of difference that she presented as evidence of their savagery. She described the jaws, skin colour, hair, lips and muscles of the non-white peoples she met, but never bothered to record much about the white colonists who often hosted her in their homes.

She was happy enough when such occasions presented themselves, and she could enjoy European foods. English duck or freshly baked bread represented, to her, a kind of reprieve from her adventures. But local foods, as strange as possible, helped her measure the difference that separated her, the white woman, from locals. Even at a time when Ida, blazing the tourist trail, was so dependent on locals for food and often housing, she used close encounters to measure differences of race and civilization. In so doing, Ida, like tourists for decades to follow, threw in her lot with empire. She wrote at length about the ways locals prepared, served and ate their foods: did they rip the cooked flesh? Did they toss pieces into the sauce? Even when she found the food tasty, she was often disgusted by the peoples who cooked it and the way they ate it. At the same time, she was proud of partaking in such eating, because with each bite of manioc or morsel of monkey, she proved herself an intrepid traveller. Even the densest jungles, by the time she visited them, had been mapped. Travel was becoming tourism, but food was an adventure.

Ship Biscuits and Bonito at Sea: May–September 1846

In May 1846 Ida departed Hamburg for Rio de Janeiro. Then, she sailed around South America to Valparaíso. From South America, she travelled to French Tahiti en route to Canton. By the next spring, she had arrived in Singapore and then sailed across the Indian Ocean to Ceylon and Madras. From Madras, she began a long overland journey across the subcontinent. She returned to Europe via Constantinople and Athens. There was no established itinerary to follow. She could choose her routes by sea easily enough, even if travel by sail was hard to endure. By land, in many places she visited, European influence did not extend far from the coast. When she returned, she published her account in German, which was quickly translated. By the autumn of 1848, she was home and famous.

Sail was cheaper than coal-powered travel, but far slower. At the very beginning of her journey, still in the English Channel, her ship lay becalmed. Some days the captain tacked into the breeze all day, just to travel a few miles. One night, the sailors roused Ida from her bunk. She worried that the ship was foundering, but they wanted only to show her the phosphorescence of a truly still sea and unmoving ship. Ida longed for steam power, even if, on her limited budget, she couldn't afford its pricier tickets.

On a steamship, she was convinced, 'the passengers enjoy good and fresh provisions, spacious cabins, and excellent society.' At sea, however, a ship with sails was at the mercy of the winds and Ida was at the mercy of the captain. The ship's captain – by law, a dictator at sea – cared more for his cargo than his customers' comfort. He determined not only the routes but the menus. As Ida suffered through a meagre diet of coffee without milk, salted cod, hard dumplings, ship biscuits and a thin cabbage soup, she decided that sailing ships 'are not fitted up for passengers'. She recorded her meals, partly in anger against the captain and partly as advice to potential around-the-world travellers: 'As regards wine, passengers should take especial care to ask the captain whether this is included in the passage-money.'[3]

Catching fish offered a respite from the monotony of the ship's kitchen. Off the coast of Morocco, crew and passengers rushed to bait hooks to lure a passing school of bonito. They caught just one, but, Ida noted, the ship's cook prepared 'us a fresh meal, of which we had long been deprived'.[4]

On 29 August the ship crossed the equator. Ida had been looking forward to crossing the 'Line' for the first time. There was an intimacy among the small number of passengers squeezed into what was primarily a cargo ship and more seasoned passengers shared stories of the 'fearful' tropical heat that would 'melt the pitch', the tar that protected the ship's rigging, and spoil their provisions. Others described the traditions of drunken celebration that marked the crossing of the equator. But when the moment came, Ida was disappointed. One of the passengers opened bottles of champagne and the passengers shook hands 'as if we had done some great and heroic deed'. The sailors soaked a cabin boy with buckets of seawater to mark his first trip to the Southern Hemisphere and the pitch didn't melt.

In the tropical heat, the food was 'just as bad as before'. But when, a few days later, the ship drifted into one of the violent storms that whip off the African coast in early September, Ida longed for doldrums: as she tried to eat, she had to steady herself and her plate by clinging to the table.

Passengers and sailors ate the same rations and together they struggled to overcome the boredom of a long voyage. For amusement, they fed stale bread to the birds that followed the ship. One of the passengers wanted to kill and stuff an albatross for his natural history collection. The sailors objected. Killing an albatross would bring bad luck and becalmed winds, they explained. The passenger released his specimen.[5]

Months later, when Ida traded sail for steam on her journey from Hong Kong, she expected luxury and good company, but was disappointed. This was her first journey on a steamship, and she bought the second-class ticket she could afford. Her cabin furniture was stained. At the second-class table, the food tasted 'execrable', and the dress was rude. 'Sometimes one of the company would appear without either coat or jacket.' She drank from an old teacup missing its handle. Having her own cup, though, was a little luxury offered to the only woman on board. The male passengers all shared two drinking glasses. Ostensibly to amuse them, an officer asked the second-class passengers to care for his two puppies. The era of steamship luxury remained decades away, but the era of segregation afloat had already begun. Even these dismal surroundings were reserved for Europeans – and their pets.[6]

Manioc in Brazil: September–December 1846

Ida arrived in Rio de Janeiro on 17 September 1846, tired and ill-kempt after two and a half months at sea. She and her fellow passengers were examined for symptoms of yellow fever, then allowed to disembark in what she called, with marked disappointment, a 'disgusting and dirty sort of square'. A small group of Afro-Brazilian vendors were hawking fruits and sweets, which would have been welcome after months of stale food. But she wrote only about the vendors. To Ida, they were 'disgusting and dirty'. Everywhere one looks in Rio de Janeiro, she wrote, 'horrible and disgusting sights . . . meet the eye'; it was a city with open sewers, and she noted that 'it is only here and there that a white man is to be seen.' Brazil, when Ida visited, still relied on African chattel slavery to support two of its principal industries, sugar and coffee. Even ex-slaves, having won manumission, typically faced lives of extreme penury.

Between 1840 and 1851 around 370,000 African slaves arrived in Brazil, but Ida focused more on the plight of Europeans. During her stay in the city, she watched the arrival of ships carrying European emigrants. 'Want, hunger, and sickness destroy most of them,' Ida insisted. The Brazilian government rewarded a lucky few with uncleared lands to cultivate, either on their own or with slaves.[7]

In Brazil, Ida wrote, the milk tasted watery, the meat dry and even the famous pineapples were inferior to those grown in a European greenhouse.

She ate manioc, a root crop that was a Brazilian staple, for most meals, though she never learned to enjoy it. Today, Brazilians call the dry, crumbled manioc 'farofa'; Ida, who saw it as a substitute for European wheat flour, called it 'flour of manioc'. Manioc, she explained, grew stalks as tall as a person, but only its heavy roots were edible. Washed, peeled and then ground 'by a negro', the mushy mass was soaked and then pressed dry. (What she didn't know or understand was that manioc must be soaked to wash away the naturally occurring and poisonous cyanogen.) 'Everyone at the table takes as much as he chooses, and sprinkles it over his plate.' In her opinion, manioc was 'far from being so nutritious and strengthening' and in fact epitomized the degenerate, inferior diet of Brazil. That degeneracy, Ida believed, extended beyond the food itself to the meal where she observed white, Black and Indigenous people sharing dishes and tables.[8]

Ida longed to escape Rio de Janeiro, and she followed an itinerary that became a pattern for the rest of her travelling life: she arrived in a city governed by Europeans and, as soon as possible, she departed, 'traversing virgin forests' in search of what she imagined to be untainted, untamed primitive peoples.

She began the first of her two journeys upcountry on a sailing ship with a Black crew and a white captain. Onboard she ate fish, oranges, coconuts, 'a considerable quantity of flour of manioc' and 'even white bread'. She was overjoyed to eat familiar wheat bread, though disappointed that she had not yet eaten alongside Indigenous Brazilians. It was the last bread she would enjoy until Christmas, when she sailed out of Brazil, around Cape Horn to the Pacific.

In November, back in Rio de Janeiro, she suffered a fever, likely her first bout of malaria. After she recovered, she joined a small group of Europeans living in Rio di Janeiro, mostly Germans and Austrians, as they travelled inland on foot. Her plan was to pass through the ramshackle coffee plantations, worked by slaves, until she finally arrived in the jungles where local Indigenous people lived. She called them Puris. By then, the population of mostly nomadic Indigenous peoples had been decimated by violence from European settlers and deforestation linked to the spread of coffee plantations.

On the road out of Rio di Janeiro, Ida carried a knife. Wary of Black Brazilians, she noticed a Black man following her and her travel companions. At a lonely turn in the road, the man – a slave, she assumed – rushed forward, baring a dagger. 'No doubt', white Brazilians later told her, the thief had just been disciplined by his owner and 'thought that it was a good opportunity of satisfying, with impunity, his hatred against the whites'. In the struggle, he stabbed Ida twice on her upper arm. At last, she managed to grab her own knife. She gashed his hand. 'The negro's fury was now roused to its highest pitch,' she later wrote in her diary; 'he gnashed his teeth at us like a wild beast.' Luckily for Ida, he fled into the underbrush when two white men on horseback rounded the bend in the road. Her assailant was later caught and 'severely beaten'. Ida met other slaves on the road but 'without any mishap, and with a continually increasing admiration of the beautiful slavery' – or, at least, of the masters who kept the enslaved beasts at bay.[9]

At the point of a knife on the road from Rio de Janeiro and later at the dinner table in a coffee plantation, Ida chose the apologist side in the debate over Brazilian slavery that was emerging in Brazilian politics. Britain, a key destination for Brazil's exports, had also begun demanding that Brazil abolish the slave trade, though not yet slavery itself. She arrived at the plantation Fazenda of Boa Esperanza at dinnertime. There was plenty to eat – except for the manioc, the food was 'very nearly in the European fashion'. As she chewed, she contemplated the slaves who swallowed manioc nearby and thought about the slave who had attacked her. She 'had an opportunity of convincing myself' that Black slaves were not as overworked or harshly treated as Europeans might imagine. Certainly, she thought, they were not treated poorly enough to turn to robbery and murder.[10] Her sympathy for white Brazilian slave owners was growing.

The next morning, her host wrapped manioc, fowl and cheese for the journey. Ida felt that each humid mile represented a step back in time from civilization to savagery. She ate manioc throughout her journey, but the further she got from Rio de Janeiro the more it struck her not as a poor substitute for European flour, but as a primitive food in its own right. The Puris simply tossed the tubers into the fire. (Baking also neutralizes cyanogen.)

Ida's expedition stopped at a coffee plantation barely cleared from the underbrush. Whites, slaves and Puris sat together on the floor in front of an open fire. To Ida, ever taxonomizing, 'the place was like a book of specimens containing the most varied ramifications of the three principal races of the country.' She watched as a 'negress and two young negroes cooked' a meal of 'primitive simplicity'. Slaves placed manioc farofa and boiled manioc roots in the centre of a table and 'everyone whose complexion was white' served themselves to fowls stewed with rice, manioc and wine. Outside, amid the animals, Black slaves ate from broken basins and hollowed out pumpkin-gourds. They consumed a mash of beans and manioc flour, a 'thick and disgusting-looking mess they devoured with avidity'. They tore dried meat with their hands. Ida thought of clawed animals. They threw the rough meat into their mouths, alternating with handfuls of manioc. As she watched the slaves eat, she became convinced of their savagery. Here, at dinner time on a roughly built coffee farm, she found herself at odds with the moral convictions of European abolitionists. In Brazil, she concluded, slavery did not seem as cruel as she expected.

In front of the open fire and helping herself to dried, crumbly manioc, she was 'tempted to believe that I was already among savages'. She spent the night on a straw mat. 'The women lay all around me.' She was boasting: she was proud to be an adventurer who ate crude food and then slept alongside slaves and Puris.

The next day, Ida departed, walking further into the jungle, further from Europe. After eight hours of walking, she found the huts of the 'Indians'. She was eager to see Brazil's 'primitives' – who, to her, were even uglier than African slaves. She described their noses as flattened, their mouths as absurdly long, their eyes thin, almost, she judged, like the 'Chinese'. 'A peculiar look of stupidity is spread over the whole face,' she wrote. The huts, covered with palm leaves, dripped from the rain. Inside, the Indians slung hammocks around a faltering fire where bananas, corn and manioc boiled and roasted. They used gourds instead of plates.

She joined the Indigenous peoples in a hunt and the 'good creatures offered me the best hut they possessed, and invited me to pass the night there'. They served what they had killed: monkey and parrot, roasted on a spit over the open fire. Ida spread her cloak on the ground and leaned against a log. She ate manioc, monkey, parrot and corn off a few gathered leaves. 'My appetite', she wrote, was 'tremendous'. The monkey tasted 'superlatively delicious', she noted in her journal. The parrot, though, was tough. She was as proud to have eaten foods unheard of in Europe as to have dined with Indigenous Brazilians. Full, she begged the Indians to dance. She seemed satisfied that the war dance left her 'affright'.[11]

A few days later, she paid £7 for a berth on a British sailing ship around Cape Horn bound for Valparaíso. From Valparaíso, she planned to cross the Pacific to Tahiti. En route, she reported in her journal, a mixed-race steward got drunk and threw himself from the rigging into the roiling seas and drowned.

The captain fed his passengers generously, she also noted. Ida was overjoyed to eat roasted and stewed fowls, duck and geese. Stewards served bread, baked fresh in the ship's ovens daily. For Christmas, they feasted on ham, rice and plum pudding.[12]

Pigs in Tahiti: April–May 1847

Storm clouds covered the moon the night Ida arrived in Tahiti. French warships anchored in the harbour.[13]

War had raged for the last several years, as the French converted the islands from protectorate to colony. The 'golden times for travellers are over', complained Ida as small boats surrounded her ship. Tahitians climbed aboard to sell fruit and shellfish. Once, she explained, Europeans arriving in Tahiti received gifts of fruits and hospitable welcomes from primitive inhabitants. In exchange for a few glass beads or red rags, travellers could even prise primitive artefacts from locals. Now, she lamented, 'they demanded money' and were 'grasping and cunning in their dealings'. She offered one of the locals a small bronze ring. He smelled it, shook his head, returned it, grasped her hand and pointed to the ring that was genuine gold.[14]

She travelled to Paya (today's Paea) as the guest of Tati, the local chief. Ida guessed that Tati was nearly ninety when she met him. Tahiti's French colonial government, which only in the last few months had imposed its power, now paid him a pension.

Tati's older son (also named Tati) began preparing a feast. In the early evening, just as the tropical humidity moderated, he killed a small pig, weighing maybe 20 pounds (9 kg). He built a large fire in a shallow pit and added stones. When the wood reduced to embers and the stones were hot enough, he added in peeled breadfruit and then the pig. On top, he piled more heated stones, leaves and then earth.

Ida already knew that roasted pigs were the main course in Tahitian banquets, and she had eagerly anticipated eating some as a guest of honour. She sat for an hour and a half with the older Tati, a French officer and his local mistress until the pig was ready. She watched as the guests and host used their hands to tear the pig into portions. Each guest received their share of the pork, along with half a roasted breadfruit and a coconut shell filled with miti, lightly fermented palm sap. The drink tasted sour to Ida, and she decreed the meat neither 'artistically cooked nor very enticing'. Pork itself wasn't an unusual food for any European, but the familiar became strange to her when she watched Tahitians eat. They ripped and tore the meat and, as she surveyed the guests gorging themselves, she decided, 'I had seen enough.'

For more than a century before Ida arrived in Tahiti, and for years after, too, European travellers had portrayed the Tahitians as noble, sensuous savages, free with their affection and lavish with their hospitality. Ida agreed that Tahitians were 'a remarkably strong and vigorous race' – but strength wasn't nobility. They ate crudely, she thought. She judged their mouths too large and their lips too thick. The women's noses, she wrote, were especially 'ugly'.[15]

Ida wrote about Tahitian women with a sense of repugnance that she associated with their sexuality as much as their looks. Tahitians, Ida wrote, were 'naturally very lazy, and above all things disinclined to work'. So, 'they have made the female portion of the community the means of gaining money.' At Tati's feast, she gazed across the table at the French officer's Tahitian mistress. Women, Ida was disgusted, were for sale by brothers, parents, even husbands, and the French were willing buyers. 'Every officer's house is the rendezvous of several native beauties, who go out and in at every hour of the day.' The war may have ended, the Tahitian queen remained in exile for a few more months, but Ida wondered 'whether the immorality of these islanders has been lessened by French civilization'.[16]

When the elder Tati offered another pig feast, Ida believed it was planned in her honour. Yet when she arrived at his land, she was disappointed that the 'whole neighbourhood' would attend. Tati had already heated the stones and wrapped pork, breadfruits and plantains when villagers rushed out of their huts to add their own provisions. Tati added a large turtle to feed the extra guests. Ida didn't understand the mutual obligations of a chief to local peoples when villagers added their own supplies to the feast and expected freshly cooked pig and turtle in return. For Ida, a feast that she had decided was meant for her was spoiled by its guests.

Ida watched the villagers eat. They 'threw' each piece of food into a coconut shell full of miti and then devoured each morsel with their hands. At the end of the meal, they drank the miti, with all its crumbs and jumbled flavours. The strange tastes didn't disgust her; the human habits did. Tahitians seemed as brutish as their feasts. Just as she saw their pig feasts as tasteless ceremonies devoid of genuine hospitality, she considered their noble savagery as only skin deep. She didn't dispute their superficial kindness. 'They readily invite a stranger,' Ida admitted, 'and even kill a pig in his honour.' But there were plenty of pigs around.[17]

Finally, nearing the end of her stay, she couldn't contain her repulsion any longer. In a French officer's quarters, sitting at the same table with his Tahitian mistress, 'I could not help telling one of the gentlemen my opinion of the matter.' These weren't noble savages. They were 'grasping and avaricious creatures'. She remembered those hands ripping pig flesh and throwing the meat into a sour drink and she thought only of beasts. 'Their only pleasures are merely animal.'

All the people needed to do was 'gather the fruit and kill the pigs'. Yet, she grudgingly admitted, the flavours were often delicious. Once, she walked the 36 miles (58 km) from Papara to Papeiti with a French officer and his 'native beauty'. They paused at the house where the woman's mother lived. Her mother kneaded breadfruit, mangoes and bananas into a paste which she baked on hot stones. It was a 'most splendid dish'. Ida enjoyed it warm with an orange sauce. When they departed, Ida noticed that the officer gave the Tahitian woman money to give her mother. She accepted the money without 'one word of thanks'. Ida, for her part, gave nothing.

When the long trek was over, Ida lodged at a French colonial fort. She enjoyed, 'in military fashion', bread, wine and bacon.[18]

Sweetmeats in India: October 1847–April 1848

On 27 October Ida set out from Ceylon to Madras. This time she travelled by steamer, and it was strictly divided by class. She soon discovered that the ship was just as segregated by race and religion.

She watched an Indian noble as he dined on deck – she heard that his name was Schadathan and that he was a prisoner of the English. Ida didn't know his crime, only that he had broken 'the peace he had concluded with' the English. She was more interested in his meal. The noble, his servants and his secretary spread rugs on the deck, and while Ida watched, the Indian noble ate fowls and pilau. Indians used their hands to eat, instead of knives and forks, Ida noted.[19] The noble's meal was Ida's introduction to colonial India: for what seems to have been the first time in her trip around the world, no one invited Ida to join the meal. Once she reached land in India, she ate separately and, though she knew that caste rules precluded such hospitality, she resented the exclusion.

'Hindoos,' she wrote, 'are divided into four castes.' Some of the upper castes 'especially the women, are almost white'. The upper castes ate modestly, mostly on rice, fruit, fish and vegetables, while the lowest castes – Ida called them 'Parias' – ate 'all kinds of offal, and even diseased cattle; they go about nearly naked'.[20] To keep their caste status, Indian Hindus could not share food with 'Parias' – or with Ida.

The emerging British empire, Ida witnessed, had its own hardening hierarchies. Late in the evening on 29 October, just before the steamer sailed from Madras to Calcutta, an Indian woman with two small children boarded the ship. A steward showed her to her second-class cabin. Her son was suffering from a bad cough, which kept awake an English woman in the nearby first-class cabin. The next night, the captain forced the Indian woman and her son to sleep on the deck, despite the passing heavy showers. Even Ida was appalled. 'No savages would have thus thrust forth a woman with a sick child.'

In Calcutta, Ida explored the profoundly segregated city. 'Black-town', the quarter of the city where Indians lived, repulsed her. The houses were 'wretched', the huts 'miserable'. She was impressed by the 'European quarter' – White Town, it was called. It deserved its reputation as the 'City of Palaces'.[21]

She also visited the house of a wealthy Indian. He had a fortune of, she guessed, £150,000. He greeted her at the door, wearing the 'most picturesque' outfit of white muslin over which he wound an impressive 'Indian shawl'. The house, though, was decorated in European fashion. Even the bookcases were filled with English poetry and philosophy. Ida noticed that the two volumes of Byron were shelved in different directions, and she speculated that they must have been just for show. She asked to meet her host's wife and daughters, knowing, of course, the rules of purdah – the religious and social practice of public seclusion of women – that made such a request uncomfortable.

At the end of her visit, a servant offered her a tray of sweetmeats and fruit. She ate alone. She didn't care for them, 'owing to the predominance of the suet'.[22] (In fact, suet, rendered beef fat, was an ingredient that would never have been added to the sweets in a wealthy Hindu man's house.) Sweetmeats, she decided, were gifts for 'principal guests' but, in addition to finding fault with their flavour, she disliked their subtle reminder that she was an outsider – to the homes she visited and to India. Sweetmeats represented hospitality, but Ida tasted them and felt that they meant that Indians and Europeans were not supposed to eat – or live – together.

As she made her way across the subcontinent, she expected, even demanded, hospitality from Indians, and when she visited local homes, she continued to make requests that would make her hosts uncomfortable: not just meeting wives and daughters but seeing parts of the house that were normally kept private from Europeans and visitors. Wealthy Indians' decor might aspire to English fashions, but retained those barriers and walls designed to keep Ida (and other outsiders) segregated and distant.

The Rajah of Benares invited Ida to visit his palace at Rhamnagur (modern-day Ramnagar) on the left bank of the Ganges. The palace was 'overcrowded' with European furniture. The paintings, framed and glazed, were 'miserable'. She gazed critically at the pictures; a 'swarm of servants' stared curiously at her.[23] Ida watched a dance and concert. Two women performed for only 15 minutes, but it was enough for Ida. 'The two sylphides shrieked so miserably that I was in fear for my ears and nerves,' she said. During the performance, a servant offered sweetmeats, fruits and sherbets. The next morning, the rajah sent her an array of sweetmeats and rare fruits.[24]

A few days later, as Ida passed through Kottah (modern-day Kota), King Ram Singh sent servants and soldiers mounted on a riding elephant with a gift of sweetmeats and fruit. In Indor (Indore), the queen Jewswont-Rao-Holcar invited her to an audience in a hall filled with servants who proffered sweetmeats and fruits, this time sprinkled with rose water. Later, they carried in pan – areca nuts and betel leaves – on silver platters. Ida felt that the pan was a digestive signal that the audience was finished, and visitors should now depart. The queen's servants sent her home with yet more fruit and sweetmeats.[25]

In Delhi, she visited the palace of the emperor destined to be the last Moghul. Everywhere she travelled in India, Ida witnessed the shifting balance of power between British and Indian. His palace, she thought, had a tawdry air and the gardens, once grand, seemed ragged. 'The present Great Mogul has so little taste,' she sniffed. The palace was dusty. 'Heaps' of rubbish marred the courtyards that had once been graced with gardens. The British, meanwhile, advised Ida not to continue beyond Delhi. The land beyond 'was not under the control of the English Government, and the people were far less civilized'. She was frightened by their stories of 'stranglers and Thugs', but she still travelled overland to Bombay.[26]

The country was on the verge of a rebellion that the British would eventually call the Great Mutiny. Resentment against the colonizers had been brewing even while Ida visited. The rebellion was sparked by rumours that the grease on the rifle cartridges used by Indian sepoys contained both beef tallow and lard. The beef would have been forbidden to Hindu soldiers; the pork to Muslims. In 1857, sepoys initiated a revolt that, the following year, besieged Delhi itself.

In Bombay, whose community of Zoroastrians, known as Parsis, included many merchants, Ida at last had the chance to eat a full meal at the house of an Indian. Manockjee Cursetjee was a wealthy Parsi who had travelled widely in Europe. As she expected by now, his house was decorated in a European style. Still, she was surprised about her host and his family's 'European manners and customs', which Ida called 'reforms'. Cursetjee's daughters had been educated in English. The eldest wrote a short paragraph in Ida's diary. They sat in the drawing room, even while Ida visited, and worked on their needlepoint.

Ida was surprised when the merchant invited her to remain 'during their meal-time'. A Parsi, he would not have followed the same strict caste rules as Hindus. The food was mostly prepared in as European a style as the house itself, and Ida ate with a knife and fork – but she still dined alone as the family and servants watched. She had watched many others eat before, including the imprisoned noble on her way to India. Now, she felt uncomfortable. 'To them', she was a 'singular spectacle'. When she was finished, the table was 'as carefully brushed as if I had been infected with the plague'.

Then the family ate. The same dishes of food that had been served on plates to Ida were now ladled onto warm flatbreads. She stared. 'They tore flesh from the bones, separated the flesh into pieces, and dipped the pieces into various soups and sauces.'[27] They threw the dripping, torn flesh right into their mouths. Ida noted that they never seemed to touch their lips with their fingers. She seemed impressed by their skill, but she still associated eating with the hands with savagery.

A few days later, she joined a European picnic to the island of Elephanta, just outside Bombay. The island, with its impressive Hindu temples, was already becoming a popular tourist attraction. When she first sailed to India in October, Ida was appalled by the cruel impact of imperial segregation. Now, as she was about to depart, she had come to relish the luxuries afforded only to British and Europeans. In the shadow of the temple, she enjoyed a picnic served by an Indian cook on tables and chairs carried by servants. 'That is what I call a simple country party!'[28]

Humans in Sumatra: April–October 1852

In 1850 Ida published the account of her first journey around the world. Her book was translated twice into English, once into French. A year later and enjoying her fame, she was ready to travel around the world again, with a small grant from the Austrian government.[29] When she departed in May 1851, she hoped to penetrate the interiors of Africa and Indonesia, travel to California and then across North America, before returning to Europe. She failed in Africa; she decided, after all, that a trip beyond the Cape Colony was just too dangerous. Instead, she continued on toward the Dutch Indonesian colony.[30]

In April 1852 Ida was en route to the colonial capital of Batavia on the island of Java. From there, she planned to sail to Sumatra. Her ship was transporting troops, mostly Indonesians and a handful of Dutch. She was appalled by the drunken outrages of the white soldiers. They seemed 'more immoral in their conduct' than 'their more uncivilized brethren'. When the ship paused at Fort Sorg, the Dutch she met struck her as similarly lacking. She described a 'deplorable' Dutch encampment of squat huts haphazardly roofed with leaves. A local man offered her housing while the ship remained in port. He had, she thought, a 'European air', and she hoped he might offer tolerably European food and more comfortable lodgings than the ship. She asked for eggs, but they arrived raw. Breakfast the next morning was 'literally tea, without milk or bread'. Lunch was just as disappointing. Half a wing of some kind of fowl was served in such a fierce curry that it burned her mouth 'like a live coal'. Two thin slices of some sort of meat were cooked to cinders in coconut oil she deemed rancid. At teatime, she picked at the basket of fruit her host offered, worrying that 'in these countries the fruit often disagrees seriously with Europeans.' 'Even with my appetite,' she wrote, 'I could eat but little of this.'[31]

Still, her short trip had a silver lining. On board, she met T. J. Willer, a Dutch colonial civil servant who had recently published a lengthy account of the Batak people. They lived, Willer told her, untouched by Dutch rule, in the Sumatran highlands and around Lake Toba, a lake in the crater of an extinct volcano. Much to Ida's fascination, he assured her that they practised cannibalism.

An idea formed in Ida's head: though Dutch officials (and Willer) warned against it, she planned to travel far into the highlands, meet the cannibals and survive uneaten.[32] She was used to tasting and describing local meals. Now, she wondered if she herself might become one. It seemed the supreme food adventure.

On 1 May, a stormy tide washed a large boa constrictor onto the ship's deck. She remembered an eating feat when, on a tiger hunt near Singapore, she had tried the 'curious' dish of snake cooked by Chinese plantation workers. Now the sailors laughed when she encouraged them to eat the drowned boa. She peeled its skin, cut a steak and grilled it. A sailor, 'the boldest among them', asked for a taste, and she obliged. Soon the others curiously tasted and 'tasted so much that, at last, I had the laugh on my side'.[33] Ida was proud to have proved herself to these men as a genuine explorer.

In Batavia, the colonial capital, which was just beginning to develop the tourist infrastructure that would later welcome around-the-world cruisers until the end of Dutch rule, Ida checked into the Hotel Nederland. Despite the comforts of the hotel, the colonial city held little interest to her. The houses were small, and the Chinese quarter was especially crowded. The Europeans kept their offices in the city itself but lived in villas in the surrounding hills. She found their villas' gabled Dutch architecture heavy and dull, and the blending of European and Javanese life inside the villas appalled her. The Dutch in Batavia, colonists 'who have nothing to do', employed legions of servants 'to come and help them'. The Dutch insisted that their servants wear livery coasts and breeches, but their feet were bare. To Ida, the sight of a 'dark brown face' topped with a 'European footman's livery hat' made the servants appear 'like dressed-up orang-outangs'. The European 'ladies' meanwhile wore Javanese sarongs and jackets during the day, but 'European full dress' when they gathered for the colonial round of 'dinners and entertainments'. She longed to see savage life, as yet untamed by empire.

Her Dutch hosts, who tried to convince her to abandon her journey to the Bataks, led her on a tour of Batavia's colonial institutions. She visited the hospital in time for breakfast. While European patients drank coffee with sugar and milk and ate white bread, Indonesian patients ate rice, vegetables, fish and meat. At the prison, she was surprised that even local inmates received meat twice a week with their rice. She found the museum dull. The best insect specimens had already been sent to Holland. She visited a new Dutch club, the Harmony, still a pillar of the colonial establishment by the time around-the-world cruisers visited half a century later. In the evening, she skipped the European theatre. She had already seen the play back at home in Europe and, anyway, she didn't have the appropriate clothes. Instead, she attended the Chinese theatre with a dinner to follow, only to complain that the actresses screamed and their 'gestures were anything but graceful'. She longed for the four acts to finish so she could try the food. The table was 'spread with "all the delicacies of the season"', at least according to her Chinese hosts. The birds' nests were the most interesting. They 'would assuredly not tempt a European palate to excess', Ida judged. She proudly found them 'delicious'. On 1 June she left the city to visit the Dutch botanical garden at Buitenzorg, but was more interested in the rocky grottoes nearby where the local Chinese harvested birds' nests.[34]

In Padang, the largest Dutch settlement on Sumatra, she attended a dinner in well-manicured gardens, shaded by coconut trees. The island's Dutch governor cautioned her against travelling into the interior. As recently as 1835, he warned, two Dutch missionaries had been 'killed and eaten'.[35] The story excited her.

On 19 July Ida finally departed coastal Padang for the Sumatran highlands where the Batak lived. She did most of her travelling by foot in the cooler mornings. Each evening, she wrote in her journal and recorded the miles she had walked on rough paths into the jungle, further from the safety of Dutch colonists and deeper into cannibal country.

On 22 July she walked 20 miles (32 km) to the house of a local Dutch resident. He had been the first Dutch soldier to lead his troops into the 'Battaker country'. Now, the territory he patrolled produced coffee on large plantations. That night, Ida recorded the prices for the spices, tea, coffee and other commodities harvested in the Dutch colony. In 1851, planters across Sumatra produced 2 million pounds (900,000 kg) of coffee. Coffee fetched 20½ 'rupees the picul'.[36] She was impressed by the growing wealth of the colony, but her goal was to visit its Indigenous peoples before they, too, were swamped by empire. Rumours of cannibalism excited her more than commodities.

A week later, Ida arrived at last at the borders of the 'Battaker country'. The Dutch had claimed this part of the region ten years earlier, and Ida believed that Dutch control meant that the locals were 'obliged to renounce their favorite table delicacy of human flesh'. Still, she hopefully wandered through the village looking for evidence of past cannibalism. Another local Dutch resident offered her a tour of the market to watch a cockfight, a 'brutal and disgusting kind of gambling'. She was more interested in the spectators and their 'most horrible grimaces and threatening movements'. She was glad to have witnessed the fight.

Each village had their own local heads that Ida and the Dutch called 'rajahs'. That evening, her Dutch guide invited the local rajahs to his residence. The Dutch resident hoped that the rajahs could dissuade Ida from continuing beyond the vague borders of Dutch rule into the Batak lands where people remained food. Ida listened as the Dutch resident and his local allies spun tales of missionaries tied alive to stakes with steaks cut off from them and eaten with salt and tobacco. The lucky ones were killed at once and beheaded, with their blood cooked into 'a kind of pudding with boiled rice'. The rajahs explained that the head, heart and liver were considered particular delicacies. They 'assured me, with a certain air of relish, that it was very good food'. Ida recorded the vivid description of cannibal feasts (accurate or not) with another kind of relish. She enjoyed the evening, proud of her growing notoriety as a 'white woman who was about to venture into the dreaded country of the wild Battakers'.[37]

After a 20-mile (32 km) trek on 2 August, Ida rested at the home of local Europeans who had only recently hacked a plantation out of the jungle. That afternoon, she enjoyed a siesta and, refreshed, joined them for tea and a rubber of whist. During their game, her Dutch hosts told of four white men who had been 'killed and *eaten*' just two years before.

On 6 August she proudly said goodbye to 'perhaps the last Europeans whom in this world I was ever to see'. She looked back at the last Dutch coffee plantation and fingered the letters she carried from colonial officials to those rajahs who 'were occasionally in communication with the Dutch'. She left behind letters for her family in case she was feasted on by cannibals. She spent the night as the guest of the local rajah. The villagers gathered 'to gaze at me'. She stared back, wondering if they had once eaten people.[38] The rajah slaughtered a buffalo calf and distributed meat around the village. The choice liver was 'politely put aside for me'. It was 'quite uneatable'. She ate rice and salt instead, 'although the calf had been killed expressly to do me honour'.

Two days later, villagers warned her against continuing. They pointed to her throat and gestured that the 'wild men' might soon cut it. Yet 'it never once entered my head to desist from my undertaking.' She spent a miserable night huddled under a hastily built hut and eating unwashed rice and a fish with its guts intact cooked by locals.

On 10 August Ida was a guest of a local rajah, Hali-Bonar, who would travel with her for the rest of her journey. For the first time, she encountered Bataks and she seized the opportunity to examine them carefully. Their lower jaws were large and prominent, she wrote in her diary. Brass plates or pieces of wood ornamented their ears.[39] Hali-Bonar ordered the villagers to slaughter a buffalo calf. She guessed that it was partly in her honour and partly to assuage the spirits who might trouble her journey. The meat and entrails roasted on spits just outside the hut where she lodged. The blood hardened into a kind of rice pudding. Her hosts offered her portions of every dish, alongside a generous piece of liver. She refused the meat and offal. Perhaps her hosts understood her refusal less as a sign of disgust and more as a strange ritual around hospitality. Whenever she refused a dish, they returned it to her. She relented and chewed the liver. At best, she confused her hosts; at worst, they were offended. Once they had eaten, she begged the villagers to put on a dance 'which is performed when a man is to be killed and eaten'. The villagers seemed reluctant, but they eventually relented. Ida described its details, especially when they appeared to 'be lapping up the gore from the dripping head'. She shuddered, thinking that she was 'entirely in the power of these wild cannibals', though, of course, they had only carried out the dance at her insistence.

Still, Ida was beginning to feel frustrated. She had only witnessed dances, not true cannibalism. Annoyed, she was increasingly disgusted by locals' hospitality and food. The smoke from the hearth irritated her eyes and she felt the men staring at her. The food 'was so excessively disgusting that I could hardly bring myself to swallow the meals they prepared for me'. The pots never seemed to be washed and the locals stirred the milk, curdled with herbs and leaves, with their hands. The villagers ate insects and the entrails of any fowls specially killed to feed Ida. Insect eating was 'an abominable kind of epicurism [*sic*]'. Still no cannibals.[40]

On 13 August, she travelled 12 miles (19 km): in the village of Silindong, armed local men blocked Ida's progress. 'They were tall robust men.' Ida examined them, delighted that, at last, she had found the hungry cannibals. She couldn't understand their words but insisted that she understood their gestures. They 'gnashed their teeth at my arm, moving their jaws then, as if they already had them full of my flesh', she wrote. 'I knew if I could say any thing that would amuse them,' she said, 'I should have a great advantage over them.' Savages, she explained, 'are quite like children' and a little joke 'will often make them friends'. In what she judged to be a mixture of broken Malay and Batak, she smiled at 'one of the most violent' of the men and told him: 'Why, you don't mean to say you would kill and eat a woman, especially such an old one as I am! I must be very hard and tough!'[41]

They laughed, and Ida believed that she had triumphed. It is just as likely that they were laughing at her odd mishmash of language and panto-mimed eating gestures. She spent an uncomfortable night there, but the next day, agonizingly close to Lake Toba, the same men refused to let her proceed. Ida still boasted that she had travelled further into the Sumatran highlands than any white person before her: the locals 'assured me', she wrote, 'that no Dutch person – by which they mean any European – had ever come as far as I now was'.[42]

Ida began retracing her route back to Dutch settlements; her fail-ure to witness cannibalism still gnawed at her. She seemed to express her frustration through disgust at the villagers who fed her on her return jour-ney. They were 'dirty beyond description', neither changing clothes nor washing their cooking pots. She saw a dog licking a baby, lapping spit-up mother's milk and rice. 'And among these people I passed several weeks, and had to eat with them out of the same dish!' No one, though, had tried to eat her.

On 23 August she arrived back in Padang and relaxed in a Dutch home, with a clean table and European food. A slice of bread and a cup of coffee seemed to welcome her back to the European colony, using local products to familiar ends. The coffee beans were grown in a nearby plantation and the milk was buffalo.

A month later, as she prepared to leave Sumatra and to sail back to Batavia, Ida fell gravely ill with a 'violent' fever.[43]

Ida in Madagascar: November 1856–October 1858

In 1856, when Ida published the account of her second journey, she dedicated it to the 'Dutch and the Dutch Governmental Authorities'. Though she considered herself an explorer, she was actually documenting the creation and consolidation of European empires, and she made clear whose side she was on.[44] She voiced disappointment or outright disgust when local peoples were, as she saw it, spoiled through their encounters with Europeans. Yet she still understood empire as inevitable progress; savages, their way of life and their foods were destined for extinction.

That same year, Ida schemed to visit Madagascar, the vast island off the southeastern African coast where the English and French jostled for influence and where Queen Ranavalona 1 tried to rebuff both. In November 1856, over glasses of champagne in Mauritius, she met Joseph-François Lambert, and became involved in his coup plot to overthrow the queen. The year before, Lambert had secretly signed a charter with Prince Rakoto, the heir to the throne. Their agreement traded land and extensive mineral rights to Lambert in exchange for a 10 per cent royalty fee and help in overthrowing the queen. By May 1857 Lambert and Ida Pfeiffer were at sea bound for Madagascar.[45]

Their plot rapidly unravelled in violence and sickness. Shortly after their arrival, Lambert suffered his first attack of 'Madagascar Fever'. On 3 June Ida also felt chills and fever. Three weeks later, the queen uncovered their conspiracy.[46] 'I consider our cause is lost,' Ida confessed. Local plotters were condemned to death and the queen exiled the Europeans, including Lambert and Ida, back to the British colony of Mauritius.

By then, however, Ida was dangerously ill with malaria. 'My strength becomes less and less from day to day,' she wrote on 4 July.[47] 'Every illness is trying,' Ida complained, but nothing matched the agony of the 'Madagascar Fever'. She could hardly rouse herself from her couch. She lost her appetite.

Ida blamed her fever on her exertions and the humid tropical air. She could not have understood the irony that, on her imperial adventure, she had at last become food. It was a mosquito, not a human primitive, that ultimately fed on Ida. On 9 October she wrote the last entry in her diary. Back in Mauritius and then home in Austria, the attacks of malaria became increasingly frequent.

On 27 October 1858, in a haze of opiates and delirium, Ida died.[48] When they later printed her obituary, American newspapers, whose offices she had visited during the last stretch of her second journey around the world, reported that Batak cannibals had 'proposed' to eat her.[49] It was how she would have wanted to be remembered: the intrepid explorer who survived local appetites and stomached local food.

2

The Comte de Beauvoir

In 1866 a young French noble, the Comte de Beauvoir, began a journey around the world. He travelled with Pierre d'Orléans, Duc de Penthièvre and an exiled scion of the deposed French royal family, and Auguste Fauvel, the duke's loyal companion and a noble. Beauvoir often described them as three 'French princes'. France was ruled by Emperor Napoleon III, and the deposed French royal family remained in England hoping for a return to the French throne, but these men demanded and received special treatment wherever they went.

Thanks to a personal intervention from General George B. McClellan, the duke had served in the Union Navy on blockade duty during the American Civil War. Towards the end of the Civil War, Napoleon III sent troops to Mexico and installed an ally as emperor, over angry American objections. By 1866, amid the political tensions, the duke, caught between his country of origin and his uniform, resigned his naval commission. For a nobleman without a country, a trip through the colonies seemed the only alternative to endless days of languid leisure in exile in England. Beauvoir and Fauvel were too low-ranking to face exile. Born in 1846, Beauvoir was only nineteen years old when he set off around the world. Though a loyal retainer of the duke, the older Fauvel had in fact served in the French navy as a lieutenant during the Crimean War.

Now, all three set off from London, sailed through the English Channel and continued south. They missed the opening of the Suez Canal by three years. In 1866, travellers departing Europe to sail around the world still had to circumnavigate the Cape of Good Hope. When they passed Africa, they didn't spend time there; instead, they stopped in the English colony in Australia before sailing to the Dutch East Indies, British Singapore and independent Siam. Beauvoir had hoped to visit the French colony in Indochina, but they missed their boat. Instead, he and his party travelled to Hong Kong to start a trip across China, into Japan and across the Pacific to California, New York and back to Europe.

Beauvoir and his companions travelled far and wide, but they were truly tourists, not explorers, the title that Ida Pfeiffer had been able to claim with more credibility. The 'French princes' followed the routes of scheduled ships and lodged mostly in hotels. Tourism, though, didn't always mean comfort. Only a handful of steamships had begun to experiment with the kind of service that segregated tourists from migrants and delivered endless service and bountiful food to their first-class passengers. Grand hotels were new, but few and far between. In 1866 the appeal of leisure travelling was still adventure, not luxuries like soft beds, good food and fine wine.

Throughout his journey, Beauvoir kept a journal and wrote letters home to his father. He relished the opportunity to record what revolted him, devoting much more space to the hardships than the rare luxuries of travel. In the South Seas, he wrote, swarms of mosquitoes 'nearly drive us wild'. In the torrid jungles 'a most painful thirst would induce us to barter a year's existence for a glass of fresh water.'[1] He bragged about the strange, sometimes foul-smelling foods he sampled – or, by necessity, was forced to eat. He also described local peoples and the cities he visited.

Everywhere he went, Beauvoir recorded his impressions of the effects of civilization on those he deemed inferior races. He travelled consciously, as a noble and as a white man, finding affinity with colonists who, serving under many flags, were partaking of the great game of empire building. Diplomats, nobles and even French legations threw open their doors to the aristocrats, whom they treated as visiting dignitaries. In fact, the three men, with their ties to the deposed royal family, found themselves more warmly welcomed in French colonies than in France itself.

Local nobles also invited the French nobles to lavish feasts in their palaces. A few of these local potentates enjoyed real authority, but most had just the trappings of it. Beauvoir allied himself with a deposed monarchy, but considered himself a French patriot. If Ida Pfeiffer travelled to see primitive life before it was submerged by empire, Beauvoir went to see empires in the making. Always aware of his status, he expected, even demanded, hospitality from white colonists and local potentates. He ate the meals served to him by local nobility but delighted in describing them as tawdry.

Shortly after Beauvoir's return home, France went to war with Prussia, the rising European power. The Franco-Prussian War of 1870–71 ended disastrously for France, upending the European balance of power and fuel-ling the French drive for overseas colonies. Eager to reassert its political clout, France, now a republic, seized territory everywhere from Southeast Asia to West Africa. In the midst of this frenzy of conquest, Beauvoir published his journal and his letters as a three-volume memoir of his journey around the world. In between publishing the second and third volumes, Beauvoir served in the French army during the war with Prussia. His books provided a tourist's witness statement of the scramble for worldwide empire. His account helped shape the chauvinism of homebound readers about the character and traits of faraway peoples, whom he often looked at with condescension or outright disgust, complaining about what he perceived as their stench, their food and their character. But he also feasted and rejoiced in settings he found paradisiacal.

London to Melbourne: 9 April–11 July 1866

The Frenchmen left together on an English-built ship, the *Omar Pasha*. The duke preferred sailing ships to steam, and as sailing ships went, the *Omar Pasha* was fast. It had even won a race from Melbourne to London. Displacing 1,200 tons, the ship sailed with a crew of 42 and could offer cabins to sixteen passengers. On this trip the vessel carried only the aristocratic tourists and a young couple bound for the Antipodes. The jovial French young men irritated the couple. 'They do not make the best of things as we do,' explained the count proudly, 'laughing at a sort of food unknown on dry land.'[2] In the first stage of the voyage, the passengers ate the ten sheep carried on board. Since nose-to-tail dining was necessary, they ate the innards and parts they would normally discard as well as choice cuts. The ship also carried chickens for fresh food and eggs, though a few fluttered away, only to drown in the sea.

The weather in the English Channel in early spring was unmerciful. Tossing waves kept the passengers awake at night. By early May, they crossed the Tropic of Cancer and the seas calmed. Schools of flying fish hurled themselves from the waves. Some left the sailing ship behind in their speed. Others accidentally launched themselves over the low deck rails. The passengers and crew collected them for the galley kitchen. Freshly fried, the fish offered merciful relief from the normal diet. The soup was made from water and pepper, and the gravy from pepper and water. The drinking water was fit only for an 'aquarium'. When the fresh food ran out and the flying fish stopped leaping, the French nobles and the other passengers dined on salt cod and cured herrings. The ship carried tinned milk, at least.

In the evening of 7 July a lookout perched on the masthead glimpsed the first lights of Australia. After three months at sea, no one slept that night amid the bustle of packing and the sounds of merry songs. 'Australia is at last before us!'[3] When morning came, the French nobles gazed through spyglasses at the craggy coast, noting the contrast between the wild scrub vegetation and the lighthouses. 'Growing civilization', they decided, was replacing 'barbarism'. After a long journey the length of Africa and then across the Indian Ocean, 'the very atmosphere of Europe is still about us,' marvelled Beauvoir. Then, agonizingly, the winds died. The *Omar Pasha* lay motionless in sight of Melbourne.

Early in the morning, they heard oars sloshing the still water. Beauvoir, excited about the chance to meet what he imagined to be local savages, wondered: 'Are they natives armed with lances?' In fact, local white merchants, selling fresh bread, fruit and meats, had rowed out to the becalmed sailing ship.[4] Later, a naval officer boarded the ship to welcome the exiled French duke. He promised the duke a 21-gun salute of welcome and invited all three French nobles to dine with the governor after they finally disembarked.

Ashore, the Frenchmen rested at a magnificent hotel as nice as any in Paris. As they dined in its sumptuous restaurant, they enjoyed a welcome from Melbourne's high society. The Melbourne Club sent a card announcing that all three had been elected as members. The Union Club promised a nomination. All the 'great people in the town' sent a 'deluge' of cards. They left the table as delighted with fresh vegetables (and the complete absence of salt cod) as they were with British colonial hospitality.[5] Revelling in the warm embrace of colonial society, they walked out of the hotel in search of Aboriginal peoples.

Beauvoir had already begun to think in starkly contrasting terms about civilization and savagery, which he equated with 'whiteness' and 'blackness'. On their first day in Melbourne, he described Aboriginal Australians' skin as black, like a crocodile's. No matter that a crocodile's skin was visibly green: the brutal comparison appealed to him. The Aboriginal people's 'woolly' hair was filthy, Beauvoir insisted. Their 'repulsive bodies' were uglier than any monkeys – the first of many such comparisons to primates he made. Their clothes, once European dress, had degenerated into savage rags – from tartan, they had turned black. They were, he declared, so intoxicated with tobacco and drink that they stumbled into the walls of the 'fine houses' built in the European fashion. And, he pointed out again and again, they smelled bad.

Smell mattered to Beauvoir. If a noxious odour today might be disgusting or just annoying, for Beauvoir, stench also warned of deadly disease. Before the articulation later in the nineteenth century of the theory that microscopic germs caused disease, Europeans like Beauvoir feared 'miasma', that is, 'bad air'. Smells confirmed for Beauvoir – and later, his readers – that the tropics were both lush and perilous.

Yet the disgust Beauvoir felt towards Aboriginal peoples was part of what attracted him to Australia. He felt privileged to witness what he framed as the march of civilization. 'I could not help thinking', wrote Beauvoir, that in about half a lifetime, steam whistles had replaced the cry of animals and supposed savages. Once Aboriginal peoples lit fires as signals to announce across the grasslands that 'white men to be eaten' had arrived, he wrote. Now, telegraphs spanned the plains.

Beauvoir walked the Melbourne streets and handed a coin to an Indigenous man. Beauvoir noted in his journal that the coin featured the English queen, tangible evidence that white nobles like the queen were victors in the struggle for civilization. In the evening, the Frenchmen relaxed in the Melbourne Club. So large, so handsome, so carefully furnished, 'it is quite equal to any Paris Club.'[6]

Murray River to Victoria: 1–21 August 1866

The Frenchmen followed the banks of the Murray River to a sprawling cattle station owned by the rancher John Capel. Large trees sheltered the river and cast shadows over the vast plain. The house at the centre of the station offered the kind of rustic wildness that Beauvoir craved. They had come to hunt exotic Australian game, taste its flesh and meet Aboriginal peoples.

In the evening, they feasted on beef, butter and cheese, all from the station. They cleaned their guns.[7] The next morning, they set out for their first hunting trip, a 'little four days war' in which they killed 120 birds and shot, without success, at kangaroo herds. Beauvoir regretted killing far more birds than they could eat but, he reassured himself, his pangs of guilt and sympathy were what separated civilized 'sportsmen', who hunted for pleasure, from the 'Blacks', who hunted for survival. The wild birds, along with domesticated beef from Capel's ranch, made for magnificent feasts. To Beauvoir, the meals seemed to represent Australia itself: domesticated enough to feel civilized, but wild enough to fascinate.

When the French nobles returned to the cattle station, Capel served them crabs and fish caught from the Murray River 'by the blacks'. It was 'a splendid bill of fare'.

Hunting again, this time further from the ranch, the French nobles stewed the tail from the kangaroo they shot. They roasted parrots on a string over an open fire.[8] Eating wild game in the midst of the wild Australian grasslands, the French nobles imagined that they were sampling the strenuous life of savages. But they were frustrated that they had not yet encountered bands of nomadic Aboriginal peoples. At last, they met 'a tribe of Blacks'. Beauvoir stared and judged: their 'half-naked wives' were 'horrible'. The nobles hired members of the 'tribe' as guides and as porters for their game trophies.

In the evening, after 'a few drops of brandy', Beauvoir and his companions wandered too far from their campsite. Bushwhacking drunk without a compass, Beauvoir depended on the same Indigenous guides he also condemned as odoriferous savages. 'After three mortal hours', lost and inebriated, Beauvoir smelt something repulsive. 'I recognize it,' he shouted, 'our Blacks are here!' The Frenchmen were ravenous and watched as their guides speared fish. 'But the one thing which strikes us, is the frightful putrid smell exhaled by the whole race at every pore.'[9] Beauvoir, Penthièvre and Fauvel ate the fish, and in the heat of the Outback with brandy on their breath, all three surely stank. But Beauvoir does not seem to have been able to smell a French noble, or at least did not think his own scent worthy of commentary.

The Chinese that he encountered in Australia's cities and later in its gold fields also reeked to Beauvoir. However, to Beauvoir their foul odour seemed different to that of the Aboriginal peoples. The Indigenous communities were harder to find, and he was excited when he smelled them and could experience what he understood as a kind of last gasp before they would be extinguished by civilization. However, his descriptions of the smell of the Chinese suggest fright and worry. To Beauvoir, their smell seemed omnipresent, drifting over the cities and gold fields like a deadly miasma.

When the nobles visited the Chinese Quarter in Melbourne, Beauvoir wrote that 'John-Chinamen' reminded him of insects, swarming over the young colony. 'Yellow as tobacco-juice', their stench 'would frighten the rats away', the very rodents Beauvoir assumed that the Chinese ate. Aboriginal peoples, hunting wild game and netting fish, helped the Frenchmen feel like manly, accomplished hunters by association. He was convinced that they would simply become extinct as they were overwhelmed by empire. Chinese foods, by contrast, struck Beauvoir as both inedible and insipid, and he connected them to his fear about the future of the colony and the advance of its civilization. The Chinese, who could survive on just a 'bag of rice', might overwhelm the 'white races' who, according to Beauvoir, required better food and cleaner air. Such concerns were familiar strains in a virulent, anti-Chinese sentiment that was sweeping across the settler societies of the Pacific, from California and British Columbia all the way to Australia.[10] White politicians, who accused Chinese workers of living on a bag of rice and a rat a day, imposed racist restrictions and head taxes on Chinese migrants. Through his tourism, Beauvoir aligned himself with a politics of Chinese exclusion, the racist restriction of Chinese migration. Within a few years of his around-the-world journey, exclusionist politics dominated migration policies in the settler societies of Australia, the United States and Canada.

Beauvoir eventually travelled to those sites, but for now, the French aristocrats rested in Victoria, attending operas and formal dinners. Just a few days before, they had eaten kangaroo with Indigenous guides. Now, footmen in powdered wigs, French cuisine and an 'immense bottle of port, adorned with ancient spider's-webs and decorated with a classic ode of Horace' welcomed them back to civilization. 'How far off already from the savages,' Beauvoir marvelled, and sipped his wine.[11]

Brisbane to Batavia: 23 October–10 November 1866

On the Brisbane docks, the nobles watched sailors loading hard tack and biscuits onto the *Hero* for the journey north to Batavia, the capital of the Dutch East Indies. Beauvoir was excited for the voyage, which would take them through South Sea Islands, which he believed were infested with cannibals. The crew reassured their French passengers that they were safe from cannibals so long as the ship's steam engines continued to function. If, however, the ship foundered on one of the many shallow coral reefs, the passengers would be a 'good breakfast'. In case they needed to escape cannibals, the captain ordered the sailors to load three lifeboats with guns, charts, salt meat, ship's biscuits and fresh water.[12]

Imperial rule still rested lightly over these islands. Britain posted only a few soldiers. When their ship called at Cape York, the Frenchmen escaped the stale air and heat of the ship to stay with the local British colonial official. Captain Simpson and a handful of soldiers led a solitary colonial life. Ships rarely visited or resupplied his outpost. 'Eight months without the sight of a white man,' Beauvoir wrote. As the *Hero*'s crew offloaded 60 tons of supplies – the only goods that Simpson and his troops would receive for the year – Simpson, the ship's other passengers and the Frenchmen trekked into the jungle. In the filtered light of towering trees, they discovered evidence of a campsite. Simpson pointed to long, hard beans scattered around the ashes of a campfire. They were remains of a cannibal feast, he said. Cannibals, he explained, ground the beans to spice 'human hash'. Beauvoir was thrilled.

Soon, they stumbled upon the Indigenous encampment. 'There they were! Literally naked, quite black, and stinking,' wrote Beauvoir. Beauvoir eyed a woman's bone necklace, convinced they were human remains. He longed for a keepsake. Beauvoir offered nails and glass beads, assuming that they would trade valued relics for trinkets. The Indigenous people bargained shrewdly. Beauvoir added tobacco. They refused. He held out an English knife. In exchange for watches, Beauvoir's white collar, the knife, his handkerchief and his notebook, the supposed cannibals offered a sash and an axe.

Beauvoir, though, was desperate for the necklace. He begged his fellow Europeans to cut the buttons from their dresses and coats and offered the buttons to the Indigenous people.[13] At last, the woman handed Beauvoir her necklace. The Europeans must have presented a strange sight as they walked back, defrocked, to the coast.

Back at the British colonial outpost, Beauvoir was glad for a European meal, however meagre the supplies. Ten days later, the *Hero* arrived in Batavia. As in Melbourne, merchants in small boats surrounded the ship to sell fruit and other foods to passengers weary of stale water and hard tack. In Melbourne, the white butcher and baker had reassured Beauvoir that civilization had truly taken root in Australia. Here, Malay vendors reminded him of monkeys, swinging around the ship's riggings like jungle vines. They sold Beauvoir tropical fruits.[14]

Batavia to Singapore: 10 November 1866–5 January 1867

'The last inhabitants of Australia of whom we took leave were cannibals with black skins,' noted Beauvoir as he gazed across the tall masts that crowded the Dutch colonial port, while 'the first to receive us on the soil of Java are Dutch custom house officers, pale and fair.' It was a striking racial contrast, but 'they softened for us the transition from savage to civilized' by their officious search of the Frenchmen's baggage.[15]

In a colony of 25,000 whites, 25 million Indonesians across many islands and, Beauvoir judged, hordes of Chinese, the nobles quickly learned the racial rules about comportment. No European should be seen on foot; it threatened their dignity in a place where the colonial governance of so few whites over so many Indonesians and Chinese felt fragile. The Frenchmen rode in a carriage even for the short distance from the port to their hotel. Beauvoir looked around at the Dutch colony. The Javanese quarter, rank with the smell of people and their cookery, clustered near the unhealthy muddy seashore. Further from the port, European merchants' offices with their Dutch gables contrasted with luxuriant tropical vegetation. It seemed to Beauvoir as if the civilization embodied by the Dutch architecture was in constant conflict with the savagery represented by locals' homes and the encroaching jungle. Beauvoir also worried that the Chinese threatened to peel back the thin veneer of civilization. He saw them everywhere in Batavia, promenading with 'their conceited strut', and wrote of his longing to pull their braided queues.[16]

The Frenchmen arrived at the Hotel der Nederlanden, newly opened in the verdant Dutch quarter of the capital. It would remain one of Batavia's grandest hotels for the rest of the colonial era. Even though Beauvoir was accustomed to Parisian luxury, the hotel – surrounded by villas, tamarind and banana trees and coffee bushes enrobed in vanilla vines – astonished him. Marble columns supported a shaded verandah where Dutch military officers lounged in cane chairs. The dining room opened to the freshening breeze but sheltered diners from the sun. Best of all, sixty Javanese servants, 'swarming like ants', rushed to lay the tables. Beauvoir decided that the 'instinct of the white race from the North' had met the 'yellow race of the equator' to produce this 'garden of fairyland', a 'verdant paradise' offering the pleasures of endless service.

A local servant pumped water into Beauvoir's bath. Another two wrapped him in soft towels. A fourth, dressed in curious red robes, offered a basket of fruit. The servant expertly split open mangosteens to display insides 'like pink snow'. Even more servants – a 'whole troop of Orientals' – waited upon him at dinner. A servant poured his ice water – at 'arm's length', Beauvoir noted approvingly. Another two changed his dishes. Another carved the roast. Another stood ready to serve coffee.

Beauvoir learned his first local phrase, saying to the servants: 'Sapade, cassi api!' On his command, one of these 'Arabian Nights figures', he said, leapt forward to light his cigar. In a letter he wrote that night, Beauvoir said he was tempted to call them 'slaves'. To a French count accompanying the

A main road in Batavia, illustration from Comte de Beauvoir, *Java, Siam, Canton: Voyage autour du monde* (1872).

duke around the world, Dutch merchants seemed to live regally, served by 'swarms' of servants, amid luxuriant gardens that appeared to grow right into their dining rooms. How, after life in 'such a paradise', could they ever return to the Netherlands to be waited upon by only four servants, Beauvoir wondered?

The next day, lunch brought a procession of dishes: salads, curries and roasts. Soon, vast lunches like this one would have a specific name: the rijsttafel. By the turn of the twentieth century, the rijsttafel, with its abundance of both food and service, would become an essential culinary adventure for tourists on around-the-world cruises. The army of servants impressed Beauvoir more than the variety of food itself, whose many plates reminded Beauvoir of his foreignness. 'As a North-man I must make some reservation,' he admitted when confronted by the 'celebrated curry'. He picked cautiously through his food and counted 84 different chilli peppers hiding in the bamboo salads and chutneys. For the French 'amateurs' unaccustomed to 'local flavour', Javanese foods lit 'fiery torments' in both his mouth and stomach. The flow of alcohol didn't help. Even worse, as he cautiously dredged with his fork through spicy sauces, he couldn't find enough meat to cut with a knife. He longed for Australian game dinners.[17]

In the afternoon, after his fifth bath of the day – a vain effort to combat the heat – Beauvoir visited the shops and miasmatic streets where Malays and Chinese, but never the Dutch, lived. A Malay shop sold sticky sweets. Another offered, he guessed, variations of chillies in innumerable saucers.

He judged the neighbourhoods, their residents and the foods they ate by how they smelled. He associated savagery, non-white peoples and, especially, the Chinese with smells that not only revolted him but frightened him as the cause of disease. For Beauvoir, the smells of food, people, mud and rotting plants merged in 'great whiffs' of disgusting smells. His distaste with locals and their foods joined his worry about falling ill in the tropics. Plants that seemed Edenic when manicured into Dutch gardens emitted 'putrid' smells and poisonous miasma here.[18]

That evening, a Dutch colonial official organized a grand reception for the French nobles. During the meal, Beauvoir stared at the 'regiment' of servants guarding a 'stunted little old man', a sultan. The sultan furiously chewed betel nuts, the seeds of the areca palm tree.

Beauvoir, like many of today's tourists, had heard about betel chewing long before he witnessed the local habit; it remains common throughout South and Southeast Asia today. Betel nut chewing excites the salivary glands and chewers' spit is often stained red. To Beauvoir, the sultan's lips looked 'hideous and deformed', and his gums seemed to be bleeding.[19] When local nobles hosted their own receptions for the Frenchmen, they offered imported wines and local cigars, but never betel nuts, which the Frenchmen were not curious to taste. The strong cigars may have stained the Frenchmen's teeth yellow, but Beauvoir never noticed.

The French nobles departed Batavia to relax in the comparative cool of higher altitudes. The botanical gardens at Buitenzorg, grown since Pfeiffer's visit, dazzled them. Like the rijsttafel, a visit to the gardens would soon become an attraction for around-the-world cruises. Ordered into shaded avenues, tropical plants once again seemed Edenic. Beauvoir wandered through the 'perfumed' groves of coffee and nutmeg plants and cinnamon trees and thought about profit, not pestilence. Outside the garden grounds again, locals selling cigars and tropical fruit surrounded their carriage. In the nearby town, attractive women 'dressed as in Eden' fanned coals heating little dishes of food for sale. The Javanese women crouched and bowed when the carriage rumbled past, and Beauvoir was delighted. Here, in Java, 'I am the Great Mogul,' Beauvoir revelled, and 'so can you be if you come here!'

The Frenchmen visited the palace of a Javanese noble, and Beauvoir noticed the servants, not the architecture. They reminded him of bees, countless in number and instinctively serving their master. He counted seventeen servants who waited on them at lunch. At dinner, when 'the native prince sits down to the same table with the French princes', there were twice as many. Still, unwilling, perhaps, to admire the local noble's wealth, Beauvoir decided that these servants couldn't cost much to maintain, given that they were doubtlessly perfectly content eating only rice. 'Like chickens', wrote Beauvoir.[20]

By the end of November, during their travels outside Batavia, the three Frenchmen fell dangerously ill. One shivered with malaria; another was miserable with ophthalmia, a painful eye infection; and the third suffered from sunstroke. (Perhaps to maintain their dignity, Beauvoir refused to admit which disease was suffered by each of the three nobles.) Despite their ailments, a local sultan organized a magnificent reception for the visiting French aristocrats. Under the shade of a banana tree, servants laid a table with heaps of fruits and a cauldron of steaming tea. Amid all this luxury and in front of the locals, Beauvoir resolved not to appear like a feverish, 'wretched-looking European'.[21] The sultan's military band performed the *Marseillaise* and Beauvoir chuckled at the irony of a revolutionary anthem being played for local nobles who were served tobacco and betel nut by armies of bowing servants. (He didn't remark on the other irony, of a French revolutionary anthem being played for an exiled French duke.) Later, as they lounged in a 'thoroughly Asiatic' garden, the servants announced dinner. Seated between the sultan's sons, the Frenchmen drank champagne.

Whatever intoxication Beauvoir may have felt from the splendour of the sultan's palace did not keep him from reflecting in his journal that a 'stifled hatred' obviously ruled relations between the Dutch colonizers and the Javanese, both humble and noble. Beauvoir described the life of a Javanese noble as the 'outward pomp of barbaric magnificence'. The French noble refused to recognize the Javanese sultan as aristocratic equals. Instead, he insisted that the sultan could do nothing more than copy Europeans. Beauvoir scoffed: 'there is much masquerading in the midst of the intoxicating perfumes of the seraglio.'[22] He delighted in being feted, but Beauvoir insisted that barbarism still lurked beneath the luxury.

On the way to their next stop, the Frenchmen shared dirt roads with caravans carrying sacks of coffee, cinnamon, quinine and tea, all bound for export. As Beauvoir counted the porters, struggling with their loads of colonial commodities, he also surveyed decaying temples and monuments. Suddenly, he recognized the Dutch less as civilizers than as conquerors of local monarchs, who now did their bidding. Yet he still blamed the victim. The fault, he decided, lay more with the character of the people than with a European demand for profit and food commodities. It's an 'Asiatic' mode of governance, he concluded.[23]

By 13 December Beauvoir had returned to comfortably European Batavia, his mood brightened and his fever broken. In his journal, he described himself as a 'colonial swell'. Even better, 'I speak Javanese.' That is, he knew enough commands that when he demanded ice water, his servants no longer brought him a hot foot bath. He boasted, as well, that he now enjoyed the 'spices and curry which are so wholesome in the tropics'. Through his own tasting, he had proved to himself that Europeans could survive in – and colonize – the tropics.

Two days later, on the French nobles' last day in Batavia, and with all three recovered, the Dutch colonial government arranged a farewell banquet. Beauvoir was busy counting. He estimated that hundreds of servants, dressed in red turbans and gold-embroidered dresses, served ninety guests. The banquet offered all that 'the greatest gourmand could desire'. The candlelight dancing off the crystal and the servants offering baskets of tropical fruit struck him as the perfect marriage of European luxury and Javanese paradise.[24]

Singapore to Bangkok: 5–20 January 1867

The French nobles arrived in British Singapore at the beginning of the new year and stayed at the Hôtel de l'Europe. A few days later, they left the hotel's colonial comforts to visit a Chinese opium den. Well into the twentieth century, this was a typical tourist jaunt in cities across the world with Chinese migrant populations. Two white police officers led the noblemen into a bamboo shed in the Chinese quarter. Writing in his journal back in the comfort of his hotel, Beauvoir described the den. Chinese men lay prone, in a stupor, on filthy mats. Every night, the police officers explained, these 'filthy' Chinese 'creatures' came to 'dream of the delights of paradise' under the influence of the vile, sickly-sweet opium smoke. The smoke blinded the French visitors, and the smell disgusted them. Beauvoir spied a pet monkey jumping on the table where the den's owner hid his account books. In his journal, Beauvoir wrote that he found the monkey the most human creature in the place.[25]

Beauvoir's initial hostility towards the Chinese that he had formed in Australia and the Dutch East Indies hardened into a visceral aversion. Yet he remained fascinated by them. From Australia to Singapore and then across the Pacific to California, he would visit their neighbourhoods before scurrying back to the comfortable confines of colonial hotels, enclaves and residences, where he would write about his disgust at Chinese foods, bodies and opium. Beauvoir believed that his sensitive nose confirmed his racial status. He worried that the progress of European empire might be rotted away from within, by Chinese who seemed able to work harder and eat less – or, at least, to eat what disgusted whites. 'I do not think that there can be any positive theory as to the immigration of this race,' Beauvoir declared.[26]

His distaste increased even on the trip to Siam, their first visit to an independent Asian nation. Their voyage on the steamer *Chow Phya* began violently. As Beauvoir watched, the Chinese first mate beat his crew mercilessly. Indifferent, Beauvoir looked away, towards a French naval ship, the *Jasmin*, which lowered her flag to salute the prince. The *Chow Phya*'s cooks were also Chinese, and they served up what Beauvoir described as a repulsive mix of mouldy fish, eggs ready to hatch into chicks and red pepper, all fried in coconut oil. The Frenchmen ate on the decks without a table. Sometimes waves broke over the ship's rails, turning their meal into a saltwater mess.

The conditions on deck, though, were 'paradise' compared to what the Malay and Chinese passengers endured below deck. They ate, slept, gambled and smoked opium among the bales of cargo. This 'human ant-hill', wrote Beauvoir, stank.[27]

In the distance, the Frenchmen spied Bangkok, the Siamese capital. Eager to disembark, they planned visits to the city's famous golden pagodas and hoped for an invitation to the royal palace. They were also wary. In Singapore, they had heard rumours of political turmoil in Bangkok. Would Siam remain independent? Would it fall under the influence of the English or the French, who had only recently claimed dominion over neighbouring Indochina? Beauvoir's biggest fear was that migrant Chinese would overwhelm both the European powers and the Siamese.

Floating houses and small boats, loaded with fruit for sale, crowded the harbour. As Beauvoir examined local Siamese up close for the first time, he decided that they looked neither European nor Chinese, but certainly 'hideous', their tobacco-coloured skin accented by mouths blood red from chewing betel nut. Beauvoir felt disconcerted and out of place. In Batavia, the Dutch had built gabled palaces and banks. In Singapore, the English played cricket and raced horses. But nothing of Europe, he said, had been 'transported' to Bangkok. 'It is Asia itself,' with all its 'strange odours', he wrote.[28]

The Frenchmen visited Bangkok's famous floating market. They bought souvenirs: tiger hides and claws, snake skins, drums and perfumes. They gazed at the boats that sold ground betel nuts mixed with lime paste for Siamese to chew. On the banks of the market, they inspected piles of kapi, shrimp's eggs and spawn, fermented in brine. At the vegetable market, they viewed piles of lotus, sago, custard apples, lychees and 'stinking' durians. The smell of the durian, Beauvoir wrote home, 'fills you with horror'. He noted that in Singapore, Europeans never served durian in their bungalows. For the French tourists, 'Siamese cookery' was for looking at, smelling and even hearing, but not tasting. Standing outside a restaurant, refusing even to go inside, they listened to the clink of chopsticks as the Siamese ate kapi.[29]

At last, on 13 January, the French nobles received the invitation they had been craving: a visit to the Siamese royal palace. King Mongkut was the first truly independent Asian ruler Beauvoir had met. Beauvoir wrote that the king resembled a monkey as he spat betel nut into a gold vase. The king toasted his French visitors with an 'abominable decoration under the name of wine'. The descriptions that Beauvoir chose to record in his journal – the betel nut and the appalling wine – capture the paradox of his visit. Beauvoir had been desperate for an invite, partly to assuage his own self-conception as a royal visitor and partly to confirm that Asian royalty was decrepit, decadent and powerless. When the Siamese king served bad wine to French royalty (no matter that the prince was an exile), Beauvoir seemed convinced that Siam, too, might soon become a colony.

To Beauvoir, Siam was the decadent, 'unadulterated East' of splendid palaces, sprawling harems and armies of servants, ruled by a king who did nothing but 'cough and spit'. Outside the palace walls, everything was filth, miasma and stench, yet the country was a 'tempting morsel' for a European power to devour.[30] In his journal, Beauvoir explained that the Siamese, by nature indolent, survived on rice and just a taste of fish, and so could hardly defend their independence. He hoped that France, led by its steamship companies, might peacefully lead a commercial conquest of Siam. If not, he feared that the Chinese, 'restless parasites' undaunted by hard work and meagre food rations, would overwhelm the country.[31]

Hong Kong to Tianjin: 8 February–6 April 1867

The Frenchmen arrived back in Singapore from Bangkok just a few hours too late to board a French-flagged steamship for the French colony of Indochina. In 1867 steam service among the Southeast Asian European colonies was possible, but irregular. Facing a two-month delay, they decided to travel instead to Hong Kong on a British ship.

Along the landing quay of the Peninsular and Oriental Steam Navigation Company (P&O) in Hong Kong, almost-naked children skimmed around in tiny pirogues and waited for passengers to throw small coins into the sea. They dived for the pennies that passengers tossed into the water.

During their time in Hong Kong, the Frenchmen dined with the English colonial governor. Beauvoir hoped to enjoy a banquet prepared by the governor's French chef. Instead, the governor treated his guests to 'a real Mandarin supper' – that is, according to Beauvoir, the kind of banquet enjoyed by Chinese royalty. In a restaurant in the Chinese quarter of the colony, they were seated in a private room, accompanied by British colonial officials and four smiling, made-up Chinese women. Servants and waiters covered the tables with flowers and food. Beauvoir counted two hundred little dishes and just as many tiny cups. The guests were permitted to take home 'two little ivory sticks, for knives and forks' – chopsticks. Nobody explained the recipes to the French guests or gave them a menu. Likely, Beauvoir simply guessed the most repulsive of ingredients based on nasty rumours of Chinese dog- and rat-eating. No doubt he joined the table jokes that a mystery meat was actually a rat.

Such a banquet would have featured local dishes, all served simultaneously. The foods would have been complex and diverse. Highlighting multiple techniques, Chinese foodways had far fewer taboos than French cookery.[32] Yet Beauvoir showed no interest in identifying the methods of a cuisine at least as complex as the French. Instead, in a letter home to his father, Beauvoir invented outlandish descriptions for the dishes that he tasted: cold fish roe in caramel, hashed dog with lotus sauce, sinews of whale with sugar sauce, stewed gills of sturgeon, dried fish and rat croquettes, shark's fat soup, stewed starfish and a sweet pudding made from fish fins. Only the fruit was simply 'preserved'. The rice wines were 'sickening', but, Beauvoir wrote, that word could have been used to describe any of the 'viands'. He recorded these ingredients, not because he was afraid to eat them, but because the banquet was as repulsive as he expected.

Beauvoir was proud of the French aristocrats' 'usually strong digestions'. The adventure was in the eating; the pleasure was in the retelling. 'Now that I've partaken of it, I must confess that it is awful.' He chose the most colourful imagery he could think of to accentuate the foul aromas, curious textures and appalling tastes of the banquet. He boasted that he could, at home, reproduce the whole 'anti-gastric combination that calls itself a real Chinese dinner' with a 'large pot of gelatine, some giblets of fowls, the sweepings of the druggist shop, and the bottom of an apothecary drawer'. To his taste, the dishes were slimy, insipid and sweet, and he was glad that he ate them. 'I was prepared for all,' he boasted, and he was pleased that 'my expectations have not been surpassed.'[33]

In Canton, the nobles visited the market in their continuing search for repulsive foods and pervasive filth. The fishmongers' street felt paved with sticky seafood waste. Beauvoir guessed that the hanging meat at the butchers' stands was dried rats, split and smoked, as well as dogs skinned for braising.[34] There were no hotels in town they deemed worthy of European travellers, so they lodged at the house of a European merchant who worked as a tea taster. The merchant demonstrated how he graded the valuable teas by steeping a pinch of leaves in hot water. He gravely sipped each cup and decided what to purchase and sell abroad. The profit of growers across China depended on his judgement.[35]

In Shanghai, the Frenchmen lodged at the Astor House, 'the least horrible hotel in this place'. They left the hotel, not to eat, but instead to watch local Chinese as they dined in restaurants. Even 'the most sumptuous' restaurants disgusted Beauvoir. At one restaurant, where 'well-dressed waiters' served wealthy merchants, paper flowers and mandarin oranges decorated the tables. To Beauvoir, the food appeared green and sticky. He described how diners used their chopsticks to shovel food from saucers to 'their huge smiling mouths'. In a humbler restaurant, the 'hardly human' customers consumed an old dog, swollen and putrid from having been dragged from the slime of the ditches (or so Beauvoir assumed). On the streets, 'stinking, creeping swarms' of desperate Chinese fed on vermin. They reminded Beauvoir of scavenging monkeys. 'Is not a Chinese town a foretaste of hell?' he asked in his journal.

Beauvoir knew that France and Britain had fought wars to extend their influence in China, seize vital ports and keep the opium trade flowing. Pekin, the imperial capital, stank of decay, he wrote in his journal. 'It is a corpse, falling day by day into dust.'[36]

Yokohama to San Francisco: 3 April–12 June 1867

The Frenchmen arrived in Japan in the spring, just as the cherry blossoms bloomed. Beauvoir recognized that as tourists they were permitted to visit Japan only because American gunboats had arrived before them. In 1853 an American fleet led by Commodore Matthew Perry sailed into Edo Bay. He returned the next year, threatening force unless the isolationist Japanese government signed a treaty permitting trade and travel. Beauvoir imagined the opening of Japan as a confrontation between the white West and the Asian East. 'We are the strongest,' he wrote. 'We do not allow a part of human society to isolate and cut itself off.'[37]

These three French nobles were some of the very first European tourists to arrive in Japan. The country was in upheaval when the Frenchmen visited, though they seem not to have been aware of it. It was the last few months of the rule of the Shogun Tokugawa Yoshinobu, the leader of the feudal, military government. Already, reformist voices called for Japan to welcome both Western visitors and their ideas. They called for both massive industrialization and imperial expansion. Shortly after they departed, during the Meiji Restoration, the shogun handed power to the emperor, whose previous role had been largely ceremonial.

The Frenchmen focused on measuring the differences between China and Japan, which they, like so many other Europeans and Americans in the years to come, understood in racialized terms. Beauvoir viewed China as a decadent, collapsing empire, and he believed he could smell its decay. By contrast, even in the early stages of the Meiji Restoration, he sensed Japanese reform. Still, he refused to acknowledge the Japanese as racial equals. The Japanese 'are bold and enterprising, amiable but as simple as children', Beauvoir concluded. In Yokohama, the first Japanese city they went to, the houses reminded Beauvoir of Lilliputian Swiss chalets: neat, clean and delicate.[38] 'What a contrast' between Japan and disgusting China, he believed. 'You leave the stagnant mud of an unhealthy pool for the clear fresh streams of running water,' wrote Beauvoir in a letter home.

They stopped at a cake seller's stand. The 'cakes are delicious'. He ate enough 'to bring on indigestion', but he blamed his own gluttony, not the food. The Frenchmen ate local foods throughout the rest of their time in Japan and marvelled at the cleanliness of the cooking. 'Indeed, Japanese cooking is far from bad; it abounds in very clean little dishes,' Beauvoir wrote. The food seemed delicate and lovely, but he missed European chops of meat. Only chicken was available. Beauvoir was convinced that the

innocent Japanese could never kill an ox or sheep. Japan was also militar-
izing; within a few years, it, too, would join the race for empire when, in
1876, the country declared a protectorate over Korea, the first step in its
eventual annexation. Even a visit to a gunboat that now flew the Japanese
flag, a gift from England, didn't change his conception of Japanese childlike
gentleness.

After China, Japan smelt fresh, redolent of flowers. The French aristocrats stopped at a teahouse and carefully removed their shoes. 'I really think
our hosts would have cried to see us dirty their pretty mats.'[39] The tourists
bathed, delighting in the pleasures of the young women who refreshed their
bath with warm water. In Kawasaki, in a splendid teahouse, they joined a
crowd of Japanese who were 'devouring with their chopsticks rice and raw
fish'. Attractive young women – 'smart coquettish damsels' – served artful
foods on red lacquered trays. The Frenchmen sat on mats to be served.[40]

By now, Beauvoir was homesick. 'I feel as if I had never been so far from
you,' he wrote to his father in May. A cruise on a French warship, stationed
in Japanese waters, and a French meal helped. For the first time, the duke
was permitted to sail under the French flag, if only for breakfast.

Eager to begin his trip home, Beauvoir shopped for souvenirs. 'We
were dying to buy everything, and to know the price of everything at each
shop,' he admitted. They fingered lacquered pots that will 'find a number of
admirers in France'. They coveted Japanese handiwork but were suspicious
of 'Eastern habits'. They bargained, convinced that the Japanese demanded
outrageous prices from Europeans even as the local merchants served the
French tourists free tea, cakes and cigarettes.[41]

The *Colorado*, a flagship of the Pacific Mail Steamship Company, sailed
into the Yokohama harbour, firing its canons in salute and in a sonorous
reminder that American ocean liners sailed in the wake of gunboats. One of
the very first ships dispatched on scheduled steam service from the United
States to Japan, the *Colorado* advertised 'splendid accommodations' for its
passengers and plenty of space for freight. 'Steam! Steam!' cried the ads.[42]
Though the *Colorado* would take them only as far as San Francisco, they
felt as if they were about to return home.

They had expected and hoped to leave immediately, but the ship was
first scheduled to load tons of tea for export. While waiting, the Frenchmen
were guests at a farewell Japanese dinner. To the sounds of Japanese music,
they entered the dining hall. Covered, lacquered dishes sparkled in candlelight. *Pièces montées* – elaborate edible sculptures – decorated the tables.
Eggs, fish, onions, carrots and other carved vegetables composed a landscape

of green fields, flowing rivers and ornamental bridges. Amid waves of a sauce that Beauvoir guessed was mayonnaise, a sculpted fisherman hauled in a catch of live oysters and wriggling stickleback fish. An expertly cut brill was magically transformed into a ship with billowing sails. The Frenchmen ate it all 'with our chopsticks'. The portions of crab, sauces and fish were small, though – 'homeopathic doses'. The French nobles had brought champagne and handed glasses to the performing geishas. When the dinner ended, their last in Asia, they took – pilfered, perhaps – their chopsticks and paper napkins 'as recollections'.[43]

After fourteen months abroad, they had passed two hundred days at sea. Yet the *Colorado* was the first ship whose first class seemed designed for pleasure travel, 'a sort of country-house life'. Each evening, Beauvoir watched the sunset over the Pacific and thought of France, drawing ever closer. On the journey home, he experienced the dawn of the era of luxury travel. A gong summoned them to dinner. An 'army of waiters' served the six first-class tables. The waitstaff included 'thick-lipped pot-bellied negroes, bearded whites and whiskered mulattoes'. Beauvoir was surprised that the head steward was Black and, disconcertingly, the white stewards 'obey[ed] a sign or look from him as though they were black'. The service, almost absurdly formal and punctuated by ringing bells, impressed him more than the food itself. He wrote nothing about the menu.

The decks far below the airy first class were reserved for Chinese passengers, migrants perhaps to California. The Chinese gathered in their own saloon to smoke, dance and eat, and Beauvoir was relieved never to see them. First class afforded the luxuries of clean air, fawning service at lengthy meals and racial segregation.

All the way across the Pacific, he never smelt 'those fearful odours which mark the track of all the Sons of Heaven'.[44]

New York to Le Havre: 2 August–3 September 1867

In 1867 the trip from San Francisco to New York still passed overland through Panama. The Golden Spike connecting the Central Pacific and Union Pacific railroads wouldn't be hammered in for another two years. The Panama Canal wouldn't open until 1914. It took the Frenchmen a month to get from the west coast of the United States to the east.

Each day, the New York newspapers announced which notable travellers – artists, entertainers, politicians, the wealthy and nobles – had arrived in town. The Frenchmen were staying at a luxury hotel, the Brevoort Hotel, reported the *New York Times*.[45] Reporters, discreetly, did not mention that Fauvel was dangerously ill. In Panama's 'poisonous swamps', Fauvel had caught a fever, likely malaria. A New York doctor prescribed quinine. Fauvel's fever worsened, and his friends struggled to warm him as he shivered. On 13 August they called a priest to deliver last rites and the next day Fauvel died.

On 24 August Fauvel's coffin was loaded onto the *Pereire* for Beauvoir's voyage to Le Havre. The two survivors embraced. The duke, still an exile, departed for England on a different ship.

Beauvoir sailed to France alone.

PART II:

THE GOLDEN AGE OF
STEAM, 1900–1945

Itinerary: ss *Cleveland*

On 14 December 1912 passengers were about two months into their cruise around the world on the Hamburg-America Line's ss *Cleveland*. Sailing between Singapore and Batavia, they dressed for dinner. The dining saloon was expansive. Between ornamented columns, a long table dominated the middle of the room. Smaller but still shared tables lined each side of the room, closer to the portholes. Electric light danced off the white porcelain, white tablecloths and silver cutlery. Colourful menus, decorated every day with different original cover artwork, greeted the passengers at each meal. Passengers were encouraged to keep the menus as souvenirs. Today's menu was well worth storing away at the bottom of the steamer chest.

Even breakfasts were multi-course meals on the *Cleveland* and other around-the-world cruises. Lunch and dinner featured appetizers, soups, fish, chops, roasts, cheeses and desserts. Today, the soup was 'Seagull-soup'. The fish was 'Fillet of Whale, Sea Rose Sauce'. The roast was 'Saddle of Seal'.[1] The menu served up jokes to mark this special day. The *Cleveland* was slipping south of the equator. In the rough days of sailing ships, sailors and passengers marked the crossing into the Southern Hemisphere with raucous festivity. Those crossing the equator for the first time splashed in tanks of salt water. Rum flowed freely and typically a sailor would dress up as Neptune, the god of the sea, in flowing clothes, a white wig and a trident. The *Cleveland* offered something more temperate. Around-the-world tourists celebrated with champagne and gentle jokes about dining on seal – 'Neptune style'. The male passengers took a dip fully clothed in the ship's swimming pool.

The saddle of seal was likely beef, or perhaps lamb. Around-the-world cruises at the turn of the century might laugh about exotic foods; they didn't serve them.

The *Cleveland* joined the Hamburg-America Line in 1909, originally scheduled for the transatlantic trade. At the time, the Atlantic crossing was a busy business, with American, Canadian, French, German and English companies all vying to attract wealthy passengers to first class and migrants to steerage, the cheap accommodation below decks. Commercial competition was also a proxy for international tensions, especially between Britain and Germany. Winning the Blue Riband, the prize for the fastest commercial crossing, was a matter of international pride. In a kind of first-class naval arms race, the major imperial powers competed to build the fastest, most luxurious and largest ships. In 1909, the *Cleveland* was a big

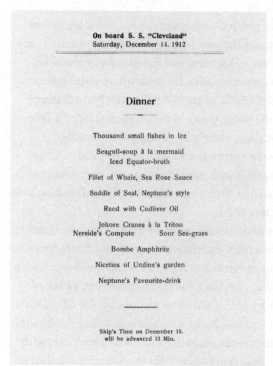

On board S. S. "Cleveland"
Saturday, December 14. 1912

Dinner

Thousand small fishes in Ice

Seagull-soup à la mermaid
Iced Equator-broth

Fillet of Whale, Sea Rose Sauce

Saddle of Seal, Neptune's style

Reed with Codliver Oil

Johore Cranes à la Triton
Nereide's Compote   Sour Sea-grass

Bombe Amphitrite

Niceties of Undine's garden

Neptune's Favourite-drink

Ship's Time on December 15.
will be advanced 13 Min.

Dinner menu on board the
ss *Cleveland*, 14 December 1912.

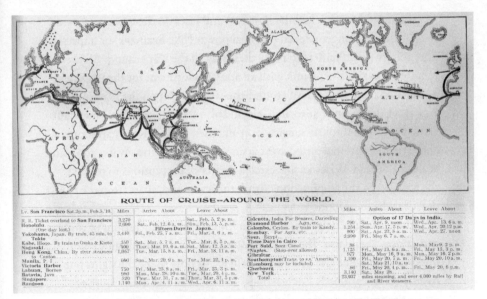

ROUTE OF CRUISE—AROUND THE WORLD.

Lv. San Francisco Sat.2p.m.,Feb.5,'10.	Miles	Arrive About	Leave About		Miles	Arrive About	Leave About
R. R. Ticket overland to **San Francisco**	3,270		Sat., Feb. 5, 2 p. m.	**Option of 17 Days in India.**			
(One day lost.)				**Calcutta,** India For Benares, Darjeeling	790	Sat., Apr. 9, noon	Wed., Apr. 13, 6 a. m.
Honolulu	2,090	Sat., Feb. 12, 6 a. m.	Sun., Feb. 13, 5, p. m.	**Diamond Harbor** Agra, etc.			
Yokohama, Japan. By train, 45 min. to Tokio	3,440	Fri., Feb. 25, 7 a. m.	Fri., Mar. 4, 6 a. m.	**Colombo,** Ceylon. By train to Kandy.	1,254	Sun., Apr. 17, 5 p. m.	Wed., Apr. 20, 12 p.m.
Fifteen Days in Japan.				**Bombay.** For Agra, etc.	900	Sat., Apr. 23, 8 a.m.	Wed., Apr. 27, noon
Kobe, Hiogo. By train to Osaka & Kioto	350	Sat., Mar. 5, 7 a. m.	Tue., Mar. 8, 5 p. m.	**Suez,** Egypt.	2,990	Fri., May 6, 7 a. m.	
Nagasaki	500	Thur., Mar. 10, 6 a. m.	Sat., Mar. 12, 5 a. m.	**Three Days in Cairo**			
Hong Kong, China. By river steamers to Canton	1,067	Tue., Mar. 15, 8 a. m.	Fri., Mar. 18, 11 a. m.	**Port Said,** Suez Canal	88		Mon., May 9, 2 p. m.
Manila, P. I.	660	Sun., Mar. 20, 9 a. m.	Tue., Mar. 22, 4 p.m.	**Naples.** (Stop-over allowed)	1,125	Fri., May 13, 6 a. m.	Fri., May 15, 3 p. m.
Victoria Harbor				**Gibraltar**	677	Mon., May 16, 9 a. m.	Mon., May 16, 2 p.m.
Labuan, Borneo	750	Fri., Mar. 25, 8 a. m.	Fri., Mar. 25, 3 p. m.	**Southampton** Trans. to s.s."Amerika"	1,190	Fri., May 20, 7 a. m.	Fri., May 20, 10 a. m.
Batavia, Java	980	Mon., Mar. 28, 10 a.m.	Tue., Mar. 29, 4 p. m.	(Hamburg may be included.)			
Singapore	520	Thur., Mar. 31, 7 a. m.	Thur., Mar. 31, 5 p.m.	**Cherbourg**	86	Fri., May 20, 4 p.m.	Fri., May 20, 6 p.m.
Rangoon	1,140	Mon., Apr. 4, 11 a. m.	Wed., Apr. 6, 11 a. m.	**New York**	3,140	Sat., May 28.	
				Total	23,937	miles steaming, and over 4,000 miles by Rail and River steamers.	

The route of the around-the-world cruise, from William G. Frizell and
George H. Greenfield, *Around the World on the Cleveland* (1910).

ship: almost 1,000 feet (305 m) long and 17,000 tons. By the First World
War, it was mid-sized, already displaced in size, speed and luxury by ships
like Cunard's ill-fated *Lusitania*.

In its brief heyday as the pride of Hamburg-America fleet, the
Cleveland was just too luxurious even for the Atlantic trade. By 1910
Hamburg-America had outfitted the ship with even more opulent lounges
and bigger cold-storage facilities to cater to around-the-world cruisers.
The *Cleveland* would leave New York in the autumn, heading east to
arrive in San Francisco in mid-winter. Technically – though passengers
didn't complain – it wasn't a full circumnavigation. Until the Panama
Canal opened in 1914, the route from the Pacific back to New York passed
through the choppy waters off Cape Horn. Those who insisted upon the
full around-the-world experience could book an optional train journey
across the United States.

The *Cleveland*, meanwhile, turned around, heading west back
across the Pacific. It was the first of what would become a flotilla of
luxury liners dedicated to around-the-world tourism. Like many other
companies entering the global cruise craze, Hamburg-America partnered
with a travel agency, in this case Frank Clark. The travel agency booked
the ship, handled the marketing and guided passengers during their
shore excursion.

If tempted tourists had the money – and fares on the *Cleveland* were steep – they no longer needed personal power (like Beauvoir) or impressive phrenology (like Pfeiffer) to make their way all the way around. All they required was a steamer trunk with an array of clothes fit for the tropics, a guidebook and money. An around-the-world ticket on the Hamburg-America Line began at $650, meals included – about what most Americans earned in a year. If tourists insisted on an airier, more private stateroom or chose to join optional onshore excursions, they paid extra. Wine, too, came at a price. The guidebooks suggested a variety of precautions to protect the traveller in the tropics: don't drink the water and, apart from the fruit, don't eat the local food.

The *Cleveland* helped establish an itinerary that generations of tourists and cruises would use. The route followed the bustling sea highways of imperial commerce and brought travellers not only to see the sights but to visit colonies, mostly English ones. Towards the end of the journey across the tropics, cruises called at Dutch, American and French colonies in Southeast Asia and the Pacific. In China, at least until its 1911 revolution, around-the-world cruises visited 'treaty ports' under the authority of European powers. Early in the new century, Canadian Pacific, Cunard, Messageries Maritimes and Peninsular and Oriental (P&O) joined Hamburg-America in offering around-the-world packages, typically with a travel-agent partner. It was easy enough, as well, for slightly more enterprising passengers to piece together their own circumnavigations on regularly scheduled first-class routes.

The *Cleveland* promised luxury. 'One hardly knows which to admire most,' read Frank Clark's advertisement, 'its imposing proportions and graceful lines, or the luxurious completeness of its appointments.' The *Cleveland* was a 'floating palace', departing New York and heading towards the Mediterranean, with a pause in Madeira.[2] In early November 1912 the cruise docked in Cairo for passengers to visit the pyramids and dine at the Grand Continental Hotel on 'Filet d'Hambourg' and 'Dindouneaux [*sic*] Americain' – Hamburg steak and American turkey.[3] The ship sailed through the Suez Canal into the Red Sea. The African coast might just have been visible to the west, but Egypt was the only part of Africa that around-the-world cruises in the steamship era typically visited. In late November the *Cleveland* docked in Bombay and passengers disembarked for an overland journey to view the landlocked sites and sights of the British colony. They gazed at the Taj Mahal, of course, but also at the battlefields of the Great Mutiny. They gasped at monuments from India's ancient history but marvelled at the consolidation of British power ever since. In Benares they shuddered at the sights and smells of the Hindu holy city where pilgrims bathed in the Ganges and where the dead were burned on pyres on its banks.

The *Cleveland*'s coal-powered dual screws and towering smokestacks promised speed. Its refrigerated holds, though, were an equal draw for tourists. They carried meat, vegetables, ice cream, wine, beer, champagne and bottled water so that passengers wouldn't have to depend on anything locally grown. Off the coast of India, around-the-world cruisers supped on 'Boiled Turbot, Butter Parsley Potatoes' and 'Braised Leg of Mutton in Burgundy'.[4]

The ship, then, pointed towards Colombo. Its menu looked to France and Europe. The left side of the daily menus – breakfast, lunch and dinner – listed the courses in German, the right in English. The common culinary language was French: passengers would begin dinner with 'Bouchées à la Reine' and end it with 'Bombe à la Constantin'. Passengers booking a trip

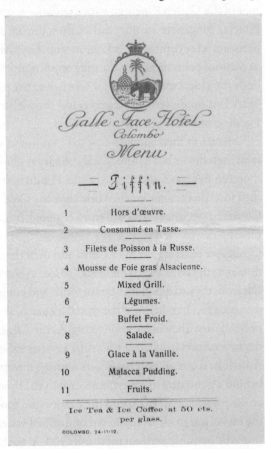

Menu of the Galle Face Hotel, Colombo, 1912.

around the world needed to know enough French culinary terms not
to face the humiliation of asking a passing steward for explanation.

French names reassuringly rooted meals in Europe, ironically, one
of the parts of the world the *Cleveland* left unvisited. Tourists often said
that they could smell the Ceylon's spices when they entered Colombo's
harbour. The smell of spices may have been in the air, but on the menu at
the Galle Face Hotel in Colombo, spices could be found only in the 'Glace
à la Vanille'. The fish was 'à la Russe', the foie gras was 'Alsacienne', the buffet
was cold and the grill was mixed.[5]

Even if they were adventurous and curious, passengers had few opportunities to try anything remotely local. In Kandy, famed for its flowers and
spices, passengers who took the excursion to Ceylon's mountainous interior
lunched at the Queen's Hotel. Alongside the Cock a Leekie soup, 'Grilled
Chicken Robert Sce' and Irish Stew, they could sample 'Fish Mowlie', a
mild curry flavoured with coconut and coconut milk.[6] It was a culinary
tour of the United Kingdom with a tentative taste of Ceylon. At the Raffles
Hotel in Singapore, savoury dishes, from tomato soup to cold turkey with
beetroot, were comfortingly Continental. Gula Malacca, a sweet dessert
of coconut palm sugar, was the only opportunity for tourists to adventur-
ously try a local speciality. In the German treaty port at Tsingtao on New
Year's Eve, for dessert, passengers could choose between 'Englischer Plum
Pudding' and 'Berlin Fritters'.[7]

Menus, in their commitment to Continental tastes, not only refused
local ingredients but ignored local culinary traditions and religious prohib-
itions. In Benares tourists gazed at the Hindu holy sites before returning to
the Hotel de Paris for lunch, where they ate 'Cold Hunters Beef' and 'Veal
Cutlets Lime Sauce'.[8] Tropical fruits tempted, by contrast. At Raffles, the
pineapples were iced.

Before entering the Suez Canal and then the tropics passengers began
dinner with caviar served on blocks of ice.[9] Aboard, there was luxury.
On land, they snapped pictures of locals and complained about constant
demands for 'baksheesh' – the traveller's catch-all word for tips, begging
or handouts. They bought souvenirs. As the *Cleveland* departed Bombay,
the newspapers laughed at the cruise passengers' spending: 'When the
American is out on holiday, he lets nothing interfere with it. They left
behind a good deal of superfluous cash in the shops of Bombay.'[10] But
cruise passengers didn't spend their money on food. Even the ice chilling
the caviar was made from filtered or distilled water to protect passengers
from the invisible perils of food and drink in the tropics.

For clients eager to circle the globe, but worried about what might infect them along the way, the Hamburg-America Line promised that a doctor and a nurse would accompany the cruise. In Egypt, at the gateway to the tropics, the medical staff organized lectures, distributing a list of 'prophylactic instructions to people travelling the tropics'. The measures, though, were 'prophylactic', not preventative. Most passengers still expected to fall sick, no matter how much Clark's staff promised quarantine and segregation from local peoples and their foods. In Batavia, the ship's passengers disembarked, and the doctor hurried ahead to the hotel to order their lunch. Even the salads, he insisted, must be cooked.

From Ceylon to Singapore, one British colony to another. Then China and Japan. The ship crossed the Pacific to Hawai'i. On 29 January 1913, as the *Cleveland* approached San Francisco, passengers sat down for their 'Farewell Dinner'. For tourists accustomed to the standards of Continental cuisine, the menu offering 'Saddle of Lamb à la Jardinière' and 'Sweetbreads à la Maréchale' suggested that they had never really ventured far from home. Perhaps the 'Parfait of Goose Liver in Madeira Jelly' reminded passengers that their first stop, months before, was in the Portuguese island.[11]

During this final banquet, at the end of their tour of tropical colonies, American tourists listened to a German band. The ship neared the United States and the world crept towards war. In the immediate aftermath of the First World War, during the pause in global tourism, the *Cleveland* was impounded in the United States and reflagged as a troop ship, USS *Mobile*, a decidedly less grand moniker. After sailing under other names, it was eventually returned to Hamburg-America in 1926, only to be broken up in 1933. For such a trailblazing ship, the *Cleveland* led a short life.

The *Cleveland* helped usher in a new age of around-the-world tourism. It offered an all-inclusive package of shore excursions and on-board comfort. Meals being included, with alcohol extra, profoundly altered tourists' relationships to locals. Tourists could see and smell local peoples, food markets and meals. Except for fruits, they rarely tasted anything local.

In the years after the First World War, the *Cleveland* was outclassed and outmoded. New ships, especially Cunard's all-first-class *Franconia*, offered even grander luxury around the world than the pre-war *Cleveland*. Ships were steaming all the way around; the menus still remained in America or Europe. In September 1934, the year after the *Cleveland* was scrapped, the *Franconia* was sailing in the heart of the tropics.

The sauce for the salmon was Hollandaise. The rissoles de foie gras was 'Perigourdine' and the mutton was 'Nicoise'. The duckling was Long Island and the ham was Virginian. The ice cream was 'Francaise'.[12] Tropical plantations provided the coffee after dessert. The water to brew it, however, was filtered and distilled.

3
Water

What might be swimming in that glass? When Pfeiffer and Beauvoir travelled around the world, doctors and tourists alike still believed that the unpleasant vapours they called miasma caused disease. But by the late nineteenth century, as concerns about foul odours gave way to germ theory, the anxieties attached to around-the-world travel shifted in kind. For European and American tourists, drinking water in the tropics became just as terrifying as eating strange foods.

As palatial steamship and grand hotels replaced cramped sailing ships, European and American tourists to the tropics redirected their worries onto their most basic need: water. Changing medical understandings of what precisely threatened tourists, however, did not render the strange smells of local foods, meals and marketplaces somehow innocuous. Rather, for many travellers and tropical medicine experts, foul odours, already cast as evidence of racial inferiority, now also testified to poor hygiene. Poor hygiene, in turn, hinted at lurking germs.

Doctors of tropical medicine, a new field that developed in symbiosis with imperial expansion and global tourism, sought to catalogue the diseases threatening both long-term colonial residents and Euro-American travellers.[1] In September 1923, for example, the *Journal of Tropical Medicine and Hygiene* reported from British India on documented deaths from contaminated water and 'neglected diarrhoea, due to eating indigestible food'. Two months later, the *Journal* noted that for travellers in India, 'fluids are required in plenty in the hot weather,' but that, since local water could kill, a whisky and soda with the evening meal or at sundown seemed a good idea. Fine wine, too, could 'promote digestion'. Travellers should bathe daily, exercise (but not to exhaustion) and swallow quinine conscientiously to combat malaria.[2]

New businesses promised to keep their customers safe with carefully managed itineraries. Steamship lines such as P&O and Messageries

Maritimes promised luxurious travels. Travel agencies, like Thomas Cook, offered guided journeys on land. Still other companies, like John Murray, sold guidebooks that explained monuments and attractions. Alongside such companies encouraging travel, new businesses promised protection. As tourists donned cork helmets, strapped on tight belts, swallowed bitter medicines (some of which they carried around in handsome, portable chests), paid a premium for fizzy water or filtered their own, they admitted that, despite beliefs in their own racial superiority, they were at risk in places where locals appeared to live without encumbrance. Alongside their racist dismissals of tropical peoples, tourists admitted their own fragility.

Yet many travellers recuperated this weakness as just another piece of evidence for white racial superiority. As another issue of the *Journal in Tropical Medicine* put it, in 1923, 'The higher [the] standard of civilization the more restricted becomes the range of diet.' It was only right, the *Journal* went on, that British travellers, confronted by cats and puppies for sale as meat in Hong Kong markets, would understand the scene as 'unwholesome, dirty, smelly, unedible [*sic*], and contaminated'.

Certainly, tourists did (and still do) suffer from disease, including waterborne illnesses. The U.S. Centers for Disease Control and Prevention (CDC) estimates that between 30 and 70 per cent of travellers will suffer the uncomfortable effects of tainted food and drink, mostly caused by bacterial infection. 'Boil it, cook it, peel it, or forget it': the CDC still endorses the 'simple recommendations' to treat local food and drink with suspicion and caution.[3]

Diarrhoea, nausea and fever convinced many tourists of immutable difference. Colonized peoples might be able to eat the strange foods and drink the water, the rhetoric went, but tourists should not. With troubled stomachs, tourists came to gaze upon locals as fascinating, a little alluring, sometimes appalling and fundamentally different.

Don't Drink the Water

As his around-the-world cruise neared Port Said, the British tourist A. C. Mole attended the ship doctor's lecture on health precautions. Mole listened attentively and hastily scratched notes in his diary. 'Native quarters, bazaars, etc. to be avoided,' he wrote. At Colombo, 'keep away from poorer quarters' to avoid diseases. Wear sunglasses. Keep the head covered. Don't get overheated or chilled. Don't taste the food or drink the water.[4]

Tourists heard such advice and worried. In 1910 Hamburg-America's *Cleveland* began its cruise around the world with 650 passengers, 140,000 pounds (63,502 kg) of meat, 103,000 eggs, 18,000 quarts (17,000 l) of milk and cream, 6,500 gallons (29,500 l) of beer, 19,000 bottles of wine, 56,500 bottles of mineral water and 3,200 tons of fresh water. The cruise organizers promised to protect passengers against local tainted meats and unsafe water all the way from Egypt to China. Even so, Charlotte Ehrlicher, the *Cleveland*'s on-board nurse, was busy. Instead of sightseeing, she wrote in a letter from India, she treated 'many cases of intestinal disturbance', sometimes 55 a day.[5] A *Cleveland* passenger, Edgar Allen Forbes, also recalled the outbreak of 'digestive disorders', including among those who had 'eaten and drunk indiscreetly while on shore in the tropics'. Forbes took photographs, but carefully avoided the local water. In Benares he snapped a picture of a local man carrying a jar of muddy Ganges water. Back on the *Cleveland*, Forbes ate ice cream frozen 'in the USA'. The ship carried 6,000 frozen bricks of it.[6]

Steamship companies and travel agencies advertised the on-board luxuries of European chefs, well-appointed dining saloons and ample cold storage for frozen foods and stiff drinks. In addition, they promised that a doctor and nurse would follow the cruise around the world; medicine, too, was a perk of first-class travel.

Europeans and Americans had long worried about their health in the tropics and, indeed, disease hampered their earliest efforts to build colonies. In alarming numbers, European soldiers, administrators, planters and residents succumbed to a variety of illnesses, from dysentery to malaria. The psychological impact accompanied the mortality rate, and Europeans openly wondered if those from the temperate zone could survive the tropics. By the end of the nineteenth century, doctors increasingly recognized bacteria, viruses and parasites as the explanation for the diseases that ravaged colonists when they arrived in the tropics. The emerging field of tropical medicine, supported by hospitals and research institutes in both colonies and metropoles, not only promised health to colonists but, in their quest for sanitation, offered a justification for imperialism.

Across the breadth of their colonies, Euro-American imperial governments trumpeted their hygiene projects, from clean latrines in a Hong Kong food market to water-filtration plants in India. Tropical medicine doctors worked alongside colonial sanitation officers and at new institutes both in colonies and metropoles, where they often treated local populations less as patients than as obstacles to effective sanitation. For such doctors, safety in the tropics was a Sisyphean goal. No matter the extent of tropical medicine or the reach of colonial sanitary projects, they warned, avoid local food and water. Sir W. J. Simpson, later the president of the Royal Society for Tropical Medicine and Hygiene, also urged travellers to the tropics to be wary of the 'climate, food, mode of life, environment and civilisation'. They should protect the digestion and avoid overeating.

Safe drinking water was 'a commodity not easy to obtain in the Tropics', declared Simpson. He encouraged travellers to stick to coffee or tea. Like many tropical medicine doctors, he advised against overindulgence in alcohol, but admitted that Europeans found wine and spirits 'necessary'.[7] In both the temperate and tropical zones, drinking water came from wells, rainfall, reservoirs and rivers, but in these warmer climates water was subjected to the 'customs of the people', Simpson explained, and became a 'liquid solution of filth'. He listed the perils: 'cholera, dysentery, filariasis, bilharzia, guinea-worm and a host of other parasitic affections'.[8]

So, as the weather warmed, the sun beat down incessantly and the *Franconia* passed through the Suez Canal, Edith James attended a lecture about staying healthy in the tropics. The ship doctor's advice was a boiled-down version of a tropical medicine textbook: dress carefully, avoid chills and drink alcohol (preferably good Scotch whisky) in moderation. Above all, eschew local foods and local water. If there was no other option, filter, boil and add chemicals to anything locals might drink.

This suspicion of locals both validated and enhanced tourists' fears. In their first few pages, the many other guidebooks available to tourists in hot climates listed the dangers. They printed reassuring hotel and pharmacy advertisements in the books' final pages. By the end of the nineteenth century, a variety of companies, including Thomas Cook, Karl Baedeker, Hachette, Michelin and John Murray, all competed to reach English-, French- and German-speaking travellers. Steamship lines also greeted passengers with their own guides. Tourists were unlikely to read dense tropical medicine journals. Guidebooks, though, distilled the inherent prejudices of tropical medicine into easy-to-digest advice for tourists. 'Europeans must drink only known, reputable water,' wrote a French guide to the colonies, published by the colonial government itself.[9]

In Tunisia, warned the *Guide Michelin*, the water is 'doubtful'. Avoid drinking water from public fountains, or at least thoroughly boil it. Better still, stick to bottled, mineral water from a European firm. All raw vegetables and any fruit that can't be peeled could be dangerous.[10] In Algeria, choose light meals that are easy to digest. Drink liquids moderately and in small gulps. As the dry season turned humid in Annam and Tonkin, germs would multiply in the drinking water. The water should not be trusted, and diarrhoea could quickly become dysentery.[11]

In Egypt, Murray's handbook praised the dry heat, but blamed persistent problems with the drinking water on the 'ignorance, superstition, and filthiness of the natives'. At least 'the sanitary service, which is under an English doctor, is greatly improved', the travel company noted. Avoid Cairo from November to February, and always beware of the 'most picturesque parts of the city'. The old mosques and the bustling bazaars were insanitary. In India, unboiled water 'should be avoided' in favour of 'light wines and aerated drink', recommended the guidebook that P&O distributed to its passengers.

Before drinking the water in your hotel, check whether it is built 'on the most modern sanitary principles'. Diarrhoea is common in Egypt, and you can expect to suffer from it. Try castor oil, Seidlitz powder, a rhubarb pill, a liquid diet and brandy, or an astringent medicine. For more severe diarrhoea, if rice jelly doesn't work, there are 'many good European doctors and chemists' in the bigger cities, claimed a Murray's handbook.[12]

As nineteenth-century guides were revised for twentieth-century tourists, they even expanded their urgent warnings. The 1891 version of the *John Murray Handbook* for visitors to India and Ceylon counselled that the hotels were liable to be disappointing and the service inadequate unless you brought your own servant. The food, 'as a rule', was not good. Except for the buffalo's hump, the meat was lean and tough. The fowls were skinny. Avoid milk and butter because of the 'promiscuous manner' in which locals fed their cows. Depend instead on tinned meats, biscuits, spirits and soda water.[13] In the updated 1919 edition, the hotels remained sub-standard. Hardly any reached the 'European standard of excellence'. The hump was still the only recommended cut of meat, though now the guide also cautioned that river fish 'does not always agree with persons new to the country'. The guidebook had become even more alarmist. Milk and water should 'NEVER be drunk until [they have] been thoroughly boiled'. Aerated water was better than plain water 'and the water in hotels and refreshment rooms should be absolutely avoided'. Never buy soda water from Indian vendors at railway stations. The guide provided instead the address for the British Ice Company, based in Calcutta, which would deliver ice by train.

The guide added a new note celebrating colonial hygiene campaigns. On the one hand, Murray's praised the efforts of the colonial government towards 'practical sanitation'. Towns and cities had 'great system[s] of filtered water'. Still, the grand projects of imperial tropical medicine could never be a 'complete success' because the government faced the obstacles of 'climatic conditions' and the 'habits of the people'.[14] The habits seemed unbreakable and, for tourists, the results could be deadly.

Alarmed tropical medicine doctors published their own guides to health abroad. 'Too often foreign travel,' noted one such guide in 1899, 'instead of restoring health is the means of sowing the seeds of disease.'[15] In the same guide, Simpson contributed a chapter that warned of the perils of Indian travel. During the worst times of the year, 'the whole place teems with the lower and smaller forms of life.' In this particular case, he meant germs. Inevitably, 'it is with difficulty they are kept out of food at table.' Avoid heavy meals and especially *réchauffés* – leftovers. They were likely to cause indigestion and dysentery. Tainted or less-than-fresh fish was 'dangerous'. Ripe fruits were 'wholesome' enough, but it was best to eat them only in the evening, he recommended. Vegetables, however, should be avoided entirely unless prepared by a 'reliable and particularly clean person'. The water for washing them must be boiled. At the other end of the tropics, Aden, for Simpson, remained 'a hotbed of the most deadly diseases, altogether one of the most uninviting and unhealthy spots on the face of the globe'. Most steamships to India and around the world, he warned, docked there.

Tropical medicine was not a shared project with local peoples. Rather, as a change imposed by colonial governments, it was an exercise in frustration that in turn added to doctors' and tourists' suspicion of locals. Typically, tropical medicine doctors believed that colonized peoples, their traditions and their foods represented obstacles to good hygiene. In their accounts, local peoples were vectors of disease rather than partners in progress. As Simpson warned, never trust a servant to prepare your drinking water. The 'necessary precautions will not be taken'. Even 'soda-water from native factories should not be drunk.'

Water represented the lurking peril of tourist travel in the steamship age. 'It is impossible to be too particular about the water drunk in the East,' Simpson stated, describing how waterborne illness assaulted organs throughout the traveller's body. Cholera, typhoid fever, diarrhoea, dysentery – the list was alarmingly long – attacked the intestines and stomach. Worms of various kinds invaded the lymph, circulatory and urinary systems. All this from a glass of water carelessly consumed. 'Every one [*sic*], therefore, who desires to escape the risk of being attacked', should avoid any water that hadn't been carefully prepared for the tourist. Even the 'public water supply', good enough for locals, threatened tourists.[16] World travel came with luxuries – and warnings.

Have a Dive?

'Water', wrote one observer in 1882, 'helps to make the character of the people.' What made one race different from the other, he wondered? Climate, he assumed, played its part. In fact, many theorists seeking to explain racial difference, from social scientists to tropical medicine experts, argued that temperate climates forced its residents to struggle for survival against the elements, leading to innovation and energy. The tropical climates, by contrast, were too generous and locals could simply live off luscious fruits. Not surprisingly, such theories about the effects of climate on the development of races attempted to demonstrate that white races were more energetic than the brown and Black. Yet these same theories raised questions about the fate of white travellers and residents in hot climes. Non-whites seemed to survive in the tropics where the white temperate races weakened. In addition, locals seemed to be able to consume filthy water where white travellers sickened. 'Does not the character of the water supply deserve to rank as equal to climate in the development of men?' this writer asked.

Water divided tourists from locals. Tourists marvelled that, despite their own fear of drinking contaminated water, locals seemed to drink it with impunity. (If locals also fell ill, tourists never noticed or mentioned it.) Travellers, when they arrived in Egypt, snapped pictures of water carriers ferrying water from the Nile back to the thirsty. Or they simply bought a postcard.

Tourists watched locals drink fresh, if befouled, water and, from the safety of the decks of their ships, they observed locals dive for coins into salt water. That, too, amazed tourists as something only locals seemed able to do. 'Hop-o-die! Hop-o-die!' called the 'Black urchins' to the American tourist Delight Sweetser as she leaned over the rails of the ship's deck in Colombo and wondered what they were shouting.[17] 'Don't you recognize your mother tongue?' replied another passenger. 'They want you to throw a coin and they are saying, "Have a dive! Have a dive!"'

She fished for silver coins in her bag as the divers pounded their bare chests – their clothing was 'microscopic' – and sang 'Ta-ra-ra Boom-de-ay!' The passengers laughed, and 'a shower of silver bits' rained into the harbour waters. Sweetser watched as five divers plunged after her coin in a 'tangle

Malays diving for money, illustration from Eliza Scidmore,
Java, the Garden of the East (1897).

of brown legs'. In a flash, they were back, holding the coin and singing for more.

The steamship annihilated space but created distance, architecturally and physically, between local divers and white tourists. As they marvelled at the divers' ability to swim to impossible depths and return to the surface with a coin safely in their mouths, tourists admitted that locals could accomplish feats they could not. The bigger the ships and the higher the decks from the water, the more tourists tossed, the harder divers negotiated.

'Have a dive? Dive for a rupee, for twenty cents, for ten, for five, for a penny.' In Singapore the divers were bargaining, and Robert Stuart Macarthur understood their cries. He tossed coins. The 'boys' scrambled from their fragile boats into the sea. They surfaced with the coins in their teeth.[18]

Coin divers were a common attraction, an opportunity for passengers to examine locals' bodies far more closely than decency otherwise would have allowed. The act of begging, combined with the divers' undress, helped tourists reaffirm their conceptions of racial hierarchy before they even landed. The divers will be 'naked', warned – or perhaps, promised – Messageries Maritimes. When the American travel writer Eliza Scidmore wrote her guidebook to Java, she selected an engraving of Malay coin divers as the frontispiece.

When Lucile Mann sailed out of Singapore for a side trip to Batavia, she watched locals – mostly young men and boys – dive for the coins that she tossed. She pitched coins, gazed at and later described in her diary the thin, brown bodies of Malay divers. One man in particular caught her fancy. He was smoking a cigar. If a coin sank nearby, he flipped the smoldering end into his mouth and eased himself into the waters. To watch his trick, she threw coins towards his tiny raft.[19]

As soon as they arrived in the tropics, tourists like Mann tossed coins to watch the locals swim. Messageries Maritimes explained to passengers that boys in rickety rafts will surround their ship before docking in Aden. They will shout: 'All to sea! All to sea!' Throw them silver coins and they will plunge into the water.[20] In New Zealand Edith James even threw coins into the colder mineral springs in the remarkable thermal area of Rotorua. In her diary, she wrote about the Māori coin divers, not the geysers.

'You no need sixpence any more,' a diver told tourists in Singapore. 'Throw it down, poor boy dive.' Another cried, 'You rich gentleman; plenty sixpence.' Sixpence seemed to be the going rate for a dive in Singapore. In Aden, the divers claimed that they could only see silver underwater and refused to dive for copper coins. Tourists were doubtful but, regardless, they threw silver.[21]

Even as they looked forward to tossing coins, tourists increasingly complained about baksheesh – the coins locals demanded from tourists, sometimes to reward a small task and sometimes just as harassed charity. In Benares Edgar Allen Forbes was thrilled with his dramatic picture of a water carrier until the Indian man held out his hand for a coin.[22] Thomas Cook was just as disgusted, noting that locals would ask for coins for even the smallest tasks they did and even for tasks they didn't. For thirty years, and multiple editions of guidebooks, his company implored passengers to keep their coins to themselves. If every tourist resolved to avoid paying baksheesh, 'he would confer a boon upon the people and upon future travellers.'[23] One traveller even recommended carrying a small bamboo stick to whip the bare legs of locals in India who came too close when begging for baksheesh. 'In this close contact there is danger of catching the plague or some other disease,' she wrote.[24]

Salt water was a source of fascination. Fresh water was a source of disgust. Locals could dive to the ocean floor and drink the local water. On the one hand, tourists could try to convince themselves that locals' ability to drink and dive was evidence of their racial inferiority. On the other, it reminded tourists of their own fragility while in the tropics. In Egypt, the guidebooks warned tourists that, if they must drink from the Nile, they should draw their water from the centre of the stream, where it was clearer. The Egyptians, the guidebook explained, drank from its muddy sides. According to one guide, the Egyptians who preferred muddy water to filtered suffered from various disorders 'in consequence of their inveterate ignorance'.[25]

Packing for the Journey

In 1906 a reader wrote to the 'Traveller's Bureau', a monthly advice column in the *Gentlewoman and Modern Life*, asking for advice about the outfits she needed for her journey around the world. The column writers had advice: bring a fancy dress and an evening frock for dinners or concerts on board, but for travel in India, pack tweed, alpaca and flannel clothing. Select tan-coloured outfits; India was dusty. And, they advised, she should make sure to pack a cholera belt.

The cholera belt was a cummerbund. What is today the wide belt that makes a tuxedo seem vintage had its origins in the desperate attempt to keep white travellers safe in the tropics. 'Let it be thin,' recommended a medical journal, but make sure the wool cholera belt covers the entire abdomen snugly to protect against evening chills. In the tropics, the journal warned, travellers were at particular risk as the temperature plunged after sunset.[26] The cholera belt demonstrates how older, vaguer ideas about the transmission of disease persisted even after the germ theory became popular knowledge. In theory, the cholera belt shielded travellers by warming the stomach and intestines, even in the hot climates. It protected tourists from diarrhoea and the worst digestive problems. By the time this reader of the 'Traveller's Bureau' was departing on her journey, many tropical medicine doctors suspected that cholera belts were little more than an uncomfortable encumbrance. They could hardly protect travellers from bacteria and parasites. Yet most doctors still recommended that tourists should put them on in Egypt or Aden and take them off again in Tokyo or Hong Kong. Even an ounce of prevention was worth the discomfort.

When tropical medicine warned passengers that disease lurked everywhere in the tropics and germs swam in drinking water, passengers packed cholera belts, desperate for any advantage in the fight against stomach trouble. Tourists dutifully wore the tight strip of wool around their stomachs in the desert heat of Cairo and in the oppressive humidity of Singapore. The very fact that passengers wore them, even in the luxury of the steamship dining saloon, reveals how profoundly they worried about their own fragility in the face of tropical disease.

Behind the freshet of warnings and travel advice, the reality remained that the fear of disease increased out of proportion with advances in tropical medicine. Even if steamship companies could guarantee luxury, tourists still felt at risk. Walter Del Mar, an American banker who decided to abandon finance to focus on travel writing after a cruise around the world, shared his recommended, detailed packing list. Bring a sun umbrella of light cotton or silk. Buy your pith helmet in Port Said or Colombo. If you are carrying letters of introduction to an ambassador, pack a frock coat and silk hat. Before you depart on your voyage, buy an aluminium water bottle, a portable water filter and plenty of capsules to purify the water. Carry your own towels, especially if travelling in India, and make sure that 'your whisky flask' was a 'large one'. You can bring it into dining cars on the railway and, often, even into hotel dining rooms. Del Mar recalled that as his ship neared the Hong Kong harbour, an unofficial welcome back to the temperate zone, the crew rolled up the canvas protectors that shielded passengers from the tropical sun. Tourists took this as a cue to remove the cholera belts that they strapped on in Port Said, where they had first tossed coins to divers.[27]

In an atmosphere of concern, the business of outfitting tropical and around-the-world travellers thrived. Sampson & Company, a menswear outlet in the heart of London, even advertised the 'complete India outfit'. Included in its sprawling wardrobe of shirts, collars and suits, Sampson & Company recommended warm flannel to protect from evening chills and linen for the extreme heat of the day. All passengers to the tropics, the shop warned, required a cholera belt.[28] No matter what they wore, however, all passengers needed to drink.

Foreign Water

Tropical medicine doctors lauded the drive for hygiene as the virtues of empire but, in the same breath, they cast the ongoing problems of drinking water in the tropics as evidence of locals' racial inferiority. Thus sanitary officials, doctors and guidebook authors warned that no matter the advances in tropical medicine, locals befouled the water and the colonies remained perilous for tourists. 'There are few travelers of any great experience who have not suffered from cholera morbus, diarrhoea, and the like from drinking water,' wrote an American doctor.[29]

Echoing guidebooks, this doctor recommended only drinking water bubbly with 'carbonic acid'. Its effervescence seemed to sooth the stomach in hot climes, a sanitary and temperate taste in the tropics. 'Avoid ordinary drinking water abroad,' warned *The Sanitarian*, a British medical journal. The journal reminded its readers that when the Prince of Wales went to India, he brought bottled mineral water with him.[30]

Consider the prince's water bottle, fizzy with carbonic acid and carried all the way from England to India. Its glass represented a reassuring barrier separating the safety of home from the perils of abroad. Its bubbles each popped a few molecules of British air. Bubbles reassured travellers that their drink truly came from a bottle, rather than being refilled by non-white hands and resold as safe and pure. Bottled water divided temperate from tropical, white from Indian, pure from befouled.

Soda water was comfortingly non-native. Del Mar even noted, with satisfaction, that 'the natives call it *vilayati pani* or *belaiti pani* ("foreign water").' He recommended it but reminded tourists that their servants would inevitably 'forget' to return the cost of the bottle's deposit.[31] In fact, imports of bottled water from Europe to tropical colonies surged in the last decades of the nineteenth century. In 1893, when the French colonial government in Tonkin measured its imports – 9 million francs' worth – they discovered that a third of those were French wines and spirits. Bottled mineral water accounted for the fourth largest category of imports to the colony. Colonial residents and tourists in hotels drank 100,000 francs worth of bottles of water that had travelled halfway around the world. If they couldn't find French mineral water, they could always buy 'Vichy water salts' at colonial pharmacies.[32]

Fear of water, the invisible enemy, acted as an impulse for segregation, driving travellers away from not only local water and drinks but local foods. Pack simple foods, like tinned meats and biscuits, recommended the London-based doctor Charles Heaton in his guide. If you must eat what is locally on offer, choose bland foods. Your concern is safety, not taste. 'A hot stimulating diet' will only make you crave water. Keep track of foods which agree with you, and those which don't. Beware the 'impure water' used to prepare your food.[33] When you are finished eating, brush your teeth with spirits, not water.

If bottled water from home could keep a prince safe (and his bowel movements regular), it might also protect the ordinary traveller. Though cruise ships packed thousands of bottles of water and alcohol, they could hardly carry enough for an around-the-world journey. Tourists were thirsty – and afraid. When William Frizell arrived in Benares on his around-the-world cruise on the *Cleveland*, he and his fellow cruisers watched Hindu pilgrims drinking the stagnant Ganges water. 'We decided to spend our coins for soda water at the hotel, he wrote. When the cruise reached Rangoon (now Yangon, Burma), the tourists checked into the Strand Hotel only to be greeted with warnings against drinking the running water. The hotel, meanwhile, raised its price for bottled soda water.[34]

Tourists' nervousness about tropical travel and growing hostility to locals were stirred into their glass of water. The big business enticing tourists to the colonized tropics developed in a curious symbiosis with the big business promoting solutions to the dangers of travel. 'The effect is marvellous,' endorsed Thomas C. Flashman. He owned Flashman's Hotel in Rawalpindi and promoted Chamberlain's Colic, Cholera and Diarrhoea Remedy. He prescribed it to travellers to his hotel and claimed 'it has never failed to check diarrhoea.'[35] Despite promises of sanitation, the water still threatened, and tourists added long lists of medicines to the cholera belts, pith helmets and dust-coloured clothing in their luggage.

'The Need is Very Urgent', read the Chamberlain's ad. Dysentery 'often results from indigestible food, polluted drinking water, or sudden changes in weather or climate'. The remedy should be in 'every traveller's bag'.[36] Charles Heaton also offered a lengthy list of medicines for travellers to hot climates. His list ran to two fine-print pages and included everything from potassium permanganate for dosing foul water to cocaine. Ads, again, were at the back of the book. Buy his list of medicines from Burroughs Wellcome & Company. Carry all those medicines in one of the company's signature medicine cases, available to 'tourists and travellers' but as used in Ashantee and Egyptian campaigns and by the Stanley expedition.[37] Thus Del Mar departed for the tropics carrying an extensive medicine chest, including carbolic acid, Cockle's pills, opium, chlorodyne, lactose-tine, solution of ammonia, glycerine of tannic acid and a clinical thermometer.[38]

Ads distilled tropical medicine into pithy warnings, accented tourists' racially tinged revulsion towards local eating and drinking habits and promised miracle solutions. Try 'Treacher and Co.'s Special Preparation for Cholera, Dysentery, & Diarrhoea'. No traveller 'in the East should be without a supply'.[39] Guidebooks enticing travellers east also assaulted them with advertisements for water filters and antidiarrheals. In its guide to passengers, the French steamship line Messageries Fluviales, for example, advertised L'Elkossam. Available from European pharmacies in the colonies, the medicine treated chronic diarrhoea, if tourists swallowed six capsules per day.

Quenching thirst was hard work. Simpson cited the latest findings in tropical medicine, warning tourists that, before they drank, they must purify water and filter it, segregating themselves from the local peoples and their microbes. Simpson recommended further treating the water with 'permanganate of potash', which, he promised, held the power of 'destroying organic matter'. Its crystals turned tainted water an alarming pink. After all that preparation, however, local water was still only 'fairly safe'.

In various colonial wars, in all corners of the tropics, colonial armies had experimented with water filters. During the Boer War in South Africa, for example, the British employed a filter which supplied 800 gallons (3,600l) of fresh water a day. Essentially, the filter, conveniently stored in a fortress tower, worked through distillation. Tourists, though, required a more portable apparatus. At the back of the guidebooks, ads for filters promised to make drinking water safe by passing it through charcoal, asbestos, magnetic carbide, spongy irony, silicated carbon or other barriers that few consumers could explain, but hoped they could trust. They couldn't. Most were ineffective and should be 'discarded', Simpson implored.[40]

Among the crowded field of companies advertising water filters to Euro-American travellers, Simpson recommended only two: the Pasteur–Chamberland and Berkefeld filters. They worked in similar ways, Simpson explained: 'It appears to depend on a sugar economy attraction which the material exercises on protoplasm of microscopic dimensions.' More simply, water was forced under pressure through tubes that blocked bacteria and other microscopic organisms. The Pasteur–Chamberland filter used porcelain filters, while the Berkefeld used 'diatomaceous earth', that is, a soft, sandy rock, which had the advantage of producing filtered water faster.[41] The filters were designed, initially at least, for large-scale purification. In 1895 Darjeeling, for example, a high-altitude refuge for British officials escaping the heat of the Indian plains, installed a large Pasteur–Chamberland filter for the municipal water supply. Companies also marketed portable versions

Pasteur-Chamberland filter, *c.* 1900, metal and porcelain.

for tourists. 'Pure Water', the Berkefeld company promised, 'absolutely free from Disease-Germs'.[42]

Like so many other advertising claims for a safe glass of water, portable filters promised purity, but delivered anxiety. Muddy water easily blocked the filtration tubes – those of the Berkefeld filter were especially brittle. Even worse, doctors experimentally and travellers experientially discovered that other illnesses, viruses in particular, passed through the filter tubes into the water. Countless suggestions to tourists about how to purify water and what to take when they fell ill anyway recognized that the colonial state had failed in its promises of safe water. Pages of ads for miracle pills, bottled waters, filters and imported alcohol responded to a desire for physical and racial segregation. They also tacitly recognized European and American fragility. They may have militarily conquered the tropical zone, but that did not mean that Euro-Americans could safely enjoy it.

So, at the back of the guidebooks, including those written by doctors, ads from hotels, outfitters and pharmacies enticed customers, travelling luxuriously, but worried and sick. The hotels promised healthy locations and safe water. In addition, the wine lists and the cuisine were European. Local – colonized – hands, the vectors of contamination, might carry bags or remove the 'night water', but Europeans oversaw food preparation.

In Cairo, the Eden Palace Hotel advertised 'perfect sanitary arrangements' in an 'exceptionally fine and healthy situation'. Eat in the restaurant. Drink in the American bar. The Galle Face Hotel claimed 'the healthiest position in Colombo', with modern conveniences promising 'health, elegance, and comfort'. In Damascus, the Orient Palace Hotel advertised its 'hot and cold running water in every room' and an 'American bar'. When in Palestine, 'drink Spinney's Minerals and Table Water'. The Bristol Hotel in Colombo advertised 'iced lager beer on draught', imported from Munich. Raffles Hotel in Singapore advertised its own private dairy farm and 'cuisine under the supervision' of a European chef. In Colombo, Calcutta, Rangoon, Singapore and several other branches across the British tropical empire, buy 'pith helmets for gentlemen. Sun hats for ladies.' If travellers did get sick, European pharmacists dispensed medicines. In Bombay, Kemp & Company advertised 'all that is purest'. In Jerusalem, the 'Anglo-American Pharmacy' sold only 'British-made drugs'. The Colombo Apothecaries was conveniently located next to the Grand Oriental Hotel. Cargills Ltd, just a minute's walk from the Colombo landing jetty, also sold wines.[43]

'An Empty Liquor Store'

After the *Cleveland*'s doctor completed his lecture about keeping healthy in the tropics, A. C. Mole and the other passengers filed into the first-class dining saloon for a multi-course meal served with plenty of wines. Alcohol had become the drink of choice on the around-the-world holiday.

For tropical medicine doctors and those who translated their medical texts into practical suggestions for tourists, alcohol seemed a safer choice than the local water. Thomas Cook, whose company blazed the tourist path around the world, would have been disappointed. He was, after all, a temperance activist, eager to prove that mass tourism didn't require alcohol. In fact, in 1841, in Cook's first foray into the travel business, he organized a special train trip from his native Leicester to a nearby temperance rally.

In 1872 Cook set off around the world on an adventure that would help turn his British travel company into a global brand. Cook sent letters describing his around-the-world voyage to the *Times of London* and to the *Temperance Record*. Later, he bundled the letters together into a booklet that served as an advertisement for an itinerary around the world without having to drink a drop of alcohol. While his journey helped convince

Thomas Cook, *c.* 1880.

tourists that travel in the tropics could be pleasurable, alcohol – even to excess – marked first-class leisure.

In his letters, Cook recorded the irritations and pleasures of travel in the tropics: Indian sleeping cars charged extra fees for bedding, for example, at a higher cost than one would pay for pillows and quilts in a shop. Ceylon's hotels were attractively set among the groves of cinnamon and nutmeg, but in his room, Cook lost the 'inevitable war with mosquitos'. Cook promised to leave behind suggestions to improve conditions for any tourists who might in the future book a Cook tour around the world. In Calcutta Cook described the Great Eastern Hotel, where each guest enjoyed their own personal servant, a remarkable luxury for the middle classes. A separate attendant made the bed, another carried out the rubbish, and still another brought the water upon which Cook depended.

To Cook and other temperance activists, it seemed as if the colonies were drowning in alcohol. Cook was dismayed: British colonists began drinking as soon as their steamship departed England for India. 'I have seen young men enter our ships who at first drank moderately,' Cook declared. By the time they disembarked, they could drink 'a decanter of brandy'.

Even in the tropics, Cook still avoided alcohol. 'We get on just as well without "the drink" as do those who take it,' he insisted. Cook described – and enjoyed – the lavish attentions of servants but said little about the safety of the water his servant offered at the Great Eastern. A devout Christian, Cook regarded Hindus as heathens and in Benares, the holy city of Hinduism, he described how idolatry polluted the water. From the deck of their excursion boat, Cook and his companions watched bathers purifying themselves in the holy waters of the Ganges. Meanwhile, partially cremated corpses floated down the river. Later, back on shore, Cook observed a priest ladling out holy river water to pilgrims. The pilgrims drank the 'dirty libation'. Cook was horrified and added Benares to the itinerary of his around-the-world package. Like pilgrims, tourists flocked to Benares. They came not to drink the waters, but to experience revulsion.

During his trip, Cook sent a letter to cheer his temperance readers: P&O ships to India and the Antipodes no longer offered free wine and spirits. Before 1871 P&O had offered complimentary alcohol to attract customers. In 1864 the traveller Cornelius Bradley, for example, sailed on a P&O ship from Penang to the United States and dined on lavish meals and flowing alcohol. At lunch, the stewards served two roasts, miraculously fresh-tasting, cold pineapples, and 'wines, beer, claret, ale, etc.'. At dinner, they served the 'inevitable wines, etc.' to accompany the many courses.

Another typical traveller, Sir Frederick Nicholson, travelled on P&O from England to Madras in 1869. The fare, he noted, was an astronomical £95, but the free drinks were almost 'pressed upon one'. The dessert wines at dinner were 'high class'. At night, in the smoking saloon, a tray of spirit bottles swung over every table. Even so, some passengers kept their private stores of port in their cabins. Only breakfast was alcohol-free.[44] By one estimate, P&O served about 1.3 million bottles of free alcohol every year until 1871. After that, the company's new policy wasn't the temperance victory that Cook anticipated. P&O kept pouring, but for profit. P&O even reminded passengers that they were not allowed personal stocks in their cabins; the company wanted to ensure it had a monopoly on alcohol on-board.[45]

'I now feel that the special work for which I entered upon this round-the-world tour is accomplished,' Cook decided, as he sailed up the Arabian Sea towards the Mediterranean and Europe. 'I think I comprehend this "business of pleasure" around the world.'[46] He did; in the decades that followed, Thomas Cook would cement its position as the world's leading travel company.

His company ended up selling alcohol too. By 1878 Thomas Cook had retired, leaving the company in the hands of his son, who found the profits from alcohol too tempting to resist. In any case, tourists were too frightened to drink the water. In 1892, the year Thomas Cook died, the company that still bore his name advertised a guided tour around the world for $1,575 (in gold). The tour included the cost of food in hotels as well as tea and coffee but charged extra for wine or other drinks.[47]

Thomas Cook helped open a tourist's itinerary around the world, but his views on temperance were at odds with both the pleasure-seekers his company served and the doctors who travelled with them. Temperance was best left in its own climatic zone. By the new century, like other travel agencies partnering with steamship lines to organize competing packaged tours around the world, Thomas Cook enticed tourists with promises of well-stocked cellars. By the time Thomas Cook and the Cunard Lines joined forces in the 1920s to offer a five-month cruise on the *Franconia*, the founder's legacy of temperance had been washed away in a profitable flood of wine, beer, champagne and cocktails. On a typical voyage, the *Franconia* served 4,000 bottles of whisky, 4,000 of wine, 2,800 of champagne and 49,000 of beer to 356 passengers. When it arrived back in North America, wrote one observer, it was 'an empty liquor store'.[48]

Delhi Belly

Around-the-world tourists emptied the wine cellar not simply because they had come to associate luxury with flowing alcohol but also because they didn't trust much else to drink. Pure water, in the end, was just a dream and the glass of water remained a tourist's nightmare. Tourists, on their way around the world, longed for an impermeable boundary that could protect them from local people, their foods, their water and their germs. No matter the size of the medicine chests they packed or how tightly they wrapped their cholera belts, tourists fell ill. When they did, their contempt for locals and their foods hardened.

As the first golden age of around-the-world tourism that Thomas Cook helped inaugurate came to an end during the Second World War, a new type of traveller invented a name for the tourists' agony.

Cairo, 1942: the 'frolic capital of the East', *Vogue* magazine called it. Before the war, all the around-the-world cruises paused here for tourists to see the pyramids before passing through the Suez Canal. Now Cairo lay in the path of Erwin Rommel's Afrika Korps. British soldiers on leave ate and drank where tourists once relaxed. The British Long-Range Desert Group was already legendary for its daring raids far behind Rommel's lines. In Cairo, the unit was known as the 'Short-Range Shepheard's Group'. They spent their leave drinking on the famous terrace of Shepheard's Hotel, Cairo's best known and most luxurious establishment for travellers. The terrace had long attracted tourists as a place to enjoy cocktails while gazing down from a safe distance on the mass of Egyptians in the street below. 'Officers entering the hotel restaurant should be properly dressed,' was the new hotel policy.

With the coming of the Second World War, travel to the tropics didn't stop and hotels like Shepheard's were filled with soldiers instead of tourists. The same ships that once carried around-the-world tourists became troop transports. Tropical medicine doctors who until then had worried about colonial residents and tourists to the colonies refocused to consider the health of soldiers serving on fronts everywhere from Egypt to Burma. The British Army still issued cholera belts, but Americans who arrived in bases as far away as India in 1942 wondered more openly about their efficacy.

Many soldiers were travelling far from home for the first time. Like tourists before them, they sought pleasure, rest and recreation when they could find it, and worried about the food and water. As traveller's diarrhoea became soldiers' dysentery, they invented names to describe the painful consequence of eating and drinking local. In Cairo the famous museums were closed, and Tutankhamen's treasures were hidden, but the bars and hotels remained crowded. Soldiers, wrote *Vogue*, were 'sooner or later laid low or double up with the absurdly named Egyptian stomach (or "Gyppy Tummy") – a most exhausting and humiliating disorder which corresponds to "Delhi Belly" in India'.[49]

In India, where the Japanese army threatened to invade through Burma, American soldiers arrived in bases thousands of miles from home. From America to India, then, 'over the hump' of the Himalayas to China, 'you can fly every inch of the way with American wings. At every stop, you can eat American chow, drink American soda pop, smoke American cigarets [*sic*]', wrote a war reporter. Soldiers might enjoy American soda, but local food and drink offered a tempting respite from Spam and army rations. While waiting for a possible Japanese invasion, soldiers of the American Expeditionary Force tried their hand at tourism. The Taj Mahal 'is counted worth seeing', but the military was worried.

The army hoped that soldiers would 'learn to fear native food'.

4

Harry Franck

'Adventure – in the grand old manner – is obsolete,' complained Harry Franck. In the latter half of the nineteenth century, faster and more luxurious steamships and trains, the spread of hotels and the proliferation of guidebooks and travel agencies had turned the around-the-world journey from exploration into a holiday. 'It requires far less courage and no more persistence to be an explorer than it does a certified accountant.'[1]

But Franck craved adventure, so he invented a challenge. In June 1904 he left his job as a high-school language instructor and set off around the world, sometimes dressed as a hobo and sometimes as a common sailor. 'It was my original intention to attempt the journey without money, without weapons, and without carrying baggage or supplies; to depend both for protection and necessities of life on personal endeavor and the native resources of each locality,' he said.

Harry had many names for his version of travel: vagabonding, tramping and beachcombing. Rather than pay first-class fares for segregated travel, lodging and dining, he would prove his courage, resourcefulness and manhood by mingling with the locals. He encountered locals most frequently when it was time to eat. Sometimes locals offered to share their meagre meals, sometimes they protected them and sometimes, as in India, they struggled to accommodate Harry while following their own religious rules. Harry typically responded with entitlement, especially when he reached the colonies, which afforded special privileges to white travellers, whatever their circumstances. Harry used those privileges as a passport and a meal ticket, often demanding to be fed.

In Europe, the food for tramps was miserable. The soup was thin, more dishwater than hearty broth. Harry cast that swill as a reflection of Europe's class structure, but when he arrived in the colonies, he complained about local food as a reflection of race. Harry, in his writing, always identified himself as a 'white man' struggling with Indians, Arabs and Chinese, whom he often described with the vilest of American racial pejoratives. He was eager to prove his courage and resourcefulness – his manhood – not by earning a fortune, but by overcoming obstacles to which most readers would have surrendered – or would have paid a first-class fare to avoid. Harry chronicled how he won his daily bread on the road by eating local, from the alms given to the poor in France to flatbreads in Syria to the spicy curries of Ceylon. Harry ate it all but enjoyed none of it.

When he returned home, he compiled his notes and diaries and began lecturing about his experiences. Later, he published *A Vagabond Journey Around the World*, a bestseller that helped him make travel writing into a long-term career. In the 1910s he took a job as a policeman in the Canal Zone in Panama and then wrote another bestselling book about it. In the 1920s he wandered around China and through French Indochina and during the 1930s he tramped across the Soviet Union. As first-class travel became more commonplace, Harry offered readers a different kind of arm-chair travel that skipped the hotels and steamship dining saloons. Tramp travel meant eating local.

Rachel Latta Franck, who married Harry at the end of the First World War, had a very different experience of food and travel, even on the same trips. Harry's was a story of conflict, about the adventure of eating local food, however contaminated and spiced. By contrast, when Rachel later published her own book, *I Married a Vagabond*, she described raising children and maintaining a household in the countries where Harry tramped. During her extended stay in China, while Harry wandered, she developed relationships with Ma Yu Shun, her cook in Peking, and her servants. She tried earnestly to learn their language. In the process, she came to appreciate their food.

A College Boast

Harry hatched the idea for a vagabond journey around the world when he was a student at the University of Michigan, attending a party. 'If only I had a few thousands,' said a classmate, 'I'd make a trip around the world.'

'With all due respect to bank accounts,' Harry replied, 'I believe a man with a bit of energy and good health could start *without* money and make a journey around the globe.'

Everyone laughed, believing, like many other people at the beginning of the twentieth century, that travel around the world was only possible for those with ample time and money.[2] But Harry knew that, at least in

America, the penniless were mobile – although they travelled for work and food, not pleasure. Immigrants arrived in steerage, the lower decks and cheapest fares on steamships. Seamen gathered in cheap sailors' homes while 'on the beach', waiting to sign onto a new ship. American tramps congregated in the seediest urban neighbourhoods, sleeping in flophouses or religious missions. Tramps travelled between cities and to rural lumber camps, mines or farms by road or rail – hitchhiking, walking or sneaking into boxcars – and they fascinated Harry.

Social workers, politicians and religious leaders blamed tramps for a host of social ills from drunkenness to revolutionary plots. Cities introduced vagrancy ordinances intended to discourage tramps from congregating in their skid rows, and the railroad lines hired special police to catch people riding the rails. Yet seasonal employers also depended on this ready pool of homeless, unemployed men who drifted between work on the docks and the harvest. And for the public, tramps became objects of fascination – not just criminalized, but romanticized, studied and chronicled. Tramps became the fictional subjects of short stories and pulp fiction novels. A new vogue appeared as both journalists and scholars exchanged their middle-class garb for baggy, torn clothes – the tramp's outfit – and hit the road. Harry read books, for example, by Walter Wyckoff, a Princeton professor who for more than a year dressed, travelled and worked as a tramp to study their lives and labour.[3]

In May 1903 Harry decided to follow suit, and began writing his senior sociology thesis, documenting his experience of life as a tramp. He worked the wheat harvest in Nebraska, joined railroad gangs on the Pacific Coast and even lived among dockworkers in England. Like so many other middle-class observers, Harry bemoaned the 'tramp nuisance'. Yet he found their mode of travel seductive: 'A certain amount of travel', he mused, 'has its beneficial effect', especially on young men 'just arrived at the age of maturity'.[4] He wrote about studying the 'graft', that is, tramps' tricks. He learned, for example, how to spin a yarn of misfortune to win food from 'some householder'. His thesis mixed a condemnation of the 'tramp nuisance' with a prurient fascination with tramps' ability to get by and travel.

After graduating from university, Harry, who spoke French, German, Spanish and Italian, took a job teaching languages at a nearby high school. Still, he yearned for the excitement of vagabond travel and when the school year was completed, he crossed from Michigan into Ontario and found a job on a cattle boat crossing the Atlantic. Every year, the British Dominion sent herds of cattle by boat to England. On the cattle ships, the animals crowded into tight pens in the lower decks. The sailors who cared for the animals joked that this was the real reason these lower decks were called steerage.[5]

In the Company of Men

The cattle ship docked in Ireland at the end of June 1904. Harry knew that his discharge papers were worth more than his meagre earnings. Without a genuine able-bodied seaman's certificate, Harry could later use these papers to pretend that he was officially a sailor and find a position on a ship crossing from Europe to Egypt.[6]

Harry hoped that his language skills would permit him to blend in with the masses of European tramps. By rail, boat and on foot, he tramped across the British Isles. Then, he made his way south from Germany towards Italy. In Venice, next to St Mark's Cathedral, he joined the 'submerged tenth' in one of the 'joints' that sold cheap meals. 'A lean and hungry multitude surged around the corner.' Each tramp grabbed a rusted fork and spoon and a battered plate and dropped a few coins into a dish. A 'wrinkled hag' slopped a ragout made from liver and tripe onto Harry's plate and another cut him a chunk from a slab of cold polenta. Instead of wine, everyone drank water that Harry guessed was drawn from the canals. At the crowded tables, 'rag-pickers snarled at cathedral beggars,' and street urchins shoved shoeshine boys. Outside, Harry noted, tourists fed the pigeons wholesome grain.[7]

In France, Harry met two tramps eating stale bread, which they softened in a nearby brook, under the shade of an oak tree. The three men decided to walk south towards the coal fields, where the Frenchmen hoped to find work. At each town, police stopped the tramps. Harry learned that it was normal for them to demand identification. 'To the French gendarme', explained Harry, the tramp on the road is a *misérable sans-sous* to whom every law against vagrancy must be strictly applied'.[8]

Harry arrived in Marseille in October 1904, during a port strike. In normal times, ships left from here to Egypt, and he planned to sign on as a sailor. Now, though, he was stranded. A monastery managed the public shelter for tramps in an austere building with the words 'Asile de Nuit' carved above its stone doorway. The 'night asylum' reminded Harry how permanent tramp poverty had become in Europe, as in America.

At the water's edge, Harry assumed the role of a beachcomber, a sailor dependent on the meagre resources of public charity.[9] As a large port, Marseille had both a bread and a soup kitchen for stranded sailors. Each day, Harry ate at both. In Europe charity, he realized, came with a side of punishment. 'No talking is allowed in the Bouchée de Pain,' read the rules pasted on the wall of the bread kitchen. Those not following the rules 'forfeit their right to the kind charity of the city of Marseille'. The beachcombers sat at rough tables, washing down stale bread with a jug of water, under the watchful eye of guards. 'Allez', the guards screamed after the men finished, commanding them to leave.

Harry joined the still-hungry beachcombers as they tramped 2 miles (3 km) to the 'Cuillère de Soupe'. At the soup kitchen, they exchanged charity tickets for a bowl of tepid, grey broth with one leaf of cabbage, half an inch of carrot and three sprigs of what looked to Harry like grass. He spied pebbles at the bottom of his bowl. 'The fates preserve me from ever again tasting the concoction,' he declared.[10]

Harry snapped photos of the beachcombers as the strike persisted and their numbers grew. Some men earned a few francs doing odd jobs. Others sold their extra clothing. Some depended on 'grafting', the panhandling and petty theft that might win a few coins or hunks of bread. These 'famished *misérables*' – Harry insisted on the tramps' dignity – shared their meagre earnings among the beachcombers just to fend off 'gaunt starvation'.[11] He would not afford the same admiration to the desperate local poor he met a few weeks later in colonized Asia.

By early December 1904 the strike had ended, and Harry signed on to the *Warwickshire*, the Bibby Line's all-first-class passenger ship bound for Colombo. An officer examined Harry's discharge papers and asked if he was, in fact, an able-bodied seaman.

'I am an A.B.,' Harry answered. It was close enough to the truth, he figured: he was, after all, a Bachelor of Arts.[12]

Bread-Sheets and Baksheesh

Colonial racial segregation began at the water's edge. The rest of the Bibby Line's crew was East Asian, so Harry ate with the white officers. In France, he had subsisted on miserable soups and stale bread. Bound for Egypt and Asia, he dined on French food: 'Valiantly, I struggled to make up for those famished days in the dismal streets of Marseilles.' At sea, Harry strategized to stand his watch – his daily duty – directly under the promenade deck, close to the passengers, who often handed him tips.

The *Warwickshire* anchored in Port Said. As he stood on deck, staring towards Egypt, darkness fell, and Harry panicked. 'In the blackest of nights, this new and unknown world was in my imagination peopled with diabolical creatures lying in wait for lone mortals who might venture ashore and well-nigh penniless.' What he pictured as 'black hordes' frightened him.[13] He considered bypassing Egypt and the Middle East altogether and continuing on to British India. A passenger, returning to his post in colonial Burma, had even offered Harry a job. But how could an around-the-world tourist – even a penniless one – skip Egypt and the Holy Land? Harry collected his wages and courage, and paid a local man to row him to shore.

It was Harry's first time outside of Europe or America but, like many tourists, he already had in mind an image of the 'East' that blended privilege for and service to white travellers with anxiety about the locals. 'A scene typically Oriental graced my landing,' Harry wrote. At the European hotels on the avenue facing the harbour, 'well-dressed white men' sipped cold drinks brought by 'black, barefooted waiters'. Harry, though, knew he could only afford 'native inns'. The white men he asked for suggestions just shrugged, but Harry was too worried to venture into the alleys where locals lived, slept and ate. To Harry, the local quarter was 'the black inferno beyond the wharves'.

To his relief, he spied a sign in English: 'Catholic Sailors Home'. He dashed inside into a shabby reading room. He felt comfortable, at last, inside among the white sailors. He followed their example, chose a book and dozed.

Two days later, on 11 January 1905, he booked deck passage for Beirut, at the time part of the Ottoman Empire. Harry planned to walk from Beirut to Damascus and from there to Palestine.[14]

On the first night of his trek, in a town on the outskirts of Beirut, Harry stopped a local woman to enquire where he might find an inn. She invited him home to eat with her family. Everyone sat on cushions surrounding bowls of lentils, chopped potatoes in oil and yoghurt. One of the men – Harry guessed that he was the woman's father – handed him flatbreads. Harry stared helplessly at the food, searching for utensils. The man tore a piece of the bread and demonstrated to his guest how to pinch a mouthful of lentils.

Writing about the experience a few years later, Harry quickly shifted from confusion to condescension. One needed 'a pair of biceps' to tear this bread, he sneered. 'Ten minutes chewing makes far less impression on it than on a rubber mat.' But it was a 'serviceable wrapper' that could cover a cooking pot, function as a waiter's tray or maybe tile roofs. He turned to racial humour: 'The Oriental is noted for his inability to make the most of his opportunities.'[15] No matter that, in Europe, the food for tramps was simply bad and nobody had invited the ragged traveller home for dinner. Once in Asia, even as a guest in a stranger's home, Harry looked down on what he was offered and, by extension, the people who offered it.

In Europe, he ate bread. No matter how stale, it was simply sustenance. He tried to transcribe the Arabic name: *gkebis*. (He meant khobez, round flatbreads that puff in the oven.) He quickly abandoned the Arabic word in favour of the more disparaging 'bread-sheets'. The flatbread was caught somewhere between staple and food adventure and, with it, Harry could describe himself as a brave, white American confronting the perils of the road and the misery of hostile Arab villages. As Harry walked on towards Damascus, sometimes begging and sometimes buying bread, he passed from tramp – the submerged working class – to *faranchee*, a white foreigner with privileges. He was eager to claim them. Walking into one village, he yelled 'Faranchee' and then asked in fractured Arabic for directions to an inn. Instead, a local man welcomed Harry and offered him a bed in his wood shed. 'I called for food,' wrote Harry – a phrase that suggests the superiority of an employer, or at least a customer, but certainly not a guest – and the man returned with 'bread-sheets'. When Harry proffered a few coins as payment, the man generously refused.[16]

Another night, in a deserted bazaar in the historic Lebanese city of Tyre, Harry encountered the owner of a 'squalid shop' dozing over his simmering sour-milk soup and a stack of stale bread-sheets. Harry prodded the vendor until he woke, grabbed some bread and ordered soup. Locals gathered, curious about the sight of a rough-looking foreigner eating bread and soup late at night. When Harry called for a second bowl, they laughed. (Elsewhere in his account, Harry wrote that locals who watched him eat chuckled at the 'power of *faranchee* appetites', but it seems quite possible that he was entertaining for other reasons – including, perhaps, his clumsy scooping up food with bread.[17])

When he was done eating, Harry turned to the bystanders and demanded a place to sleep: 'I am a white man, looking for an inn,' he said.[18] A local offered him a bed for the night in his home.

Later, when he transformed his private diaries into a published book, Harry emphasized his bravura in the face of what he expected would be danger. He described his daily efforts to eat as a struggle with savage locals who gnawed 'bread-sheets' with their 'fangs'. In fact, these locals usually showed him hospitality, though he rarely acknowledged it as such. When he demanded food from a villager who handed him two stale pieces of bread, he said, 'they were as tender as a sea boot, as palatable as a bath towel.' That didn't stop him from commanding more. The woman shook her head. She had none left to give.

From Beirut to Damascus and back again, when Harry made clear his hunger, he was often welcomed and sometimes refused, but never, really, threatened. Once, in the pitch dark, he stumbled into a Bedouin camp. '*Faranchee*', they cried, startled by the sight of an American walking the road at night. Terrified, Harry crawled silently away from camp 'after the fashion of the West', using the night as his camouflage. Later, he admitted that the Bedouins might simply have been greeting him. Was it 'Oriental hospitality', he wondered?[19]

By mid-February he was back in Egypt, this time in Cairo. He gathered with Egypt's local poor as they crowded underneath the famous verandah at Shepheard's Hotel where tourists and white British residents sipped tea and drinks. The poor surged in the street below hoping that someone would emerge from the hotel to pay them for some simple errand – and tourists invented tasks just to watch the crowd jostle for coins.

Harry joined the crowd of locals more for the experience than for the money. After all, white tramps and beachcombers shared details with him about the graft they enjoyed here in Egypt, which ran along lines of racial solidarity: Christian missions offered them free meals, and the diplomatic consuls and white residents were generous with charity. An agent for Thomas Cook, eager to help a white tramp, even offered Harry a letter of reference to a contractor, who in turn handed Harry money.

'The Americans', a German tramp explained to Harry, 'there are dozens of American missionaries, judges, merchants, engineers, and . . . Gott! the tourists!' Tourists on Nile cruises led by Thomas Cook readily gave handouts to white tramps. 'There's your rich harvest.'

'Ever think of going to America?' Harry asked the tramp.

'Never,' he answered. 'Never again a white man's country for me! Here, a white wanderer is an isolated case of misfortune, far from his native shore,' explained the German. In Europe or America, he would be just another reviled tramp.

Harry agreed. For 'the penniless adventurer of my race', Cairo was 'paradise'. Even the soup kitchens meant for white tramps were generous, thought Harry as he stared into a quart of soup garnished with 'cubes of meat'.[20]

Harry planned to travel up the Nile to visit the ancient Egyptian landmarks. His comrade, the German vagabond, explained to Harry how to see the sights while living off graft. Drop in on English residents or missionaries, he suggested. Tourists, too, were invaluable resources. 'Above all, never let a boat load of tourists go by without touching them.'[21]

He found this advice easy to follow. Thomas Cook had long warned tourists against liberally giving charity to locals, dismissing their demands for spare change as bothersome baksheesh. Harry agreed, complaining: 'Tis the national anthem of Egypt, this cry of backsheesh,' he complained. (In fact, we might understand baksheesh as a strategy for claiming just a small amount of the immense profits from tourism – a kind of informal entrance fee as locals claimed control over their local monuments and heritage.) But Harry saw himself in a different category – a white man, and therefore deserving of handouts. They came, as his German friend had predicted, readily.

An English station master offered him a meal and bed in his telegraph office. Another Englishman, the superintendent on the railway line, gave him a free ticket straight through to Aswan. He travelled in the third-class compartment, surrounded by locals. Like them, he bought dates, fish, boiled eggs, sugar cane and 'soggy bread-cakes' from hawkers that surrounded the train at each stop. Just outside Luxor, at a hospital run by American missionaries, Harry pretended to be a mechanical engineer. The missionaries paid him $2 and fed him dinner in exchange for Harry's opinion on how to fix a contaminated drinking water reservoir. (Evidently, Harry made the same suggestions the Egyptian engineer had already made.) In the famed Valley of the Kings, the Englishman in charge of an archaeological dig cried out to his employees: "'Ere, lads, pass the 'at for the Yank."[22] And to evade entrance fees charged to single sightseers, Harry used his white skin to blend in with tourist parties. He saw the temples and tombs for free.

Once he had seen Egypt's sites, Harry was eager to move on to India. Paradoxically, the same white privilege that fed him ashore made it difficult to sign on as a sailor on a ship passing through the Suez Canal towards India. The steamship lines were unwilling to pay the higher wages white sailors in Egypt expected and, in addition, the lines sought to maintain strict segregation at sea. The stewards and officers were white, but the crews – which Harry would need to join – were largely Indian. Instead, Harry stowed away in a lifeboat on the *Worcestershire*, another all-first-class Bibby Line ship. When the ship passed into the open waters of the Red Sea, he emerged and presented himself as a stowaway. The furious first mate threatened to send Harry to work off his passage as a stoker, shovelling coal alongside Indian sailors in the ship's sweltering engine rooms.

Harry complained that a white man, even a stowaway, had rights and privileges: 'The Hindu fireman would never have ceased gloating over the sahib who had been sentenced to the degradation of working among them.' The captain instead gave him easier work on deck.[23]

The Muck and Mire

White men in spotless cotton suits and jackets greeted Harry when he landed in Ceylon on 13 March 1905. 'In garb, they were men of means,' he wrote, though in fact these were 'vags', indolent 'beachcombers' looking, albeit not very hard, for work on a passing ship. In the meantime, they enjoyed their privileges, stretched out in the shade of a veranda. On the grass below, two 'natives' poured tea for any '"comber" who tossed a Ceylon cent at their feet'.[24] For the 'the white man of the peripatetic mood', Harry had discovered 'Eden'.

Later that day, at the table of the 'The Original and Well-Recognized Sailors' Boarding House of Colombo', Harry watched as two servants prepared the evening meal. Wearing just breechcloths, the servants squatted near the kettle over a wood fire. They scratched 'savagely' and 'sprang up to plunge both hands into the kettle'.

They scooped handfuls of rice onto Harry's plate and topped it with chopped fish curry. He helped himself to bananas and a jug of water.[25] The water was warm, discoloured and bitter.

Over tea, coconut cakes and bananas at breakfast the next morning, Harry chatted with John Askins, an Irishman who had wandered throughout India. Harry had enjoyed graft in Egypt. In Ceylon, he was eager to find paying work. Like Harry's comrades in Egypt, Askins enjoyed the privileges of being a white man in the colonies. Askins suggested he join the police. After all, Askins estimated, half of Colombo's white policemen were once beachcombers.

Harry hurried to the police station. 'An American!' said the police superintendent, 'What a shame! Had a beat all picked out for you.' Harry was the right race, but the wrong nationality. The superintendent encouraged him to travel to the American colony in the Philippines.[26]

Harry was disappointed, but not discouraged. Life was cheap in Colombo, even cheaper, he soon learned, if he slept in the shade of trees and ate at a local restaurant favoured by beachcombers. When he entered, 'a dozen white men bawled out a greeting.' In South Asia, the vagabonds imitated locals and ate with their fingers. At first, Harry was disgusted. As a 'naked boy' served a heaping plate of rice, bananas and curries of vegetables, meat and shrimps, Harry realized that 'I must learn, like my companions, to dispense with table utensils.' He watched as the practised beachcombers excavated a hole in the mound of rice and dumped in the curries. They mixed it all together, like a '"board-bucker" mixes concrete'. An English beachcomber sitting next to him had 'received careful Singhalese training', plunging his fingers, straight and rigid, into the rice mixture and, then, sucking the food into his mouth with a long, quick breath.

'I imitated him,' said Harry, 'gasped, choked, and clutched at the bench with both hands.' Tears ran down his check.

'Hot, Yank?' the Englishmen chuckled. 'That's what all the lads finds 'em when they first get out here.' When they finished eating, the beachcombers threw the leftovers on the floor.[27]

The food was spicy, but there was plenty of it. 'Hunger and thirst come often in the tropics,' Harry recalled.

Harry sailed for Madras, the major port of southern India. He worked briefly as a streetcar ticket officer, a job only open to white men, and saved money for the most ambitious adventure of his tramp around the world: a trip across India by rail and then to Siam on foot through the Burmese jungle.

In the first stage of the journey, he tramped with two other American 'hoboes': Marten, a former clerk for the British Steam Navigation Company,

'Five white bums on park bench', Colombo, 1904, photo by Harry Franck.

'Our cook', 1904, photo by Harry Franck.

and Haywood, who had come to the British colony after serving a sentence in New York's famous Sing Sing prison. They knew that white men could travel by rail at a minimum of cost. The ticket collectors, Harry explained, were typically Eurasians, that is, mixed-race men. Railway work gave them employment and limited power over Indians, but they were 'deferential to white men and no match in wits for beachcombers'.[28] Sometimes, instead of paying their fare, the three hoboes turned to racial violence and threats. A Eurasian collector demanded: 'Ticket, please, sahib.' 'Go to the devil!' Marten threatened. 'Don't ever tell a sahib again that he's stealing his rides.'[29]

In April 1905 Harry scribbled in his diary that Haywood 'assaulted' an Indian (to whom Harry referred, in his diary, with the n-word) for insisting that the white tramps pay their fare.[30]

Harry soon learned that the law dictated that local colonial officials could pay for a third-class fare to the next district for any 'beachcomber who wanders inland'. Harry noted, 'this ideal state of affairs is well known to every white vagrant in India.'[31] Officials even handed beachcombers 'batter'

– money with which to buy food. One rupee a day, just for travelling while white, wasn't enough for the tramps to eat in the kinds of restaurants or hotels typically favoured by tourists. They could, though, afford local food.

In his diary, Harry phonetically transcribed the words he needed to know to eat local: 'pawnee = water … rootee = bread, bas = enough, gilayver = sweets'.[32] To eat the 'messes' for sale in the marketplace or hawked on station platforms, Harry boasted, 'requires an imperturbable temperament, an unrestrainable appetite, and a taste for edible fire'.[33]

Though British colonial officials happily gave Harry money, Hindu food vendors were reluctant to take it. Harry travelled in India at a time when caste lines, which assigned hereditary social positions to differing groups across India, were hardening, encouraged by British colonial governance. British imperial rule employed caste in governing India, even allotting administrative jobs based on caste, thus linking religious segregation to racial segregation to produce the social order of the colony. White British residents and tourists alike were outside of the caste system, but they were still implicated in its beliefs about ritual purity and pollution, which regulated interactions at the table. Their touch could pollute food and render it inedible, ritually forbidden to observant Hindus. Harry, though, dismissed caste as 'silly superstitions', and continued to cross its lines by commanding food from Hindu vendors. He treated caste as an insult to the privilege he demanded, and he attacked it with a blizzard of racist insults and comic stories. Only 'the ignorance and sterility of a brain weakened by centuries of habitual desuetude', he declared, could truly explain caste practices.[34]

Harry understood caste and empire via American models of racism. When he encountered Indian servants or shopkeepers, he thought immediately of the '"mammy" of our southern States'. He compared segregation in India to 'caste in an American street-car', but here, he felt on the wrong side of its restrictions. The Indian shopkeeper, Harry wrote, 'smirks so benignly', even as they were quietly 'cursing the *sahib* and his entire race'.[35]

'Go where we would, the cry of pollution preceded us,' Harry wrote.[36] A street vendor selling green coconuts demanded that Harry throw away his own shell after he drank its water. Another vendor insisted that he smash his clay dish after he ate, and restaurants turned him away with the sign 'For Hindus Only'. 'White men' could not enter.[37] Standing far away from a vendor's open pans, Harry pointed. The vendor filled 'sacks' of stitched-together leaves with the food and, wary of touching, dropped the food into Harry's outstretched palms. The vendor pointed to where the vagabond could eat – alone.[38]

Elsewhere, as an Indian assistant clerk filled out the paperwork for Harry's batter and free rail ticket, Haywood reached to drink from the clerk's pitcher of water. 'Don't touch that, sahib,' cried the clerk. Harry, infuriated, wrote that the Indian 'spoke like a man on who had suddenly fallen the task of launching a first-class battleship'.[39] The British Empire might escort the white tramp around India, but a simple request that Harry respect religious mandates made Harry feel like an outcast.

In Trichinopoly, in South India and today's Tiruchirappalli, Harry wandered the marketplace, eyeing fried coils of pastry, cakes, balls of sweets, chapatis (rounds of baked 'bread-sheets') and cubed potatoes, covered in a green sauce spiked with dark, red chillies. Harry reached out to touch a sweet he wanted. The vendor screamed. Haywood, with whom he was still travelling, just laughed: 'Oh, Franck's gone and polluted his pans of sweets.'[40]

'Beyond the shadow of a doubt, the Hindu heartily deserves an occasional chastisement,' Harry fumed. Evoking ritual pollution was key to 'the subtle ways in which he can annoy the white man'. Haywood, especially, turned to crime and violence when he felt his racial status threatened. He picked Indians' pockets and stole from street vendors. At a station outside Madras, he attacked a fruit seller who sold overpriced bananas 'long past the stage when it could appeal to a sahib taste'.[41]

Harry, for his part, heaped scorn on locals, whom he described as eating rotten food. Around the market in Vizagapatam, a port city on the Bay of Bengal and today's Visakhapatnam, he wrote that Indians crouched, 'clawing at scraps of half-putrid food'. To Harry, they appeared like 'ruminating animals', chewing, staring at 'the vista of squalor beyond'. To the north, in Puri, Harry bought curried potatoes and 'greasy sweets' from 'iron-voiced' station platform vendors. In the bazaar, only a 'vicious-faced youth' agreed to sell him milk but yelled when Harry tried to put his clay drinking pot back onto the 'worm-eaten board' that doubled as the stall's counter. The vendor ordered the white tramp to smash the now-untouchable pot on the cobblestones.[42]

Notions of ritual pollution were less important to Islamic vendors, but Harry looked down on them as well. In Delhi, a Muslim vendor promised mutton, a welcome relief from days of eating vegetarian, but to Harry, the bones in the stew looked suspiciously small. Ultimately, he chuckled, Harry – 'the light-skinned vagrant', he called himself – was too happy for any kind of meat to 'inquire into the status of the pure food law'.[43]

After 4,200 miles (6,760 km) of third-class train travel across India, Harry arrived in Calcutta. He left behind Haywood and Marten and found a new travelling companion, Gerald James, a tramp from Perth, Australia. Together, they planned to tramp across Burma to Bangkok. They could reach Chittagong easily enough by train and continue east to Rangoon by steamer, but eastern Burma, though still part of the British Indian colony, lacked a comprehensive rail system. They would have to walk to Siam, eating local all the way. Harry knew that 'native "chow"' was cheap and, crucially, that there were few notions of ritual pollution in predominantly Buddhist Burma. If he had the money, Harry could buy food easily enough from locals.

However, between them, Harry and Gerald had very little money remaining. They spent some of these savings on a meal at the beginning of May 1905: 'A shriveled Hindu' reluctantly sold them 'a stale and fly-specked breakfast'. Harry assumed that the vendor was frightened by the 'sahibs'.[44] By the time they entered Burma at the end of the month, their money was gone. The hungry pair demanded food from a vendor in exchange for Harry's cotton suit – which, clean and white in Ceylon, was now ragged, threadbare and stained brown.

'We want something to eat,' yelled Gerald, 'you missing link.' He shook the vendor so hard the cigarette dangling from his mouth fell on his sleeping children.

'This is a very jungly place,' the Burmese man protested, 'there's only native food. White men cannot – '

'Jumping Hottentots!' Gerald held out the filthy suit as payment. The shopkeeper and his wife prepared European bread.

'I have worked for Europeans,' explained the shopkeeper, 'I know they cannot eat native bread.' Harry and Gerald ate the toast and demanded fish curry and rice.

At another village, Harry exchanged his solar topah – the hat meant to protect his white skin from the tropical sun – for food. When trade goods ran out, they began stealing. 'We chose a well-stocked booth in a teeming village,' explained Harry. They ordered food from a shopkeeper and his wife, who smiled and brought rice and a vegetable curry. They ate, then left without paying.[45] 'I'm sorry to work this phony game on you, old girl,' said James to the woman.

Whenever they were hungry, the white tramps took to eating and fleeing, expecting anger, even mobs. More often, the locals laughed. Once, a vendor called them back and handed them handfuls of fruit. Harry and Gerald liked to think of themselves as 'two witty sahibs'. Villagers, though, met theft with hospitality.[46]

'H.A.F. and Siamese soldiers', 1904, photo by Harry Franck.

Harry and Gerald also encountered white residents, living in splendid isolation in the jungle. 'Holy dingoes', Gerald gasped as they approached one bungalow. 'I'm a Hottentot if it isn't a white woman.' Harry asked for water, but the English railway official and his wife felt compelled to feed European food to any white traveller, no matter how threadbare they appeared. They offered lunch, but Harry, who thanked them, explained that they had eaten just three hours ago in a village hut.

'What! Native stuff?' the white woman shuddered. The Englishman offered lemonade or seltzer.[47]

At another English house, a missionary's wife handed them a compass and a bottle of 'Superior Curry Dressing'.[48] They carried the bottle all the way to Bangkok, as a souvenir, not sustenance. By the beginning of June 1905, Harry and Gerald were sunburnt and feverish with malaria. They were desperately hungry but complained of food poisoning from the little food they scrounged from locals. 'Nearly sick,' Harry wrote in his diary, 'from bum food'.[49] Dazzled by the tropical sun and starving, they encountered a troop of Burmese soldiers.

The Burmese sergeant laughed and gestured to the jungle, as if to say there was plenty of food. Harry watched as the soldiers dug roots. Others caught frogs and lizards. 'Best of all was the lizard currie,' recalled Harry.

'James and I ate more than our share.'[50] They had tried to cross the jungle by demanding food – on occasion violently – from locals, but they were ultimately saved by the willingness of the Burmese to feed them.

Harry's travel thrust him and his companions into close contact with locals, and his own racial prejudice could lead to violence. In Bangkok, Harry and Gerald booked deck passage, the cheapest fare, to Hong Kong. On the *Paklat* most of the deck passengers were Chinese. They slept and ate in open air, regardless of the weather or sea conditions. Typically, white travellers could afford more luxurious classes, and Harry and Gerald were oddities to the Chinese passengers. During a meal, a Chinese man approached, curious about Harry's camera. Harry was skittish and aggressive. Harry pushed him and the Chinese man fell, shattering his rice bowl. During the ensuing brawl, Gerald badly injured his spine. The last time Harry saw Gerald was when he checked him into the charitable municipal hospital in Hong Kong.[51]

By the autumn, Harry had returned to the United States. He began lecturing about his tramping experience around the world. Packed audience halls and a New York publisher convinced him to describe his journey in a book.

It took Harry five years to turn his journals and letters home into a book. *A Vagabond Journey Around the World*, published in March 1910, kept intact the same racist epithets he had scrawled when he initially encountered locals in the colonies, for he saw no reason to alter his immediate sense of contempt. But the book did revise his experience in other ways, minimizing episodes of weakness and fright in service of a story about a white man realizing a college boast, triumphing over caste rules, surviving local food and laying claim to the fullness of his racial privilege.

And it was a success. Forty years after publication, when the book was in its eighteenth printing, Harry recalled that it had climbed to the 'top of the "best-seller" lists, and stayed there for months'. The book was also popular in Europe and throughout the British Empire. 'I could hardly believe my royalty statements' or the 'flattering letters' from readers.[52]

Harry may have craved such flattery; certainly he enjoyed boasting about it. In the privacy of a letter he wrote home from Ceylon, Harry admitted that shortly after his arrival in Colombo, he was pickpocketed and lost all his journals from the first stages of his journey. He spent days painstakingly reconstructing from memory his time in Europe and the Middle East. In the finished book, he omitted the theft and instead he described barging into the locals' houses to demand food. He insisted that the families greeted him silently – 'silent joy' at the 'honor of welcoming a white man'. They were 'speechless with awe and veneration'.[53]

Rachel's Story

Rachel Latta married Harry in 1919. They met during the First World War, when she served as a volunteer at an army hospital in Paris. As a cavalry lieutenant, Harry censored soldiers' letters home. After the armistice and his discharge, Harry departed for a defeated Germany and resumed his vagabond writing career.

After Harry finished his book *Vagabonding Through Changing Germany* (1920), and with the urging of his publishers, he and Rachel decided on a tramp honeymoon through the Caribbean.[54] In Cuba, for example, Harry decided they should abandon the tourist hotel for a Cuban family home 'to get the feel of the country'. Harry wrote. Rachel studied Spanish and tried to make friends with 'daughters of the house'. They stayed for two weeks, 'martyrs', she wrote later, 'to the "feel"'.

This was the pattern for the first years of their marriage. Harry tramped and wrote. Rachel cobbled together a household and eventually raised their first children. Their son was born during their Caribbean trip and their daughter, almost two years later, in China.

On 15 April 1922 Rachel, Harry, and their son sailed for Japan, en route to China. Harry had plans for two new books about tramping across Japan, the Japanese colony in Korea, and then China.[55] In Tokyo, their first stop in Asia as a family, Harry arranged a stay with a railway company official at his house. Their hosts served them three trays with bowls of rice and soup, plates of fish and an assortment of small dishes. They added 'bread of a sort' and butter, a gesture to their American tastes. Harry sampled a dish of 'brownish liquid'.

'Suffering tom-cats. It's poison,' yelled Harry. It was soy sauce. Their Japanese hosts laughed politely, but Harry's loud suspicion of food in East Asia was obvious. Rachel put their son to sleep on unfamiliar tatami mats. Harry went for a walk.[56]

Harry began planning an itinerary for his tramp in China that would take him to the Russian frontier in the far north and across the Gobi Desert in the west. Rachel worried about how she might find a house to rent in Peking. Rachel went with him as far as Korea where she and their toddler son planned to set up house. She was nervous, especially about running a household with Chinese servants and cook. In July, as they neared Peking, she wrote to her sister asking for a copy of the *Boston Cooking-School Cookbook*, the standard collection of American recipes, explaining, 'I'll probably have a lot to show my Chinese cook if I have a house to keep.'[57] In Peking, after an arduous search, she found a house with those conveniences she associated with the West: coal-heating and hot water.[58]

While Harry had a habit of running roughshod over cooks, servants and vendors, then quickly leaving town, Rachel, staying in one place, cultivated longer relationships. She keenly felt her dependence on the skill and knowledge of her five servants. 'Coming from servantless America, five seemed a great plenty for three people,' she wrote. Across the barriers of language, it was her job to manage them.[59]

Sometimes it went poorly. Rachel fired a nurse after discovering her opening the toddler's hygienic bottle with her teeth, and then had to hire another. She fired another servant for stealing coal. Others, she treated with affection, in particular the 'marvelous cook' Ma Yu Shan. At first, she communicated with him using signs. After their first month together, he had taught her a few words. 'My little old cook is good to me and spoils me,' she wrote home to her sister.[60]

Household staff with Rachel Franck's son, 1922. Ma Yu Shan is on the far left.

In early October, Rachel began taking Chinese language lessons, but struggled with the tones. Once she sent out for firecrackers to mark the Fourth of July. The servant returned with bananas.[61] She depended on Ma Yu Shan to order food from the market. 'I am studying Chinese pretty hard,' wrote Rachel. 'I can talk fluently about stoves and food and babies.' She boasted to her parents: 'now the cook says I talk very well ... The cook is a dear.'[62]

Rachel and Ma Yu deepened their mutual trust and understanding. She and Harry had expected edible oddities in China, and Harry had even written about his expectation of needing to consume 'fried rats' as he tramped across the country.[63] But Ma Yu Shan recognized what the family desired and stretched his shopping and cooking to include it. For breakfast, Ma Yu prepared persimmons, hot millet, eggs and bacon.[64] One lunch, served in a bowl, looked to Rachel like a blooming plant, with leaves of chopped spinach and flowers of iridescent shrimp. ('Food in China', she wrote later, 'must taste good and smell good and be good to look at.')[65] For dinner, the cook mixed eggs into a clear soup to spin delicate ribbons. He roasted pheasants or snipes with baked water-chestnuts or French-fried potatoes, Rachel wrote, 'as only a Chinese can make'. For dessert, he might make 'Peking Dust, a wall of glacéd nuts and fruit with a heap of grated chestnuts inside'. The dessert is 'scrumptious', said Rachel.[66] At Thanksgiving, he explained to Rachel that there would 'not be a foreign chicken' at the market. Instead, he roasted small game birds and served them with hollowed-out persimmons, filled with fruit salad. Chocolate cake followed, and Rachel and her young son thanked Ma Yu Shan in Chinese.[67]

'Will the *taitai* have Chinese or foreign food for dinner?' Ma Yu would ask, using a Chinese title of respect. Sometimes, she requested 'Chinese food' and he placed a boiling copper pot in the centre of their specially made Western-style dining table. Rachel and her son used their chopsticks to boil paper-thin slices of lamb meat and liver, seaweed, noodles and cabbage in the hot pot for soup. 'I wanted the small boy to learn to use chopsticks,' Rachel remembered.[68] But they enjoyed Ma Yu's interpretations of Western foods too. 'I supped alone to-night,' she wrote early in her stay to her sister, 'on squabs and potato chips and apple sauce, with a heap of grated chestnuts and white-of-egg frills to top it off.'[69]

Harry, meanwhile, wrote to relatives in the United States that he had 'escaped from domestic captivity on the evening of the 23d of October and was neither seen nor smelled again until the evening of December 21st'. He was humbled when he returned to his family. 'As you know, I have a very good opinion of myself as a cute guy, and especially in the linguistic,' he confessed. He believed that he could 'spiel Chinese' well enough to order servants about, but Rachel had quickly exceeded his abilities. When Harry returned, he wrote, 'a squint-eyed gentleman dropped in the day before Christmas, and it took some two hours before I succeeded in kicking him out again.' Rachel, meanwhile, chatted amiably in Chinese. 'I could not even understand,' admitted Harry.[70]

Rachel had developed close ties with the cook, and Harry knew that the family dined satisfactorily, regardless of whether he was at home or on the road. But he was distrustful and suspected that the cook cheated them. 'It is taken for granted by all foreigners in China that their cooks believe a certain legitimate "squeeze" is attached to the job,' Harry said, meaning that cooks pocketed leftover change from market vendors, who themselves regularly overcharged white foreigners. Harry wondered 'just how much our cook manages to lay aside' from the money he was given to buy food from the market. Proudly, he noted that even if the Francks could afford it, they didn't pay their cook more than the standard low wage. 'The moment you pay a servant more than the market price,' explained Harry, 'he takes you for a gullible victim.' It was, according to Harry, 'the Chinese way of thinking'.[71]

Harry also complained about the cook's signature Peking Dust dessert. To Harry, the 'infamous' dessert was 'exactly the consistency, though by no means the splendid taste, of sawdust'. He knew, though, that the 'member of the family with most influence in the kitchen' enjoyed it.[72]

Rachel enjoyed other Chinese dishes and recorded them in her diary. After dining at a Chinese restaurant in early January 1923, she wrote, 'Had shark's fin soup, pressed chicken, bamboo, duck, lotus seeds and a million more things.'[73] In late March, she gave birth to their daughter and, just two months later, she packed up and prepared to leave Peking, with her two children, to meet Harry in Shanxi province, where he was beginning his tramp towards southern China. She would set up another household, though more briefly, in the south. On one of her last days in Peking, she went out to enjoy a 'Chinese feast' of what she called 'most elaborate and endless dishes'. She also wrote letters of recommendation for her servants, at least some of whom quickly found new positions with her help.[74]

On 1 June Rachel and her two young children boarded a train to leave Peking. As the wife of a travel writer, she was used to an itinerant life, but today she was teary. 'I wanted to stop the train and get the servants and go back to the little house,' she remembered. Over the course of about half a year there, she had learned an impressive amount of Chinese, forged a friendship with her cook, cared for her toddler son and given birth to her daughter, but now she was plunging back into uncertainty.

Fear resurrected old prejudices, and Rachel was frightened. The train was passing through areas of China that had been plagued by bandits and warlords since the 1911 revolution that overthrew the Qing Dynasty and culminated in the creation of the Republic of China. Just two weeks before, she recalled, bandits had waylaid a train from Shanghai to Peking and robbed the 'foreigners' aboard.

She spent the day on the train worrying about bandits and feeding the children from a 'basket of excellent food' their cook had given them. She needed only to 'order a dish of hot rice' and boiled water from the train porter.[75] She decided to boil the water again on an alcohol stove, balancing it carefully against the train's vibrations.

After she put her children to sleep, their train passed safely through the most perilous areas. When she went to sleep, though, she dreamed that bandits robbed the train and kidnapped her and her children. In her nightmares, she subsisted for 'three weeks' on 'Chinese food and unboiled water'.[76]

5

Durian

Like most passengers on the SS *Cleveland*, the American tourist Paul Junkin marvelled at the amount of food and water the ship carried when it departed San Francisco in 1909 for its cruise around the world. Their first stop was Hawai'i, known for its pineapple plantations. A few weeks later, the *Cleveland* would call at the Dutch East Indies, with its harvests of tropical fruits. Still, the *Cleveland* brought its own fruit to the tropics. In San Francisco, the ship loaded four train carloads of California oranges, four of grapefruits, one of lemons, two of apples and one of pears and grapes, and 43,000 quarts (41,000 l) of tinned fruit.

All that fruit, alongside tons of meats, vegetables, water and ice cream, comforted Junkin. Knowing that dinner was reliably temperate on a ship bound for the tropics, he planned his food adventures hoping to stay safe. He did not intend to eat full meals of local food: that was a taste too far. Fruit, though, tempted.

To help him remember the natural abundance of the tropics, he kept a list of the names of the fruits, nuts and a few spices he encountered (and, later, he published his list in a book). Some were comfortingly familiar and temperate. Others were so exotic, he could only guess at their spelling:

> thirty kinds of bananas, mango, orange, citron, lemon, mandarin, pomelo, shaddock, lime, grape, avocado, fig, cocoanut, vanilla, strawberry, roselle, papaia, mangosteen, kumquat, loguat, monstera, sour sop, custard apple, cherimoya, macademianut, betel nut, dates, mountain apple, rose apple, water apple, cayenne cherry, bush cherry, jambolana plum, water lemon, guava, grenadilla, tamarind, cacao, castor bean, annatoo, ginger, cashew nut, mammee apple, star apple, oil palm seeds, tuna, ohelo berry, carambola, bread fruit, durian, pomegranate, otaheite, gooseberry, peach, apple, cherry, apricot,

kukei nut, bhel fruit, indigo, sapodilla, longan, leitchee, wii, poha, wampii, cinnamon, cinchona, vegetable ivory palm.

Junkin wrote lists but sampled cautiously. In a letter home, he described passing a restaurant in Batavia with his fellow tourists, en route to their hotel, and watching an 'Asiatic' reach into the serving dish, smell a piece of fried fish, replace it and select another. The tourists did not stop there but did pause to buy fruit from 'native peddlers'. Junkin wondered at the 'native fruit stands' overflowing with tropical fruits but remembered that 'we were warned to be careful about eating them and for this reason kept a check on our appetites.' He bought only a few samples and a souvenir photo of fruit vendors, displaying their wares in woven baskets.[1]

He didn't sample the durian. Among the cornucopia of tropical fruits, the durian inspired special fascination and increasing horror. Travellers such as Junkin seemed to relish encountering it in markets in Southeast Asia, chuckling at the locals who clearly loved it, and describing its odour with often absurd comparisons. Quick to the hyperbolic, they likened durian to rotten onions, reeking cheese and sewer gas. Junkin followed suit, declaring it 'really awful, reminding me very much of Canton'.

Junkin, like so many other tourists, could not imagine that locals could be connoisseurs. Yet they looked forward to harvest, cast expert eyes on trees to judge when the fruit might ripen and weighed the pleasures of one varietal against the other – much as the tourist, safely back on their steamship, might with vintage wines. Locals knew how to carve the durian expertly, removing the hard spiky rind while leaving the large lobes of fruit, each several inches long, pristine. Typically, they ate the fruit raw by scooping out the pale, yellow lobes.

Tourists such as Junkin imagined that the local love of durian was a more animal hunger. To abhor durian helped tourists separate themselves from local inhabitants. Taste, too, was part of the segregation enforced by empire. Ships, trains and hotels all restricted access to the colonized. They were the luxury refuges of the colonizers. Cities in colonies segregated white colonizers from non-white colonized, with white areas in the parts of town deemed healthier. Understandings of race, too, had hardened, strictly divided into hierarchies. Visitors who loudly proclaimed their disgust at durian were casting judgement on locals who undeniably loved it.

Outside the durian's spiny shell ripened a history of conquest and the articulation of difference. But whether tourists knew it or not, the durian was also wrapped up with the subtle ways colonized peoples, in turn, could laugh at tourists.[2]

The Fruits of Empire

Just a few hours outside of Singapore, enthused an American tourist in 1883, 'all the rich-flavoured coloured fruits of the tropics are here – fruits whose generous juices are drawn from the moist and heated earth.' As she tasted an abundance of new flavours, she decided that fruits were the 'wealth' of the tropics.[3]

She was right. For Euro-American colonies, fruit was big business. Bananas and pineapples, especially, were already plantation crops by the time around-the-world cruises became popular. Fresh bananas as well as tinned and fresh pineapples had become familiar flavours and staple ingredients for consumers in the temperate zone. They hadn't, however, entirely lost their exotic appeal. Around-the-world tourists were loath to try local cooked food, but fruit was a different matter. They had tasted tropical fruits at home and were tempted to try them warm from the tree and bush. Maybe, here in the tropics, the pineapples would be fresher, juicier than at home.

Tourists cautiously tasted fruit as a tropical tourist attraction. Other Euro-American visitors, though, travelled and tasted for fortune. Botanical explorers, journeying alongside tourists, hoped to find tropical products that could be marketed to temperate consumers. They searched for some new fruit or unfamiliar strain they could cultivate in orderly rows in plantations. In their letters home, their diaries and, if they wrote them, their published memoirs, botanical explorers revealed another secret: they also travelled for pleasure and excitement, crossing paths with those tourists on scheduled around-the-world journeys. As one botanical collector admitted, Borneo was rich in fruits from mangosteen to durian, but 'if one would enjoy them a journey to the East is unfortunately necessary.'[4]

Tourists and botanical explorers stayed in the same hotels, visited the same sights and – crucially – dreamed about a future when bustling plantations owned by Euro-Americans replaced quaint local markets. Both leisure travellers and professional botanical explorers were astonished by the abundance of fruits in local markets, and they fantasized about the export potential of choice fruits. Markets were picturesque, but whether travelling for profit or pleasure, Euro-American visitors imagined a future of imperial plantations. British traveller Florence Caddy, though entranced by the tropical fruits she enjoyed on her luxurious yachting holiday to Siam and Malaya, wondered how much better these fruits might taste if they were cultivated by British growers rather than local farmers. When tropical dwellers learn from colonial planters how to cultivate for flavour, 'we shall have fine fruits from our trans-oceanic empire,' she declared with imperial zeal.[5] One of the supreme pleasures of tourism, Caddy realized, was the opportunity to sample rare tropical fruits that those at home could never dream of trying. Steamships had brought travellers from Europe or America, but on long journeys home fruits were difficult to save from rotting.

Tourists and botanical explorers alike firmly believed that the fruits they encountered in the tropics could be sweeter, riper and more profitable if only they were grown in plantations. The commercial quest for the next big imperial commodity aligned with the experience of tasting for adventure while on holiday. Tourists who relished the chance to sample fruits unheard of in Europe or America and botanical explorers who dreamed of the next commodity also crossed paths at botanical gardens. Everywhere from British Singapore to the Dutch East Indies, imperial botanical gardens, like local markets, were prime attractions. The pleasure traveller W. Basil Worsfold, typically, was astonished by his visit to the Buitenzorg botanical gardens near the Dutch colonial capital at Batavia. He sketched the trees and fruits and ambled along the garden's resplendent paths.[6] Botanical gardens, in all their manicured splendour, offered a vision of abundant tropical nature, tamed and ordered by colonial botanists. The exotic grandeur also reflected the desire to turn tropical bounty to fortune. The British and Dutch empires had built an infrastructure of botanical gardens. Botanical specimen hunters found and categorized tropical commodities and fruits and these gardens nurtured cultivars that could be grown commercially.

In the shade of towering palms, the big business of colonial food met modern tourism. The *Cleveland* carried temperate food for its cruise passengers. Other ships carried fresh or tinned tropical fruit back home again. The webs of steamship lines also carried plant seeds, clippings and seedlings from continent to continent, linking together botanical gardens the breadth of empires. By 1840 Kew Gardens outside London had blossomed from a private royal plant collection into a public institution at the centre of a British imperial network of gardens. The botanical garden cultivated the idea that tropical nature was, like colonial peoples, in need of civilization and development. In Singapore the botanical gardens became an official government department in 1874. Rubber cuttings spirited out of Brazil, nurtured in Kew and then cultivated in the Singapore gardens formed the commercial backbone of the valuable Malayan colony.[7]

As an official at the botanical gardens boasted, Singapore was also becoming a fruit 'emporium', growing seedlings in the gardens and exporting fresh and tinned fruit to all corners of the empire. In 1886 the Colonial and Indian Exhibition in London showcased the products and peoples of the British Asian colonies, including fruits. The exhibition highlighted public fascination with tropical fruits and their commercial potential. The displays of fruits 'afford proof of numerous undeveloped resources of our colonial possessions', marvelled one observer.[8] By the time of the exhibition, commercial fruit industries were growing in Britain's colonies in Singapore and Malaya.[9] Ethnic Chinese entrepreneurs owned many of Singapore's fruit canning companies such as Chop Lian Soon & Company, which packed tins of pineapples and preserved mangosteens, guava, jackfruit and papaya for export to Hong Kong, Shanghai, Japan, Europe and the United States.[10] But no one was exporting durian.

The United States developed its own botanical infrastructure especially after 1898 and the country's war with Spain. When the United States tightened its grip on a vast tropical empire, American botanical exploration flourished. By then, bananas were already the curved yellow pillars of the U.S. empire, food for those thousands of miles away from their site of production, and coerced, dangerous labour for those who did the growing and the transporting.[11]

New colonies meant new commodities. Just as the United States was consolidating its own tropical empire, the botanical explorer David Fairchild was travelling around the world in search of fruits and vegetables. A remarkable number of the treasures he sent home became big American business. He spirited out seeds from Mexico to spur the production of avocados in California. He brought back dates from the Middle East and mangoes from the French colony in Vietnam. With his friend Eliza Scidmore, he helped introduce flowering Japanese cherry trees to Washington, DC. Once, on a train journey in England, he boasted to his seatmate, a 'typical burly business man of the confident British type', that ever more 'foodstuffs consumed by the British public' would come from the American tropics.[12]

Fairchild knew that he was a lucky traveller, a botanist, paid to circle the globe in search of seeds and plants that could excite American diners and enrich American planters. His job was to evaluate 'the passing show of foods which have been offered to me on the tables of the countries through which we have traveled'.[13] In a Java hotel, where Fairchild often went to enjoy the rijsttafel, a local 'coolie' arrived, selling fruit. Fairchild knew better than to choose a durian because he knew that 'none were allowed in the hotel'. 'Few Europeans can endure' its pong, he explained.[14] Even Fairchild, the seasoned culinary tourist, struggled to taste the fruit, repulsed by the 'odor of the rotting durians' that he later encountered in a Javanese marketplace. Tasting the fruit was 'a major operation which I could not force myself to undergo', he admitted.[15] He still wanted the seeds, however, not to cultivate into plantations, but to complete a collection of tropical oddities.

'I had gathered together many interesting seeds,' Fairchild reported from Java, 'among them some of the durian.' He bought a durian for its seeds, but as the day warmed, the smell became overpowering. 'So, I turned it over to one of the boys to eat and to clean the seeds.' Fairchild collected what only his servants could stomach. Even the seeds stank 'with the unmistakable durian odor'. On the steamship home, Fairchild wrapped the seeds in peat. Then, he secured them in tin containers and put them on the sill of the porthole. The 'charming Judge from South Africa' in the cabin next door still complained.[16]

Fairchild's collecting was a curious public–private partnership. He journeyed around the world in the service of the U.S. Department of Agriculture, and his many plant samples, including those pungent durian seeds, piled up in the department's laboratories and warehouses. However, his patron, Barbour Lathrop, an eccentric Chicago millionaire with his own case of wanderlust, paid the bills for Fairchild's peripatetic collecting. Lathrop shared Fairchild's belief that foreign plants could thrive on American soil in Florida or in new colonies. Lathrop underwrote Fairchild's visit to Java and then his excursions around the world in search of new cultivars. Lathrop also imagined a cornucopia of tropical fruits cultivated by American farmers and planters, but he threatened to cut off his patronage if Fairchild attempted to introduce 'the d---n tree' into the United States. By the twentieth century, even the word 'durian' had become a curse.[17]

So, Fairchild surrendered the 'spectacular' fruit to its local cultivators, like the 'head hunters of Borneo' who, he explained, 'will commit murder for the possession of it'. Maybe, someday, a 'refined durian', bred without the smell appreciated by locals, could be cultured by a white horticulturist. Maybe, it 'may become the rage and be carried back and forth across the Tropic of Cancer by airplane'.

As his ship steamed from Java, Fairchild thought of the future and imagined 'the first plane to arrive at some north custom-house with the durian'. It would 'create a sensation among the officials', but not a good one.[18]

Fairchild, though, had different ambitions for another tropical fruit. From the local vendor selling fruit to soothe the palate after his rijsttafel, Fairchild chose mangosteens. He savoured its white, cooling flesh and crowned the mangosteen the 'queen of fruits'.

Professional botanical explorers such as Fairchild were tastemakers on the move. Just like tourists travelling around the world purely for leisure, botanical explorers described exotic fruits to avid readers back at home. Perhaps one day those readers might become customers, tasting a new fruit imported to domestic markets. In 1920 the botanical collector and former United Fruit Company employee Wilson Popenoe published his definitive handbook of tropical fruits, their taste, growing habits and commercial potential.[19] Despite his corporate training, Popenoe's authoritative book depended on tourists' tastes. He moved seamlessly between the natural history of a plant species and evaluations of taste drawn from individual accounts of Western travellers. Local popularity didn't matter for Popenoe. 'The durian', he judged, 'occupies the same position today which it held when first observed by Europeans in the fifteenth century – that of a semi-cultivated fruit of great importance to inhabitants of the Malayan region.' When he relegated its economic potential to that of 'miscellaneous fruits', he noted that because of its 'disagreeable odor', Europeans abhorred it.[20]

Popenoe was a professional traveller whose career depended on evaluating the taste and commercial viability of the durian and many other tropical fruits. Ordinary tourists also tasted them, however hesitantly. They delighted in the experience of sampling tropical fruits common in the tropics, but rare, or unheard of, in the temperate zone. They boasted about the taste of pineapples that were riper and more juicy than the pale imitations that somehow lost their flavour on the long trip to temperate tables. One tourist's bargaining with a Chinese vendor selling luscious pineapples evoked a mixture of gastronomic pleasure and musing on the challenge of commercialization. The pineapples were just 'half-a-cent each' and, as he relished the warm juice, he thought about other pineapples gathered not quite ripe and shipped to American and European customers. Metropolitan consumers 'will buy it because it is foreign, rare, and expensive' – a mere hint of the deliciousness of the tropics brought home to the temperate zone.[21] Together with botanical explorers, tourists imagined what fruits might whet the domestic appetite and, in addition, they anticipated the

Postcard of Malay man
with durian.

day when more and more tropical fruits could be cultivated in vast plantations. Some fruits, especially the luscious mangosteen, seemed to represent
the untapped potential of the tropics. Tourists and botanical explorers, too,
pictured local durian eaters as fascinating. In their minds, however, they
weren't connoisseurs or knowledgeable growers.

For these Euro-American travellers, the durian exemplified the perils of
life in the tropics and the vast difference that separated the white traveller
from colonized peoples. Some tropical fruits became big colonial business
– pineapples and bananas, especially. The durian, by contrast, never became
a colonial commodity, even though travellers were awed by the scale of its
indigenous commerce. Tourists and botanical collectors alike recognized
that the durian, with its smell and size, could never travel beyond Asia. Even
if the buying and selling of durians crowded marketplaces from Singapore
to Sumatra, the business remained solidly in the hands of local peoples.

Durian was big business but never a colonial one. The American tourist Charlotte Cameron arrived in Singapore in 1924. She was astonished
to hear that '200,000 of this vile-smelling fruit is shipped here for the

Singapore market.' But, apart from the odd fruit that tourists might sample, these were delicacies for the colonized, not the colonizers.[22]

Capon Meat with Sugar and Rosewater

The sheer variety of tropical fruits had long astonished Euro-American visitors to the tropics, but they had not always expressed such aversion towards the durian. In fact, when Europeans recognized how locals relished the fruit, they were at first curious as to why. In the early fifteenth century the Italian explorer Nicolo Conti offered what was perhaps the first European account of durian. 'The taste varies like that of cheese,' he wrote. A century later, the durian's flavour reminded the Dutch traveller John Huyghen van Linschoten of blancmange.[23] The historic European dessert at least shared its pale yellow colour and soft, creamy texture with the durian. The comparison between the durian and a much-appreciated dessert, made from luxury ingredients such as almonds, highlighted Linschoten's recognition of durian as something locally enjoyed. In the 1850s the naturalist Alfred Russel Wallace tried the fruit during his botanical adventures in the Malay Archipelago. He compared the durian's creamy pulp to a fine European cheese.[24] He recognized that the strong smell could hinder one's desire to taste, but he learned to like it, and framed the durian as a tourist attraction. 'To eat durians', he noted, 'is a new sensation worth a voyage to the East to experience.'

Soon enough, other visiting Europeans were expressing less curiosity about the durian, and more wariness, or even outright disgust. In 1864 the French naturalist Henri Mouhot described his encounters with the durian on his journeys to Indochina. Even in the jungle, he wrote, it was hard to be near a ripe specimen – however much locals enjoyed it.[25] A British visitor to Dutch Batavia described the fruit as 'admired by the natives' but 'disagreeable to foreigners'. Another tourist agreed, this time in 1913: 'Throughout Malaysia it is considered the most delicious fruit. Europeans, of course, generally revolt at the unpleasant odor.'[26]

Some travellers described the smell, but not the taste – hinting perhaps that they never had the courage even to put the fruit in their mouths. Of course, smell and taste are closely entwined. One American noted as much, after first tasting a durian: 'smell and taste are so nearly twin that they generally act as monitors to one another's protection.' According to a British traveller, the durian encapsulated the health perils tourists faced when eating in the tropics. In addition to the 'horrible smell', he believed that durian had a 'strong laxative' effect. He quoted Wallace's once laud-atory description of durian and then rejected it with a Latin curse: 'Credat Judaeus non ego.' That is, 'I don't believe a Jew.'[27]

In 1895, when Mark Twain set off on an around-the-world tour of the British Empire, he too sought the durian. By then, it was a well-known edible – but, for most tourists, revolting – stop on the tourist trail. Twain wrote, with some disappointment: 'There was a great abundance and variety of tropical fruits, but the dorian [*sic*] was never in evidence. It was never the season for the dorian. It was always going to arrive from Burma sometime or other, but it never did.' Twain had heard that the taste was mild, but he was eager principally to experience the smell, 'a stench of so atrocious a nature that when a dorian was in the room even the presence of a polecat was a refreshment'.

Twain's published book about his around-the-world journey used his trademark comic stature to offer a critique of the British Empire. His book, *Following the Equator*, cemented Twain's position as one of the United States' leading anti-imperialists. Even as that country was also emerging as a global empire, Twain denounced the rapacious imperial hunger for new lands to conquer. Yet his anti-imperialism didn't require Twain to reject the idea – indeed, the science – of racial hierarchy. Instead, he structured his narrative as an eyewitness account of the imperial struggle between savagery and civilization – even if he felt that those claiming the mantle of civilizers often acted with cruel barbarism. Across the tropics, Twain sought out the durian because it meant so much to the imperialists as a sign of savage nature.

Twain never did taste – or smell – the durian, but because readers at home knew about the fruit, he felt compelled to offer his own comic description. The fruit was more than botany; even in the words of an American anti-imperialist, it was a judgement on locals, how they lived and how they ate. He wrote that the Hindu holy city of Benares – where the fruit he never tasted doesn't even grow – 'is as unsanitary as it is sacred, and smells like the rind of the dorian'.[28]

Curry, Death and Durian

Tourists came to see locals eating durians. They wanted to smell the fruit, but only a scant few ever attempted to taste it. When American Lucile Mann arrived in Singapore on her 1937 voyage around the world, she went shopping. It would be weeks before she managed to purchase the fruit

Lucile Mann's photographs of durian vendors and consumers, Singapore, 1937.

itself and gather her courage to taste it. In the meantime, she bought a postcard. Mann's postcard, a typical tourist souvenir readily available in Singapore, posed the fruit as if in still-life painting.[29] She snapped her own photographs whenever she encountered the fruit: durians piled at markets; locals eating durians; durians taken right from the tree.

Tourists picked and chose their tastes carefully, wary of strange fruits and hidden germs. An experienced world traveller, Charlotte Cameron, went to see the nearby markets and then took a drive around Singapore's Chinese and Malay neighbourhoods. 'Such messes! Such smells!' She watched as the Chinese and Malay enjoyed 'feasts' on the streets. They seemed 'obviously delighted', and Cameron recorded her revulsion. 'To us', she wrote, it was the 'most unappetizing food'. The dried fish looked as if it was preserved in 'the days of the Ark'. Grilled octopus tentacles and meat on sticks – probably satay – must 'form a happy hunting-ground for insects', she decided.

Amid the street foods, Cameron noted, stalls also sold durians to eager local customers: the 'nasty odour of the durian fruit, which they love, overwhelms all the other nauseous odours'. She compared the fruit to an onion custard, flowing through a gas-pipe and then seasoned with garlic. Thankfully, she planned to have fled the colony by 'the height of the durian season'.[30] She knew that Malay and Chinese diners loved the durian. Their appreciation fascinated tourists like Cameron as much as the fruit itself. So, when Cameron recorded the extent of the trade in durians to Singapore all the while judging its aromas, she was commenting on locals' tastes. She was, at the same time, measuring racial difference.

There was a pattern to the way tourists by the end of the nineteenth century described their durian adventures. They competed to describe the fruit's aroma in the most outlandish ways (even if those brave tourists who actually tasted it often recognized that the flavour is rather mild).

An American diplomat on holiday in Sumatra was typical when he evoked death, decay and excrement in describing durian. Tasting the fruit, he wrote, was like 'eating bad eggs and decayed fish over an open drain'.[31] The fragrance of ordure and death repelled tourists, but they were excited to have smelled the fruit – precisely because locals ate durian with such obvious delight. When tourists decided that the durian smelled of a morgue at night, rotten onions, decaying fish or sewer gas, they were judging locals as much as describing a fruit. Tourists often noted that when they tried the fruit, but couldn't stomach it, as was generally the case, they handed the leftovers to locals, mostly servants.[32]

Travellers' obsessive focus on the fruit's rotten odours was accented by what they believed was a primitive, animalistic way of harvesting the fallen fruit. Notably, the durian was eaten at the moment of its putrefaction. Often the fruit not picked like the apple from the branch itself, but harvested when it dropped. When it fell, the fruit might crack its hard shell, described by many late nineteenth-century tourists as covered with 'tubercules' rather than spikes. 'Ladies', said one 1878 description, should regard the durian 'with extreme disgust'. The odour of the fruit was 'foetid'.[33] Tourists typically evoked 'rotten onions', 'stale eggs' and 'rotten cheese'. Wallace had once compared durian to fine cheese; by the twentieth century, the cheese had rotted. The comparison to cheese – rotten cheese in particular – is revealing. Everyone knew that cheese was essentially decayed milk, but the cultural context of cheese turned putrefaction into refinement. When Burbidge described the flavour of durian as 'rotten cheese', he extracted the refinement of cheese and substituted decay.[34]

Marking the shift from a strange, but deliciously tasty fruit to a reeking tropical oddity beloved by Malays, the popular British humour magazine *Punch* in 1929 even published a satirical poem on the subject. The magazine described a merchant ship officer who refused to transport durians. Singapore was a cornucopia of fruit overflowing with pineapples, mangosteens and 'thousands more', said Jake the tourist. He tried to bring durians on board, but an officer blocked his path. The officer had sailed the length of the empire to transport odoriferous copra, rotting oyster shells, sago, even animal hides, but he drew 'the blinkin' line' at durian. 'This ain't no perishing garbage-tank.' He made Jake 'heave those overside'. The uneaten, sinking, stinking fruit had become a comic symbol of the disgusting side of empire and a potential commodity lost to colonial commerce. The desire of Europeans and Americans to protect themselves from smells they associated with racial inferiors had trumped taste. Durian might be a 'delicacy' for Malays but for Europeans – and this ship's officer – 'a taste for it cannot easily be acquired.'[35]

The durian's stench (more than the fruit's taste) helped visitors mark the differences that separated them from locals. The tourist Charles Walter Kinloch on visiting Singapore and Malaya declared his own civilized status by describing his 'repugnance for offensive smells'. He recognized durian's local popularity. He also admitted that tasting the durian and overcoming the stench required 'courage'. Yet he insisted that it was not fear but his refinement that prevented him from eating the strange fruit. After all, who could eat a fruit that smelled like the 'fowl [*sic*] and offensive atmosphere of a common sewer'?[36]

The 'queer fruit' was adored by 'natives of Java', noted another visitor, but 'detested by Europeans and Americans for its unpleasant odor'. Odour first, and taste second, measured the distance between 'natives' and 'strangers' for A. B. Morse, an American missionary travelling in Siam. 'This is the most delicious of the delicious, the concentrated, sublimated quintessence of deliciousness.' But only 'to the native taste'. The refinement of the Western sense of smell meant that tourists' could only feel nauseous – proof enough for Morse of how different sensual responses revealed the primitiveness of non-white locals and the civilization of the white American tourist. Based on tourists' accounts like these, Wilson Popenoe relegated the durian to the category of 'miscellaneous fruits' with little commercial appeal, even though, he admitted, it had 'great importance to inhabitants of the Malayan region'.[37]

Assured of their racial differences, travellers turned the experience of watching locals eat the fruit into a kind of spectator food adventure. One family discovered the durian on a brief coaling stop in Padang in Sumatra en route home. From a distance, they watched locals under a tree with 'some strange kind of fruit spread out before them'. Coming closer, they were overwhelmed by the 'nauseating smell', but still eager for a taste that locals clearly craved, the tourists bought a fruit and took it on board. The durian's odour contrasted with the civility and manners of the Western steamer and assaulted the family as they dressed for dinner. The family resolved to try the fruit, though not before 'several ladies retired'. Only the father proved capable, but a few mouthfuls later, he handed the leftovers to the servants. They accepted it, he noted, 'with bows'. The pleasant relationship of service re-established for this family and the sense of difference confirmed, they watched the servants 'in their quaint turbans . . . in a circle round the durian, each with his hands and mouth stuffed full'.[38]

Virtually all tourists passing through Southeast Asia described the durian and they relied on a small number of comparisons: rotten onions, Limburger cheese, stale eggs and soured cream. The idea that a sensory experience was 'like' something familiar and utterly Western can represent a kind of domestication, every bit as important as the hybridization of cultivars in turning wild fruit into a plantation commodity. Travellers relied on a colonial vocabulary of metaphors and similes, understandable to their side in the imperial relationship. In translating the durian's taste for the domestic audience, tourists' descriptions ripped the fruit out of an autonomous nature and seized it for empire: from the East but understandable (and disgusting) to the West. Tasting across a geographic divide might hold out the potential for respect and communication – but this promise of breaking bread isn't the same thing as sampling durian. Domestication and colonization, even without commercialization, mattered. Augmented by colonial service economies, tasting the same fruit marked the boundaries between European and Asiatic.

Even Twain laughed that 'there is a fortune' in the durian. 'Some day somebody will import it into Europe and sell it for cheese.' Europeans and Americans lucky enough to encounter a durian did indeed smell cheese; they just thought it was rotten.[39] No one would deny that the durian smells

Postcard of Malay boys eating durian.

strongly. There were both chemical and biological explanations for the durian's smell. Popenoe, for example, explained that the durian's aggressive odour came from sulphur compounds with a touch of butyric acid. Chemicals alone, though, can't explain Cameron's aversion or Mann's hesitation. In a theory still generally accepted today, the British biologist E.J.H. Corner postulated in 1949 that the durian tree developed strong aromas, protective oversized shells and sweet fruit to entice animals to transport, replant and fertilize seeds with their bowels.[40] Evolution alone, however, can't explain travellers' violent reactions as they gazed at local peoples eating the fruit. Think of a strong food smell: perhaps a soft cheese? Grilling meat? What makes a strong smell repellent and what makes a food disgusting or alluring?

When we smell and try to describe odours, we rely on either adjectives – pungent, strong, spicy – or metaphors to suggest that something either has aroma (which is generally good) or stench (which is generally repulsive). Tourists' combination of comparisons of durian to familiar products such as cheese or eggs and adjectives like rotten or stale separated durian from temperate foods (like Camembert cheese) whose strong flavours testified to the consumer's refined taste. Western descriptions of durian could simultaneously demonstrate the tourist's conquest of the tropics while still condemning local taste.

Smell especially helped harden personal likes and dislikes into perceived racial traits, as accelerating imperialism strengthened the boundaries
between colonized and colonizers. As tourists focused on smells, they noted
that the fruit appealed as much to locals as to animals. Local people seemed
to have more in common with native animals than they did with European
visitors, tourists insisted. After all, only locals loved durian. When tourists
watched locals eating durian, they thought of animals lusting after a seductive, addictive fruit. 'At the height of the durian season,' the outdoorsman
Caspar Whitney wrote, 'all animal kind in Malay, two-legged and four-
legged, is animated by an insatiable lust for the fruit itself.' Running amok,
the two-legged's savagery was revealed in conflicts with each other over the
ownership of trees and with jungle beasts with whom they competed for
fruit. Among animal and local human, the desire for fruit was enough 'to
fill [them] with savage anger against whatever stands in the way of satisfying its appetite . . . All durian eating Malays – man and beast – are aflame
with erotic fire,' wrote Whitney.[41]

Tourists used such evidence of shared taste to argue that locals' seasonal
durian gorging unleashed animalistic savagery. In tourists' accounts, such
frenzied eating seemed connected to another presumed racial trait. The idea
of running 'amok' took a Malay word and imported it into English to refer
to moments of inexplicable frenzy and violent rage. Euro-American observers never forgot its linguistic origins and cast running amok as an essential
Malay racial trait, a savagery that lurked below the surface until possessed
by a vengeful animal spirit, a 'common occurrence among Malays' according to a tourist guidebook. The season of ripe durians seemed to have this
maddening effect. 'The durian', noted Whitney, 'brings . . . great madness
of conflict upon those that taste of its passion-stirring flavor.' Ultimately,
such fruit-fuelled running amok proved to Whitney the need for imperial
control. In durian season, he told his American audience, the rice paddies
were neglected, and Malays became 'howling, quarreling' men. The imperial
'resident becomes a peripatetic Lord Chancellor, whose waking hours are
filled with civil suits, and whose nights are made sleepless'.[42]

Tourists were marking the lines of social, racial and cultural difference
when they recounted the durian's disgusting taste and smell while in the
same breath marvelling at the local lust for durian. Disgusting, though, isn't
a synonym for inedible. Travellers, even as they found the durian repulsive,
admitted that it was edible. Durian's uniquely colonial history placed it
into a different context than, for example, a cheese whose aggressive flavours excited the connoisseur. Southeast Asian durian, by contrast with

French Camembert, was a tropical fruit, and its odours marked a Western consumer as an outsider in the fruit's indigenous climate, as an intrepid tourist. For one traveller, the durian's stench was so 'abominably disgusting' that 'few *strangers* will permit the slightest approach to familiarity with its taste or odour.'[43]

Stench, disgust and the reality of local appreciation turned this traveller into a 'stranger'. As empire hardened distinctions between strangers and locals, the allure of the durian was linked to its status as something that locals loved and tourists learned to dislike. Durian existed within the context, less of odoriferous European foods, than of other tropical fruits. If other fruits, especially the mangosteen, represented the enticing side of the luxurious tropics, durian represented its savagery and dangers.

Cameron believed that, for visitors from the temperate zone, the tropics posed perils. Tropical fruits in all their abundance testified to the luxuries accessible to the tourist, but durian reminded her of the dangers of life in warm climates and made her think of tropical medicine warnings. The American travel writer Eliza Scidmore, too, began her guidebook to Java by listing the 'appalling' mortality rates of early colonial Batavia.[44] A few days of sightseeing in the 'moist, enervating heat' could reduce a tourist to 'limp condition', she warned, and staying 'fit' was critical. Water must be boiled or, better, imported, advised a 1914 guide. Unripe or overripe fruit was a particular hazard. Fruit excited commercial desires but also aroused fears of 'the terrible maladies that prove so fatal . . . in tropical regions'. For those who liked spice, warned a guide, curry could be 'a joy', but 'like other violent delights it is apt to have violent ends' and 'surfeits of tropical fruit' could be hazardous.[45]

The durian offered an exotic taste of tropical abundance and a foreboding notice that Asia was never quite conquered. With ripe fruit within, spikes without and a powerful stench throughout, durian reminded travellers that the tropics may be ripe for commercial development, but travel within them remained unsettling.

When, by the nineteenth and twentieth centuries, travellers insisted that they could share neither the table nor the appetite preferences with locals, the durian became an edible imperial boundary. Allure met disgust at the dividing lines of race and empire. 'The very report of this fruit stinks nowadays in the nostrils of Europeans,' wrote one guidebook, 'so much have people written describing its smell.' But 'Asiatics pay high prices willingly.'[46] Guidebooks warned tourists about the durian's alarming odour, in fact, to entice them. 'While in Penang, the traveler', read a guide, 'should not fail to become acquainted with the famous Durian.' During the season, the fruit filled 'native markets and stalls'. The primary attraction was the sight of the fruit sold in picturesque markets and of locals eating it. If tourists gathered their courage to sample, the guidebook reminded them to do so 'out of doors'.[47]

Another tourist guide to Malaya and Singapore even encouraged visitors to assemble a 'collection of Malayan smells', olfactory souvenirs of the tropics. Lucile Mann listed her collection in her diary: incense, fried fish, native hair oil, orchids on the table and 'unsanitary whiffs better not analysed'.[48] In her list of the 'smells of Singapore', Mann didn't include the sweaty odours of white colonists or other around-the-world tourists, uncomfortably dressed in linen suits, tight cholera belts and heavy pith helmets. Instead, she noted the smells of local Malay, Tamil and Chinese people and their foods, spices and fruits. Smells, sometimes even more than sights, could convince tourists that they had truly travelled vast geographic and cultural distances. Except for the durian, Penang was 'of no great interest in itself', noted the guidebook.

Tourists visited the fruit markets, marvelled at locals' open-air meals, coughed at the durian's stench, guessed at the colonies of germs and ate at their hotels. In Singapore, Cameron stayed at the Hotel Europa. Electric fans cooled the rooms and the Chinese servants, 'always in white, are clean and attentive', she approved. The rooms were pricey, but food was included. For those tempted after watching Malays, Tamils and Chinese eating on the streets, 'a curry, so beloved of the Easterner, is usually on the menu,' she noted. Cameron tried her exotic foods in the 'white, and spotless' hotel. After the meal, she enjoyed the fruit. 'Those who are partial to pineapples, can surely feast, as this fruit is served at every meal,' said Cameron, 'also bananas' – never durians.[49]

Eating Outside the Hotel

Fruit markets were tourist attractions. In Java the noted American travel writer Eliza Scidmore visited the market with a servant whom she had hired locally. Scidmore was curious but ignorant. Confused as to how to open the hard-shelled fruits, she was dependent on her servant. He carried baskets of fruit back to Scidmore's hotel and then out onto the veranda. In the guidebook to Java that she later wrote, she described the tastes and smells of exotic products that those at home could never try and narrated a gustatory itinerary for the lucky few who might one day travel.

Climbing for coconuts,
from William G. Frizell
and George H. Greenfield,
*Around the World on the
Cleveland* (1910).

After indulging in the pleasures of local bananas, star fruit, rambutans and mangosteens, Scidmore turned to the spiky durian. A simple whiff of the durian convinced her that she had made a mistake: durian should not be eaten inside a civilized hotel. Locals were always 'munching it inconveniently to windward', but Europeans described the fruit with 'bitterness and contempt'. In her hotel room, surrounded by rinds and spilled juice and confronted by the durian, she realized that a single fruit could segregate Asian from European. Scidmore chose the side of Europeans. Appalled by the odour of 'onion and stale egg', she never seemed to have worked up the courage to be one of the 'intrepid ones' and taste it.[50]

Alexander Hume Ford, the journalist and passionate promoter of tourism to colonial Hawai'i (and famed as a popularizer of surfing), did taste the fruit. He and a travelling companion began their first day on holiday in Java with Dutch pancakes in one of Batavia's luxurious European hotels. They drank coffee from beans grown on a plantation – 'the real strong essence of coffee'. Next stop: the Harmonie Club. The whites-only club that Ida Pfeiffer visited in its early years had become a pillar of Batavia's colonial establishment. The hotel and then the segregated club reassured the tourist from Hawai'i that colonial rule was not only firm but comfortable. The local market, however, was a food adventure. Twenty or thirty small stalls, all in a line, each offered their specialities. Ford looked – but didn't taste – until he came to the end of the line where there was 'nothing but fruit'.

Ford leaned towards the stall owner. 'Durian?' he asked.

The stall owner nodded and led Ford into the open air towards a pile of spiky fruit. He gestured towards his nose. Europeans, white customers, he seemed to say, need to hold their noses when opening it.

Here, at last, was the supreme food adventure. 'For twenty-five years,' Ford explained, 'I had been longing to sample the durian.' He and his companion brought their durian back to the hotel. His companion took a bite. 'I thought he would go into convulsions,' chuckled Ford.

Then, the European hotel owner arrived and demanded that they remove the fruit. 'It was', he explained, 'the first durian that had ever been opened in the hotel.' A 'corps of native servants' removed the durian 'a mile away', but not before Ford tasted and saved the seeds as a souvenir to bring home. It was the durian that 'I ate in my pride,' he said.[51]

Carveth and Zetta Wells also learned their lesson: never to eat a durian in a hotel. Relaxing at the Gap Resthouse, a 'palatial stone building' built as a healthy high-altitude, cool refuge from Malaya's tropical climate for both colonists and tourists, the American travellers looked forward to a meal of roast grouse, shipped in cold storage all the way from Scotland. Carveth had smuggled a durian that he had bought near the coast all the way uphill to the hotel. He left the fruit in his luggage, guarded by servants in the hall. 'I could smell it. Probably everyone else could too,' he recalled. The other guests protested about the aroma of 'custard, turpentine, and rotten onions'.[52] The Wellses were asked to take their fruit as far away from the hotel and the dining room as possible.

First grouse, then durian – the Wellses retreated to the lawn to attempt a tropical dessert, all enabled by the pleasures of colonial service. They watched as the servant hacked open the fruit. Proudly, they finished it. English guests, though, complained about the durian smell on their breath. When he later wrote about eating his durian outside a colonial hotel, Carveth insisted that Ali, their servant, was visibly impressed.[53]

Guidebooks reminded visitors that the durian had no place in a civilized colonial residence or hotel. The durian, 'greatly prized by the natives, is never admitted to European tables on account of its fetid odour', explained a guidebook to Java and Sumatra. Yet guidebooks also explained how to eat the durian. If 'not too disgusted by it', visitors should only eat the fruit 'at a moderate distance from inhabited places'.[54]

Hotels declared new rules, banning the durian. The fruit must be eaten in the open, far from verandahs, dining tables or, for that matter, anywhere where white people gathered. One British observer even chuckled at the exotic prospect of a durian in the heart of London. A single durian would 'infect Fleet-Street'. 'Householders' would rush to check their sewers and drainpipes and the 'Inspectors of Nuisances' would investigate. Even a question would be raised in parliament. Locals may crave it but 'the stranger' avoids the 'awful effluvium'.[55]

European and American travellers hated the smell, but nonetheless felt drawn to buy a durian after watching local peoples relishing it in Singapore, Malaya or Java. Yet tourists were not eating durian *like* a local: buying it from a market or waiting for the ripe fruit to drop from the tree. Rather, like Scidmore, they enlisted locals as servants to fetch them the harvest of the exotic East. The way travellers tried their durian and then described the taste reinforced colonial power relations, of service and domestic labour. Durian tasting required servants to open and present the fruit. Visitors might not 'find servility' in British Malaya, reported a guidebook, but 'you will find . . . a universal and ready disposition to oblige you merely because you are an *orang puteh* [white person]'.[56] As Scidmore tasted tropical fruit, she admitted to a fantasy 'of the tropics to have a small black boy climb a tree and throw coconuts down to me'. Rather than trying to cut through the spines, one guidebook advised tourists to let local Malays open the fruit, and then to take 'it boldly in your fingers and eat it'.[57] Empire was an exotic destination and the adventure of being served durian was a key attraction.

Tasting Durian, Seeing Empire

'Well, Abdullah, what have you in view that can tempt one to a ramble?' said the tourist Fannie R. Feudge to her servant. The 'foreign tourist', she admitted, easily succumbs to the 'Oriental love of ease'. Yet today was set aside for culinary tourism. As she sipped her morning coffee, she delighted in Abdullah's service. 'What a picture he was as he stood there . . . with his jet-black moustache and bronze-brown complexion, one small hand placed over the heart in token of his absolute devotion to the foreign sahibs.'[58] As much as she enjoyed the luxury of servants, she was convinced he was cheating her by overcharging for the fruits he fetched from the market. Still, Feudge understood that she depended on her servant if she wanted to try the exotic fruits of empire.

So, she collected her sketchbook and market basket and set off with Abdullah. Tourists such as Feudge enjoyed the experience of having servants as much as the exotic foods. Mann was also proud of her successful durian tasting, but during her travels she was never more contented than watching the sunset over the jungle, a gin drink in her hand, cooled by the breeze of a punkah-wallah, the fan pulled by a servant. She thought all kinds of 'nice thoughts about the tropics'. Service brought a comforting sense of power to tourists, especially those like Mann who didn't employ domestic workers at home. There is also another side to colonial service and culinary tourism: they realized that as they tasted, savoured or rejected strange foods, they were being watched, often with amusement.

Abdullah led Feudge to see some of the culinary sights of the Straits colony, including coffee and black pepper plantations. At lunch, she visited a local house and her Malay host and hostess challenged Feudge with increasingly exotic dishes including turtle steaks and a Malay curry of shrimp and cucumbers. For dessert, the hostess placed the 'far-famed durian' in front of Feudge. Feudge knew that the fruit was loved by 'Orientals' who would pay high prices at the market, but she was one of those 'strangers' who could not abide its 'disgusting' smell. Feudge, on the verge of fainting, dashed from the room and the host followed, laughing. He commented on her weakness and her foreignness: 'You have not been in this country long enough to appreciate this rare luxury.'[59] It had been a tense meal and hard to digest not only because of the strange foods and smells but because of a thinly veiled eating competition. The host and hostess went to lengths to prove to Feudge that, despite her expectations of obsequious colonial service, she remained an outsider.

Tourists enjoyed the racial privilege of servants, but the act of tasting represented a fleeting moment when tourists – strangers, as they revealingly often called themselves when they described their relationship to the durian – acknowledged themselves as out of place and weak in the tropics. At the dinner table or in the marketplace, a tourist's first durian taste was a chance for locals to laugh at the stranger.

For a brief moment, the unwillingness of tourists to eat a fruit so self-evidently tasty had become not only a source of humour but an opportunity for locals to affirm to tourists that they were out of place in the tropics. Similarly, when Florence Caddy arrived at the court of the sultan of Johore, she enjoyed the kind of reception expected by British aristocracy. Yet she blanched when the sultan served a durian. Laughing, the sultan gave Caddy a present of eight redolent durians when she departed on her yacht, a not-so-subtle reminder that she was merely a visitor to the tropics. She might have been politically powerful, but she had not mastered the tropics. Maybe, the sultan suggested, she might eventually learn to enjoy the taste of Malaya.[60]

When Caddy, Feudge and so many other travellers recounted their encounters with durian they knew that the fruit was an economic bonanza. An 1870 estimate claimed that a single tree could earn its owner the substantial sum of $50 and during their season, fruit filled the markets.[61] Yet through their pinched noses, travellers sensed only disgust, curiosity and allure – not profit. They bought souvenir photos, not durian farms.

Colonial photo souvenirs of market stalls overflowing with durians reveal the workings and profound limits of colonial capitalism as it unrolled in the tropics. Smells, so vividly described in texts, linger in photographs like Mann's. The otherwise mundane photo of a colonial marketplace became a tourist keepsake to illustrate (likely for others at home) a reeking tropical oddity. It is easy to imagine Mann marvelling to friends how much a single stand fouled the surrounding street. Yet the Malay merchant appeared unmoved.

Tourists played a vital role, in symbiosis with botanical collectors and gardens: they evaluated the taste of the fruits and imagined their appeal to temperate appetites. The next banana or pineapple might yet be growing in the tropics. But disgust could create blind spots to the vibrancy of indigenous trade that grew out of local taste. Local markets remained just that, catering to local merchants and customers, though fascinating to tourists.

So, durian remained far removed from colonial conquest and colonial capital. It was and remains big business – just not one in which Europeans or Americans played a role.

6

Edith James

In the roiling waters of the Bay of Biscay, Edith James began to feel nauseous. Not the kind of person who permitted others to witness her discomfort, she retreated to her cabin to endure seasickness in private. Edith opened the pages of her new leather-bound journal, picked up her scissors and glue and pasted in the first page of her tourist brochure: 's.s. *Franconia* World Cruise 1926 (Under the auspices of Thomas Cook)'. Off the French and Spanish coasts and bound for Madeira, where she would meet the *Franconia*, the grand Cunard liner, Edith anticipated tropical pleasures. Cunard and Thomas Cook enticed world travellers in verse:

> There's a sun that shimmers, a breeze that croons
> Of fronded palm trees and blue lagoons,
> And the drowsy glamour of tropic noons ...!
> Afar from politics, crimes, and courts,
> From business troubles and stock reports.

She glued the poem into her journal.[1]

Edith never worried about stock reports or business troubles. In fact, she circumnavigated the globe twice and this journey on the *Franconia* around the world in 130 days cost $2,000 (about $35,000 today). She had enough money, but few ties back in England – except those of patriotism. Her extended family were rooted in the empire. Her father had been a high-ranking naval officer. One of her brothers had lived for decades in Australia and they would be reunited, though only for a few hours, on her second trip around the world. Another brother was buried in Singapore. When she visited the island imperial outpost, she pasted a picture of herself standing next to his grave. In the middle of the Pacific in the final weeks of her around-the-world trip, she confessed that 'if I had a home I should be homesick, but I love the sea, and it has been a magnificent voyage.'[2]

Edith James on the deck of the *Franconia* with unknown passenger, *c.* 1926.

Edith travelled a lot. She began her tourist life with trips to Europe, following the tried-and-true routes of the Grand Tour, the popular genteel itinerary around Europe. She went to Switzerland and Germany in her youth in 1900. Twenty years later – when she decided she was too old to marry – she booked her ticket on the *Franconia*. She was simply a 'sister to all men', she declared, even if she preferred the company of white people and demanded polite subservience from the service workers she encountered in hotels and on railways and ships.[3]

Edith's circumnavigations demonstrate how the golden age of steamships reproduced in extreme ways the segregation of Euro-American empires. Thomas Cook's luxury really meant the promise of European foods all the way around the globe. The British travel agency organized Edith's first-class tour around the world on the *Franconia*. The company wove the webs of hotels, service and hospitality that enabled tourists such as Edith to travel in ways isolated from local peoples. Edith's wanderlust compelled her to witness an imperial world where the British sun was setting, and the American was rising. Everywhere, from the *Franconia*'s dining saloon to the shore outposts of American possessions, she regretted what she saw as the decline of restrained British civilization and the rise of American Jazz Age opulence. As much as she might admire an architectural masterpiece or verdant jungle, as she travelled, she viewed the world as teetering on a precipice, with disorder, bad manners and rich Americans as an unfortunate future. When she complained in New Zealand on her second voyage about a poor portrait of the Prince of Wales, she belied a deep-rooted concern that she was travelling at the tail end of the era of British power.

When Edith toured, she wrote detailed journals. When she returned to England, she closed her diaries and led a rather private life. When she wrote or received letters, she never kept them. Sometime before she died, she donated her hard-bound travel journals, with the occasional postcard, brochure, poem or picture pasted inside, to the Royal Geographical Society. The society supported the great explorers of the far reaches of the world and of the British Empire. Perhaps Edith, who so craved the formality and rules of the British imperial upper classes, believed that her tourist journals deserved to sit on the same hallowed shelves as the personal effects of Ernest Shackleton and David Livingstone.

Her journals included a few personal photos. On deck, she once posed wearing a long black dress, its sombre cut tempered only by a lace collar. En route to the tropics, she wore her plush fur stole. Looking directly into the camera, she seemed to demonstrate more how to behave on a tour than how to enjoy it. In her world, the tourist should dress right, speak right, act right and – except for fresh fruit – avoid eating anywhere or anything a local might enjoy.

Waiting for the *Franconia*

The *Franconia* sailed from Liverpool on New Year's Eve, 1925. Before it circled the globe, it needed to fill its staterooms with Americans wealthy enough to pay for an around-the-world trip. In the 1920s many British tourists still felt the pinch of wartime austerity. By contrast, this decade was one of prosperity for the United States, and to Edith's regret, she soon realized that the *Franconia*, though a British-flagged ship travelling to mostly British colonies, was designed to pamper Americans. The United States now controlled a formal empire that included possessions across the Pacific from the Philippines to Hawai'i. The Panama Canal, completed in 1914, linked the Pacific to the Caribbean and the American colonial possession of Puerto Rico. Informally, American corporate and military influence reached even further, especially in the Caribbean and Latin America.

While the *Franconia* neared New York, Edith journeyed on a different vessel, the *Balmoral Castle*, bound for Madeira. She planned to meet the Cunard liner on its return journey across the ocean. This was, in part, because the weather mid-winter in the mid-Atlantic promised a rough crossing – sunny days waiting in Madeira seemed more comfortable – but also because Edith, by instinct, disliked the United States and Americans. When she finally arrived in America at the tail end of her voyage, she confessed in her journal: 'What do I think of New York? Nothing.' Just a city of tall buildings with rude people who say 'yah or yup'.

When the *Franconia* headed west eventually to travel east, the sun was setting on an empire that Edith treasured. The British Empire, she believed, set the standards for manners and morals and, above all, it appropriately ordered the relations of all the world's peoples. Though curious about the local and Indigenous peoples she watched from the distance of the package tour, she was vexed by Americans who were white enough to be dull and *nouveau riche* enough to be gauche. On board the *Franconia* and too nervous to venture beyond the protective umbrella of Thomas Cook, she spent the next few months of her life in the comforts of British luxury decrying the end of British manners and the rise of a new order.

The *Franconia* that left New York on 13 January to pick up Edith nine days later was actually the second Cunard liner to bear the name *Franconia*.

Launched in 1910, the first *Franconia* – Cunard traditionally named its ships after ancient Roman colonies – set a standard for opulence. Five years later, however, it left the transatlantic trade to become a troop ship. In 1916 a U-boat torpedoed and sank the first *Franconia* (luckily with no troops on board). After the war, Cunard lay down its successor, hoping to turn the page on the Great War and to revive the company's fortunes by escorting tourists to the far corners of the twilit empire.

So, in mid-January 1926, Edith was growing bored in Madeira, eating the local fruit, waiting for her ship and worrying about the drinking water. It must be boiled, she wrote, because of typhoid.[4] She complained, 'there really is nothing for visitors to do here – only watch the natives.'[5]

Cocktails and American Dishes

'Great fun getting away,' she confided to her journal on 22 January, delighted to escape Madeira at last. As the *Franconia* nosed into the Atlantic, she had no one to wave to, so she wandered around the liner. There are 'miles of corridors', she enthused. In her cabin again, she pasted postcards of the ship into her journal. At 20,000 tons, the *Franconia* was twice the size of the *Cleveland*. Yet by the interwar period, as steamship companies rushed to produce faster and bigger ships to attract tourist money, the new *Franconia* was only a mid-sized ship. In its luxuries, however, the *Franconia* 'ranks among the superliners of modern times', read some of its initial reviews. On the upper decks, the ship boasted swimming baths, a gymnasium, even squash courts. Below decks, it was designed with vast cellars to carry alcohol and bottled water.[6]

The *Franconia* was a new kind of ship built at the dawn of the age of tourism. Cunard chairman Sir Thomas Royden, well aware that his company increasingly depended on tourist dollars, described the ship as the most 'magnificent vessel' afloat. Its single, sloped funnel and its dramatic prow promised speed. Inside, the ship featured a maze of first-class lounges, including a half-timbered, oak-panelled smoking room that evoked a quaint British inn, a nostalgic touch designed primarily to appeal to Americans. Pewter plates and original Elizabethan armour and etchings decorated the lounge. A model of Columbus's *Santa Maria* graced the mantelpiece, linking the old and new worlds.[7]

Built in an era that Sir Thomas acknowledged as 'difficult', the *Franconia* was designed purely for luxury and tourism, a departure from Cunard's pre-war business plan. These were difficult times, not because

First-class dining saloon, ss *Franconia*.

Cunard lacked for wealthy passengers, but because it lacked for migrants. Pre-war, Cunard earned substantial profits from cheap tickets purchased by migrants to America. However, as the *Franconia* completed its first sea trials off the coast of Scotland, the United States slammed its doors to immigrants. In 1924 the United States passed the Johnson-Reed Act, which essentially prevented immigration from Asia and set restrictive quotas on migration from Europe. Cunard, and other companies in the transatlantic trade, now sailed with empty third-class and steerage. Sir Thomas knew that restrictions on migration to the United States represented 'a serious loss of business'.[8]

If American nativism threatened the British company, Americans' curiosity about the tropical world might also save it. The *Franconia* was grand evidence of the company's new strategy to replace the revenues from migrants to America with the fares of American tourists. In the uncertain world of post-war travel, Cunard introduced its new 'tourist type of travel'. Tourist class filled the lower decks of other Cunard ships and offered cheaper travel with a few extra amenities. Cunard's American offices happily reported that 'such accommodation has appealed to a large section of the public in America.'[9] For a smaller but wealthier section of the American public, Cunard designed the *Franconia* for all-first-class, around-the-world cruises organized by Thomas Cook. Complementing its neoclassical reading room, cosy garden lounge and hotel-style dining saloon, the ship offered a hairdresser's, sweet shop and, for those who patronized the sweet shop, a dentist. The dentist, the company assured, was American.[10]

'The Cruise Supreme!' tantalized Thomas Cook and Cunard, with 'cuisine and service unsurpassable'.[11] The *Franconia* circled the globe annually between its launch in 1923 and the beginning of the Second World War. In the summer, when the *Franconia* plied the scheduled Atlantic service, the ship bore 2,000 passengers. For its around-the-world tours, it carried only four hundred, all in first class.[12] On Edith's cruise, three-quarters of the passengers were American and most of the remainder were British, with a handful from Europe and British dominions in Canada, South Africa and Australia. Most were businessmen or lawyers, professors and artists with the time and money to afford the long trip. A few notables joined Edith's cruise: John H. Clarke, a retired justice of the Supreme Court of the United States, and Francis Edwin Drake, a tourist from Cleveland who was retracing the naval adventures of his ancestor Sir Francis Drake. The theatre producer F. Ray Comstock travelled with filmmakers, photographers and writers to collect material for his new comedy: *A Hop Skip and Jump Round the World*.[13] Over the next months, they would collect 348 inane questions posed by the ship's company to the ten Thomas Cook staff members – comedy to entertain those who could afford a theatre ticket, but not an around-the-world cruise.

In this new post-war era of fewer migrants and more tourists, British austerity and American wealth, the *Franconia* was a British-flagged ship heading for mostly British colonies with mostly Americans on board. The *Franconia* was an institution of interwar round-the-world tourism, but other agencies and steamship lines offered their own cruises. As they faced increasing competition, Cunard and Thomas Cook aimed to set the standard for the around-the-world holiday by introducing new destinations, including Surabaya and the Seychelles.

'The cuisine and service conform to the highest standards of the Cunard Line,' Thomas Cook promised. In her early days on the ship, Edith revelled in the gastronomic luxury: 'Such food!' she declared on her first day aboard, 'Everything I like. I counted over 60 dishes for lunch, and 56 for breakfast.'[14] Typical of ship life on a long voyage, the tourists began to organize their community. They formed committees: one to decide on the music and concerts, another to arrange dances and still another fancy-dress balls. Edith avoided them all. Instead, she retreated to the solitude of a good book and the refined quiet of the lectures given by the tour director.[15] She wasn't eager to join an on-board community dominated by Americans.

Within a few days of sailing, surrounded by American accents and, even worse, their manners and music, the spit-and-polish luxury already seemed tarnished. Edith had 'only' a steward, stewardess and cabin boy to look after her. She asked the stewardess about who would serve her in the night.

'I am on duty until 10:30,' the stewardess shrugged. Edith registered the conversation in her diary. It was the kind of impertinent response Edith believed characterized a ship filled with Americans.[16]

Even worse, Edith got to know her fellow passengers, and she didn't like them. After only four days at sea, she complained to the tour director about her American roommate. That night, Edith boasted in her journal that she now enjoyed a four-berthed cabin all to herself. The next night, though, with the *Franconia* docked in Monaco, she confronted yet another drawback of Americans. At the restaurant in the Hotel Negresso, the band played jazz. When the band played anything 'American', her shipmates applauded. Edith decided it was 'perfectly horrible music with screeches in it'.

Back in the solitary comfort of her cabin, she scanned the tour pro-gramme, which listed the names of her fellow passengers. The American passengers were 'very rich', she wrote, but 'so ignorant'.[17] She comforted herself that while the Americans might have money, at least the British had manners and, for the moment, a bigger empire. Americans 'have no class' decided Edith, as she watched them, especially the younger set, enjoying a fancy-dress ball. 'One girl ought to have been spanked.'[18] By the end of February, she changed her table in the dining saloon, fleeing an American. 'I could not stand that vulgar American woman any longer.'[19]

American appetites also appalled Edith. She counted the lunchtime desserts of an American clergyman at her table: lemon pudding, baked apple, ice cream with a wafer. 'Pig!' she wrote in her diary.[20] Americans at the table – and particularly at the bar – were especially infuriating. Perhaps it was the effect of u.s. Prohibition (an American woman confessed to Edith that they all drank so much at sea because they couldn't on shore), but Edith counted in horror as a sixteen-year-old American drank five glasses of Champagne, even after cocktails. 'Quite out of control,' Edith judged. 'Were I a mother with daughters nothing would induce me to bring them on a voyage like this. One girl of 18 came out as a child, with pig tail – now looks a middle-aged woman, *and* so fat.'[21]

Still, Edith felt a special pride when Americans were impressed with Britain's empire. In India she enjoyed watching them as they learned about the famous Indian Mutiny of 1857. She 'swelled visibly each time' she overheard the Americans praise 'our work' in India.[22] Yet when the ship docked in American possessions, her hostility returned. In mid-March General Leonard Wood, the American colonial governor of the Philippines, hosted a reception for the *Franconia*'s passengers – Edith was 'not at all impressed'. Even the 'horrid photo of our Prince of Wales', a diplomatic gesture for a British-flagged ship, angered her. Touring outside Manila, she was convinced that the American colony was failing. She reasoned in her journal that 'natives', instead of cultivating rice, seek education and run for elected office only to escape American government. 'They would prefer English' rule, she declared.[23]

By the end of April, Edith complained that she had heard enough of Americans' 'horrid voices and perpetual talking – and such vulgarity'. As her dislike metastasized, she wrote in her journal: 'It is time the voyage was over for people's private histories are coming out, and although immensely rich there are many disreputable people.' Some had even been divorced more than once. On the other side of the Pacific, on behalf of her late father in the Royal Navy, she couldn't help being impressed by the Panama Canal. In May Edith and her fellow cruisers visited the memorial for the American battleship *Maine* in the Havana harbour, whose sinking sparked the American war with Spain and the subsequent expansion of the U.S. empire. In front of this monument to American power, she resolved in her journal that she would never travel with Americans again.[24]

Still, when she first embarked on the *Franconia*, Edith confessed her desire to eat the exotic foods of these strange peoples: American dishes, such as 'soft neck Clams' and 'Cream Squash'.[25]

An English Ankle and Tea in Ceylon

A few days into the tour's rail trip across British India, Edith pasted a picture into her journal of a beggar on a rail platform in Agra, in the shadow of the Taj Mahal. Two weeks later, Edith watched a British woman, a 'nice young widow', entering a train carriage. In front of both Indians and Americans, the woman raised her 'short tight skirt'. Her bare ankle harmed our 'prestige', Edith scolded.[26]

In Bombay Thomas Cook had arranged private rail cars and Edith unfortunately shared a four-berth cabin and a shower with two American women. She noted (and appreciated) the smoked glass and shutters of the first-class cars. They shielded the passengers from the sun and, at least when they were aboard, the windows guaranteed that tourism was a one-way gaze. She enjoyed watching as the Indians on the platforms struggled to keep warm in the February chill; 'very picturesque', she declared to her journal.[27] Edith considered the comfortable rail compartments and elegant hotel dining rooms as the glory of the empire, but the beggars she confronted on railway platforms everywhere from Bombay to Agra were just as much local colour as the monkey she also saw on the Agra platform. In exotic India, monkeys, Hindu corpses whose burning she witnessed in Benares and the Parsi dead consumed by vultures in Bombay were tourist attractions.[28]

For Edith, much of the appeal of an around-the-world tour was watching the locals. In Cairo she pasted into her diary the handout from the day's excursion organized by Thomas Cook. The handout encouraged tourists to marvel at the 'types of people you never knew in existence'.[29] Later, in Benares, she recorded a tourists' cocktail of horror and fascination. 'The blackies were like ants everywhere', she wrote. 'I have often wondered what leprosy was really like: now I know.' She took tea back at the hotel and ate dinner on the train. Edith went to bed disappointed at not having seen an elephant.[30]

Edith may have protested the white English ankle, but she gazed (and recorded in her journal) the most intimate sights of locals. On an excursion to Kandy (in Ceylon), she watched the 'natives doing their washing' and stripped-down men labouring on tea plantations. They had 'thick hair on their chests like animals'. Later that day, she complained that men from the ship's company – Americans, likely – left their coats open for afternoon tea and dinner. 'It is dreadful!'[31] In Malaya, she bought typical postcards of locals and their plants. One was of a Malay man and woman in front of their house; he was holding a durian. In Japan, she bought pictures of Japanese women. One woman was having her hair set; another bathed in a tall wooden tub. Edith was surprised when a 'Jap' came up and snapped her picture, 'why I can't think'.[32]

When she described local people, she resorted to familiar racial epithets (some even borrowed from Americans). In India, local peoples were 'blacks'. In Korea she borrowed from white Americans their derogatory term for African Americans. When locals demanded 'backsheesh', she was annoyed but she didn't blame the inequalities of her empire. 'One little man slapped his little tummy so hard we all got up to see what it was. It was to show his hunger.' Edith remembered his grinning face and the 'whitest teeth possible'.[33]

Often, after a visit to some crowded colonial city, Edith admitted that she would have preferred to remain on board. As much as locals were 'picturesque', they were attractions that talked back. In Benares she watched the spectacle of, first, a child marriage – the bride was five and the bridegroom was twelve, she wrote – and then a funeral. She peeped, uninvited, into a temple, all 'crowded by these black people'. With a slip of a foot, however, tourist detachment became tense encounter. A tourist from the *Franconia* tripped and pushed against a sacred cow. A crowd of locals surrounded the woman in anger. 'She flew for fear they might attack her,' Edith wrote in her journal that evening. In the fine print of their brochure, Thomas Cook reserved the right to change the itinerary, especially if it seemed unsafe for a shore excursion. In mid-March Cook's called a meeting of the ship's company to share the unfortunate news that an outing to Peking and Canton had been cancelled after another pleasure ship had been fired upon and some tourists kidnapped. Thomas Cook had to pay 'thousands of pounds to free them', but Edith and the other passengers were furious. Perhaps to assuage the disappointment, the *Franconia* hosted a St Patrick's Day dinner and the next day, en route to the Philippines, Edith pasted photos of Indigenous Igorot peoples posed outside their hut.[34]

The grand arrival of the *Franconia* in a new port was part of the attraction of a first-class around-the-world tour. Tourists enjoyed reading local English-language newspaper accounts of their ship's arrival. In fact, Thomas Cook encouraged local governments to host formal receptions for the visiting *Franconia*. In the Japanese colony of Korea children welcomed cruise passengers on a visit to their school. The children waved Japanese and American flags and wrote 'Welcome' on the blackboard. Missing the British flag, Edith found the ceremony 'dull'. A presentation about soya beans was even worse. We 'use it for oat cakes and cattle feed', she sniffed. Edith preferred the cheering reception in Beppu, Japan. As she enjoyed dishes of English biscuits and delicious, if weak, tea served by 'little Jap girls', she felt like a queen, she wrote in her diary. In Manila the company listened to a prison band and watched the Filipino prisoners exercise. 'I hear this prison does immense good,' wrote Edith. She also described in her diary the Morse code message the prison sent to welcome the ship while it was still at sea: 'Welcome to the FRANCONIA passengers.'[35]

Concerts and receptions like these served many purposes. They generated newspaper coverage, which in turn provided free advertising to Cunard and Thomas Cook. When they served tea, sang songs or sent a Morse-code message from a jail, locals also seemed to be offering the kind of obsequious service that travellers like Edith expected and relished. In practice, though, even if tourists like Edith landed with a strong sense of their superiority, on a shore excursion, they depended on locals, especially for transportation. Edith had been particularly excited about riding in a rickshaw, but the human-drawn carriages often ceased to be exotic transport and became a perilous collision between frightened tourists and local men. Across Asia, whenever the *Franconia* docked, Thomas Cook organized a 'perfect army of rickshas'.[36] Once this army left the docks, however, Thomas Cook's authority disintegrated. Rickshaw pullers, as hard workers as any in the colonized tropics, recognized that tourists were essentially helpless, but carried plenty of money. In Kowloon 'the coolies were troublesome,' complained Edith. Once out of sight of Thomas Cook staff, they simply dropped their chairs and demanded extra fares.[37] Tourists had a similar fright in Manila when rickshaw pullers carried two 'of our ladies' into the 'native part of town' and refused to continue without extra pay.

Edith had learned a lesson. In the privacy of her journal, she could use all the racial epithets she wanted, but ashore and away from the safety of Thomas Cook staff, 'one might get in a fix with the natives'.[38] In Shanghai, for example, she recounted the story of tourists caught in the midst of a fist-fight between two rickshaw pullers. They 'cried out for a guide, or Cook's man'. None came, and Edith longed for the safety of the ship.

After the day's excursions were completed – survived – and dinner enjoyed either in a hotel or back in the ship's welcoming dining saloon, Edith opened her journal and described the day. She wrote more about the people she saw than the palaces, temples, ruins and monuments she visited.[39] In Egypt, rather than a souvenir picture of the pyramids, she pasted a postcard of a Cairo water carrier and his 'primitive' goat skin water bag. 'The old Cairo still clings to primitive life,' she wrote, as if to remind herself that on the eastern end of the Mediterranean, she had encountered a fascinating, strange and ultimately unsafe way of drinking water.[40]

From Cairo to Hawai'i, Edith treated local foods and drinks as sights and smells to describe, not exotic things to sample. 'Extraordinary looking food', she declared in a Hong Kong market. Chickens barbecued until dark brown hung next to an array of fruits and vegetables. The sheer variety of fish astonished her. Some were tiny. The large ones looked like salmon and she estimated that there were 'tons' of prawns and lobsters. None were appetizing. In Japan, she collected picture postcards of fish sellers and 'cooks', including of two Japanese women cutting turnips sitting on the floor.[41] She dined on board.

For Edith, food markets like these were as fascinating as monuments or temples. But she enjoyed visiting them for the disgusting experience. Seeing and smelling were enough; tasting was an adventure too far. In Delhi she walked through the cramped alleyways of the famous Chandni Chowk market, returned to the ship and wrote in her journal: 'native shops – dirty and noisy'. In Dutch Indonesia, she pasted a picture of a Batavia market scene and recounted the array of 'eatables' in the markets.[42] Like other tourists, she bought postcards and souvenirs of cloth and wood – never cooked food.

She observed workers in a Colombo tea factory, a stop on their shore excursion. As the guide led them into a room filled with squatting women sorting tea leaves, she also realized uncomfortably that an overly dressed British woman, dutifully wearing her sun helmet, could also be a source of entertainment. When Edith and the tour entered the room, the local women burst into laughter. 'We amuse the natives as much as they do us,' Edith admitted. Those tea leaves, for Edith, had another meaning. Shrivelled, dried, packaged and exported, Ceylonese tea embodied the segregated tastes of imperial Asia. Inscribing in her journal the guide's lessons, she noted that the tips of Orange Pekoe tea were the 'choice bits'. The larger leaves were inferior and the 'stalks sold to natives'.[43]

'56,000 lbs of Beef'

The *Franconia* offered plenty of luxury in its staterooms, private baths and gyms. The heart of the ship, though, was its coolers. Passengers expected plenty of choices at each meal, but during its 30,000-mile (48,280 km) cruise the ship restocked its meats only twice, and never in the tropical zone. It refuelled its engines at most ports.

Edith asked the ship's stewards for a tour of the ship's stores. '56,000 lbs of beef augmented at two ports, 19,000 lbs of lamb' were the impressive figures she recorded in her diary. Like so many tourists who toured below decks, Edith was bewildered by the sheer amount of food and drink an around-the-world ocean liner carried. The vast stores were architectural evidence of the everyday suspicion of the kinds of food available at the *Franconia*'s many ports of call. Edith was eager as well to visit the ship's 'iron cow', which mixed distilled water with powdered milk to make the ship's milk, cream and butter.[44]

Iron cows and cold storage – Cunard designed its luxury liner to avoid anything locally edible. A vast swathe of the earth, from Cairo to Honolulu, represented a food desert for tourists like Edith. When the ship docked, European hotels greeted passengers at the wharf with runners ready to carry their heavy luggage. Hotels were oases where passengers like Edith believed that they could safely eat and drink.

In the midst of the apparent plenty of local markets, Thomas Cook made sure that its tourists looked at but didn't taste cooked food. Before disembarking in Sumatra, the company warned tourists 'never to buy food from natives'. In Ceylon, Edith enjoyed the perfect colonial meal, except for the 'native dance with horrid music'. Fifty waiters followed the ship's company on their walk and served them their picnic lunch. There were even ices, despite the tropical heat.

Departing from her habitual displeasure, Edith revelled in Thomas Cook's service. In the luxury of a special train in India, Edith recalled that a 'black man' waited on her and her travel companions. He appeared regularly with tea and 'to dust us'. While they ate 'good' meals in the dining car, Indians outside begged for food. Edith carefully kept her coins hidden. In her diary, Edith described the sandwiches and drinks that awaited them on their arrival at the Elephanta Caves outside of Bombay. A wonderful luncheon at the Taj Hotel welcomed them back to Bombay. 'Cooks are wonderful,' she exclaimed. 'I never saw such care for the inner man on board,' she marvelled. At sea, after an early tea, they ate a breakfast 'of everything'. Then at 11 a.m., they drank chicken broth or, in a nod to the climate, iced tea. They finished only in time for a large lunch. Mid-afternoon brought tea and, soon, dinner. Before bed, servants offered sandwiches and drinks. If only the men had the decency to close their jackets, Edith would have been truly happy.[45]

Food was an attraction for Edith – just not anything cooked at local homes or markets. She might share the leftovers from her picnic lunches with servants, but she wouldn't eat their food. On the steamer during an optional excursion from Cairo to visit the ancient Egyptian ruins, Edith marvelled at the picnic carted by servants from the hotel. Ancient Memphis and Sakkara were fascinating enough, but it was the day's menu that she listed in full in her journal: '1 whole tin of sardines, A large piece of boiled fish, 3 blocks of different cheese. 3 rolls. Butter. Parcel of fancy cakes. 2 oranges. 1 apple. Salt-sugar-pepper-toothpicks.'[46]

'We feed on all occasions,' she confided joyfully to her journal. On board the *Franconia*, Edith scanned the menu, laboriously counting the offerings (63 on one occasion). Onshore, they dined at hotels. In Benares visits to the sights along the Ganges were timed around meal service. They lunched at Clarke's hotel. Then an outing. Then tea. They dined on the train. In Bombay they lunched and dined at the Taj Hotel, in Shanghai at the Astor House and in Singapore at Raffles, where she was amazed – and displeased – at the number of wealthy Chinese permitted into the immense ballroom.

The meats she ate were European animals from cold storage, but the fruit was often tropical. She tasted her first papaya at a hotel: 'Not so nice as melon.'[47] Amid the obvious precariousness of local life around her, the sheer numbers of unfamiliar fruits that she saw at markets evoked the abundance of the tropics and the luxuriousness of travel. In Kandy, at the end of the railroad line, she discovered a Ceylonese cornucopia: coconuts, pomegranates, jackfruits, mangosteens and 'heaps of things I have never heard of'. Their guide explained the difference between date and coconut palms.[48]

In Kandy, the abundance of local fruit was too tempting for Edith to keep to the safety of the hotel. She had planned an early bedtime, but when she heard about a nearby night market, she headed out for a bit of local colour. Amid the locals wearing 'coloured shawls and sarongs', and unfamiliar vegetables and fruits, she gathered her courage and asked a stall owner the price of a single mangosteen. The vendor 'insisted on my eating one, and would not accept money'.[49] Edith understood the gifted mangosteen as the appropriate deference paid a European tourist, but was that anonymous vendor intimidated by her demands (no doubt in commanding English)? Did he make the safe choice of an inexpensive, if ingratiating gift? Or was his gift of the mangosteen an expression of pride in the deliciousness of the local and an invitation to other tastes?

In Java, on an outing to Buitenzorg for the botanical gardens, she tried to remember the name of the fruits served at the hotel. 'Ramboltan – Lockoe – Gervek – as well as I can write them out from the waiter', she wrote.[50]

As the *Franconia* neared Hawai'i, Edith read the Thomas Cook pamphlet, opened her journal and described the local fruits and vegetables she expected to see. Some were plantation crops, others were indigenous, but Edith didn't differentiate. A few were familiar, like pineapples and bananas; others were exotic, like avocado pear and guava. Taro demanded explanation. 'Taro', she wrote, 'grows in mud like a potatoe [*sic*].' Hawaiians pounded it to make poi, a sticky savoury pudding that she remembered when she would return to the islands on her next journey. When the ship docked, she bought a postcard of locals preparing poi and pasted it into her journal.[51]

Honolulu 'natives' preparing poi, postcard collected by Edith James.

In Hawai'i she pasted in a picture of a lei vendor, smiling broadly and holding out flower necklaces. Hawai'i, though, also felt American. After months of curiosity about American foods, she finally tried her 'first American lunch, and everyone grumbled about the black waiters'. Edith also complained about a salad of pineapples and bananas. For once, she disliked tropical fruits because she was now in a country and an empire she openly despised. In the midst of tropical flowers and fruits, she noticed an advertisement pasted all around Honolulu: 'Hot Dog on a bun.' After months of avoiding local foods, maybe she wondered if this Hawaiian food was truly canine. It was, she discovered later, American: a 'sausage on a roll, split and hot'.

Chewing Gum

The *Franconia* continued its journey ever eastward. Edith and the other passengers, however, could only recall the warm juiciness of tropical fruits fresh from local markets through picture postcards. Before landing in San Francisco, the ship's stewards required the passengers to throw all their fresh fruits into the sea.[52] Plenty of tropical fruit made the long journey from Hawai'i to the mainland – often in cans – but these exports were plantation commerce, not tourist souvenirs. If the International Dateline was an invisible line that divided East from West, Orient from Occident, those floating fruits marked the passage from colony to metropole.

As the fruit was tossed in the turbulence of the *Franconia*'s wake, Edith realized that the tropical part of her journey was finally over. On the mainland, Edith felt comfortable at last to venture outside of the hotel for food. She found American food served in restaurants different, often disagreeable, but at least safe.

Edith, though, was disappointed to leave behind the pleasures of service and servants that she had so enjoyed, for example, on colonial India's trains. In Santa Cruz, California, in mid-May, she recorded the discomfiting experience 'of doing without chamber maids or men'. When she wished to be called at 6 a.m., she was awakened not by colonial tea in bed but by a ringing telephone. She was 'obliged to get up to stop it'. Edith made her way across the country in safe comfort, but without the colonial trappings and formality she cherished. In Washington, DC, her chauffeur even chewed gum. 'Perfectly disgusting', she wrote. In Bombay, she had praised the luxury of the Indian servant who served her meals, but in Boston, she complained about African Americans, especially when they waited upon her table. 'I <u>can't</u> get used to them, and dislike them waiting on me. They are so free and easy.' Without the attractions of exotic peoples, American modernity left her cold.[53]

In her New York hotel, she discovered that she was now on the 'American plan'; she could eat only at designated mealtimes, though it was safe to eat at one nearby restaurant, at least, and she admitted that the salmon tart followed by custard with coconut was delicious. In Ceylon, coconut was exotic; in New York, it was garnish.[54] Tropical products were just so omnipresent that she didn't comment on the coconut in the dessert. She missed her lavish breakfasts on board, but American food had its strange attraction. She discovered that American drugstores served sandwiches, ice cream and drinks, and in Niagara Falls she admitted that 'food is very different here.' She called over a waiter to explain the strange salad of shredded white cabbage tossed with a creamy dressing. Coleslaw, he shrugged.

Edith sampled the American foods that had sparked her curiosity at the beginning of her journey. She ate them without fear, though often with contempt.[55] In India she dined only in hotels and on board the train. She nibbled a mangosteen in Kandy. In Japan she sipped sake (and hated it). Yet only in Hawai'i, already emerging as a tropical holiday paradise, where the American settler empire met its colonial empire, would Edith finally taste local foods prepared by local hands. But that courageous step required another trip around the world.

Edith's Fingers

On 27 May 1926 the *Franconia* arrived back in Britain.[56] Just two and a half years later, in late November 1929, Edith prepared to circle the globe again, but this time, she travelled on the Peninsular and Oriental (P&O) ship ss *Mooltan*. Less elegant than the *Franconia*, the *Mooltan* was also less likely to attract American tourists. It was bound for Australia. From there, she would stitch together segments to New Zealand and from there to Fiji and Hawai'i.

The *Moolton* steamed out of port in a gale and fog. 'The dishes went [on] walks on their own account,' Edith wrote in a fresh, new journal. By the time the boat docked in Port Said for its passage through the Suez Canal, the weather had calmed, and Edith returned to her favourite pastime. She watched the locals, especially men who dived for coins tossed by passengers. When they caught a coin, 'they put it into their cheeks until they bulged out.' Two days later, in Aden at the mouth of the Red Sea, Edith was glad that lunch was served on board. 'The hotels looked horrid and the natives dirty.'

Food on the *Moolton* reminded Edith how much she loved the indulgence of around-the-world travel. 'How they do eat on board,' she exclaimed. Early risers could enjoy tea, biscuits and fruit, even before an 8.30 a.m. breakfast. Later in the morning, depending on the weather, passengers could snack on ice cream or beef broth in the comfort of their deck chairs. Lunch was at 1 p.m. and tea at 4.30 p.m. The seven-course dinner began at 7.30 p.m. In the evening, those passengers who lingered in the lounges to play cards helped themselves to potato crisps, olives, sandwiches and drinks.

For all that excess, Edith still wasn't entirely comfortable; there were 'blacks on board'. This was a passenger ship, not a designated cruise, and p&o sold tickets to any who could afford the high prices of first class. In her diary, she yearned for stricter segregation. 'I may be wicked,' she wrote, 'but I do not like to see the blacks mixing with the whites.' In the dining saloon, the stewards had the temerity to place 'a black' opposite Edith and between 'two white ladies'. No one spoke to him. Even worse, some of those 'blacks' were wealthy, even more so than Edith, the inveterate leisure traveller. Rumours spread on the ship about an Indian rajah who had reserved five separate cabins and then had them made up into a suite.[57]

The rumours broke the monotony of the long ocean trip across the Red Sea towards India and Edith, for all her segregationist yearnings, was fascinated. When an acquaintance joined a private dinner cooked by a private chef in the rajah's cabin, Edith listed the menu in her diary. First, fish, then chicken. The curry, scented with saffron, was 'not like ours'. The small grains of rice were also 'unlike ours'. At least at dessert, the ice cream was 'like ours'. Her interest in the dinner was comparison, not shared tastes. After dinner, the rajah served port. The mixture of disdain and prurient curiosity to which Edith subjected the rajah in her diary must have slipped into her table manners in the dining saloon. Edith wasn't invited to dinner.

In Bombay, by early December, the rajah disembarked, to the 'shrieking of natives'. In Honolulu Edith was happy to have local women drape a lei around her neck, but when 'natives' threw flowers at the rajah, she was appalled. 'I am told', she repeated a final rumour, 'he has a million a year.' Still, she wrote, '99½ per cent of the people are starving in India.' Edith wasn't eager to visit India again, she realized. She remembered India not for its flowers, but its dirt, people and danger. Before the ship set sail again, this time for the Antipodes and the South Sea isles, she recorded a bit of travel advice in her diary, as if to remind her future self to avoid the subcontinent. 'If you travel,' she warned, 'you might be sick at many things you see.'

Once the rajah disembarked in Bombay, Edith dashed off to find a steward to beg a private tour of the rajah's cabin: three bedrooms with two extra rooms connected into an expansive sitting room.[58]

When the boat reached Australia and she disembarked, Edith's mood soured. Everything she witnessed made her feel like her orderly colonial world was truly coming apart. Even Australia seemed in upheaval. Though Indigenous Australians remained profoundly marginalized, Australians had just elected a new 'rowdy' Labour Government, which 'seems to give everybody the right to freedom, which with them means vulgarity, rudeness and pushing', she complained. In Sydney, a hotel waiter answered her 'with an "ugh".[59] En route to New Zealand, she observed that Māori people boarded her ship. She was relieved that they remained in second class.

After her disappointment in Australia, New Zealand felt like a respite and Christchurch was a comforting small city, 'so English', she approved. Even the 'tiny slum children' had the decency to curtsy. Outside the city and off the ship, the Māori seemed both enticingly exotic and excellent servants. At Rotorua, the famous area of geysers and hot springs, guided by a Māori woman wearing 'native dress', Edith visited the geysers, which obligingly erupted after their Māori chauffeurs tossed in soap. (Soap can force geysers to erupt, though at the cost of destroying their natural plumbing systems.) Māori boys dived into the cold springs to collect coins tossed by Edith's tourist group. Māoris, she wrote, 'cook and do their washing in the geysers'. She eagerly enjoyed a naturally boiled lunch, but the foods were English and served by the Indigenous guides. Back on board, she glued a picture of 'Maori beauties' into her journal.[60]

En route from Auckland to Fiji, she pasted pictures of Fijian types. The small steamer on which she had booked passage unfortunately also carried a cargo of huge pigs for Suva and Tonga and first class again wasn't a fully white, English refuge. A Samoan chief was 'a huge mass of black flesh'. At least he spoke English perfectly and before they landed, he invited Edith and other passengers to visit his island home.[61]

Edith was curious. She imagined savage Pacific isles abundant with fruit. An invitation to a chief's house was enticing, even if she didn't plan to eat anything – or expect to be eaten. Fiji, she declared in her journal, was only a half-century removed from cannibalism. Once it became a British colony, she explained, Fijians realized that human flesh tasted too salty. Visiting a local Anglican church, she imagined that the baptismal font was once a hollowed-out rock to cook tender children. Now colonial subjects, she believed, Fijians ate pork, instead of people, and luxuriated in tropical Pacific abundance.

After lunch at the Royal Pacific hotel, Edith took a drive through Fijian villages. She stopped to ask a man sitting at his doorstep 'if he was contented'.

'Perfectly,' he replied.

She assumed that she knew why. 'He had everything he needed, yams, sweet potatoes, paw paw, pineapple, bread fruit, cocoanuts, guavas.' If he wanted something both calming and celebratory, he drank kava, 'their drink', she explained, made from a root 'chewed by beautiful clean-mouthed girls'. Kava has a mildly narcotic effect. Edith understood his contentment as laziness. In the midst of all that fruit and intoxicating drink, Pacific islanders were too 'indolent' to plant gardens.[62]

Everyone appeared so happy. Too happy, she complained. After a leisurely day visiting Fiji's attractions and drinking the water from green coconuts chopped open by her driver, Edith criticized those locals who 'refuse to work under a white man'. Some of the other passengers attended a local Fijian wedding and took part in the kava drinking. If they managed to drink the kava without a 'grimace', the wedding guests applauded. With all its kava drinking, the wedding, too, seemed distasteful. Kava, 'if drunk to excess', she wrote, 'makes the legs useless'. There was a blindfolded boxing match (a window was broken) and then a 'boy' imitated a preacher reciting a psalm. But the description was all rumour; Edith again wasn't invited. She remained back at the hotel, pasting pictures in her journal of 'natives climbing for coconuts' and of a Fijian chief's house.[63]

Edith wrote authoritatively about kava – but never tasted it. Instead, she drank from fresh coconut, insulated in its hard shell. She marvelled at wild custard apples but condemned Fijians for enjoying the natural bounty. She was a full-time leisure traveller who disparaged locals for not work-ing hard enough. Amid all those contradictions, she was eager to visit the Samoan chief's house – 'the "blackie"' from the ship. He invited the pas-sengers to his house, the first non-white house she had ever entered in all her travels. The chief was hospitable, though careful to serve only fresh fruit alongside British drinks and sweets. Still, his guests had to eat without plate, knife or fork, complained Edith.

Later that day, she pasted a picture of a 'native pig feast'.

By the end of March 1930, Edith was back in Hawai'i, angry again at the casual service from American hotel staff.

'How do?' greeted the Royal Hawaiian Hotel's doorman.

'No, I do not approve of the free and easiness!' she fumed.

Despite her distaste, she enjoyed the view of the hotel's coconut tree garden that framed the sea beyond. Relaxing in the hotel, Edith thought about a fellow passenger, lying ill in a Honolulu hospital with dengue fever. The tropics had their luxuries, but also their germs. 'I am very careful' in the tropics, wrote Edith. She swallowed quinine pills and washed vigorously with harsh carbolic soap. She packed her own towels.

Here in Hawai'i, towards the end of her second circumnavigation, Edith set aside her fears and her distaste for locals and their food. She set out from the Royal Hawaiian Hotel in search of poi. She knew that

Indigenous Hawaiians scooped poi with their fingers from a small bowl. She just didn't know how it tasted.

She drove out from the hotel to a house owned by a Hawaiian man she called 'David Kaafez'. Likely the visit was an excursion organized by the hotel. His house appealingly mixed primitivism – it was built of grass and leaves – and American hygiene; the colonial government insisted on a concrete floor, she explained. David ate 'everything without being cooked', especially fish and poi. He demonstrated to Edith that Hawaiians showed their delight with poi by sucking their fingers 'with a great noise'. She photographed David eating poi, a souvenir for a food adventure two around-the-world trips in the making.

David handed Edith the poi. She reached for the bowl and was about to plunge a finger into it.

'No,' he chided, 'wash first.'[64]

The Occident Calling

Edith disliked the last leg of her journeys. Across the Atlantic towards England, the weather turned rough and the passengers became tetchy.

On the *Franconia*, she had read, cut out and pasted a poem Thomas Cook and Cunard included in their 'last log'. Edith was convinced that the lure of the East, its exotic peoples and flavours, also represented dangers and discomforts. She had gazed enough at Arab men in Aden diving for coins, Māori women cooking in geysers and fruit-sellers in Ceylon and Singapore. 'I'm sick of the Mongol and Tartar/ I'm sick of the Jap and Malay,' read the poem. She longed for 'crowds that are white and clean'. Not that she ate any of it, but 'I'm wary of curry and rice all/ commingled with highly-spiced dope.' All that spicy food, the poem reminded, came with carbolic soap, mosquitos, vermin and flies. To draw in its customers, Thomas Cook had promised 'tropical breezes and sunshine that dazzle my eyes'. To ease passengers home again, the company reminded them that tropical breezes also blew infections. For all the pleasures of luxury travel, Edith heard the 'Occident calling'.

She ended her journal: 'Oh! Lord, but I want to go home.'[65]

7

Mangosteen

This was the story: Queen Victoria craved mangosteens. The British queen ruled an empire that stretched across the globe and its never-setting-sun-ripened fruit in Malayan jungles and West Indian plantations. Yet, the story continued, she had never sampled a mangosteen, the supremely delicious fruit of the tropics that just didn't lend itself to travel or transplant. The hard, purple-brown rind protects milky-white segments, flecked with nectar and sweetly fragrant. There were different versions of the story of the queen and the mangosteen. Some said that in reward for just a taste of its tropical deliciousness, Queen Victoria promised a knighthood.

Uncommon in supermarkets in Europe or America even today, mangosteens tantalized European travellers to Southeast Asia since the 1700s. The fruit's small round shape, with woody leaves at its top, looked enough like the temperate apple to seem familiar. But the perfumed segments inside hinted at the exotic. Tourists who used appalling metaphors to describe the durian struggled to describe the mangosteen. As they sought mangosteens in local markets and devoured them with abandon, tourists thought only of the seductive abundance of the tropics. Nature in tropics seemed especially generous. In fact, tourists such as Edith James gazed at local peoples and then concluded in their diaries that tropical nature might even be too generous. Fruits grew too freely, too sweet – and when the fruits of the jungle were so easy to collect, it rendered the locals lazy. Java, especially, appeared to tourists like Eden, and the mangosteen seemed to be Eden's apple.

When they first encountered the mangosteen, European travellers, seduced by its flavours, wondered if it might be something more than a tropical treat and a favourite of the locals. Maybe it was a miracle medicine, a 'fruitaceutical', to use a contemporary word. The tropics were lush with fruit, but travellers worried. Long before they realized that malaria was transmitted through a mosquito's bite, travellers blamed the tropics themselves. Based on medical fears of miasma as the source of disease, the

Mangosteen postcard, early twentieth century.

enervating heat and humidity bred indolence; at worst, it caused fevers. Until the middle of the nineteenth century, travellers in Southeast Asia believed that the mangosteen's cooling qualities countered the dangerous heat of the tropics.

Over the course of the next few decades, the belief in the medical benefits of the mangosteen faded, as European understandings of the cause of disease changed to focus on germs and as suspicion of local communities increased. Yet the mangosteen seemed immune from the antagonism tourists focused on the durian. If the durian represented the perils of the unhygienic tropics, mangosteens became an edible emblem of the tropics (even if visitors stopped touting its miraculous health benefits). Tourists sought out the mangosteen, so much so that the fruit became an edible stop on the tourist trail, but none of them knew exactly how to grow a mangosteen or how locals harvested them. Instead, it seemed to tourists that the luscious mangosteen in all its perfumed sweetness embodied the exotic abundance of the tropics.

If, by the early twentieth century, tourists could eat English roast beef in the heart of the tropics, what local tastes did tourists actually sample as food adventures? Mangosteens were the perfect fruit for tourists like James, so reluctant to try local foods and so concerned about the dangers of infection. The enticing flesh of the fruit, after all, was safely quarantined in the hard, protective and inedible rind. Neither local hands nor local germs could contaminate this small fruit, which, humble on the outside and fragrant inside, seemed a safe food adventure for all.

Like James, tourists visited markets as attractions but imagined vast plantations growing exotic fruits for a curious homebound public. More than any other fruit, the mangosteen symbolized the temptations of the tropics and its illusive prospects of wealth from harvesting its bounties. Tourists wrote in their diaries and described the fruit in their published travelogues or private letters home. Botanical explorers, meanwhile, yearned to turn private food adventures into imperial industries. With all its 'deliciousness', declared the American botanical explorer David Fairchild in 1915, the mangosteen deserves 'the special place accorded to it by all who have ever tasted its snowy white pulp'. He thought of Queen Victoria and crowned the mangosteen the 'queen of fruits'.[1]

The name stuck. From the mid-nineteenth century to the Second World War, every few years plant explorers like Fairchild publicly promised that the Queen of Fruits would soon arrive on grocery shelves – and, of course, on royal tables. The profit fantasies of planters and plant hunters, encouraged by the curiosity of tempted tourists, met the reality of rotting. If mangosteens grew at all in cultivated colonial plantations, the fruits decayed long before they could be marketed and sold. Only the story of a food adventure denied the queen of the British Empire remained.

The Wonder Drug

Ida Pfeiffer savoured her first mangosteen in Singapore in September 1847. Pfeiffer thought of the British colony as a gigantic cornucopia, overflowing with luscious fruit. Of all the varieties she sampled, she judged the mangosteen superior. As big as a 'middling-sized apple', the mangosteen's rind was deep brown on the outside, scarlet inside. The sections of the fruit were creamy white and melted in her mouth with 'an exquisite flavour'.[2]

In the era of her two journeys around the world, the mangosteen was already well-known but impossible to find in the temperate zone. For almost a century, Europeans, longing to wring profit out of the bounty of their Asian colonies and West Indian plantations, had praised the fruit's flavour, but struggled to grow it or ship it home.

Pfeiffer experienced the luscious pleasures of the tropics. Later, as she lay shivering with recurring bouts of malaria, she also experienced its dangers. For generations, local peoples had turned to mangosteens for more than flavour. The fruit's rind, in fact, has some antimalarial benefits. Europeans, like Pfeiffer, seemed unaware of local uses, however. Instead, they believed that the fruit cooled, providing natural protection against the torpor, fever and digestive disorders they associated with hot climates. John Ellis made his fortune as a merchant in London before going out to the Caribbean in 1764. Once in the tropics, his commercial zeal merged with a passion for botany. From his base in the Caribbean, he looked to the East Indies in search of profitable plants to transplant, especially the mangosteen.

The fruit was delicious, maybe even the 'most pleasant fruit of any yet known', he declared. For the British facing life in the tropics, he believed that the mangosteen's value was also medical. Nothing could be 'more useful to the sick, than this delicious fruit', Ellis promised. Both the succulent flesh and the dried rind offered a miracle cure for 'almost any disorder', from dysentery to fevers. Ellis shared the story of a French doctor struck down in Batavia by a 'dreadful putrid fever'. His friends assumed that he would die, but the doctor recovered after 'sucking this delicious and refreshing fruit'. In fact, Ellis claimed, when 'sick people have no relish for any other food they generally eat this with great delight; but should they refuse it, their recovery is no longer expected'.[3]

The mangosteen seemed a wonder food, the original fruitaceutical, perfect for Europeans in the tropics where illness intermingled with abundance. A French missionary serving in Siam, Jean-Baptiste Pallegoix, judged the mangosteen 'very healthy'. The fruit 'exhaled a sweet perfume'. The mangosteen was cooling and refreshing, perfect for Europeans in the tropics. Even its bark, he wrote, offered an antidote to dysentery. By contrast, he judged the durian dangerously 'heating'.[4]

In the early decades of the nineteenth century, as the French, British and Dutch competed for colonies, they agreed that the mangosteen was a wondrous fruit, as good for health as it was for the palate. The pioneering zoologist Frédéric Cuvier, in his *Atlas de Zoologie*, described its 'sweet perfume' and delightful taste. The fruit was, in addition, ideal for the sick, 'whatever their illness'.[5] A Dutch colonist writing from Batavia was just as enthusiastic about mangosteen as a delicious fruit and wonder drug. He compared the mangosteen to the mythical 'apples of Hesperie', fruit from Greek myths tended in an idyllic garden at the edges of the world. 'Fragrant and so exhilarating in taste', he wrote. They were 'refreshing', especially for those inflicted by tropical illnesses.[6]

In the context of early nineteenth-century beliefs about health and sickness, refreshing or cooling were more than descriptions of taste. These were medical properties. Perilous foods were too cold or, more typically in the tropics, too warming. The European digestion needed protection. Even Pfeiffer tasted tropical fruits with trepidation. Europeans believed that some fruits, especially the durian, were dangerously 'warming', an exotic fruit to eat only in moderation, if at all. The mangosteen cooled, but not chilled. When the French physician and botanist Michel Étienne Descourtilz described the mangosteen as 'very refreshing', he meant that its cool qualities could help cure the European traveller. The mangosteen differed from other fruits, and he assured Europeans that they could enjoy the fruit in whatever quantity they liked 'without being uncomfortable'.[7]

In the waning years of the nineteenth century, however, understandings of the cause of tropical illness shifted. Tourists echoed tropical medicine doctors and blamed germs, teeming in drinking water, for their fevers and diarrhoea. Cooling lost much of its medical meanings and mangosteens turned into an easy food adventure: comfortably segregated from its environment and from non-white hands by its hard rind, the mangosteen seemed safe. During his visit to Singapore in the 1860s, the American journalist Charles Carleton Coffin was eager to visit the famed fruit markets. The vendors recognized that tourists were fascinated by the diversity of local fruits. They crowded around Coffin and tried to sell him durians and mangosteens. Coffin avoided the durian after trying the fruit a few days previously on the boat to Singapore. It reminded him of 'fried onions, stewed garlic, burnt feathers, singed hair, assafoetida [sic], all sorts of doctor's stuff, and the odor of skunks'. One of the passengers angrily tossed the fruit overboard and ordered the stewards to sprinkle the dining saloon with disinfectant. The fruit had no place in European-only first class. The mangosteens, though, were 'juicy, cooling, delicious'.[8] F. M. Huschart also regarded mangosteens as safe adventure. When he arrived in Java in 1907, he was sick to his stomach, 'no doubt a reflex of the indiscriminate eating while going through India'. Still, in Java, Singapore and on the boats in between the two colonies, he and his fellow tourists enjoyed mangosteens. The mangosteen fruit, he decided, was 'the most delicious of any in the world'.[9]

Tourists increasingly avoided local foods but sought out mangosteens. The American tourist Isaac Newton Lewis worried about the unhealthy environment of the tropics when he left for his around-the-world tour in 1887. Writing from the comforts of the first-class saloon on the Messageries Maritimes' *Tibre*, Lewis insisted that a trip around the world still required 'something more than money'. Even leisure time was not enough. The traveller needed 'health, intelligent attention and, not least, great physical and moral strength and courage'. Despite the increasingly indulgent atmosphere of regularly scheduled steamship travel, Lewis packed carefully and fearfully for his trip. Warm wraps, he decided, would be necessary for cool evenings; light suits for the days; and a close-fitting helmet for the sun. He was just as careful about his eating, convinced that proper diet (and 'travelling first class') could overcome the perils of tropical travel. During his cautious travelling, he sampled the mangosteen. The size of a 'common apple', the mangosteens seemed 'so artistic'. As if he was shucking an oyster, with his knife he sliced the hard rind to reveal the 'creamy-white sacks'. He popped the segments into his mouth so quickly, 'there was not time to think either of malaria or poison.'[10]

To combat malaria and virtually everything else he thought he might catch in the tropics, Lewis also swallowed regular doses of quinine, processed from the bark of the tropical cinchona tree. Dutch and English expeditions collected seeds from the tree, native to Peru. Colonial botanists in Java nurtured seedlings into profitable trees. By the 1890s, Dutch plantations in Java, where local workers harvested the bark, supplied much of the world's quinine. Quinine seemed a new miracle drug – this time astringent, not sweet. Cinchona had become big business in the natural environment of the mangosteen.

The Bang-Upest Fruit

On the journey all the way around the world, tourists stopped to taste mangosteens. Even Phileas Fogg, the fictional hero of Jules Verne's *Around the World in Eighty Days*, pauses his race so that he can eat the mangosteens his trusted manservant Passepartout has purchased in a local market. Fogg eats a lot of them, several dozen in fact. For him their white segments are 'an unequaled joy'.[11]

If Verne's novel, translated into many languages, helped propel the enduring craze for around-the-world travel, it echoed depictions of mangosteens as the most superior of tropical fruits. 'We tasted a mangosteen for the first time this evening,' the British tourist Mrs Howard Vincent recorded. 'The fruit inside is white, and has the most delicate flavour. I should call it an insidious flavour, for you hardly know of what it consists, but it is most delicious.'[12]

When around-the-world tourists visited markets, they turned their noses up at the durian, but relished the mangosteen. Mangosteens represented the sensual promise of the exotic east; durian represented its dangers.

On his visit to Singapore, the American traveller H. Allen Tupper Jr wandered around Singapore's botanical gardens and paid a 'native' to climb a palm tree to fetch him a coconut. He was more interested in watching a local man climb 'with the rapidity of a monkey' than in tasting the fresh coconut water. Next up was a visit to the fruit market to enjoy a basket of 'delicious mangosteens'. After watching a 'brilliant' Malay funeral procession, he sailed for Ceylon 'where the spicy breezes blow'. Before departing, he bought and saved a postcard of a mangosteen, showing the fruit carefully sliced in half to reveal its ripe segments.[13]

Mangosteen tasting had become a tourist rite. In 1927 the American journalist Robert Casey and other tourists from his cruise followed a local guide around Java's markets. A vendor tried to entice him with freshly fried vada, a round, fried snack with a hole in the middle, made from a lentil and rice batter. 'I didn't taste any although the smiling proprietor tried to take me on as a customer.' Instead, Casey and his group hurried towards a fruit stall where their guide haggled with the vendor for mangosteens, their stems braided attractively together. Casey guessed that the guide was bargaining for only six fruits – just a taste for the tourist party. Instead, the guide purchased a full string, or three dozen mangosteens. 'It looks as if we shall have enough mangosteens to fill all our wants for the next few months.' He joked that he would try the durian only if his catarrh got worse and the nasal congestion prevented him from being able to smell.[14]

Paradoxically, though so many tourists in this era tried the mangosteen and enjoyed the experience, they also claimed that the flavours were

Mangosteen still-life postcard.

indescribable. The mangosteen might look like an apple, said tourists, but nothing in the temperate zone resembled the taste. By contrast, they found the durian's smell easy to describe. Tourists turned to familiar and repulsive things that smelled strongly – sewers, cheese, onions, garlic – and added in rot. The mangosteen, in its indescribability, widened the gap between exotic tropical and familiar temperate. An 1878 novel described two young, wealthy women, Amy and Marion, friends on holiday from their boarding school, on a cruise around the world. Their friendly ship captain, Fay, introduced the two women to mangosteens even before they arrived in Saigon. Marion was busy trying to sketch a local 'shanty under some palm trees' when the captain invited her to sample the fruit, 'the queen of East India fruits', he promised, 'and one that you will never know when to stop eating after you once taste it'.

Marion was reluctant. She had found that mangoes tasted like turpentine. She never even tried the durian after Fay described its smell of 'deceased' cats and dogs and 'decaying elephants'. Despite that vivid account of the durian's odour, Fay – like so many real-life tourists – couldn't express the mangosteen's taste. 'The flavor is unlike any other in the world,' he shrugged. 'I cannot describe it.' Still, Fay promised: 'The first time one tastes a mangosteen is an epoch in the history of a life.'

Marion swallowed a segment, closed her eyes and sighed – 'rapture too deep for utterance'.[15]

Descriptions like Fay's said little about mangosteens, but a great deal about the exotic tropics: mysterious, seductive and, potentially, ripe for colonial commerce. An American traveller in Java leaned out of train windows to buy fruit from platform vendors at every train halt. Some of the fruits were excellent, but 'others unsuited to our organs of smell'. Disgusted, it was easy for him to describe the durian's stench: 'a sewer, only much more so'. The mangosteen, though, tasted and smelled delicious. One had to peel the outer husk to reveal the white segments inside. The pulp 'melts away in your mouth', he told *New York Times* readers. Happily, mangosteens were as safe as they were delectable. 'Ripe mangosteens are harmless as ripe peaches.'

The actual taste, though, was illusive. The mangosteen 'has a taste which nobody can describe any more than he can tell how a canary sings or a violet smells'. The mangosteen was – simply – the 'bang-upest fruit'.[16]

God's Creation in the Tropics

'Java!' enthused the French travel writer Jules Leclercq in 1898. Of all the 'enchanted isles' bathed in the tropical sun, none could match the Dutch colony for its 'delights of climate, the sweetness of air, the fertility of soil', he wrote. The memories of his visit lingered. 'The more I grow old,' he said, 'the more I'd like to return to taste its charms again.'[17]

The mangosteen grew throughout Southeast Asia. In season, it filled markets in Singapore. Tourists especially associated the mangosteen with verdant Java. They sought out the fruit in urban Batavia or bucolic Buitenzorg, the Dutch colonial botanical garden. The mangosteen helped tourists imagine the tropics as abundant in its natural gifts and Java, in particular, as a primitive paradise. Java with its mangosteens became Eden.

Decades before it had become a destination for round-the-world travellers, before Leclercq declared it a model colony and before eating mangosteens became a tourist attraction, Java was a battlefield of European empires. In 1811 Sir Thomas Stamford Raffles helped lead British forces against a combined Dutch and French army. (Thousands of miles away, Napoleonic France had annexed the Netherlands and created a puppet state, the Kingdom of Holland.) Raffles became Java's Lieutenant Governor. Life in the tropics for European colonists remained perilous. In fact, Raffles's wife died of fever in Java while he was governor. She was buried at Buitenzorg. Despite the hardships, Raffles still believed that Java would one day prove a valuable colony. The island was blessed with a rich botany, especially its 'indigenous fruits', he noted.[18] 'The *mangústin*,' he wrote, has 'on account of its acknowledged pre-eminence amongst Indian fruits... been termed the pride of these countries'. Locals, meanwhile, were 'passionately attached' to the durian, he observed.

British rule in Java proved short. In 1814, as part of post-Napoleonic peace treaties, the colony returned to Dutch rule, and Raffles departed for Singapore, the British bastion. Once restored, the Dutch ruled Java harshly. Colonial officials forced Javanese farmers to plant export crops and required them to work on Dutch plantations for sixty days a year. In the era when Pfeiffer visited Java and other islands in the Dutch East Indies, the Dutch remained at war, this time with local rulers of small kingdoms resisting Dutch control. The Dutch were expanding their empire throughout the Indonesian archipelago. By the end of the century, when Leclercq arrived on holiday, however, the Dutch were eager to recast Java as a tourist destination and the mangosteen helped define the island as a tropical paradise. Java's colonial Dutch government invited tourists to visit 'God's Creation in the Tropics'.[19]

'The island of Java', Leclercq believed, 'was the most fertile in the world'.[20] Unspoiled, the virgin jungle seemed to him like the very first 'ages of the world'. Like many other travellers to the Dutch colony, Leclercq marvelled at both Java's primitive tropical bounty and its commercial productivity. He arrived in Buitenzorg during a downpour, but as he made his way to the nearby Belle-Vue hotel, he already felt as if the rains had extinguished the 'heats of hell'. Even the coolness that followed seemed 'delicious'. From the hotel verandah, he gazed across the unbroken tropical panorama towards the botanical gardens and the jungle beyond. 'Terrestrial paradise', he decided.

The colonial botanical garden tamed the natural abundance of Java into scientific and commercial order. Primitive beauty turned into imperial profit. Leclercq walked its carefully groomed pathways, marked by resplendent flowers. Vines that reminded him of Eden's serpent draped over the trees. Alongside all the 'botanical riches' of Java itself, the garden was cultivating other tropical products – and testing their appropriateness for the colony's plantations. Here grew the palm oil trees from Guinea, there the *Laodicea* plant from the Seychelles which grew a special, rare fruit. He didn't have the opportunity to taste it.

Instead, Leclercq left the botanical gardens and went in search of local fruit to sample at the local market. The lane to the market felt like a 'pathway in paradise'. The Javanese men and women haggling with the fruit sellers wore bright-patterned sarongs below their waists and little above. The children were nude. On their 'chocolate-coloured' shoulders, vendors carried cooking pots, baskets of fresh greens and live chickens, and, of course, bananas, durians, pineapples and mangosteens.[21]

Travel writers such as Leclercq and the American Eliza Scidmore toured Java for pleasure and profit. They each later published travel guides that praised Java as a tourist's paradise. Java, wrote Scidmore, was 'an oasis in travel', especially for 'round-the-world travelers'. Ignoring the Dutch colony's violent history of conquest and plantation labour, Scidmore cast Java as the 'summer isles of Eden'. In the early morning, before the tropical heat forced colonial residents to retreat to midday naps, Java felt like the 'dewy freshness of dawn in Eden'.[22]

After sampling the rijsttafel in a Batavia hotel, Scidmore tasted her first mangosteen. She decided that it was 'nature's final and most perfect effort in fruit'. A few days later, she visited Buitenzorg. To Scidmore, the botanical garden felt like 'a valley of Eden'. In the hands of Dutch gardeners, Scidmore mused, 'it seems as though nature and the tropics could do no more.' The Dutch had tamed and manicured the abundance of the jungle into profitable paradise. She turned her umbrella upside down and filled it with sweet-smelling frangipani flowers. All around, mangosteens grew on 'benevolent trees'.

After Scidmore left the orderly colonial botanical garden with its grand visions of colonial commerce, she, like Leclercq, visited the local market. Just outside the Buitenzorg gate, the market sold the staples of Javanese life. It 'most delight[ed] and divert[ed]' tourists, explained Scidmore. Amat, her 'mild-mannered Moslem servant', led her through the market and haggled with vendors for 'heaps of splendid fruits' for her basket. He explained the names of each 'strange fruit' and demonstrated the tricks for cutting their hard skins to reveal the flesh inside. Some, like the Java banana, were coarse and disappointing. The salak, a scaly-skinned fruit that grows on a palm, was pleasant enough, but anodyne in flavour, she decided. Then, she ate the 'fruit of fruits, the prize of the Indies and of all the Malay equatorial regions' – the mangosteen.

Come to Java in November or December, 'if only to know the mango-steen in its perfection', Scidmore recommended. The fruit on the tree might look like 'dark-purple apples' and, in the market, Javanese used the stems to braid the mangosteens together. They looked to Scidmore like gigantic clusters of grapes, but the fruit's flavours and aroma were like nothing in the temperate world. First tart, then sweet, the mangosteen offered 'all the delights of nature's laboratory condensed'.

Scidmore tasted the white segments of fruit and thought of '*neige parfumée*' – perfumed snow. It is 'a harmless and wholesome fruit . . . that one may eat with impunity'. The mangosteen could seduce tourists into a trip to Java, to Eden itself. Suggestive of how the mangosteen had lost its appeal as miracle medicine as it had become a tourist attraction, Scidmore found herself wishing that the mangosteen could in fact cure tropical illness. She wished the fruit was 'something antimalarial', a sweet substitute for the bitter quinine that she swallowed each day. Instead, as Scidmore enjoyed the aromatic sweetness of the fruit, her mind drifted to the Garden of Eden. Scidmore wondered if the mangosteen was 'a forbidden fruit', one that was 'wicked' or, if indulged, 'a little of a sin'.[23]

Market outside Buitenzorg, illustration from Eliza Scidmore,
Java, the Garden of the East (1897).

Eating the Queen's Fruit

As Scidmore savoured her mangosteen in the market outside the Buitenzorg
gates, she also thought about the British queen. Scidmore offered her own
version of the myth of the royal reward for mangosteens. Despite years of
tourists' delight, she explained, the 'offer by the leading British steamship
company of thirty pounds sterling to the ship-captain who will get a basket
of mangosteens to the Queen is still open'. Scidmore changed the story
slightly to reflect the reality that despite the webs of steamship lines, the
mangosteen was stubbornly a tropical treat only for tourists and locals.[24]
The mangosteen, Scidmore explained, simply didn't travel to temperate
Europe or America. Even refrigerated in modern ships or with the rinds
coated in wax, the white segments rotted into brown pulp.

Other tourists claimed that the British queen promised a knighthood
in exchange for mangosteens. Still others substituted the Dutch for the
English queen. In 1910 Paul Junkin relished a mangosteen in Batavia on
his around-the-world cruise on the *Cleveland* and claimed that the Dutch
colonial government 'has tried very hard to send the mangosteen to their
queen and has offered a considerable reward to anyone who will succeed'.
The fruit was the edible crown jewel of the colony and the Dutch queen
longed to taste it, but 'all efforts have been unsuccessful.'[25]

Tourists genuinely liked the mangosteen; many truly loved it. They especially relished the privilege of eating something the British queen could not – or the Dutch queen, depending on who was telling the story. Americans, in particular, enjoyed eating the fruit denied the very rulers of the colonies they were steadily turning into tourist destinations.

When William Jennings Bryan, the American politician and presidential candidate, travelled around the world with his family in 1905, he went to evaluate European colonies at first hand. He returned with 'increased admiration for American institutions'. When he left on holiday, Bryan remained the standard bearer of the Democratic Party. He had also already emerged as a trenchant critic of the U.S. zeal for imperial expansion in the tropics. In 1908, when he again ran for president a third and final time, the mangosteen was on his mind. The mangosteen, wrote Bryan, 'melts in the mouth, and leaves a memory of mingled flavors'. Queen Victoria, he explained, offered a prize of 'thirty pounds' to anyone who could send her a ripe mangosteen.[26]

Bryan insisted that his trip around the world was a private citizen's holiday. Nonetheless, during his journey, he sent dispatches to American newspapers and magazines and, after his return, he published a book. He visited the standard tourist sites, but he exploited his political prestige for better access and closer looks. In Buitenzorg, for example, the garden's director led Bryan on his tour. Even with a politician's special access, Bryan carried the tourist's standard guidebooks. In Java, for example, he read Scidmore's guide to prepare himself for the cornucopia of fruit.[27]

Bryan agreed with Scidmore: few places on earth as Java have 'been so blessed by the Creator's bounty'. Java – the 'beautiful', he called it – should be included in any 'tour of the world'. In Buitenzorg, he thought of Eden, but also of empire. The director pointed to a vine with curious, porous bulbs, each with ants living inside. The ants, the garden's director explained, protected the plant from pests. Bryan was unconvinced. He had heard the same defence of imperialism. 'Some of the European nations have defended their occupation of Oriental countries on the same theory.' Like ants living off a tree, colonialism 'is always a burden to the natives', insisted Bryan.

Criticism of empire didn't necessarily produce respect for locals. Bryan believed that the same endless tropical summer that nurtured luscious fruits had also rendered the Javanese, and other tropical peoples, indolent. They laboured only when forced and force was exactly what the Dutch employed, Bryan explained. The Dutch colonial government not only proscribed what colonized people could grow but demanded 'one day's labour in seven'.

Bryan asked a Dutch colonial resident: 'What, then, have the Dutch taught the Javanese?' The colonist laughed. 'We have taught them to pay us their money.'[28]

Bryan sweltered in the tropical heat. He read Scidmore's guidebook, and, on her recommendation, he tasted the mangosteen. In the cooling, sweet segments, he detected the limited promise of empire. After all, this anti-imperialist American politician and tourist had enjoyed a fruit the British queen could not. The fruit didn't travel, proof enough for Bryan that the benefits of imperial trade were a chimera. The locals raised their own food and ate their own fruit. They produced their own clothes and only rarely wore shoes. What could a colonized consumer want to buy from Britain, the Netherlands or the United States – especially if they already had mangosteens?[29]

Back in the United States, Bryan prepared for his last presidential campaign, this time against an arch American imperialist, William Howard Taft (the former American governor general of the new colony of the Philippines). After 'reveling in mangosteens', declared Bryan, he returned home and ate an apple. Why eat the tropical mangosteen when the temperate apple sufficed, he asked. He munched the apple. In the temperate zone, 'we not only have an abundance of both the necessaries and the luxuries,' he declared, 'but we escape the torments of the tropics,' from bothersome mosquitos to contaminated water. For Bryan, the rotting mangosteen that the queen couldn't eat represented the false promises of empire.[30]

Other tourists disagreed with Bryan. They thought about the queen and imagined that if they could only solve the problem of rot, they would earn a fortune. For tourists who marvelled at the reach of Euro-American empires, the prospect of profit was as seductive as the taste. Tourists imagined Eden but dreamed of plantation agriculture. Like 'hundreds of other people', the tourist James Macauley confessed, he attempted to return home with mangosteens. Watching Javanese selling the fruit in local markets, he fantasized about the money that could be earned 'if the fruit could be transported to London'. He bought extra mangosteens and wrapped some in paper; others he buried in sawdust. He even tried to seal the hard rind hermetically in hot pitch, but he might as well have tried to import 'a snowball'. Arriving home to rotted rinds, Macauley finally admitted that the luscious mangosteen 'is essentially a tropical fruit'.[31]

The brown mush of the rotted mangosteen came to embody the locked commerce of the luxuriant tropics. Because it didn't travel, the fruit retained its exotic appeal as a special privilege of the tourist. Tourists sought out the mangosteen in tropical marketplaces because imperial commerce couldn't bring it to them. In 1928 an American tourist and his companions first encountered mangosteens in a local marketplace. 'No time was lost.' They leapt out of their car and 'Purchased, tasted, and mumbled our appreciation between bites.' He enthused, 'It is worth a trip to the tropics and all the attendant dangers and discomforts thereof just to have all the mangosteens you can eat, for it has appropriately been named "The Queen of Fruits".'[32] Like so many others, he struggled to describe the flavour. 'It is neither sweet nor sour, nor acid, nor bitter, nor pucker . . . you must taste it to find out. When one comes to such a point as this all language fails.' The vast apparatus of imperial transit also failed. 'The mangosteen is too delicate in texture to keep very long,' he wrote, but he still packed thirty mangosteen saplings to bring home. They died.

For American tourists and botanical explorers, their mangosteen adventure also became a parable of the rising power of their country. Just as the British or Dutch empires had cultivated other tropical plants for profit in their network of botanical gardens, botanical explorer David Fairchild confidently expected that new American tropical possessions in Hawai'i and Panama could produce mangosteens. Tourists had made the mangosteen famous and now Fairchild, on his own tour around the world, had a plan: transplant mangosteen seedlings, mature trees on plantations and harvest the fruit for domestic sale. Ordinary Americans who couldn't afford the around-the-world cruise, Fairchild promised, could then sample at home the mangosteens the British queen never tasted. The mangosteen, however, proved the greatest failure of Fairchild's long career of botanical prospecting.

In 1896 Fairchild arrived in Java and hurried to Buitenzorg. For the next eight months, he lived in a tourist hotel just outside the garden gates. Typical of hotels catering to around-the-world tourists, lunch was the exciting meal of the day. Fairchild's first lunch introduced him to two of Java's famed tourist food adventures: rijsttafel and the mangosteen. A parade of turbaned waiters offered rice, followed by curries, fried fish or chicken, and a massive tray of fish, baby corn, peanuts, coconut, mango chutney and many other choices he could neither identify nor remember. Once he had dumped various dishes onto his rice, the waiter poured over a fiery 'curry sauce'. The first bite 'started something, whether it was digestion or not I do not know', he admitted.

At last, before Fairchild retired to his room for a siesta, a 'coolie' passed along the hotel's covered verandah with a basket of mangosteens.

Singapore fruits, a popular postcard subject from the early twentieth century.

He showed Fairchild how to cut through the hard shell after the botanical explorer tried fruitlessly to open it with his fingers. 'There, lying loosely in a pink cup, were five ivory-white segments glistening with moisture.' The flavour was 'indescribably delicious.'[33]

'I wanted to see this fruit on the American market,' decided Fairchild immediately.[34] Two years later, in 1898, after hostilities ceased in the war between the United States and Spain, the former emerged with a vast tropical empire that stretched from Puerto Rico in the Caribbean to the Philippines. In the years after the war, plant explorers and government officials together sought to identify profitable tropical crops to grow in plantations in new American possessions. 'Uncle Sam', assured *Good Housekeeping*, 'is literally ransacking every corner of the globe for dainty and novel foods with which to tempt the appetite of the epicure, and also the person of more moderate means.'[35] Later, botanical explorers hoped that Panama, where the United States began constructing the canal that would link its Caribbean and Pacific empires, could cultivate fruits right on the shipping lanes to the temperate zone.

As early as 1900, after his return from Java, Fairchild organized the Office of Foreign Seed and Plant Introduction within the Department of Agriculture. The office would carry the fruits of empire to American possessions and, from there, to American tables. He began his campaign to commercialize mangosteens. His first challenge was exporting mangosteen seeds and seedlings out of Java. He coated seeds in paraffin to prevent rotting. Fairchild thought of Java as a primitive garden with its many fruits that could simply be plucked from its trees by primitive peoples. He promised that the fruit could be improved by imperial science. If the mangosteen had been 'within easy reach of some great metropolis of white people', he fantasized, 'there would have been millions of dollars invested in its culture and thousands of acres planted with the beautiful trees'.

The British and French had long tried to cultivate the mangosteens for export. The French had introduced the mangosteen to Saigon around the turn of the century and Fairchild admired French mangosteen plantations, however small.[36] Yet the French plantations could only sell to local customers, including French colonial residents. They couldn't ship the fruits back home to France. Fairchild looked across the span of the now expansive American empire and sought to better the French, English and Dutch at their own fruit. He wanted to ship fresh to the temperate zone. 'What the profits would be if they were sold for such fancy prices as would be offered by the fruiterers of any big metropolis can be easily imagined.' Fairchild had already begun calculating profit.[37]

Where the British, Dutch and French had failed, Fairchild was convinced that he could succeed. First, he tried Florida, but its occasional chills killed the young trees. Then, Hawai'i. Planters managed to keep the trees alive, but only two ever fruited. He tried coating the fruit in wax for shipment. The wax failed, the fruit rotted and the trees, susceptible to diseases, soon died. The fragile mangosteen resisted all colonial efforts at commercialization.[38]

Puerto Rico or Cuba also seemed like ideal locations to Fairchild, but though planters could grow the trees, they didn't seem to fruit. Maybe the Canal Zone in Panama would be more successful. Fairchild helped deliver twenty mangosteen plants to Panama, but the experimental garden there soon failed.[39] The American canal was hailed as an engineering marvel, but on its banks, mangosteen seedlings withered and died.

Fairchild tried yet again in Panama. This time, government botanists fostered a few trees. In 1925 the New York Times breathlessly announced that mangosteens would soon arrive in America. 'Queen Victoria,' the newspaper delighted, 'with the luxuries of the world at her beck, longed for something that even the resources of the British Empire could not procure for her.' Tourists had long returned with stories of a fruit that tasted of 'nectar and ambrosia', but never with the fruit itself. 'So the Queen of England never tasted mangosteen.' Now, though, the fruit, sold in heaps in the markets of the Dutch East Indies colony, was coming to America – in ten years. The fruit was worth the wait, the newspaper assured its readers. 'When it finally does appear in our markets, ten years hence, it may create a new industry.'[40] They never arrived, and Fairchild never explained the fate of the trees.

In 1935 Americans still had to travel if they wanted to taste mangosteens.

A Greengrocer in Manchester

The next year, across the Atlantic, a reporter for the *Manchester Guardian* peered through the window of a typical British greengrocer's shop. New fruits had filled the shop over the last century, thanks in part to botanical explorers. Throughout the temperate zone, the variety of available tropical fruit was 'richer' than ever before. Yet the mangosteen was still not for sale. 'Inside the faded purple shell, the size of an orange, there is an arrangement of gloriously coloured sections which melt in the mouth like ice-cream,' *The Guardian* tantalized. Travellers had first tasted the 'ambrosial fruit' centuries before; maybe one day 'the swift-moving commercial aeroplane' could fly the mangosteen from the tropical to the temperate zone.[41]

Throughout the era of Euro-American empires, botanical explorers kept promising that mangosteens would soon feature on greengrocers' shelves. As early as 1775, John Ellis provided detailed models of boxes that he believed could keep mangosteen seedlings alive on the long journey away from Java. Shipping boxes like these actually helped a few mangosteen plants and seeds survive their long journeys from Java to Ceylon, from Singapore to London, and from Penang all the way to the Panama and the West Indies. But the saplings didn't survive replanting. In 1870 a British civil servant posted in Penang, Major John Frederick Adolphus McNair, shipped mangosteen seedlings to the governor of the colony in British Guiana. 'It would be interesting to know what becomes of these plants,' he wondered.[42] They died. A few decades later, just as Fairchild was failing to grow mangosteens in the Canal Zone, Robert Derry, a gardener of the Royal Botanic Gardens at Kew, admitted that 'the mangosteen is not a good traveller.' Even so, he tried to ship seeds from Singapore to Jamaica by coating them with beeswax.[43]

Canals were dug. Steamships replaced sail. Aeroplanes promised a new way around the world. But mangosteens still rotted and seedlings died because of fantasies that tastes once reserved for tourists might one day be available to the homebound public. If only the mangosteen, that 'divine combination' of flavours, could find its way to English shops, mused one hungry observer in 1875. 'The public benefactor who could bring Mangosteens from Malaaca would give our frugivorous people an unknown delight.' The profits would be 'beyond the dream of avarice'. All the evidence of dead plants aside, he refused to be daunted. 'We shall be told, of course, that the thing is impossible,' but beef and mutton could now sail from the Antipodes or South America to Britain. American apples could arrive fresh on ice to Bombay. Surely, the 'sunny world of the East' could one day 'become our orchard', he hoped.[44]

Colonial regimes constructed plantations for export crops from cinchona to tea, but not mangosteens, apart from the small French plantations Fairchild visited. Those aircraft that the *Manchester Guardian* hoped would bring mangosteens were by the end of the decade instead ferrying troops. The American military during the Second World War even trained its pilots in how to look for mangosteens, durian, bamboo shoots and other tropical foods in case they were shot down over the Asian and Pacific jungles.[45]

Post-war, the writer Charles Morrow Wilson, who once worked for United Fruit Company, again promised that the 'queen of fruits' was coming soon to American tables.[46] By then, Fairchild had retired to his home and garden in Florida, which he named 'The Kampong'. The word 'Kampong' was Javanese for 'village'. He surrounded himself with tropical plants, wrote his autobiography, took pride in the cornucopia of fruits and vegetables he had brought to America and regretted the fruitless effort to bring mangosteens to America.[47] By the 1960s the *New York Times* admitted that although Fairchild (as well as the newspaper) had promised Americans mangosteens 'in a few years', they were 'as scarce as ever'. Adding to their propensity to rot and for the seedlings to die, botanists discovered that mangosteens were liable to carry plant diseases. The U.S. government imposed quarantines – even if someone had figured out how to import mangosteens. The ban on importing mangosteens, especially from Thailand, remained in place until 2008.

The myth of Queen Victoria and the mangosteens refused to die. As recently as 2007, the noted food writer David Karp confessed that he was a 'big time mangosteen addict'. His addiction was hard to feed. Inspecting a wooden model of a mangosteen that he kept on his desk, he thought back to the first fruit he tasted 'half a lifetime ago in Singapore'. It was 'thrilling, intoxicatingly luscious, so evocative of the exotic East' – and still almost impossible to find in New York. 'Queen Victoria', he insisted, 'reportedly offered a knighthood to anyone who could bring her a specimen in edible condition.'[48]

The story has endured, yet it just isn't true.

Green Treasure

The true story begins in a novel. *Green Treasure*, published in 1948, chronicles the post-war journey around the world of Burr (and his pet monkey) as part of a plant exploration expedition. Though Burr is a fictional character, his dreams of becoming wealthy growing mangosteens was shared by both tourists and botanical explorers alike. Burr treasures his dog-eared copy of David Fairchild's *The World Is My Garden* and he knows the myth about Queen Victoria's reward for mangosteens. He explains to his grandmother that the queen had even once offered £100 for a taste of the fruit. Before setting sail, Burr tries to convince his grandmother to convert her Florida farm (near Fairchild's famed Kampong) into a mangosteen plantation. He decides to make his fortune selling mangosteens, even before tasting them.

He tastes his first mangosteen in a market in Penang. At the market, Burr turns the mangosteen over in his hand and recalls Fairchild's method for eating it, a technique the real-life explorer had learned from an unnamed servant. Burr cuts the hard rind carefully and plucks out the segments. He gives the first segment to his monkey and eats the second himself. The juice fills his mouth, refreshing and cooling. Like Fairchild before him, Burr can't describe the flavour, but he considers eating a hundred of them.[49]

Burr's version of the story of Queen Victoria and the mangosteen blended fact and dramatic fantasy. Burr recounts the story to his companions on the expedition: the Duke of Northumberland tended two mangosteen trees in the greenhouse of his British country estate. In 1855 both trees flowered. Two fruits ripened. He sent one mangosteen to the queen, explains Burr. The duke honoured the other fruit with a banquet and then cut down the trees.[50]

In fact, letters and journal articles hidden away in the archives reveal that Queen Victoria had sampled mangosteens more than once. The Duke of Northumberland had indeed ripened two mangosteens and sent both fruits to 'her Majesty for the royal table', a British horticultural magazine later recalled.[51] It is unlikely that he cut down such valuable trees as Burr claims, but there is no record of them producing additional mangosteens. The fruit was the treasure from the 'sultry clime' and the 'most exquisite of all fruits'. Riper than the nectarine, better than the grape or strawberry, with segments like an orange and a husk harder than a pomegranate, wrote the magazine. Those ill from tropical climates would be helped by its cooling properties. After all, the magazine reminded, on Captain Cook's journey around the world, the fruit protected sailors against 'putrid fever'.

Queen Victoria ate mangosteens again in 1891. This time, J. H. Hart, the superintendent of the Royal Botanic Gardens in Trinidad, sent her mango-steens carefully wrapped in pine wool.[52] Most rotted, but, miraculously, this time, a few arrived safely. George Monro, a leading fruit merchant in the Covent Garden market in central London, also received one of the rare examples. He cut the fruit open and showed it to his best custom-ers. 'I should like to try some and if sent, will do all I can to get a trade for them,' he reported.

Except for the odd gift to the queen, mangosteens just didn't travel. Neither the real-life Monro nor the fictional Burr ever found a temper-ate market for tropical mangosteens.[53] Instead, mangosteens remained the tourist's food adventure.

8

Juanita Harrison

On 15 September 1928 – a Saturday – Juanita Harrison boarded a train bound for Bratislava, Czechoslovakia, on the shores of the Danube and a gateway to ports and parts further south and east. An hour and a half later, the train collided with another heading north. Juanita's train derailed, killing 26 people. That night, she confessed to her diary: 'I cannot write about Reck [the wreck] yet as the thoughts are very sad.'

Juanita remained silent for two days. Then, she opened her journal again to describe how she survived the wreck with more than simply a black eye; she was left 'terribly heartbroken' over a German woman whose dying words she couldn't even understand. When the trains collided, Juanita was thrown across her third-class compartment. Stunned by a concussion, she found herself searching frantically for her copy of *Bradshaw's Continental Guide*, 'the book that means everything to me'. Then, she crawled into a turnip patch alongside the rails to help local farmers care for the wounded. Even in her dazed state, Juanita recalled the loveliness of the German woman. She had 'beautiful great blue eyes' that matched her sparkling engagement ring. Juanita rested the dying woman's head on a pillow of rolled-up turnip greens and listened as the woman hoarsely repeated words in German. 'I just loved her,' Juanita wrote. The girl died in her arms. 'I felt terribly heartbroken.'[1]

A few days later, safe in Budapest, she sought solace at a picnic. She wasn't an invited guest, but quickly endeared herself to her Roma hosts. They assumed that she was Italian and laughed when Juanita assured them that she was an American pleasure traveller with a black eye.

Juanita's eight-year journey around the world from 1927 to 1935 reveals how conscious, respectful tasting could produce an affectionate politics of understanding. From Budapest she travelled to Belgrade where she found a bakery that roasted pigs when it had finished its breads for the day and the ovens were empty, but still hot. Juanita was already a seasoned traveller and, fearless, she knew the tricks needed to find a good meal. When a young woman left the bakery carrying a suckling pig 'just as Brown as Molasses', Juanita followed behind her, right into a small café's kitchen. To the songs of a small orchestra, Juanita feasted on sliced pork and peppers. The musicians were, she guessed, 'a mixture of Oriental', but the waiters, like the Roma at their picnic, couldn't quite place her. In an unknown café, eating local foods, Juanita knew that she was safe and happy again.

'I'll love it here,' she decided. As she ate, the owner tried to show off his English. He might be sorry for his boasts, she chuckled to herself. She decided to return tomorrow with a long list of questions for him. This was a 'second class café where you find them so naturnal. What a place to forget a Reck.'[2]

Juanita preferred third class even to second class. Ida Pfeiffer had travelled third class out of necessity – Juanita by choice. Juanita followed a set of rules never listed in any tourist guide like *Bradshaw's*. She mingled, flirted and made friends wherever she travelled. She learned a few words in different languages, enough to find work and to order just what she longed to eat. She tasted the local foods, not because she was in search of exotic food adventures, but because she was curious and hungry. She forged friendships at the table and those friendships transgressed artificial barriers of race and class, fundamental to the way empires functioned.

By the time she left on her journey, Euro-American tourists typically lived a segregated existence. They ate in their own hotels, dining cars and steamship saloons, rarely encountering locals other than servants and waiters. Not Juanita. By her own choosing, she evaded the strict lines that kept tourists separated from locals, simply because no one could quite place her. At that Roma picnic, they guessed she was Italian. In Aleppo, they assumed she was Arabic. In India, if she wore her red scarf, she appeared Indian and heading to China, she looked forward to being Chinese.

At home in the United States, though, the colour of her skin marked her as African American. Abroad, she never tried to 'pass' and thus claim all the privileges reserved for white travellers. She carried an American passport that helped her cross national borders, but she used her heritage as a kind of global passport to join the communities she visited, if only for a few days.

Juanita began her diary as a private memoir. When she ended the odyssey, it became a bestseller. She had dreamed of circling the globe ever since she left school after a few short months in Mississippi and began working as a domestic. When she arrived in Paris near the beginning of her voyage, she went to work for Mildred Morris, an American living abroad. A writer herself, Morris was enthralled by the idea of an African American woman working and eating her away around the world. Morris introduced Juanita to editors at Macmillan. Juanita was nervous, hesitant at first to let Morris edit her diary into a book. Then, she relented. Macmillan was an established New York company which had published many travel accounts of elite travellers. Juanita knew that her circumnavigation was unique.

Juanita demanded that Morris leave intact all her spelling errors and quirks of language. In her diary and private letters, Juanita spelled phonetically; she had spent little time in school. Morris agreed and never turned misspellings back into spellings. Certainly, Morris's light editorial hand emphasized Juanita's humble origins, but not quite her 'blackness'. Morris neither corrected Juanita's spellings nor forced her language into the crude Black 'dialect' featured in so many novels, films or vaudeville acts of the era. Juanita herself owned her mistakes, just as she also boasted of her ability to speak enough French and Spanish to find both employers and food.

Unoffended by dirt and disease, Juanita wrote a book about going off the first-class trail in order to discover the 'wide, beautiful world'. Through adventures all the way from Europe to Asia and the Pacific, she described her idea about how to circle the globe: travel third class, because only Europeans (or those who looked like them) could travel first class. Never be a tourist; blend in. Make friends with the locals and eat what they ate.

A Passport with 22 Stamps

It was a beautiful June morning in 1927 when Juanita, third-class ticket in hand, arrived at the North German Lloyd Pier in Hoboken, New Jersey, to begin her journey around the world. She had packed a pair of blue dresses, apron caps and her references. She had a plan: when her money ran out, she would find a job wherever she was stranded. She would work long enough and save enough until she could travel again. The boat sailed early in the afternoon to the sounds of a German band and the shouted farewells of passengers. Juanita was glad that no one came to say goodbye to her; sadness would only taint her departure.

More pragmatically, she used the time others spent on long goodbyes to prepare for the ocean crossing. First, she chose the upper bunk. Never sleep below someone with seasickness, she reasoned. Then, she sneaked into the first- and second-class areas, where she filched softer towels and sweeter-smelling soap. The upper-class writing lounges offered better paper, 'the kind you love to touch so much'. She appropriated a few sheets for her journal. By the time her cabin mates returned from waving their goodbyes, Juanita had tucked away first-class luxuries into her third-class bunk.[3]

Juanita was able to enjoy the pleasures of world travel because of her sheer tenacity and ingenuity, not an inheritance. Born in Mississippi (or so she claimed in her book) in 1891 to a poor African American family, her formal schooling finished by the time she was ten. She wouldn't sail from Hoboken pier until she was 36 years old but, later, she wrote to a friend that she had hatched her plans for world travel when she was just eleven.[4] In her early years working as a domestic, she had managed to save $800 in a Denver bank account. When the bank went bankrupt, Juanita was left with only enough money to buy a cheap train ticket to Los Angeles for a fresh start in California.[5] There, she went to work for Myra and George Dickinson. George was a real estate broker in the booming city and helped Juanita invest her slim earnings. Soon, she could count on an investment income of about $200 a year – not much, but enough to begin her travels. Myra became a close friend and Juanita dedicated her book to her. More privately, she valued Myra's letters, which seemed to greet her in every new city. Other former employers may have claimed to be friends, but Juanita knew why they were often slow to write. She suspected that they were afraid that she might ask them for money.

After leaving the United States in 1927, Juanita worked as a domestic servant in England to save money for a trip to Paris, where she met Morris. Morris first imagined Juanita as the subject for an attractive magazine article. She crafted a biographical sketch and showed it to Juanita. Juanita chuckled at the idea of reducing her complex life to a 'short sketch'. Morris was eager enough to record Juanita's memorable life that she set aside her own writing and proposed to help Juanita turn her private diary into a book.[6]

On 26 February 1928 she said goodbye to Mildred Morris. Book contract in hand and money in her pocket, she left for the south of France, then Italy and Central Europe. Her train derailed in September. By November she had arrived in Cairo, and in Colombo early the following spring. From Ceylon, she toured India from Bombay in the south to Darjeeling in the Himalayan foothills. By early August 1929 she had reached Burma. Then she made her first U-turn, returning to Europe. She would travel, working her way across Europe for the next four years, eager to visit China, but thwarted by its famine and civil war. In May 1934 she turned east again, crossing the Soviet Union to Korea, Japan and, at last, China. Juanita celebrated the new year in Shanghai. After a short visit to the Philippines (and an abortive attempt to visit Singapore and Java), she boarded the ss *President Lincoln* in April 1935, bound for Honolulu. On 9 May 1935 she woke up from a nap on Waikiki Beach and decided that her long journey was over.[7]

Outside Europe, skilled ladies' maids and governesses were in demand, especially from wealthy British colonial residents, and she was confident that she could find work anywhere. She confided her Mississippi and African American origins to only a few trusted employers, such as Myra Dickinson or Morris. When she worked abroad, Juanita's employers assumed that she was European, that catch-all imperial phrase meaning 'white'. In Cairo she worked for a young English couple. Juanita chaperoned their six-year-old daughter through the rarefied world of British colonial life. First to the club, beautifully set along the banks of the Nile, for field hockey and tennis. Then, tea, bath and bed. Finally, Juanita was free for the night to visit one of her many favourite local places for a dinner of beans, tomatoes and salad. 'I felt good,' she recalled. Sometimes she dined with one of her new local friends. An Egyptian acquaintance invited Juanita to a 'native sweet shop'. She tasted 'something pleasant and yet not sweet'. The sweet tasted curiously 'like mint'.

With some savings, she was ready to travel again. Luxor, Aswan, then across the Red Sea – 'India may be the next place I stop to work.'[8] In Bombay in June 1929, she answered an ad in the *Times of India*. The position was 'open for a European lady only'. She quit after a week and looked for a new position. In their advertisements, employers often requested a photograph to confirm that applicants were truly European. Juanita was tempted to send a picture of herself with an Egyptian water jar on her head. 'Think what a turist miss not to do such things,' she laughed. She found a new job, this time as a nurse for an older English woman. She also left that job quickly. The British woman, rather dramatically, assumed that she was on the verge of death. 'I got tird of getting up at 2 a.m. to write out dying remarks,' Juanita explained.[9]

In Bombay, even as she was still searching for the right position, she opened a letter sent all the way from Czechoslovakia with $200 in compensation for the railway accident. 'I don't feel I can use it for Globetrotten.' She wanted to work for her train fare.[10]

Except for her memorable trip across the Soviet Union, Juanita mostly followed the routes and timetables of established railroads and steamship lines. She bought her tickets at Thomas Cook and collected her mail at American Express, but 'Cooks nor American Express do not know anything about good and cheap Hotels.' Their clients were usually wealthier and refused to sleep anywhere near locals. Once, Juanita even returned to an American Express office to boast to the clerks about the low cost of the room in a hotel catering to locals that she had found by herself.[11] When possible, she preferred to buy ship tickets from Asian steamship companies that allowed her to travel third class.

In May 1935 Juanita counted 22 stamps in her passport. In Hawai'i, almost all the way around the world, she napped, ate and decided her travels and her book were concluded. 'I have it all set up until I die and the two Books are not included,' she wrote to a friend.[12]

Travel Third Class

In September 1928 Juanita crossed from Europe into Asia, from Sofia to Istanbul. Settled into the third-class carriage, she regarded her fellow travellers, curious about the meals they had brought on the train. A Bulgarian peasant couple ate brown bread and boiled chicken gizzards. A Turkish family boarded the train and Juanita made room for their children and worldly belongings. As she nodded off, 'a nice gentleman' sat down in the compartment and instead of sleeping, she chatted with him in broken French. They shared the sweet honeydew melons he bought from a platform vendor. A month later, Juanita left Syria by train heading for Nazareth. At Damascus, an Arab man, laden down with bags of food, badly cut his finger as he struggled to board the train. Juanita ripped her handkerchief in half and used it to stop the bleeding. Hungry, but unable to speak any Arabic, she gestured that she would like to buy some of his groceries. He spoke to a Syrian woman in their crowded apartment and she in turn translated into Spanish for Juanita. At the end of this long chain of translations, Juanita understood; the Arab man repaid her quick first aid generously, giving her far more food than she could eat. So, she shared the abundance around their third-class compartment. 'I always have salt and pepper so had a feast.'[13]

First and second class, she warned, were the same the world over. The third-class world, though, was 'so interesting'. Here, passengers became friends. Sometimes, she helped amuse their children and, when she didn't have food for a long journey, passengers on cheap tickets seemed the most generous. There's 'always a full House in the Third Class', she explained, and that meant more than close quarters. It was camaraderie. 'Thats why I like it.' On a train in Egypt, 'We ate sugar cane most of the night.' By the next morning, 'the coach looked like a cane field,' laughed Juanita.

Juanita thought of herself as a 'stray Bird', a solitary traveller who could always find friends in third class. Amid laughter, broken conversation and plenty of food, third class treated Juanita 'as though I am a Countrymen of Theirs'. When she passed around her American passport, her fellow passengers, whether on a train or on board a ship, were astonished. After all, most Americans and Europeans travelled first class. Thieves, too, rode first class. Once, on a train Juanita was riding, 'a man riding first class' had several hundred pounds stolen. In third class, 'I have left change in my coat and went out,' she boasted, 'and never have it been taken.'[14]

However much she enjoyed her time and meals in third class, she also knew that she was breaking written and unwritten rules. Time and again, her desire to travel third class confronted the legality and conventions of colonial segregation. Ticket collectors tried to bar Juanita from boarding a ship from Chittagong to Rangoon because they heard her spoken English and assumed she was white. European – white – women were not allowed to travel as deck passengers, they insisted.

'If they didn't like it they must pay the differents,' she replied and pushed her way on board into third class in a tourist's challenge to the imperial colour line. She defied colonial norms and enjoyed it: 'everything is going lovely now' – especially the food. For its third-class passengers the ship to Rangoon offered Hindu or Muslim messes. Juanita chose Muslim, mostly for its chicken curry and rice. Here, on the other side of the racial barrier, the curry was fresh and delicious. 'The curry doesn't tast nothing like the dryed curry powder we get' back in the United States.[15]

She confronted – and thwarted – the same segregation en route to Canton in 1934. The English steamship companies that plied the routes from Shanghai to Canton refused to let European women travel third class. First class was an expensive '95 dollars' and without any of the fun of travelling third class. 'I told them I wouldnt waist my money traveling with other Europeans,' said Juanita. 'I prefer a Chinese or Japanese boat as I want some interest.' The Chinese tramp steamer she chose wasn't particularly 'Handsome' but, loaded down with bread, butter and coffee to share, she expected 'a Royal treatment'.[16] The trip further south, from Canton to Singapore and Java, though, was impossible when she couldn't find a Japanese or Chinese ship. Rather than pay more for segregation, Juanita turned her sights towards Hawai'i instead.

With her ambiguous skin colour and disinclination to accept the privileges of whiteness, Juanita challenged the colour line. Still, she shared a few tips about how a resourceful traveller could enjoy some of the pleasures of first class, whether soft linens or a comfortable waiting room. At night in Egypt, she slipped into the first-class railroad waiting room, enjoyed cooling fans, and ate a box of local sweets she had purchased. She did the same after a meal of fried fish in Jaipur. 'I let the fan go through the night,' said Juanita, 'the next morning my washing was dry.' A few days later in Agra, she snuck into an empty first-class coach parked on a sidetrack. She relaxed with its leather couches, electric lights and fans. Travelling by ship among the southern Philippine islands, she made friends with the Filipino cooks who prepared meals for the first- and second-class passengers. The third-class deck had a window that looked directly down into the kitchens. Her new friends, the cooks, passed up to her the luxurious first-class food, a triumph of friendliness, ingenuity and a well-placed window over a rigid on-board class system. 'They are delighted to serve me,' she boasted.[17]

Blend In and Never Be a Tourist

In February 1929, on the outskirts of Cairo, Juanita chuckled as she gazed at a crowd of American, French and German tourists and their 'awful' outfits. 'I don't blame the native for staring at them,' said Juanita. Dressed just as the guidebooks warned in order to avoid Egyptian heat and desert flies, the white tourists wore ugly white sun helmets, cholera belts, breeches and leggings. To locals and to Juanita, the tourists looked like circus clowns.

Two years into her around-the-world journey, Juanita knew that she wasn't a typical tourist. 'I am the poorest girl that ever travelled alone,' she boasted. Without a bottomless pocketbook and an itinerary from Thomas Cook, her travels depended on her ability to blend in and forge friendships. She arrived 'in a town as though I was going to spend my life there'. She watched what the local women wore and then spent a few hard-earned coins to copy them. In Cairo, she returned to her hotel to fetch her veil when her hat seemed too conspicuous for the city's poorer neighbourhoods. In the Middle East, that scarf and 'little French cap' helped her blend in with both Arabs and Jews. 'I have a very Oriental looking scarf I ware most of the time,' she said, and 'everyone think I am Arabian.' When she wore the cap, 'they take me for Jewish'. Jewish, Arab, Chinese, Indian – locals assumed that she could be anything but American. It was deliberate: 'I am willing to be whatever I can get the best treatments at being.'[18] She prided herself that locals never seemed to be able to place her, assuming instead that she must be native. She loved her two months in Japan, for example, with 'The

Kind and Gentle People' because she 'lived with Them as a Countryman and not as Tourist.'[19]

Dressing the part broke down barriers between tourist and locals. 'You are not the cold English type,' admired an Egyptian merchant. Friendships with men had particular benefits and challenges. Juanita enjoyed her flirtations and the dinners that followed, and at least once, she hit a man when romance turned threatening. The merchant invited her 'to a dinner of chicken, rice, radishes, and olives'. It was delicious: 'my heels was just smiling,' recalled Juanita, even as she schemed how to avoid following the man to an empty apartment where he promised 'an auful good time'.

'We'd better not go together,' lied Juanita.

'You're quite right,' he agreed, 'a wise little girl.'

She promised to follow the merchant through the dark streets and deserted bazaar to the apartment. Instead, she disappeared to the docks and onto a ship to India.[20]

Blending in offered flirtations, the occasional free meal and a few good friendships. It was also quietly subversive. Juanita knew the rules that separated colonized from colonizers where she travelled, just as Jim Crow laws governed race relations at home. Juanita's skin colour and heritage might have kept her at the back of the bus or segregated train cars in her native Mississippi. Abroad, if she kept her passport hidden, her ambiguous skin tone allowed her not to pass as white but to blend in. Passing – the ability to move unnoticed into the dominant racial group – was the long legacy of slavery in the United States. The reality of coerced sex across the colour line had produced the diversity of skin tones, even if 'blackness' was, both socially and legally, a matter of heritage. In the era Juanita travelled, passing, the visual ambiguity about race and colour, troubled strict Jim Crow segregation. Popular American films and novels, for example, reflected anxiety about and fascination with the ability of some to slip across racial lines.[21]

Juanita used her own mixed-race heritage to be anything or anybody she wanted to be and to cross into neighbourhoods where Europeans – those with obviously white skin and European dress – felt threatened. As she travelled, her American light-skinned 'blackness' transformed into 'Egypt and Indian brown'.[22] In Naples Italians ignored her if she didn't wear a hat; if she put it on, they asked if she might be Chinese or Japanese. In Aleppo locals assumed she was Chinese. Elsewhere in Syria, they thought she was Arab. In Cairo she made herself 'so native like with my vail', that she could slip into wedding celebrations. 'I go to a native wedding feast nearly every week,' she exclaimed.[23] Yet when she needed a job, she could also be European.

When she travelled, Juanita used her indeterminate self, accented by local garb, to challenge the imperial colour line. The perfect society was 'betwixt and between', she mused in Darjeeling, the Himalayan hill town where Nepalis mixed with Indians of all castes as well as with the British. Colonial residents fled to the hills to escape the heat of the plains. In Darjeeling, 'you have a fine time' with a low caste just as with the 'highest Hindoo', she wrote. Any traveller, if they were willing, could enjoy a $5 hotel stay – expensive – followed by a 5-cent restaurant meal – cheap, and with locals. The views of the Himalayas were glorious, but Juanita called Darjeeling 'this Wonderful Place' because of its racially and socially jumbled environment.

When Juanita turned what would have been 'blackness' in the United States into racial indeterminacy in the colonies, she chose the pleasures of blending in over the privileges of passing as European. A station attendant en route to Bombay could never have guessed that in the United States she was segregated into inferior railroad cars. To him, Juanita looked 'European' and due the privilege of a more private compartment. Juanita refused. Instead, she joined 'the lowest cast' women in third class. In the crowded compartment, she climbed into the luggage netting, and had a 'great time'. As she stretched out in the netting, swinging as the train jostled, she felt comfortably at home. Lower-caste women are 'jolly', she decided. Before she slept, she contemplated her own skin and outfit. With her red shawl and black veil, 'no one would think I had seen Broadway.'[24]

Tourists gaped at locals (and, in return, locals laughed at them and their cholera belts and sun helmets). Benares with its bathing ghats, fakirs and funeral pyres had shocked Thomas Cook. He added it to his around-the-world itineraries so tourists could recoil at the filth of this sacred city. Juanita, though, judged the river water clean, even if it was yellow in colour and filled with Indians and devout Hindus bathing. She followed local women into one of the temples and joined them in their worship. 'I touched my forehead,' and the women nearby smiled. Later, she visited the burning ghats where the dead were ritually cremated.

'It is not at all horrod to look at anyway,' she noted. After all, 'I am quite Hindu now.' While she was trying to catch the eye of a holy fakir, a 'not quite as holy' man asked why Juanita was travelling alone. 'A good Flirtation,' she decided, 'was just the thing after the funeral Pyres.' Then, she went to buy fruit and a third-class ticket to Calcutta.

When, on occasion, passers-by recognized her as a traveller, they flirted or stared. Juanita didn't mind. Enjoying a cheap street meal of baked sweet potatoes in Shanghai, she drew a crowd, curious about a tourist willing to eat off the street. Of course, that meant that the vendor gave her 'a nice size one'. Later, when she boarded the Chinese steamer bound for Hong Kong, she wrote to Mildred Morris: 'I'll be eating Chinese food and dressed up just like a coolies wife.'[25]

Eat Everything

In February 1928, at the beginning of her trip, Juanita scaled the fence to sneak into the Jardin d'Acclimatation in Paris. The botanical garden displayed not only tropical fauna but tropical peoples. The garden hosted travelling human shows, popular European entertainment that showcased the strange habits, bodies and clothes of so-called primitive peoples from tropical colonies. Here, in Paris, Juanita was curious to see women from the French Central African colonies in their re-fashioned village. Unlike other tourists, she arrived not to gawk (or pay her admission fee) but to mingle. As the women cooked a meal, 'they took a fancy to me', she boasted, 'I think they saw I had some of their blood.'[26] The women wore ornamental discs in their lips and Juanita noticed that when they talked, spittle dribbled from their lips and into the common dish. Yet, when they invited her, Juanita joined their meal. In the midst of a colonial exposition, in front of a staring French audience, Juanita offered her third rule for travel: eat everything, no matter how strange or possibly unsafe.

If locals ate it, the food must be good, just like the chicken in a Muslim restaurant in Rangoon. The owners didn't speak English. Instead, they gestured, inviting Juanita into the kitchen. She lifted lids on bubbling pots and pointed to the dishes that interested her. 'I knew better than to touch any thing with my Christian Hands,' but she teased, reaching out her fingers almost to the pot's lip. Everyone laughed. She noticed that her dishes were scrubbed separately and with a little laugh and a gentle joke, she turned her cheap dinner into a shared meal with the owners. 'They have been very good to me.'[27]

She ate everything and preferred to dine with locals, like a hospitable family she met in Naples. She knocked on their door to ask for directions to a restaurant but was privately pleased when the family's father instead invited her inside for spaghetti. He 'did not look to clean but he sure did cook clean'. The food was delicious. 'I never ate any spagitti that tasted so good.'[28]

Once, Juanita wrote to a friend that she did 'not live to eat', but ate to live, a curious enough claim for someone who so clearly relished a good meal. She was explaining why she refused to join the Morrises for their formal dinners. She ate to live, but specifically to live alongside locals in their humble surroundings. She preferred a small restaurant down the street from Morris's splendid apartment where she could enjoy a cheap four-course meal. In Damascus, 'arabic food', she said, was 'so good', especially the 'delicious' small dishes. In Colombo, it was a 'great joy' to visit the local markets with delicious food for less than '40 cents'.[29]

She feasted in restaurants that catered to locals. In Canton 'I enjoyed the food of many delicious Chinese dishes,' agreed Juanita, after her room-mate at a local women's hostel and two local men treated her to lunch. In Istanbul, she sat back in her restaurant chair after a 'good feed' of potatoes and smothered lamb. The lamb, she guessed, must have been cooked together with the string beans, tomatoes and okra. She loved the taste and the price (less than 50 cents), but best of all, she enjoyed the warm welcome and the flirtation. The head cook 'tryes to make love to me', while a waiter pulled out her chair for her to sit on. Another opened the door to usher her right into the kitchen where she pointed out what she wanted from the casseroles. The owner smoked a hookah, patted Juanita on the head and made sure that the waiters didn't overcharge. Sometimes Juanita passed by the restaurant – she had become a regular – and pretended to have lost her way.

'Madame Madame,' called the cooks.

She smiled. 'I know I am welcome.'

She particularly liked the aromas (and low cost) of Colombo's curries. At a 'native' restaurant, she savoured a wonderful dinner of eight side dishes piled onto a heaping bowl of rice. 'When I would empty one the boy would rush to fill it.' Later that evening she boasted about the meal to her new Sinhalese friends at the YWCA, a hostel just a few blocks from the beach and ringed with fruit and coconut trees.[30] The YWCA offered rooms to both European and local women. It, too, was segregated. European women, even in a humble hostel, enjoyed those racial privileges that Juanita rejected. At the YWCA, servants prepared the 'Anglos' a 'dainty bit to eat'. Juanita chose to eat the 'Indian food'. She joined the Sinhalese women in meals of curry and red pepper and, like them, ate with the fingers of her right hand. 'Of course I like to see them do that.'

Juanita practised a kind of food politics that rejected both race and class privileges. Even one of her new Sinhalese friends was appalled by Juanita's willingness to meet everyone and eat everything. 'Well my Friend gave up trying to make a high-class Sinhalese out of me.' Instead, Juanita bought a ticket to the circus, sat in the men-only section and accepted a gift of pan. The man on her left bought her the green leaf, dabbed with a paste she thought looked like toothpaste, and topped with tobacco leaves and betel nuts. Floods of tourists before her had remarked with disgust at the red mouths of pan chewers. Juanita, though, delighted in the appalled gasps of her high-caste friends. The pan sweetened her breath but made her mouth sore. When 'I begain to eat my dinner with red pepper I jumped out the Chair.' She had chewed her fill of pan.[31]

Juanita's food politics, at the table, on the train, on board ship, in the bakery, on the street, even sitting at the circus, merged breaking bread with building friendship. The amity that came from sharing food trumped fears of unknown ingredients or lurking germs. In Syria, she had resolved not to eat the bread after visiting a dirty flour mill. A pair of oxen turned the mill wheel while treading on the threshed wheat. The flour seemed the same colour as the nearby dusty road. Then, she watched three 'girls' baking bread on a street corner. They patted flat rounds of dough and slapped them onto the sides of their earthen oven. 'When the Eldest Girl took one of the thin cakes and gave it to me', her resolve slipped. 'I had to eat it and found that it tasted ever so good.' The four women – three Syrians and an American tourist – sat laughing and talking far into the night.[32]

In Ceylon, she chewed pan, in Syria, dusty bread and in Cairo, she drank tea flavoured with amber paste. In China, she discovered that smaller restaurants and street vendors offered dishes that 'you haven't the courage to eat'. But *she* ate them and discovered 'delicious' foods that she knew would appall other travellers. She recommended the snake, served 'a la King'. She bought her meals from street vendors who carried their ovens on poles. They sliced pork into strips and fried them with cabbage and onions. Her lunch, spiced with curry powder, simmered slowly. It tasted 'perfect'. For dinner in Canton, she joined students at the local university and recorded the many dishes they shared. The most delicate and delicious was braised cat – a 'tom cat' she joked, inspecting the stewed neck. Unfortunately, she didn't get enough of the cat and instead feasted on 'Chop Suez' – chop suey – garnished with bird heads and feet. She joked about the tom cat, but was happy enough to eat it, especially with such enjoyable company, the 'Boy group', she called them. They tossed peanuts at each other, and she felt natural and 'at home'. The next day, in the narrow streets across from her room, she watched her neighbours buy what she suspected was dog meat. 'I was looking forward to smelling it cooking.'[33]

Finally, in Swatow, at the tail end of her East Asian travels, Juanita discovered a street treat that she was too timid to taste. In the street stalls, she explained, they cooked large centipedes and she was tempted after she watched locals eat them 'with so much gusto'.

'I came near buying some,' she admitted, not because eating centipedes was a food adventure, but because they were so 'relished' by the people around her. Here, at the very moment when her palate reached its limit, she found the essential lesson of her travels. As she watched locals eat insects, she knew that 'theres not so much difference in Human Biens.'[34]

Third-Class Food Politics

On her travels, Juanita prayed in mosques, carefully removed her shoes outside Hindu temples and attended Catholic services. 'Hindooes had the same right to think they were right as the Buddish,' she declared. 'When you get it all added up,' she reasoned, 'I would have been just as well pleased to be a Hindu.'

And, if she had been a Hindu, she preferred to be lower-caste. On a train from Madras in April 1929, Juanita grabbed a 'good snug place'. High-caste Indian women typically rode third class, she explained, because they didn't want to and weren't permitted to mix with Europeans. Juanita was barefoot, wearing her shawl, 'looking auful casty'. When a high-caste woman entered the crowded compartment, she assumed Juanita was low-caste. She 'wanted me to get out', realized Juanita. 'I don't mind being high cast but I want to be a low cast too.'[35]

Juanita gravitated towards the lower orders, drawn by what she believed was their genuine gentleness. Aboard the Messageries Maritimes's *Chantilly* steaming from Rangoon back to Ceylon and then Port Said, an Indian passenger died in an on-board accident. The Indian sailors, to Juanita's tearful astonishment, treated the dead passenger tenderly. There was 'no roughness in the Indians', she marvelled, and 'the lowest cast seem to be the most kindest.'

Juanita's allegiances lay with the lower orders, the downtrodden, the lower castes, those opposing empire and those with whom she ate on trains and boats. In India, she vowed to save her money in order to 'give a little more to' poor servants. In colonial India, with all its racial and class divisions, it was far too easy for a tourist to feel rich but, for Juanita, years of domestic service all added up to solidarity with India's many servants. Even a third-class traveller like Juanita lodging in a humble inn had a servant to cook for her, one to bring her meals, another to heat water and another to take out her 'night glass'. Other travellers complained bitterly about Indian servants' inevitable requests for coins. Juanita, though, was sympathetic. 'They serve so quiet and faithfully it seem a shame to give so little.' As she prepared to leave India for Burma, she looked at her dwindling savings and decided: 'Tomorrow I will have a great time paying off the 5 or six men servents.'

She witnessed anti-colonial violence at first hand, especially in Bombay when an English resident warned her that trouble was brewing. The English woman urged Juanita to leave the tense city. Troops patrolled the streets, but with her olive skin and red scarf, Juanita had a passport across colonial lines. She 'walked right into the dangerous neighbourhood' to enjoy potato cakes fried brown and served on dried leaves with a 'very good tarty sauce', tamarind perhaps. 'Samplein the dishes', she subtly stated her allegiances. Especially after her conversation with a 'nice' Indian professor, she was convinced that 'India are very anxious for Home rule.'[36]

If tourists beginning with Ida Pfeiffer aligned themselves with an imperial system that built comfortable hotels, Juanita recorded the heart-felt passions of new friends. 'I know that People all the way to Burmer are displeased and want home rule.' The United States, too, deserved its criticism, including from outsiders. On board the *Chantilly*, a Hindu, angry at how Americans seemed to misunderstand India, threatened to travel to the United States to write a book about 'all the Black side of America'.

'That's a good idea,' replied Juanita.[37]

The sympathies she developed at the third-class table helped shaped an edible anti-imperial politics that, during her trip across the Soviet Union, became a sympathy for communism. Juanita described a politics of and from third class. She was immediately sympathetic to the Soviet Union, entranced by Leningrad and by Lenin himself, the only world leader she ever quoted. 'Learn, then learn some more,' she copied his slogans from propaganda posters into her diary. Soviet propaganda may have touted ideal communists as industrial workers or collective farmers, but Juanita described them as fellow train travellers – a socialism of the third-class compartment. She crossed race, caste and class lines from Paris to Rangoon, but 'Here are no cast, and class,' she admired, 'no who's who.'

She boarded a Soviet train steaming east from Moscow across the vast country, which, paradoxically, offered her normal third class (an irony of Soviet travel and tourism that she ignored). The bunks and blankets were soft and, for eight days, she enjoyed comfort, friends and good food. At each

Juanita Harrison, 1936.

station, she and her coach companions took turns in buying fresh butter, roasted chickens, melons, pork sausages, cream cheeses and boiled eggs to share among the compartment. Here in a new social experiment that she was glad 'to see . . . while its in the making' she re-distributed the cast-off luxuries given by previous employers. An admirer wanted to treat Juanita to a roasted chicken, but she refused. 'I only accepted from Those I could give a silk dress to.' In exchange for a 'nice piece of roast pork', she pulled out a dress from her suitcase and handed it to one of the young Soviet women. 'There were never one less lonely than I am,' she wrote in her diary.[38]

Villa Petit Peep

In April 1935 Juanita embarked on the last leg of her journey from Kobe to Honolulu by steamer. In the tropical sun, she wore a short skirt, jumper and Chinese slippers, 'then I skip all over the deck like a sea guile' to the delight of the Filipino and Chinese sailors, cooks and stewards. They 'sure does enjoy looking at me'. While Juanita enjoyed the sunshine, below decks, the Filipino cooks argued with the Chinese kitchen staff. 'To my greatest pleasure', she played peacemaker. Once when the sea was particularly rough, the Filipino 'Boys' were bed-bound with seasickness and Juanita took over the kitchen for the sailors' and third-class passengers' meals. The Chinese cooks cut up the chicken and prepped the vegetables. Soon, 'I had a big pot of wonderful stewed chicken with onion celery tomatoes and mushrooms' simmering on the stovetop. The sailors crowded around the kitchen door. Those that couldn't squeeze into the kitchen peered through the portholes. 'I had on my bright Pink apron and a large bright red silk Handkerchief on my hair,' said Juanita.[39]

In Honolulu, she decided that her travelling days were at an end. On Waikiki Beach, she watched the surfers. Later, she joined a 'a real Hawaiian Picnic' with dancing, barbecued pigs and steamed sweet potatoes, and planned her 'little future nest in Hawaii'.[40] She finished writing a pair of articles for *Atlantic Monthly*. She closed her journal, added a few letters from former employers and sent the finished manuscript to Morris. Meanwhile, she found work with an American military family. He was a lieutenant serving on a submarine and expected war soon.

Juanita worried about war and about her book. 'I wish that the Book could be sold for much less. I like best to give pleasure. I need so little change.' When the book was published, she didn't even open her free copies. She visited the local bookshops in Honolulu, hoping that they weren't planning on stocking it. She was chagrined to hear that they had already ordered their copies. She didn't want to 'be troubled with publicity'.[41]

Even without her help, the book was immediately popular, far more than her publishers ever imagined. One month after its release, it was already on its third printing. By 1939 on the eve of the war she feared, Juanita's memoir was on its tenth printing. By then, tourists had published vast shelves of books describing their around-the-world travels. Juanita's book stood out among other 'endless restrained, civilized, and timid descriptions of the Seven Wonders', wrote one reviewer. Such books described world travel, certainly as a luxury, but just as much as a 'thankless struggle against vermin, insidious diseases, exotic but soiled costumery, thieving servants, bad food, unspeakable lodgings, intolerable weather, and other forms of unpleasantness'. There were 'few whose author's natural habitat was third-class or no class at all'.[42]

'I give you Juanita, the perfect cosmopolite!' But what kind of cosmopolite? A Black one, most reviewers (and, likely, most American readers) declared. Juanita was 'a Mississippi coloured cook who, at the age of 36, threw over sauce pans and skillets for steamships and far horizons', read a review in a St Louis newspaper. Locals in India or Syria may have wondered about Juanita's inconclusive origins. Reviewers did not. They described her 'dark skin – for Juanita is an American Negro servant girl earning her way'. According to reviews, Juanita did not blend into local populations. Instead, she 'passed'. She 'can in the East "pass for" an Asiatic or Oriental woman', read a review in the *Washington Post*.[43]

Readers and reviewers enjoyed her book's occasional raciness and its omnipresent optimism. Yet they read her account less as mixed-race mobility than as an 'American Negress' Odyssey'. Once they re-established Juanita within American segregation, reviewers returned to her misspellings. Her observations in all their erratic phonetics flowed from 'heart of girl', the *Los Angeles Times* wrote.[44] Her admiration for the world she encountered, especially its 'beauty and edibility', was, for one reviewer, simply 'unfashionable and childlike'. Such readings echoed throughout the American press, which refused to acknowledge her mode of travel as powerful politics. They chuckled at her language, less as poetics, but to mark Juanita as both Black and primitive. 'The little dark woman has a pagan approach to things', sniggered a reviewer. 'As the children see loveliness, so also does she.' Juanita 'loves her victuals' but that, too, was simply a primitive, childlike trait. She 'requires little else to make a "gelourous" day', laughed a Philadelphia reviewer.[45]

Here was the irony: her book was so widely reviewed and read because it really *was* good reading, especially after the piles of dreary, repetitive travelogues that ended up on reviewers' desks. Yet it wasn't so much that her political darts went astray, but that her politics of food, flirtation and friendship was a hard one to grasp in intensely segregated America. Juanita had published her diary about how, as a mixed-race woman, she joyfully criss-crossed the imperial colour line. Readers, even enthusiastic reviewers in African American newspapers, described a story of a Black domestic worker's unlikely odyssey. 'In fact, the main significance of Miss Harrison's book is that a first-class colored servant girl can make her living anywhere in the world,' wrote a review in the *Afro-American*.[46]

Juanita took a photograph for the book's publicity campaign. Authors typically posed; Juanita danced. Spinning, hair flowing free, bare foot on a beach, wrapped in a sarong, she looked up at the photographer. In tropical light and shadow and far enough away from the camera, no reader could really ever place Juanita within strict racial categories. With the money from her articles and the promise of more from her book, she bought a tent that she pitched on a beach. A friend built her a portable floor. She decided to call the tent 'Villa Petit Peep', in case visitors should want to peep inside. The radical essayist and African American activist William Pickens peeped inside on his way to a political conference in Honolulu in September 1936. Pickens and Juanita cooked a meal on the beach and ate at one of the park tables. Then, they paddled in the waves with 'a group of brown and mixed-blood children' in the shadow of the Royal Hawaiian hotel, luxury lodging for around-the-world cruisers.

Nine years before, Juanita had stopped off in New York to visit Pickens and his wife. He remembered Juanita's resolve. 'I'm going to Europe. I don't know how, but I'm going,' she told him. Now, Pickens listened to the speakers at the conference and thought of Juanita's trip around the world. The speakers explained how the French ruled Indochina, the English governed Fiji and the Americans were colonizing the Philippines. 'We have certainly made the Filipinos pay for all the "help" we gave them,' wrote Pickens. Here in Hawai'i, 'we have made life a lot less paradisaical for the aborigines.' Juanita, at least, offered a different model of inter-cultural relations.

Juanita never published again. In the final pages of her diary, she gave one last peep. From her tent on the beach, she gathered hibiscus flowers and wild-growing papayas. On Friday evenings, she watched the students dance at 'one of the high-class Hulu Schools'. Sometimes she had 'a little glass of wine' and a dance with friends. When she 'felt Spanish', she visited their saint days festivals. Other days, she joined 'Chinese gatherns, Japanese, then Hawaiians'. In Villa Petit Peep, her mind travelled back to Palestine, India and Ceylon. 'Smiling faces stands out before me.'

Then, she ate 'a nice Pineapple the sweetest that grown'.[47]

9

The Rice Table

Before the Second World War, around-the-world cruise ships and packet boats from Singapore arrived at the quay at Tandjong Priok (today's Tanjung Priok), the harbour closest to the colonial capital at Batavia. Tourists were ready to toss coins in order to watch the Javanese men and boys dive. Small boats, piled high with fruits for sale, swarmed around steamships. Ashore, local men clamoured for work, ready to carry the heavy bags of first-class passengers – Dutch as well as European and American tourists – after they disembarked.

From the harbour, it was an easy drive along the canals to the hotels that catered to European travellers. (The category of 'Europeans', white tourists from the United States learned, included them too; 'European' was the local catch-all term for 'white'.) When they passed through the old town, travellers saw Javanese families splashing and washing their clothes in the canals that the Dutch had compelled Javanese workers to dig. The canals seemed to have followed the Dutch from Europe, a city-planning example of how the power of empire enabled the Dutch even to transform landscapes. But the verdant tropics couldn't be contained. Tropical blossoms dropped their vibrant petals into the stagnant waters.

Dutch men walked openly with Indonesian women and their mixed-race children. Tour guides on the around-the-world cruises described this racial mixing as a unique fact of the Dutch colony. Until the later decades of the nineteenth century, the colonial government discouraged white women from settling in Java and other Indonesian islands. Dutch men, who spent years in Java as colonial officials, soldiers and merchants, developed sexual relationships with local women. This surprised many European and American tourists, especially those who had already visited British India, Malaya or Singapore, where mixed-race children were shunned within colonial society. 'Former Dutch residents have left their impress in more respects than one,' winked one visitor as he wandered Batavia. 'There are pretty forms and beautiful faces among this hybrid race.'[1]

In contrast to the intimate and often sexual relationships that had characterized relationships between Dutch men and Javanese female domestic workers, including cooks, in private homes, urban segregation kept the races apart. Guidebooks encouraged tourists to marvel at the crowds in the Malay quarter, and to sniff the odours of the Chinese neighbourhood, but their carriages continued onto the straight avenues of the Dutch part of town, where tropical trees and climbing blossoming vines wove themselves around gabled buildings. That's where their hotels were located, and where tourists would sample the culinary ritual that had become a key attraction of around-the-world travel, one that – like the streets of Batavia themselves – reflected both cultural mixing and imperial hierarchy: the rijsttafel.

The rijsttafel, or rice table, was a substantial luncheon meal, eaten formally – that is, taken at the table with lavish attention from servants – while wearing informal, Indonesian-influenced clothing. The dish was Indonesian in many of its flavours and ingredients, but Dutch colonial in tradition and practice.[2]

What had become a hotel attraction by the late nineteenth century had more private origins in the colonial households where Javanese cooks prepared food for single Dutch men or Dutch men whose wives remained in Europe. When Dutch women began arriving in the colonies and assumed domestic responsibilities, including directing cooks, the imperial taste for Indonesian flavours was well-established. New cookbooks even offered newly arrived Dutch women guidance, especially in overseeing the preparation of the rijsttafel. The rice table became a regular feature of the Dutch colonial day.[3]

Later, with the rise of tourism, the rijsttafel moved from the relative privacy of the colonial home to the grand hotels. In Batavia, the famed Hotel des Indes and Hotel der Nederlanden competed to offer the most impressive rijsttafel. Diners – around-the-world tourists among them – sat down to heaping plates of rice. And then the parade of waiters – servants, as tourists called the Javanese men – arrived. Each carried silver tureens or platters holding a variety of dishes and ingredients. In their spices, their ingredients and their cooking technique, most dishes had clear Indonesian origin. A few were – from the perspective of tourists – comfortingly Dutch.

Tourists were impressed, excited and daunted. They described the rice table in their private diaries and in the books and newspaper articles they published when they returned home. Often they admitted that they failed to eat their way through the vast arrays of chilli-spiked dishes, but they understood it as an imperial ritual remade into tourist attraction. For author Aldous Huxley, the rijsttafel was the greatest food adventure of his 1926 around-the-world journey, and 'truly Rabelasian'. The 'Rice Table', he wrote, 'must be seen, and eaten, to be believed. Without the co-operation of the gullet, faith cannot swallow it.'[4] The experience was never really about the food alone: tourists were there, too, to be waited upon, by a parade of servants who allowed them to share in the sense of white colonial power. The meal seized Indonesian culinary practices to satiate the Dutch and tourist appetite.

Wonderland

Early in the nineteenth century, before the rijsttafel became a spectacular attraction to tourists, visitors to the Dutch colony already noted the abundance of servants and foods. When the Comte de Beauvoir arrived in the Dutch colony and stayed at the recently opened Hotel der Nederlanden in 1866, he counted sixty servants laying the tables in the dining room. Before dining, he cooled off in a bath hand-pumped by a servant. At lunch, he wrote with delight, 'we are waited upon by the whole troop of Orientals', including one servant just to pour iced water. 'I believe,' he exclaimed in his diary, 'if I wished for a dozen dishes, and particularly if I could call for them in the native dialect, I should give employment to the twelve men in red who stood behind my chair!' Beauvoir felt as if 'I were turning into a pacha'. The food itself disappointed him. The chillies were resplendent but he found the portion of meat, atop the mountain of rice, rather scanty. Still, he thrilled to the exotic atmosphere and the adventure of having a 'celebrated curry' delivered by an army of servants.[5]

By the turn of the twentieth century, as Dutch rule strengthened, hotels opened and the tourist trade increased, the kind of heavy meal that impressed Beauvoir had become the culinary ritual of the rijsttafel, a combination of hybrid cuisine and colonial service. The rijsttafel brought to the table a colonial system that enabled the mobilization of massive numbers of servants; an interest in local tastes and ingredients; and the development of a public infrastructure of luxury hotels and sprawling private homes. Beauvoir, and legions of tourists who followed, were astonished when during their visits they witnessed long caravans of Javanese porters carrying sacks of spices and coffee. The rijsttafel was the gluttonous manifestation of export statistics.

The Dutch colonial state was proud of its abundance, and eager for tourists. By the turn of the twentieth century, the Dutch colonial government of Indonesia had opened tourist bureaus in Europe and the United States to entice tourists to what it called 'the civilized part of this great colonial possession'.[6] The message was clear: 'Visit Java.'

By then, the around-the-world cruises all paused in Batavia. In addition, the Koninklijke Paketvaart Maatschappij (or KPM, the Royal Packet Steam Navigation Company) provided easy, comfortable transit from Singapore as well as longer-distance service from Holland via Marseille or Genoa and the Suez Canal. Insulinde, proclaimed KPM (which liked the lyrical appeal of an ancient-sounding name for the verdant archipelago), was 'God's Creation in the Tropics, in all its fulness, diversity, and overwhelming majesty', ready to welcome visitors 'without danger, for if it be not sought, there is no land in the world that can be travelled through with greater safety'. 'Without great fatigue or expense', tourists could escape tropical heat for the easy outing to the famous gardens at Buitenzorg. Those who felt more adventuresome, however, could scale active volcanoes, visit the jungles and hunt tigers or wild boar. The 'man of science' could collect bounties of flowers and exotic plants or, like Ida Pfeiffer years before, encounter 'races of mankind little known'. The KPM declared: 'a wide field is now opened.'[7]

Before boarding, the KPM recommended that travellers should visit a clothing outfitter, where they could buy a solar topah and gloves. (These should be carried in a metal can, to protect the kid leather from both insects and tropical humidity.) For formal outings and to dress for dinner, men required a black frock coat. These items were *de rigueur* for any tropical destination, but the dress code in the Dutch East Indies, the KPM noted, required some extra apparel: several sets of pyjamas, for times – as when eating the rijsttafel – when formality was relaxed. Women who were keen to wear local sarongs would need to buy them in Batavia upon arrival, since they were only available in the colony itself.

En route, the KPM cruise encouraged travellers to experience 'Dutch customs and mode of life' while still on board. The dress code matched that of Batavian hotels, so tourists could become accustomed to the 'Indian *négligé* dress', though they were reminded to never appear outside their cabins in the same pyjamas they wore at night.[8] The cabins were airy. The dining saloon was luxuriously decorated, accented with Dutch Delft tiles. The decks were wide and shaded from the tropical sun. Javanese servants were omnipresent, circulating between the deck chairs offering iced drinks and filtered cold water. The company organized life on board to match the divisions of the Dutch colonial day. People were to awaken early, around 5:30 a.m., for coffee or tea served in bed by a servant. In the cooler mornings, passengers were encouraged to enjoy the shaded decks. Around noon, the KPM proudly served the 'Dutch Indian rice table in all its detail'.[9]

Once they'd landed, travellers on around-the-world cruises typically headed for the Hotel der Nederlanden or the Hotel des Indes, which was also host to a government welcome office.[10] The Nerderlanden lay at the end of a verdant court. Palms and Madagascar flame trees, blooming in ebullient red, flanked the road leading to the entrance. Ficus trees and tall tamarinds shaded the sprawling building itself. Over-hanging eaves, protecting guests from the frequent tropical downpours, formed a lengthy gallery, onto which the bedrooms opened directly. Guests lounged in reclining chairs and called for cool drinks, including iced lemonades. Servants did their bidding, washed clothing and hung them out to dry on clotheslines spread along the open gallery, and squatted on the ground awaiting further commands.

The Dutch writer Augusta de Wit described her arrival at a Batavia hotel as 'surprise, a shock, a revelation'. De Wit was born in Sumatra, the child of a colonial official, but had grown up in the Netherlands. Returning to Java in 1894 at age thirty, she wondered, 'How shall I describe the indescribable[?]'[11]

W. Basil Worsfold, a British journalist working in South Africa, was similarly surprised by the Hotel der Nederlanden in the 1890s: he compared it to an ancient Roman bath. The men lounged on easy chairs, sipping iced drinks from tall glasses. The 'ladies' wore pyjamas and 'opposite you', he pointed out, was 'a little Dutch maiden'. Her golden hair and white skin 'contrasts with the dark complexion of her *baboe*, or nurse'. Back at home, tourists would feel embarrassed dressed this way, even in the privacy of their own dressing room. 'Here you feel perfectly at ease – such is the magical effect of climate,' Worsfold marvelled.[12]

If they hadn't learned it en route to their destination, tourists quickly realized they needed to follow strict etiquette around dress to fit into Dutch colonial society. European wool suits and heavy cotton dresses were swapped for linen or light cotton pyjamas. Married women wore Javanese sarongs like wraparound skirts, their ankles bare. (Unmarried women were expected to wear more conventional European clothing.) Newly arrived tourists were often publicly shocked, but in their private diaries and letters home, they admitted that in the enervating heat, any state of undress was welcome, however immodest. Such garb was acceptable in the hotel courts and at the rice table, where men often made some concession to formality by wearing loose cotton jackets. In the evening, European tradition resumed: for dinner and visiting, European frock coats and dresses were required.

But first, tourists needed their midday meal. They waited for the gong to sound. Then, foreign hotel guests, typically English or American, followed the more experienced Dutch along the shaded gallery to the dining room. The vaulted dining room opened to the garden to capture the freshening breeze. Its tall ceilings were designed to swallow the midday tropical heat. De Wit described the scene: there were white pillars, through which she could see the blossoming shrubs and trees of the garden. 'Here is, indeed, "un étouffement nouveau",' said de Wit. This was a curious choice of words in French to describe the rijsttafel – 'a new choking'.[13] Like so many other tourists, de Wit delighted in the exercise of imperial power, but the novelty of the meal mixed with the discomfort of the flavour and the experience.

The maître d' gave the order, and the rijsttafel began.

Their First Rijsttafel

Tourists typically noted that the maître d' was, as Percy Stone put it in his 1927 account of the rijsttafel, the 'only white attendant in the dining room'. When the American journalist John Gunther visited Java in 1938, he too was relieved that a Dutch headwaiter, recently arrived from Amsterdam, directed the meal service. 'The headwaiter, a sleek and rosy-cheeked young man, comes first,' Gunther explained. He was your ally, ready to remind you which of the forty 'odd dishes' goes on each plate, especially 'if you are a novice'.[14]

The cooks and other waiters were Javanese. The waiters – tourists typically called them servants, or boys – wore colourful turbans, white cotton European dress coats, sarongs and no shoes. Their bare feet suggested subservience and reinforced the rule of silence: they did not speak. While the Dutch headwaiter might murmur advice to novice tourists, the local waitstaff quietly piled boiled rice onto diners' oversized plates. Then, a parade of waiters lined up with silver trays of condiments and curries in front of the tourists' tables.

The rijsttafel was as intimidating as it was novel. Inexperienced tourists wondered whether they could refuse some dishes or when to begin eating. Inevitably, at their first rijsttafel, they let the waiters serve them everything, a spoonful of each dish. The food kept coming: servants brought noodles, fried chicken, fish, duck, coconuts, curries, sambals, omelettes and salads. Tourists tried to emulate the more experienced Dutch diners but, by the time they began eating, they often found that their food had gone cold. Fearful of anything made by the hotel's Javanese cooks, tourists counted the different chilli peppers. An orchestra played European songs – or, as when M. F. Bridie and her around-the-world cruise with Canadian Pacific lunched at both the Indes and Nederlanden – American jazz.[15] Everyone drank Dutch gin.

Some tourists referred to the meal using the Dutch word 'rijsttafel'. Others translated the meal into English, as the rice table, or blended in a bit of French to accent its high class: 'riz tavel'. Tourists never learned if there was a Javanese word for the Dutch midday meal.

'The *rijsttafel* is superhuman,' marvelled the American tourist and journalist Robert Ripley on his visit to Java.[16] 'I shall never forget my first experience of the thing,' wrote de Wit in 1900. 'The meal itself', de Wit wrote, 'is such as never was tasted on sea or land before.' At first, she assumed that the main dish was just rice and chicken. But then the waitstaff began serving 'all manner of curries', eggs, fried bananas, fowl's liver, fish roe, palm shoots, pickles and sauces, 'an entire system of things inedible'. Intending to feel like a 'conquering-hero', she nevertheless heaped her plate and 'fell to'. Already bewildered by her ride through the town and by 'the strangely-accoutered crowd', de Wit now felt foreign in a European hotel.[17] The Dutch colonists around her seemed to tuck in with gusto, but her throat burned, and her eyes streamed from the spices. Sips of gin didn't help. A more experienced diner quietly advised her to dab her tongue with salt. 'I had the almost bodily sensation', she wrote, 'of the dividing chasm' between the Netherlands and Java, 'on the unknown side of which I had just landed. And it fairly dizzied me.' Later, she called her first rijsttafel 'agony', and wrote, 'I vowed to myself I would never so much as look at the rice-table again.'[18]

She did, however, become a noted novelist and, despite her agony, in 1911, the KPM reprinted de Wit's entire, lurid description of her first rijsttafel in their on-board guide. The steamship line encouraged tourists sailing for Batavia to try their first rijsttafel while still on board, promising 'numerous highly-seasoned side-dishes (sambals) and the curry sauce'. For those 'who lack either the courage or the inclination', the KPM offered enough European dishes to 'take the keen edge off his appetite', such as roast fowl, minced beef, fried fish or 'other European side-dishes'. Once the rice had been cleared, they could rest assured that there 'is always one more course of European dishes', including meat, vegetables and potatoes.[19] Hotels did something similar: after waiters cleared the dirty plates of rice, stained with side dishes, they served the potted or fresh meat the Dutch and tourists called 'biefstuk'. The rice table ended – mercifully – with coffee and fruit. The waiters offered mangosteens, if they were in season.

On the whole, few tourists seem to have remembered, or bothered to record, just what it was they ate. Exotic dining and curious tasting rarely went together. In 1927, Percy Stone wrote that, along with other American tourists, he scrupulously avoided the 'native vegetables', which threatened his 'perfect digestion'. He referred to the dishes simply as 'the curry that is a favorite throughout the tropics' and as the 'mysteries of the kitchen'. One English travel columnist, who ate her rijsttafel at the Hotel der Nederlanden, wrote: 'No one could ever tell me all the constituents of the famous Rice-table of Java.' Anyway, she never asked.[20]

Even those who marvelled at the experience and recommended it to others often found the flavours too foreign. In its spicing, noted one tourist, the '"riz-tafel" may not appeal to the English palate'.[21] An official government tourist guide to Java also quoted de Wit in admitting that the primary appeal of the rijsttafel was the challenge of eating it. The 'gods of Javanese cookery alone' knew what it was the Javanese cooks prepared for the 'master's table, for whose digestion let all gentle souls pray'! The rice table was a 'complicated' meal, the guide explained, 'all strongly spiced and sprinkled with cayenne'. The 'uninitiated may come to grief over it', but it was 'one of the most remarkable things in the Hotel life in Java'.[22]

Instead of being impressed by culinary techniques and flavours drawn from across Indonesia, diners remembered the overall sense of abundance of both food and, perhaps even more importantly, service. An American tourist in 1902 explained: 'Every hotel in Java serves the most distinctive and remarkable meal called the rice-table.' Each diner is given two plates and 'then comes a seemingly never-ending stream of natives'. When Thomas Reid ate at the Hotel des Indes on holiday, he praised the 'punctilio and excellence of the waiting of the Javanese table boys'; a resident of British colonial Singapore, he was used to the omnipresence of servants, but the display at the rijsttafel was still remarkable.[23] Percy Stone noted that while some lesser hotels had only eighteen servants for the 'rice tafel', the Hotel der Nederlanden had 21. The hotel, he claimed with pride, is the 'social center of the place, so twenty-one is accepted as proper'. Robert Ripley recommended tourists eat the rijsttafel at the Hotel des Indes, for 'it requires twenty waiters to serve it', and they 'march in single file, each with a different course on his head, and place a little of each on your plate'.[24]

In an article he later wrote for *Harper's Magazine*, the American tourist John Gunther put the number of 'boys' at the Hotel des Indes' rijsttafel at 'twenty or twenty-five'. But unlike most diners, he also marvelled at the 'amount of labor and skill' that went into the cooking. He learned the names of a few of the dishes and, even, the recipe. 'Curry sojoer' required chicken, a local kind of nut, saffron, a sort of ginger, coriander seeds, some Dutch gin and, of course, plenty of chillies. Yet he punctuated his descriptions of the food with descriptions of the service, dramatizing the 'parade' as if his readers were right there in the dining room with him. 'You have no more than thirty seconds to think about' the curry sojoer, he wrote, before the heat hits and more servants arrive. Your plate 'is piling up', because the 'boys are still coming along'. The helpful headwaiter urges you to make space on your plate of rice for more food. There are two soups, fruit to cool the palate, spicy gravies to heat it up again, as well as fried bananas with some cold salmon. But: 'No time to dawdle. The hot-plate boys are here again.' With the beef, they bring aubergine, onions and poached eggs. Peanuts garnish a 'meat loaf' of chicken and sweetbreads. 'The boy' brings noodles made from rice and garnished with baby corn. When Gunther imagined he had reached his limit, the headwaiter encouraged him to eat a bit more. 'You need dynamite now to stimulate the jaded tongue. It comes.' The 'twenty-fourth' boy arrived with a plate of condiments. 'Each', Gunther wrote, 'will lift the hair from the skull and cause tears to flow.'[25]

For around-the-world holiday makers, the rijsttafel was a must-see, must-eat food adventure, and one of the few times tourists tried local flavours. Tourists ate dishes cooked by Javanese chefs using ingredients and recipes drawn from across the Indonesian archipelago, accompanied by Dutch potted meat and gin. But while the menu involved some hybridity, the diners were emulating the Dutch. When tourists tried the rijsttafel, they were eager to experience the white racial privileges claimed by the Dutch and extended to visitors.

The very infrastructure that the colonial government built to attract tourists, especially those travelling around the world, provided visitors the opportunity, and the guidance, to live like a colonial. 'It is of great importance to regulate one's mode of living and habits according to those of the country,' the KPM advised tourists, calling the rijsttafel 'a nice weighty introduction to the Dutch colonial character'. It also introduced tourists to the pleasures of colonial power by promising servants on board the KPM ships who were 'prompt, quiet, and polite' – traits reasoned as being 'peculiarities of the Malay race'.[26] Another guidebook reassured tourists: 'The native servants are very quick and willing to do the visitor's commands.'[27]

Lucile Mann had no servants in her small Washington apartment, but when she visited the Dutch colony, she enjoyed the luxury of being waited upon. The 'Call of the east' she wrote, was always 'Boy'. When she ate the rijsttafel, she marvelled that twenty 'boys' made an endless chain of servers.[28] Like other tourists, she watched the Dutch eat indigenous flavours, aped their manners and counted the servants. The rijsttafel wasn't just a meal. It was a colonial ritual of domination.

Tourists recognized as much. De Wit may have disliked her first rijsttafel, but she also noted that it was 'food on which to grow up to (colonial) manhood'.[29] The American travel writer Eliza Scidmore described the 'riz tavel' as having 'sacred, solemn, solid feeding function'. Gunther called the rijsttafel at the Hotel des Indes 'a sacrosanct performance', and was convinced that it introduced one to 'the complicated life of the Netherlands Indies'.[30]

The Visitor's Commands

Tourists might marvel at the parade, practising and taking pleasure in their own sense of power. Yet they also described feeling caught in a subtle battle with those who served them. In their diaries or letters home, diners admitted that they felt judged by those who paraded past them bearing silver trays. For Huxley, the rijsttafel began awkwardly when he entered the hotel dining room and sat down. 'A little old yellow waiter, looking less like a man than a kindly orang-utan', handed him a Dutch menu that the waiter knew Huxley couldn't read. Huxley regarded the waiter's batik handkerchief, tied around his bald head, and asked for the rijsttafel. Huxley's quick turn to ugly, racialized language belied his unease.

Huxley ordered in broken Dutch: 'Ane Rice Tafel for mich.' He admitted that he probably sounded as if he was speaking a mixture of German and 'Lowland Scotch'. He hoped he had ordered correctly. In the unfamiliarity of the Dutch colonial dining room, Huxley longed for the servants in British India who could understand English. 'Indian servants', he approved, seemed like 'pieces of moving furniture'. During the rice table, however, the 'machine' that 'waits upon you at table is human' – even if he was barefoot and quiet. 'Its eye is critical; the expressions on its face are comments on

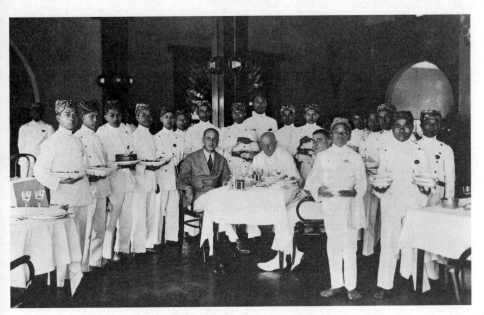

Serving the rice table in an Indonesian hotel, 1930–40.

your words and actions'. As he struggled to surmount the mountain of food, Huxley felt 'judged and condemned to an eternal derision'.

Huxley recognized that readers at home in England would assume he exaggerated the sheer scale of the parade of servants. It was, however, 'the truth, literal but unbelievable' about the rijsttafel. In what struck him as an oppressive atmosphere of too much food, served by Javanese servants he did not trust, Huxley worried that they had cheated him of a few 'dishes I was entitled to'. Yet the food did not seem to have made much of an impression. He wrote that there were vegetables, dried and fresh fish, some variety of sausage, pickles and a 'a queer kind of unleavened bread, and various other things which I cannot at the moment remember'. He stirred the various dishes together with the rice on his plate, complaining that a 'trough would be a more suitable receptacle'. He sighed and leaned forward to 'shovel the immense and steaming mound of food' into his mouth.[31]

In that tense atmosphere, Huxley ate his rijsttafel and, as he digested, he considered the meanings of 'gluttony'. It might be a deadly sin, but Huxley realized that gluttony was central to the ritual of the colonial hotel meal; diners were literally gobbling up tropical abundance, commercialized for the benefit of the colonizers. Yet as a demonstration of colonial power, the rijsttafel confronted the reality of the segregated colonial hotel. If tourists were 'eating up the colony' and displaying colonial power through sheer gluttony, Huxley realized, they could only do so under the gaze of those serving them the food.

Helpless, hapless tourists depended on the attentions of their servants at Batavia's hotels. 'Our own experience,' warned a British tourist, 'was that we were left, almost invariably, to the tender mercies of the servants.'[32] The rijsttafel gave tourists the chance to dine like a colonial, but that also meant eating spicy, exotic foods under the eyes of Javanese. As the food piled up on the American tourist George A. Dorsey's plates, he came to see the meal as a competition between the tourist diners and the parade of fourteen servants. Already full, he perspired from the spices. As more servants arrived with more dishes, his plate suddenly reminded him of the 'heaping garbage can of a Chinese restaurant'.[33]

Tourists worried that behind servants' impassive expressions lurked contempt. Even popular souvenir photos of the rijsttafel unwittingly captured the colonial contest. Most of the images that remain in archives today seem to have been designed to capture the food parade as a moment of triumph. Taken just before service begins, as the waiters line up, and the food and its chillies have not yet vanquished the European tourists, they reflect a colonizer's gaze of Java as exotic, tamed and ready to serve. But the subjects do not always cooperate.

In a 1930s souvenir photograph, for example, white diners sit ready at the table, their dishes still empty. The servants are lined up, no shoes on their feet but silver platters in their hands. There is food on the platters, but unrecognizable at a distance; it was, after all, of little consequence compared to the parade itself. The servants are in suspended animation, as though forever waiting to serve the tourists who might later display the photograph as memory of their holiday. Yet the waiters gaze back at the camera, directly, but impassively. Their expressions were precisely what troubled travellers such as Dorsey and Huxley. They express neither pleasure in service nor understanding when tourist diners were inevitably overwhelmed by the food and the spice. Their uniforms, posture and bare feet suggest discipline, but their faces withhold consent.

In another photo from the Hotel der Nederlanden, as the food parade curled around the table, one of the Europeans, trying to get a place in the photo, leans awkwardly around the servant who claimed the foreground. In that gesture of impatience, the parade had become less abundant service than encirclement.

Meals could be tense. Once the food arrived, tourists had to select or refuse strange dishes and then taste foods they couldn't recognize. The fragility of their authority became clear. The American tourist and travel writer H. M. Tomlinson, for example, remembered that a Malay waiter 'firmly disputed' his fumbling Malay commands.[34]

Tomlinson should have read his tourist guide more closely. Beginning in the early decades of the twentieth century, tourist guides to the Netherlands Indies printed an especially detailed list of vocabulary and important phrases. In fact, all the guides, including those produced by the Java government and those from the KPM, published an identical list of terms and phrases. The list intended to help tourists, not to understand a passing conversation, but to command servants. In effect, it represented instructions on how to recapture control in the subtle push-and-shove with servants. Useful terms for measurements were included. 'Semoewa' meant all; 'stengah' meant half. (This latter term was particularly useful; stengah was also the name of a watery gin drink.) For money: 'Wang perak' was a silver coin. The guide helped tourists spend that money, or at least to negotiate with Javanese vendors or servants: 'Brapa doewit' asked 'how much' and 'tida kassi' meant 'won't give it'. 'Ini satoe talen . . . boewat bajar coolie', offered the servant a small tip.

The list included plenty of words to discipline servants. 'Pigi' told a servant or another local to 'be off'. 'Soedah, habis perkara' ordered them not to bother you anymore. There were commands for each moment in the established ritual of daily white colonial life in the Dutch East Indies. 'Jonges minta kartas toelis dan penna tinta' told the 'boy' that you wanted writing paper and a pen. 'Minta ajer blanda' ordered bottled water. 'Saja maoe pigi di Bogor' told your servant that you wanted to depart on the first train to the Buitenzorg gardens. 'Pigi di kamar bola Harmonie' took you to the Harmonie Club. The guides even gave tourists the responses they expected from servants.

'Baai tosan' – all right, sir.

'Saja toean, saja djaga' – yes sir, I will take care.

The guide provided the script to negotiate the long parade of servants at the rijsttafel. When the Dutch headwaiter – the official racial ally – couldn't help, the tourist had a list of commands.

Don't want rice, before it was heaped onto your dish? 'Tida makan nassi.'

Willing to eat rice, but too squeamish for the spicy food? 'Minta nassi tapi tida maoe sambal.'

If you told the waiters, 'minta ajam, telor dan ikan sadja', you ordered only chicken, eggs and fish, rather than the curious vegetables and curries.

The Food Parade, Hotel der Nederlanden, Jakarta.

Nervous even about the chicken? 'Minta biefstuk sama salad.' You've ordered just beef and salad. The list included terms for key food staples, but not names or explanations of dishes. 'Kassi satoe bottel anggoer merra no. 10' ordered 'Claret no. 10'. 'Minta boea' commanded the servant to bring you fruit.[35]

After the meal, the Dutch typically escaped the heat and napped. Later in the afternoon, as the temperatures moderated, servants tapped gently on tourists' doors. They brought tea. The guidebooks recommended that tourists follow the Dutch model and bathe again. After that, 'European garments are worn' for visiting and eating dinner.

'Dinner is perfectly normal,' wrote Huxley, meaning European. Worsfold, too, called it 'much like an ordinary *à la Russe* dinner', except with more vegetables; it would be a comfort for tourists too squeamish for the rijsttafel.[36] 'I half believed the rice-table, the sarongs and kabayas, and the Javanese "boys" must have been a dream,' wrote de Wit as she looked around the dining room at dinner. Then, 'a lean brown hand' reached out to change her fish course for asparagus.[37]

After dinner, those tourists lucky enough to wrangle an invite could visit the colonial clubs such as the elite Harmonie Club. Still, without saying exactly why, the guides suggested that under no circumstances should tourists enter a Javanese coffee house. Maybe the guides were warning them against water or food that might be tainted; perhaps they were reminding tourists that they couldn't expect the same service in a local restaurant as in a local hotel.

Learning to Pick and Choose

Most around-the-world tourists spent only a few days in the Dutch colony. Tourists who wanted to travel beyond Batavia and Buitenzorg required a special permit, and the handful of visitors who stepped off the tourist trail still tended to stay with Dutch colonial friends and hosts. They observed local habits and wandered around the marketplaces, but they ate in the privileged comfort of the colonial home. Sometimes, when they returned to the grand hotels, they boasted that their longer sojourns with colonialists had taught them how to expertly enjoy the rijsttafel.

Carrie Catt, the founding president of the International Women's Suffrage Association, took a working holiday around the world in 1911–12. She saw the sites, but she also visited allies in the women's suffrage movement, including those in both Java and Sumatra. Catt worked hard to 'gladly follow the fashion of the country'. She happily dressed in the 'native' – and here she meant Dutch colonial – fashion, shedding heavy European clothes for light, flowing cottons. She learned to sleep in the afternoon and to drive out from the hotel to go visiting fellow suffragists as the tropical sun set, but before the mosquitos swarmed.

Eventually, Catt learned how to eat the rijsttafel. 'Of all the culinary surprises I have ever met,' she marvelled, 'this takes the lead.' During her first three days, spent in a Batavia hotel, the endless procession of dishes confused her. A 'crispy wafer' must be made of egg, she guessed. The 'Irish potato' was probably fried in coconut oil. The dishes kept coming – fried aubergine, roasted bananas and corn fritters. Crabs and shrimps arrived both fried and in croquettes. She refused several meat dishes. In the end, she admitted: 'I do not know what we have not had.' Of the 23 dishes offered by the servants, she sampled twelve on her first day, underlining the number in her diary for emphasis. The second day, she tried eleven dishes. 'To-day nine', she wrote in her diary at the end of her hotel stay. It was all prepared 'by native cooks' – and, here, 'native' actually meant Javanese.

The rijsttafel 'is doubtless not so complicated in a private house', Catt guessed – and hoped – as she was about to set off on a tour of the Dutch colonial archipelago. She visited schools, homes and markets. Occasionally, she drank tea with Javanese and Sumatran locals. Once, she watched some villagers eating at a local food shop. They ate rice topped with beans, sliced jackfruit, dried fish and a kind of fried banana. 'We have these at the rice table,' she noted in her diary. She ate with 'native' suffrage activists – by which she now meant, again, Dutch colonists. By the time she departed the Dutch colony a few weeks later, the rijsttafel had become a regular part of Catt's day. On one particularly hot, humid day, 'we rested, took naps and I read my guidebook,' Catt recorded in her diary. 'Rice table was served at one o'clock.'[38] Like tourists at hotels, she counted the servants, even at a rijsttafel in a private home. 'Seven boys' paraded past; in her diary, she underlined 'seven'.[39]

Lucile Mann, who travelled around the world with her husband William in 1936–7, also had time to adjust. They dashed through Hawai'i and Japan but spent several months in the different islands of the Indonesian archipelago. William Mann was the director of the National Zoo in Washington, and the Dutch East Indies had an abundance of wild animals, some of which he hoped to buy. When the Manns arrived in Batavia in early April 1937, they went straight to the Hotel des Indes to sample their first rijsttafel. Lucile expected to enjoy both its spicy flavours and its colonial origins.

That evening, Lucile admitted to her diary that she 'probably expected too much in the way of gastronomic delight'. First came boiled rice, ladled from a silver bowl. Then, curried chicken, steak, baked fish, fried coconut, three preparations of cucumbers, peanuts, fried bananas, chutney, shrimps, and fried and salted eggs. Then more: gravies and sauces and even 'spaghetti'. She needed an extra plate for her 'overflow'. By the time all the dishes were served, and she began to eat, the food, though spicy hot, had become cold in temperature. To the overwhelmed Lucile, it all seemed rather 'messy', and reminded her that she didn't yet know how to eat like a colonial.

During their tour of the colony, however, the Manns got to know local Dutch colonists well, especially local animal merchants, and shared with them their private rijsttafels. By mid-May, when the Manns returned to Batavia and the Hotel des Indes, she dined on hotel rijsttafel again. 'I am learning to choose,' she proudly recorded.[40] By contrast, H. M. Tomlinson never did get used to the rice table. The sheer amount of food overwhelmed him. 'It is not a meal but a buffalo wallow,' he complained. He watched a practised Dutch diner who piled his plate with chicken, eggs, nuts, prawns, seaweed and bamboo shoots. The colonist arranged his moustache, adjusted his glasses and dug into the 'discoloured muck' of rice, stained with sauces and gravies. Tomlinson, however, declared himself 'vanquished' by the array of food. 'I felt it better to creep silently away, leaving my own dinner unfinished,' he admitted, deciding that he 'ought to keep away from Java'. Still, he told tourists, however much he liked the hotel ritual, it was 'remarkable; and watch it you must'.[41]

The Last Rijsttafel

The heyday of the rijsttafel ended with the Second World War. By mid-February 1942 Singapore had surrendered to the Japanese army and everyone staying at the Hotel des Indes realized that the Dutch colony, and its abundant resources, would be the next Japanese target. The Japanese had already landed in Sumatra, but not before retreating Dutch, British and American soldiers dynamited the valuable oil wells. In the hotel gallery, shaded from the 'intemperate sun at noon', anxious Dutch colonists asked British refugees from Singapore and Malaya: 'Will the Japanese actually capture these islands?'

Meanwhile, Javanese 'boys in impeccable whites scuffle with bare feet' as they served Dutch beer and European cocktails before the rijsttafel began. For many Europeans, it was their last rijsttafel before they fled. On the eve of the impending fall of the Dutch colony, they ate 'the luncheon curry'. As they dined, and as the servants paraded, the orchestra played 'Somewhere Over the Rainbow'.[42]

Three years later, the war was over, and Indonesia declared its independence from the Netherlands. By the time the journalist Rafael Steinberg arrived in Indonesia on assignment for a 1970 instalment of Time-Life's 'Foods of the World' series, the rijsttafel, with its numerous waitstaff, was understood as a relic of imperialism. Steinberg never tried one. Instead, he enjoyed a prasmanan feast, a postcolonial buffet in which diners served themselves. The Hotel der Nederlanden had been demolished the year before and the Hotel des Indes would fall the year after. The feast inaugurated Steinberg's culinary tour of independent Indonesia. After the banquet, he left Djakarta (the postcolonial name for Batavia) satiated but with his 'appetite aroused' and ready of a 'gastronomic tour of the country'. Steinberg was guided through the country by two men with expertise in its cuisine: George Lang, who had run the Indonesian government's restaurant at the 1964 World's Fair, and Fritz Schild-Tameng, a Djarkata chef.

Four cooks had worked all day to prepare the prasmanan, preparing both 'Pan-Indonesian' dishes and others that were local to their own respective regions and islands. Unlike past tourists, who lumped the various styles of curries, sambals and gravies together, Steinberg was curious about the recipes and origins of each dish.

He recognized the satay. The grilled meat, basted with soy and served with a spicy peanut sauce, was as national a food as Indonesia might offer, he judged. Satay came in almost endless variety, a diversity that matched the archipelago itself. In Java, satay, made from beef, goat or chicken, was common street food. In Bali, locals made satay from minced sea turtle and coconut. In Makasar, satay featured shrimp, Steinberg explained. He sampled a variety of satay at the feast. Steinberg also garnished his rice with trassi, a dark red sambal made from fermented shrimp, and with petis, a pungent, salty fish sauce. He ate longing, rice steamed inside banana leaves. When overwhelmed by the chillies, he sipped tjintjau, a 'welcome' drink, made from vine leaves and sweetened with sweet-bean paste. The drink tasted to Steinberg like a mixture of ice-tea and jelly – but better.

For the benefit of readers familiar with the tourist attraction of the past, Steinberg compared the prasmanan to the 'old-time rijsttafel', and he counted the dishes: there were 52 on offer, he wrote, and it took him three hours to sample them all – motivated, he explained, by curiosity as well as 'courtesy'. There were no servants to count.

He was also quick to explain that, while 'epicures the world over' thought of the rijsttafel as the epitome of Indonesian cookery, it never was. For Indonesians, even the word reminded them of 'past humiliation'. True, the rijsttafel might seem a typical enough Indonesian meal in that it was built around the staple of rice, garnished with various sambals and small dishes. But the difference in the service and scale – as well as the rijsttafel's second course of European meat – mattered. Dutch colonists, 'with an abundance of servants, money and leisure', turned 'an indigenous style of eating into an ostentatious display of fine cooking, opulence and power'. It was a 'food parade', proof of imperial might. Steinberg quoted the words of an Indonesian he met: 'There are no rice tables in Indonesia today but there is rice on every table.'[43]

PART III:

AEROPLANES AND THE AGE OF MASS TOURISM, 1945–75

Itinerary: Pan Am

June 1945: the Second World War wasn't yet over, but Pan American Airlines – Pan Am – was already taking reservations for around-the-world holidays by aeroplane. Flight enthusiast Russell Sabor and his wife, from Dubuque, Iowa, booked the first tickets.

At the end of the war, Pan Am was planning for a tourist boom. The airline had already ordered new planes to fly along the same routes recently followed by armies and navies. They would land on runways originally built for bombers. Battlefields would become tourist sites.

Post-war, the airline immediately began planning an around-the-world itinerary, but leisure travel by air created new challenges. Where would passengers sleep? Where would they eat when on the ground and what would they eat in the air?

Pan Am executives realized that there was a lot at stake politically and economically in planning an itinerary around the world. Pan Am's founder and president Juan Trippe thought of his airline as the unofficial flag carrier of the United States and imagined that the priorities of American foreign policy matched his desire to send tourists – most of whom would be American – all the way around the world.

In the immediate post-war period, as the world rebuilt itself and struggled with Cold War tensions, countries jostled to build airports and raised money to build hotels. They were eager to attract Pan Am flights and branches of InterContinental, the airline's new hotel subsidiary. Trippe promised that if the hotels were built, tourists, armed with dollars, would arrive – even in the most unlikely of destinations. Pan Am's itinerary around the world was the story of the rise and fall of post-war mass tourism.

English Food and a Bottle of Heinz Ketchup

October 1927: Pan Am's origins were humble. The fledging airline flew mail back and forth between Florida and Havana, the Cuban city that would eventually become first a tourist haven, and then a revolutionary capital. By the eve of the Second World War, Pan Am had grown spectacularly, with routes the length of South America and over the oceans. Trippe called his planes Clippers, a romantic name that evoked the history of fast American merchant ships that had traded across the Pacific in the nineteenth century. Pan Am's enormous flying boats island-hopped across the Pacific to Hawai'i towards New Zealand, the Philippines and China.

June 1939: Pan Am inaugurated Clipper service across the Atlantic using Boeing 314s, its largest, most modern flying boat. Sabor was one of the 'Original 15', the very first passengers who flew on Pan Am's inaugural transatlantic flight. The fares were high, and the service lavish. In 1941, with the United States still neutral, Pan Am flew 375,000 passengers to and from 62 countries and colonies.[1]

December 1941: in a cloud of sea spray, the *Pacific Clipper* took off from the American naval base at Pearl Harbor in Hawai'i, a scheduled stop en route to Auckland, New Zealand. The captain, Robert Ford, couldn't have known that the Clipper was flying west just as the Japanese naval fleet sailed east. When emergency radio codes crackled over the flying boat's radio, the Pan Am flight crew realized that their way home was blocked. The *Pacific Clipper*, one of only a handful of aeroplanes that could travel such long distances, was too valuable to fall into Japanese hands. Ford and his crew decided to continue flying west, all the way around.[2] The route home from Auckland crossed Australia and Java, and eventually to Karachi in British India. The crew then flew across Africa, before crossing the Atlantic to Brazil. The plane flew north to safety.

After travelling 31,500 miles (50,694 km), the Clipper landed in New York on 6 January 1942. Edward McVitty, a Pan Am engineer, boarded the plane and noticed that someone had scrawled in crayon on the bathroom door a reminder to conserve safe water. Despite the trip around the world, McVitty discovered 'all-English foods' in the galley kitchen and a bottle of Heinz ketchup.[3]

The *Pacific Clipper*, and the rest of Pan Am's Boeing 314 fleet, entered military service. In 1943, when President Franklin Roosevelt flew to Casablanca to meet the British Prime Minister Winston Churchill, he crossed the Atlantic in a Pan Am Clipper. On the way home, he celebrated his 61st birthday in the air. While flying over Haiti, Pan Am served the president caviar, olives, celery, pickles, turkey with dressing, green peas, potatoes, cake and champagne.[4] The pilot drank coffee.

To Our Standards

December 1945: at last the war had ended. The first commercial flights from the United States to Europe and Asia had only just resumed when a Pan Am Douglas DC-4 departed New York on a 20,000-mile (32,187 km) survey flight halfway around the world. Pan Am assembled a 28-person expert committee to scout new routes, attractions and hotels. Bruno Candotti, the airline's commissary superintendent, joined the expedition. His job was to plan how the airline would feed its passengers while in the air and where passengers might sleep and dine on the ground.

The uncomfortable journey left Candotti exhausted and feverish. Yet it also laid the foundation for around-the-world tourism by air, Pan Am's flagship service. Condotti lodged in army barracks and fraying colonial-era hotels. But within two decades, Pan Am's jets would fly around the world to more than eighty countries and InterContinental would construct hotels on every inhabited continent except North America. In the process, the airline and its hotels proclaimed the first-class hotel and the jet airliner as the global beacons of American capital and modernity.

Candotti and the committee landed in Brussels, near the war's first and last battlefields. They continued as far as India. Wherever he visited, Candotti recorded numbers of local hotel rooms, wages and the standard of service available to future tourists who probably had not yet traded army helmets for sunhats. Candotti tasted the food, considered whether the water was safe to drink, checked on supplies of tinned goods and recorded the prices and quality of local ingredients. In Brussels, he ate at the airport where the only restaurant was still run by the British Royal Air Force. At least the 'kitchen is clean', he noted. In town, because of rationing, restaurant and grocery prices were set on the black market. Athens remained under military control when he arrived. According to GIs, 'the food and accommodation facilities are terribly dirty.'[5]

In his travel notes, Candotti carefully copied out the French and Turkish menu from the Ankara Palace, the leading hotel in the Turkish capital. Dessert, he wrote, was 'Peches Melba' ('Saftalili Donurma Veya Meyba') and a reminder that grand hotels still mostly offered continental dishes. Although tap-water was available, Candotti didn't recommend drinking it. Ankara seemed 'an oriental city that wants to look modern and does in certain parts', and the local authorities organized a cocktail party for Pan American staff. 'Gifts were exchanged, handshaking, and salaams', before the committee 'flew towards Damascus' and the Orient Palace hotel, a pre-war, colonial relic.

Post-war, the Orient Palace in Damascus promised 'delux', but only 'in Oriental fashion' with a kitchen that was 'not too sanitary', declared Candotti. He warned that customers must add 10 per cent gratuity to all meal costs 'if you don't want to be poisoned'. The French forces occupied the airport and had mined fields near the runways. Vegetables and meat (mostly mutton or camel) were available in the city itself, but they were inferior and tainted. Dysentery and typhoid were endemic, he noted, and water was 'doubtful'.

Wandering around the bazaar, Candotti remarked that Baghdad 'actually "Stinks"'. He quickly abandoned his sightseeing. Sanitation fell 'below any possible description' and though labour was available in kitchens and dining rooms, workers 'must be trained to our standards' if Pan Am decided to fly to Baghdad.

In mid-January Candotti landed in Karachi, where he bunked in British army barracks. British officers had requisitioned the Killarney, the only hotel. Even in such conditions, Candotti envisioned Pan Am flights soon landing at the large airport. In his report, he warned that Pan Am agents posted to Karachi would have to negotiate the bewildering South Asian world of servants. The 'regular houseboy' would never wash dishes and 'if you try to make the cook wash dishes, you won't have a cook.' 'Local foods', he wrote, were all 'inferior to American standards'. In the tense atmosphere on the eve of India's and Pakistan's independence, he noted, Americans 'are about the only whites tolerated here'.

Candotti travelled as far as New Delhi, before returning via Cairo. In late 1945, east of India, the wounds of war remained too raw for pleasure travel. Japan faced the mammoth task of domestic rebuilding and islands across the Pacific remained military airbases. In addition, Candotti had fallen ill after weeks of bumpy flights, uncomfortable hotels and suspicious foods. Yet he was feverishly optimistic. 'When one sees some of the aircraft used by foreign lines, it makes one wonder how people dare to fly in them. Since they do, it shows clearly that aviation is here to stay,' the ill airline traveller noted in the report he sent to the Pan Am headquarters.

A Few Specialities of the Land Landed

June 1947: *Clipper America*, a Lockheed Constellation, took off from New York on Pan Am's first scheduled around-the-world flight. The plane offered greater comforts than previous Clippers or Candotti's converted military transport. It travelled faster and, with a new pressurized cabin, the Constellation could fly high enough above the clouds and storms for a smoother ride. However, the piston engine plane's range remained limited. Pan Am's route around the world was determined partly by technology and partly by the shifting allegiances and politics of a world emerging from war and heading into a Cold War.

All the way around, Pan Am's Clippers landed where they could and where they needed to, not necessarily where tourists yearned to go. Pan Am's first flight around the world headed east across the Atlantic, across Europe and Turkey towards Karachi, Pakistan. Planes were flying over a rapidly changing globe. India's and Pakistan's independence arrived, in fact, the same year that Pan Am launched its around-the-world itinerary. The Clippers flew over the lines of partition to Calcutta in independent India. From Manila to Shanghai to Tokyo, the flight refuelled at Wake, Midway and Hawai'i, islands just a few years before fought over by Americans and Japanese.[6]

Food writer Clementine Paddleford joined the inaugural flight. She immediately recognized that the airline was competing with steamships. Especially at the bar, the tourist flight tried to replicate the luxury of the around-the-world cruise. On regular flights, the mixed drinks would cost 50 cents. Paddleford drank for free on this first flight and the message was clear: a luxury holiday should be boozy. Before the Second World War, the first transoceanic Pan Am flights followed steamship routes; they were, after all, flying boats. Post-war, as pressurized planes replaced flying boats, Pan Am traced new routes that placed cities such as Karachi in West

Pakistan and Dacca in East Pakistan on the itinerary. A cruise ship could carry much of the meat, water and alcohol its passengers would consume. By contrast, Paddleford explained that Pan Am commissaries at each stop loaded food for the on-board meals. She reassured future passengers that the menus were mostly American. On her first dinner, she ate grapefruit maraschino, hearts of celery and radishes carved into flowers, filet mignon with potatoes and – like Roosevelt four years before – green peas. There was ice cream cake for dessert and the galley was stocked with ham sandwiches and fruit for night-time snacks.

At each stop, however, Pan Am offered a surprise meal choice: 'a few specialities of the land visited'.[7] Even on this very first flight around the world, Pan Am introduced the safe food adventures that characterized both its political approach and its tourist appeal for the next thirty years of around-the-world leisure travel. A few local tastes provided the spice a post-war, postcolonial holiday required.

Pan Am was convinced that this flight would usher in a golden age of world tourism. Soon after Candotti's journey, the airline reported that hotels in Europe were 'now rehabilitated' and Latin America 'wants tourist dollars'. Veterans also were 'eager to re-visit war scenes', exchanging guns for cameras.

Yet barriers remained. The Cold War had begun. 'Statesmen see war danger increasing,' noted Pan Am in 1948, and postcolonial unrest and anti-colonial politics seethed in places such as India and Pakistan. In Europe, black markets persisted, and the airline reported: 'food abroad still scarce and inferior'.[8] Tourists were eager to travel, but they needed safe food to eat and hotels where they could sleep. Pan Am was convinced: 'If a good hotel is built, travelers will find their way to it.'[9]

New Horizons

October 1959: the world shrank again as Pan Am replaced its piston-engine propeller planes with Boeing 707 jets on the around-the-world flight. The new jet Clippers could travel further and faster. The flight from San Francisco to Honolulu that had taken thirteen hours in 1947 was now just under five hours. By jet, flying time from Calcutta to Karachi had fallen from six hours and fifteen minutes to under three hours.[10] The around-the-world flights by piston engine had taken off once a week. Now they left twice daily. Pan Am flight 1 headed west; flight 2 headed east, and they crossed paths somewhere over Nagpur, India.

Pan Am Clippers.

The 707s heralded the Jet Age, but Pan Am imagined that they were merely the first planes in a jet fleet. Soon, Pan Am would inaugurate the wide-bodied, double-decked 747s and announced contracts for the supersonic Concorde and an even bigger Boeing supersonic aeroplane. Boeing scrapped plans for supersonic jets and Pan Am, faced by mounting fuel costs during the oil shocks of the 1970s, never flew Concordes.

The enthusiasm for more and faster jets contributed ultimately to the airline's demise, but, for the moment, Pan Am's executives were convinced that world tourism would expand indefinitely. Once a privilege of the wealthy, leisure travel and around-the-world trips would become a middle-class pleasure, Pan Am assumed.

June 1963: Pan Am still admitted, 'if you want a vacation, East Pakistan is not the place to go. Not for a long time, anyway.' Pan Am had a long list of complaints: 'The poverty, the filth, the flies, and mosquitos . . . the strange foods, the odors, the tap water you don't use even for brushing your teeth.' Still, 'visiting East Pakistan is a truly moving experience.' In 1963 the Shawbagh Hotel was the only hotel to advertise grand colonial comfort. According to Pan Am, it delivered a 'third class experience'. Sparrows nested in the dining room. Vultures perched in the outdoor covered gallery waiting for the 'latest dumping of hotel garbage'.

An InterContinental Hotel was coming. Through its InterContinental subsidiary, Pan Am was building a network of hotels that catered to American travellers, indifferent to the older appeal of colonial luxury and curious about local cultures. In Dacca the hotel would be 'properly air-conditioned and managed'.[11] Around the world, InterContinental competed primarily with Hilton. Hilton, in turn, would eventually sell its international hotel interests to TWA, Pan Am's biggest airline rival.

The trip around the world after the Second World War, and in the midst of decolonization and the Cold War, blended liberal politics and American pleasure. Pan Am advertised its itinerary through the testimony of happy passengers. J. O. Furby reflected on the benefits of his holiday around the world: 'Finding out that people the world over regardless of colour of skin or nationality are basically very friendly, hospitable, and helpful.'[12] Dining out was crucial to the itinerary designed to build understanding. 'Enjoy their food – all as a new experience. Don't be so foolish as to insist on ham and eggs and refuse foods you've never seen or tasted,' recalled a 'Dr. V. R.'

'Go forth without prejudice – go to enjoy and not to reform,' a 'Miss E. G.' suggested. Trying local food was the gustatory demonstration that American tourism would share the benefits of American technology and prosperity with the postcolonial, non-communist world. In 1955, Trippe told the International Air Transport Association: 'There can be no atom bomb potentially more powerful than the air tourist.' The bomb brought destruction; the tourist produced goodwill with dollars. Bring $50 bills, recommended an experienced around-the-world tourist. Dollars abroad represented Pan Am's commitment to tourism as mutual benefit. Pan Am in the air, InterContinental on the ground and tourists around the world would win the 'race between education and catastrophe'.[13]

American tourists sought new horizons and the world needed the dollars they would spend lavishly, reasoned Pan Am. The airline defined a strategy of bringing tourists, not to established sites, but to new locales, especially in the tropics. InterContinental imagined each of its hotels as a miniature United Nations with room service and filtered water.

July 1967: a Pan Am 707 took off on the airline's 10,000th flight around the world. Pan Am's around-the-world itinerary 'has helped to shrink our globe, to conquer distance and time. In a quite literal sense it has made all of us around the world neighbors.'[14] By then, Pan Am's around-the-world flights had flown 200 million miles (more than 300 million km), the equivalent of forty round trips to the moon.[15]

Around the World to the Moon

July 1969: twenty-year old Jeffrey Gates watched the Apollo moon landing and the next day he called Pan Am to reserve a round trip to the moon for himself and the wife he hoped he would meet one day. By the end of the 1960s, in the final years of the golden age of mass tourism, on the eve of the oil crisis, space flight held more excitement for the youthful Gates than a trip around the world. Gates joined about 90,000 other customers between 1969 and 1971 in reserving a place on one of Pan Am's prospective trips to the moon. Pan Am, in its typical enthusiasm for tourism, hoped that flights might depart at the beginning of the new century. It sent Gates a souvenir card confirming his reservation. In fact, by 1991, Pan Am, a victim of soaring oil prices, global conflict and changing regulations of airlines, was bankrupt.

Gates kept the card: 'first around the world, first to the moon', it read.[16]

10

Myra Waldo

'**B**on Voyage and Bon Appétit', read the cookbook's dedication page, 'on this trip around the world to all those who love travel and fine food.' In 1954, Myra Waldo, the food consultant for Pan American World Airways, compiled recipes from the airline's staff and published *The Complete Round-the-World Cookbook*.[1] A few months later, a Boeing 377 Stratocruiser, the double-decker flagship of the Pan Am fleet, took off to circle around New England – an around-the-world journey in seven courses. The flight featured foods from Myra's cookbook.

The Stratocruiser, a plane designed for tourists but based on a bomber design, featured a cocktail lounge on its lower deck. Guests, drawn from the nation's press, from the *New York Times* to *Gourmet* to *Seventeen*, gathered there to begin their culinary trip around the world with kamano lomi – Hawaiian salmon. Camarones con salsa de almendras – shrimp with almond sauce – came from Ecuador. The salad was Italian, the beef was Flemish and the ohn htamin – coconut rice – was Burmese. The Champagne was French. The cheesecake was 'good old American', read the airline's press release.[2]

The Complete Round-the-World Cookbook proved a bestseller. Home cooks, Myra believed, were really tourists, eager to leave on holiday or to reminisce at the table about trips already past. With her cookbook, as virtual tourists, they could circle the globe without ever leaving their own table.

On-board, abroad and in print, Myra married tourist pleasures to home cooking 'on this trip around the world to all those who love travel and fine food'.[3] About halfway between the Austrian brennsuppe, the cookbook's first recipe, and Venezuelan arroz coco, the last, Myra visited India and Ceylon – former British colonies, now both independent nations. The right kind of tourist 'approaches the food without any restrictions'. If they were willing, Americans would fall in love with South Asia's curries, and they

Myra Waldo launches her *Round-the-World Cookbook* on a Pan Am flight, 1954.

would realize that the versions they once ate at home 'were not authentic'. A few years later, Myra would also write local dining guides so that New Yorkers, at least, could find authentic world foods in their own city.

Visit India; try the Chicken Korma. 'Morgee korma', she translated. The dish appealed equally to Jet Age travellers and to home cooks eager for unfamiliar, but not particularly daunting, tastes. Myra's version, and thousands of other recipes that in the decades after the Second World War flowed from across the globe through cookbooks into the American home kitchen, added spice to the American diet – literally a host of spices and metaphorically an exotic taste. Myra offered two versions of the spice mixture for the dish. The 'Indian korma mixture' blended coriander, turmeric, cumin, black pepper and a scant ⅛ teaspoon of ground chilli. Myra measured a pinch of authentic heat for an entire 3½-pound (1.4 kg) chicken. Need something simpler? Add two tablespoons of curry powder.[4]

The spices flavoured – gently – an otherwise familiar American dish: marinated and sautéed chicken. That, really, was both the point and the politics: if an American chicken could become Indian with just a few tinned or packaged ingredients, how different could its peoples be?

Myra helped introduce the genre of around-the-world cookbooks that reached the zenith of their popularity between the 1950s and early

1970s. Many, like Myra's, linked themselves to corporate brands, often travel companies or packaged spice companies. Others were more overt in their political allegiances. If the United Nations united many flags, the around-the-world cookbook promised to find cultural harmony in many recipes. This was a dinner-table liberalism, the firm belief that travel could build understanding, especially if tourists shed their revulsion towards local foods. Liberalism was truly on holiday around the world.

Drink bottled water, but sample something the locals ate. Myra's cookbook, and others like it, offered real and virtual itineraries all around the world. Yet the final taste of the dish mattered. Transformed into a dish palatable to Americans, Myra's 'morgee korma' would have tasted as strange to home cooks in India as it did exotic to home cooks in the United States. As an Indian dish morphed into an American main course, it seemed more like an edible souvenir than a shared meal across cultures. For Americans, Myra's cookbook did help familiarize some of the flavours of the world that previous generations avoided. It also made Myra a celebrity, one of the best-known and most prolific cookbook authors of the post-war generation. She used that fame to branch out; she soon wrote advice books about travel, dieting, even marriage. There was a common theme in her writing: eating around the world was, she promised, the answer to how to travel, lose weight and even enjoy a happy marriage.

How the World Eats

A few years ago, I helped my mother pare down her cookbook collection. Buried beneath more up-to-date Chinese cookbooks, I discovered a dog-eared, stained copy of Myra's *The Complete Book of Oriental Cooking* (1960).[5] Myra joined a pantheon of American cookbook authors who emerged from behind the anonymity of dust jackets to model ideal living in an era of post-war prosperity. Julia Child explained how to cook French food. James Beard described the right way to entertain. Myra knew that a post-war generation that had learned to travel and was beginning to re-learn how to eat needed advice: where to stay, where to visit, what to eat and what to avoid.

'I don't know when I've enjoyed myself more,' said Myra, simply by refusing the standard continental hotel menu.[6] In each of her books, she played a role, like an actor on stage. She chose the role of ordinary tourist when she wrote the cookbook for Pan Am and, later, for its InterContinental Hotels subsidiary. She capitalized upon the renown from her airline work to edit the 'How the World Eats' column for *This Week*, the Sunday magazine inserted into newspapers across the country. When she wrote travel guides, she played the role of Pan Am travel agent. In other cookbooks, she adopted the character of a newlywed or a dieter, eager to slim while trying new dishes, though she never assumed the part of professional chef. Instead, she described herself as a married home cook who circled the globe in person on Pan Am and, virtually, in her own kitchen.

Myra's cookbook lurked at the back of my mother's cookbook shelf because her books were rooted in a historical moment. Of Myra's books, only her soufflé cookbook remains in print. Myra is less remembered yet was one of the most prolific of this post-war celebrity-cookbook-author generation. If today's home cooks value authenticity, the around-the-world cookbooks that became so popular in the decades after the Second World War valorized the attraction of jet travel. Exotic dishes such as murgee korma represented stops on a tourist trail and Myra recommended meals that picked freely from the spicy foods, especially of Asia and Latin America.[7] 'Spice' can be a metaphor, suggesting a departure from the mundane – adding spice to life. Spices were also ingredients, suggestive of real foods and places, and when Myra published her first around-the-world cookbook, real spices had begun to fill American pantries. Real spices also evoked travel and adventure. Myra and other world food cookbook authors reimagined spices – and the foods they flavoured – as exciting, exotic, but still accessible. Such cookbooks valorized gastronomic encounters as a source of postcolonial racial reconciliation, but with all the contradictions of modern tourism written into the recipe. Foods, the hard work of cooks around the world, became a source of pleasure for (mostly) white tourists.

Around-the-world cookbooks were especially popular in the United States during the Cold War. They were written for tourists, real and virtual, but weren't for sale in the very places that supplied the raw stuff of recipes. These cookbooks gestured towards sharing tastes across cultures but, in fact, they produced recipes for Americans to cook at home and they often included advice about where to travel to taste the authentic recipe. They were passports to travel virtually, to relive a past holiday or to plan the next trip. Applying familiar cooking directions to a select few exotic tastes, around-the-world cookbooks invited Americans to eat something other than British or continental standards. Myra wrote publicly what so many travellers already privately realized: British cooking in England was bland. When prepared in hotels in its former colonies, it was barely edible.

French cooking could taste spectacular in France, uneven and overpriced in the United States and unpalatable in most other places.

Especially in the United States, around-the-world cookbooks were a wildly popular genre.[8] These cookbooks dashed across the world and grabbed recipes from as many places as possible. They chose their recipes based on their appeal and accessibility to American home cooks. The foods they promoted were not necessarily notable, traditional or symbolically important dishes. Rather, they were exotic but unthreatening foods that fit neatly into a lexicon of lunch, dinner, breakfast, snacks and *hors d'oeuvres*.

Around-the-world cookbooks packaged foods from the places where tourists might visit and tentatively sample the local fare. They helped familiarize Americans to exotic recipes and ingredients. Even the two biggest packaged spice companies that stocked grocery shelves printed their own world cookbooks. Try 'Ging Boortha' ('hot savoury prawns'), recommended Spice Islands in its cookbook. Of the sixteen ingredients, ten were Spice Islands dried spices and herbs. Indian foods were 'artfully blended, exquisitely seasoned dishes', not 'a one-sided cuisine of palate-paralyzing sameness', the spice company explained. 'International dining', advertised Spice Islands, offered 'flavors exotic and familiar.'[9] How the recipes might have tasted to those who produced the spices in the first place didn't matter much to those who wrote the cookbooks.

Around-the-world cookbooks were often advertisements for brands, especially those offering consumers a chance to see the world. Like Myra's, many were published by companies either promoting global travel or with global reach. Among travel brands, Hilton and Sheraton all published around-the-world cookbooks. ITT, Avon, Tupperware and magazines from *Good Housekeeping* to *Women's Day* also published world cookbooks.[10] The excitement with world cooking culminated in 1968 when Time-Life began publishing its sprawling 'Foods of the World' series, blending recipes and accounts of travel adventures.[11]

Lesley Blanch in her 1955 cookbook, in typical fashion, promised an adventure 'around the world in eighty dishes'. Lunch in Turkey, dine in Lapland, and the next day have breakfast in Portugal and dinner in the Congo.[12] A world war and 'the increase in international travel' whet the appetites of a 'newer generation' for spicy foods, Blanch explained. Myra was part of that generation. During the war, her husband was in the navy, and she worked for the American Women's Volunteer Services, so she was able to shop at army or navy commissaries abroad and began collecting local recipes.[13] Myra and her husband, as well as thousands of American soldiers, returned home hungry for Asian and Mediterranean tastes. Between 1948 and 1956, sales of McCormick's dried oregano alone rose 5,200 per cent. 'Americans today', the company enthused, 'enjoy more interesting, more varied and more satisfying food than any nation has ever known before.'[14]

Around-the-world cookbooks obviously appropriated dishes and ingredients from places of the world that were once colonies and now independent nations. Yet even corporate cookbooks promoted a dinner table liberalism, arguing that the growing taste for spice reflected a desire for new global encounters and a liberal belief that both real and virtual taste travel could produce a politics of understanding in an era of decolonization and the Cold War. The Women's Club of the Army Language School printed its own world cookbook in 1953; NATO published its own four years later.[15] Before either of these, the United States Committee for the United Nations published *Favorite Recipes from the United Nations*.[16] Food, as a reminder of 'those fundamental elements common in the life of all of us', was a perfect representation of the liberalism behind support for the United Nations. Optimistic post-war liberalism encouraged a focus on shared humanity and universal rights, in effect, avoiding and ignoring the legacies of race and racism that had produced not only empire but fascism.[17] 'If we are increasingly aware of those fundamental elements common in the life of all of us,' the United Nations began its cookbook, 'basic similarities and needs can unite human beings around the world far more than their differences divide them.'

Such a politics, overt in a political cookbook like that of the United Nations Committee and subtle in a branded world cookbook like Myra's, helped link food adventure to tourism and liberalism to pleasure travel, both real and armchair. 'Knowledge of another's way of life, and the pleasure derived from that knowledge,' wrote the committee to introduce its recipes, 'will help to contribute to that awareness which precedes mutual friendship and respect.' The committee recommended its cookbook for 'unusual food bazaars' or 'progressive dinner parties'.

To write its cookbook, the committee turned to foreign offices, embassies and legations in the United States for recipes and then passed those recipes to the American Home Economics Association to translate, test, measure and, frequently, replace ingredients. Dinner table liberalism clashed with the reality that traditional ingredients were hard to find and frequently repulsive to Americans. 'Some ingredients like the one word "organs" eluded our comprehension but aroused our anxiety,' the committee wrote.[18]

How to Write an Around-the-World Cookbook

Step 1: Start With an Airline

Post-war aeroplanes, trading speed for space, offered a different gastronomic experience than pre-war ocean liners. If steamships advertised multi-course meals in vast dining saloons, airlines served trays at seats and drinks from rolling carts. Steamships sheltered timid passengers in their dining saloons, even while in port. On the *Franconia*, Cunard and Thomas Cook set Edith James's daily schedule and planned virtually her every meal. When Pan Am passengers landed, they disembarked. The complete around-the-world jet journey demanded eating more than grilled meats and boiled vegetables.

Pre-Second World War steamship companies encouraged passengers to save their elaborate daily menus as souvenirs; Pan Am printed Myra's cookbook and shared her recipes in its in-flight magazines. As a hard-bound brochure for the adventures awaiting Pan Am tourists, the cookbook also offered around-the-world travel to anyone with a kitchen, money to spend on ingredients and a few Western-style pots and pans. Myra's 'Mahi Biriani', the airline magazine promised in 1969, is 'a good dish to whip up at home'. Marinate fish (halibut or cod, North American alternatives to local Bengali fish) with some yoghurt, garlic, ginger and cumin. Add the fish to fried onions and rice. Boil with water, tinted with saffron, for a 'taste-tickler' familiar to Americans as boiled fish, but in its spicing and methods, likely unfamiliar to a Bengali home cook. The airline hoped the recipe tempted the tourist to travel. 'There's more to Pakistan than meets the eye,' Myra promised through the dish.[19] Myra linked the genuine experience of travel to American dinner parties through dishes plucked from world cuisines.

Step 2: Travel Around the World

Myra often reminded readers that she was a professional tourist and a wife, not a professional chef. An airline selling around-the-world holidays turned to Myra to promote local foods through domestic home cooking. She blended her work for Pan Am with holidays with her husband. Travel, like cooking and dining, was a couple's pleasure, she believed, and she designed her recipes for women to prepare for their husbands and guests.[20] Travel, she promised, could enliven a domestic (in all its meanings) monotony of meat and two veg.

Mahi Biriani recipe,
Clipper (1969).

Gourmet recipes

There's more to Pakistan than meets the eye. Food, for instance, that titillates the palate and yet is fairly simple to prepare. Although we wouldn't recommend that a stewardess overnighting attempt this Pakistani taste-tickler, it's a good dish to whip up at home. It's fish and rice and the recipe is taken from Myra Waldo's "The Complete Round-The-World-Cookbook," published by Doubleday & Co., Inc., of Garden City, N.Y. Pan Am employees need pay only $2.75 for the $4.95 best-seller. The Pakistanis call this one:

MAHI BIRIANI

2 cups rice	2½ teaspoons salt
1 cup sour milk, buttermilk or yogurt	2 cloves garlic, minced
1 teaspoon cumin seed	2 pounds halibut or cod,
½-inch piece fresh ginger, chopped, or	in one piece
1 teaspoon powdered ginger	½ teaspoon saffron
1 onion chopped fine	¾ cup boiling water
	3 tablespoons butter

Wash the rice thoroughly in several changes of water. Soak in cold water to cover for 15 minutes. Bring to a boil in the same water and cook for 10 minutes. Drain. Combine the milk or yogurt, cumin seed, ginger, salt, and garlic in a bowl. Add the fish and turn it several times in the mixture. Marinate for 30 minutes. Soak the saffron in the boiling water for 10 minutes.

Melt the butter in a large saucepan. Add the onion and saute for 10 minutes, stirring frequently. Remove the onion and set aside. Place the fish and the marinade in the saucepan. Spread the rice over it. Spread the onion on top and sprinkle with the saffron water. Bring to a boil, cover, and cook over low heat for 35 minutes.

If you have a recipe you'd like to introduce to the rest of the world, send it along to: CLIPPER editor, Room 4524, Pan Am Bldg., New York, N.Y. 10017. Don't forget to include your full name, title and address.

Step 3: Add Local Travel Agents

Myra asked Pan Am employees across the globe to send recipes and details on local eating and drinking customs. Agents gathered 'culinary information' from nearby hotels and restaurants and, even, 'local gourmet groups'. Myra then tested the recipes in her home kitchen, replacing ingredients that were too hard to find and others that were 'not in accordance with American taste by reason of excessive sweetness, spiciness, and so forth'. Her recipes reassured a reluctant home cook through 'small changes in order to make them more acceptable to the American palate'. As she tested recipes, substituted ingredients and translated cooking techniques into familiar methods, Myra transformed local foods from forbidding dangers into tasty tourist attractions. She offered travel, not as observation, but as interaction, however limited and guided. 'In this atomic age,' noted Myra, 'our neighbours *are* the Patagonians, the Zulus, and the people next door.' Still, neither Patagonian nor Zulu recipes made the list of culinary stops on her around-the-world journey; Pan Am did not fly to southern Argentina or South Africa. 'The world of travel', Myra said, assuming the role of a Pan Am agent, is really about 'the observation of the life and ways of others'. You can only spend so many hours gazing at ruins or palaces; the real attraction is the 'spirit of inquiry'. Myra wrote in the same way she travelled, encouraging around-the-world tourist couples and home cooks alike to 'eat what others eat'.[21]

Her recipes referenced places and countries, but, less so, cuisines and cultures. If the around-the-world cookbook evoked an itinerary, then the recipes were souvenirs. The postcard is a visual reminder of a famous attraction and, similarly, her recipes acted as gustatory mementos.[22] Postcards sold views that mattered to tourists more than to locals. Myra's choice of recipes focused less on the daily meals of locals and more on what tourists might be more likely to encounter if they tentatively ventured beyond continental menus. In former colonies like India, this meant that dishes like 'Mulligatawny Soup' or 'Kedgeree' once consumed primarily by British colonists now became standard souvenirs.

Step 4: Choose a Familiar Ingredient

'Chicken', Myra said, quoting the famed French gastronome Jean Anthelme Brillat-Savarin, 'is a canvas upon which the cook can paint.' That aphorism hints at Myra's secret to world cooking: there were many recipes, but only a few methods. Any housewife with the loosest knowledge of Western cooking could produce exotic food by starting from a base recipe. A simple 'sautéed' chicken – the vocabulary remained French – could also be passport to India. Chopped onions, tinned broth, yoghurt and a few teaspoons of pre-ground spices oriented the dish to India. Added pineapple chunks, raisins and a splash of rum sent it to the South Pacific. '*Pollo, galinha, huhn, gai, Poulet, hens, kip, kykling, kana* . . . they're all chicken,' wrote Myra.[23]

The around-the-world cookbook removed recipes from their regional, cultural, historical or traditional contexts. Their appeal lay in the ability of home cooks to reproduce them, alongside other dishes from elsewhere, as part of a global food adventure. In the end, Myra's recipes, organized alongside those from other nations and its ingredients carefully reduced and replaced, seemed more familiar to American readers than to those who might otherwise have laid claim to those dishes.

Step 5: Travel Around New York to Collect Exotic Ingredients

Need ingredients to make 'Otak Otak – Fish, Straits Chinese Fashion'? Indonesian and Malay ingredients remained a tough find, but Edward Jurrjens imported a few. All one had to do was write to him at a post office box in Farmingdale, New Jersey. In an era when home cooks needed to contact importers at post office boxes, Myra knew that they would have struggled to find coconut milk, the base for her sauce for otak otak. She provided a substitute. Combine milk with dried coconut, easy enough to find at many post-war grocery shops. Boil, let sit, strain and discard the pulp. Flavour chopped fish with ginger and a pinch of pre-ground turmeric.

When Myra promoted home cooking, she was far less insistent on authenticity than she was when she later evaluated ethnic restaurants in New York. Miso may have been difficult to find and tasted strange, but when Myra recommended substituting beer, Japanese food became both familiar and exotic. When recipes preceded ingredients to American tables, Myra selected recipes for her cookbooks based on which flavours she could replace, approximate and domesticate.

Step 6: Serve Exotic Food at a Dinner Party

Myra adapted the otak otak recipe for the American dinner party. Place the fish and milky coconut in aluminium foil or parchment. At a time when Malaysia was just emerging from its anti-colonial insurrection, few American home cooks could source banana leaves, the fish dish's more

Advertisement for *The Complete Round-the-World Cookbook* (1954).

traditional wrapper. To spice up the dinner party: 'have each person open his at the table.' Smaller servings 'may be used as a hot hors d'oeuvre', she recommended.[24]

Myra omitted a great deal from her recipes, starting with the less-than-appetizing accurate translation. Myra provided the Malay name as a *soupçon* of authenticity, but her translation was bland: 'Fish, Straits Chinese Fashion'. In Malay, however, otak means 'brains'. The coarse-chopped fish, tinted yellow from the turmeric Myra required, and from spices such as lemongrass and chilli powder that she quietly omitted, resembles scrambled brains. In urban Indonesia, otak otak was common street food. Myra turned it into an exotic dinner party starter. What emerged was an around-the-world cuisine, flown metaphorically to the American table on Pan Am jets, simple enough to cook and easy to approach. Thus, Pan Am invited its passengers to send the airline a recipe 'that you'd like to introduce to the world'.[25]

How to Please your Husband

In 1958 Myra invented a typical American couple: Jane and Peter. 'Everyone enjoys good food – especially husbands,' and Myra decided to write a cookbook for new brides like Jane.

Before the war and before she went to work for Pan Am, Myra had many jobs. She designed modern furniture. She helped write a couple of dictionaries. During the Second World War, Myra directed, produced and acted in a training film for the American Women's Voluntary Services. Then, she began 'cooking and gathering recipes from all over the world'. Pan Am described her cookbook as a personal passion. The airline preferred to present Myra as a housewife serving up around-the-world flavours, rather than as a paid food consultant. Myra, too, stressed that she wrote her cookbook for 'the American housewife' keen to experiment with new dishes to feed her husband. Myra's husband was a 'seasoned traveller' and a war veteran who didn't mind 'tournedos one night and tufoli the next', explained Pan Am.[26]

Myra was a travel guide and a corporate consultant, but she travelled and cooked in the guise of an ordinary American wife, as eager to try new tastes as to please her husband. She never actually named her husband in her writing. (He was an attorney named Robert J. Schwartz.) Instead, she described the travelling unit of 'we'. 'We enjoyed these dishes abroad,' she introduced her recipes, 'and our guests have enjoyed them too.'

Myra offered her own history of how American couples such as Jane and Peter came to enjoy food adventures. After the First World War, they 'gradually' began to appreciate European, but still 'foreign' food. Soon, Italian and French restaurants opened across the country. After the next war, Americans learned, first as soldiers, then as tourists, to like foods from 'the entire world'. Exotic, spicy foods should be savoured at special occasions by couples, she believed. 'Foreign foods and foreign recipes', she declared, 'are becoming increasingly popular, particularly with young married couples who enjoy entertaining frequently and informally.'[27]

'Every bride wants to please her husband' – at the table. In Myra's first-person narration, Jane worked outside of the house, but she still had dinner ready when Peter returned home from his export-import business. The couple had guests, arguments and wine with dinner. Myra wrote the cookbook in the guise of Jane's diary of her first year of marriage. 'What a wonderful trip to Mexico,' Jane's diary (and the cookbook) began, 'the perfect honeymoon.' Home again, Jane wrote her resolutions in her diary: learn to cook and plan meals in advance. Market once a week. Learn about spices. Try new recipes, no matter how unusual they might seem at first.

'Since I've been married,' Jane wrote, 'I've learned that anyone can cook.' She was ready to show off for a friend who tended to 'play the great intellectual'. The menu for her first dinner party featured American classics with a French accent. While her guests debated between Mozart and Beethoven symphonies, Jane served seafood crêpes followed by chicken and dumplings in a wine sauce accompanied by a green salad. She made the seafood filling with tinned crab and a can of condensed cream of mushroom soup (a frequent secret ingredient). Dessert was banana cream pie.[28]

As she developed her kitchen confidence, Jane experimented with exotic flavours, accented by spices and herbs. She prepared recipes from Japan or Mexico for special occasions. When a client of Peter's came to dinner, she mixed curry powder and a cup of moist coconut with Italian dried pasta and two cans of cream of mushroom soup to make spaghetti curry. Frank Winslow, a neighbour's brother, had married a Japanese woman while on an army tour of duty – 'her name in English is, believe it or not, Peach Blossom.' When they came to dinner, Jane cooked sukiyaki with tinned bamboo shoots, spring onions, soy sauce and sherry. Myra's version of the Japanese dish was easy enough to make at the table in a chafing dish. 'I don't know where I ever got the idea that Japanese people eat nothing but seaweed soup and raw fish,' Jane noted in her diary. She enjoyed the saké Frank brought and Peach Blossom liked the chocolate roll for dessert. It was a 'simple but international menu' and a little gesture towards 'international relations'.[29]

When Jane cooked world food, she used the same pots and pans she used to make her everyday Western meals. Jane produced world food with chafing dishes, sauté pans and cream of mushroom soup. For female home cooks (especially those with day jobs), Myra promised ease and familiarity. She added spice to marriages but demanded authenticity only when she travelled and dined out.

How to Travel

'What a wonderful age we live in!' cheered Myra in 1965 to introduce her travel guide to Asia.[30] About a decade after she began her consultancy with Pan Am, Myra started writing travel guides that advised couples on what to eat and what to avoid while on holiday. 'Travel to foreign lands', Myra celebrated, 'has become a way of life for Americans.' Many travelled as soldiers to Korea and, later, Vietnam, but Myra, despite her own wartime experiences, thought only of holidays. Myra pushed the military realities of Cold War hotspots far into the background as she promoted Asia's comforts. Her guide to Asia, for example, didn't include a chapter on Vietnam.

Her cookbooks and guidebooks, together, advised Americans about how to adventure with food. The sights she recommended, meanwhile, repeated those in any other travel guide. Whether a potential traveller read *Myra Waldo's Travel Guide to the Orient or the Pacific* or, for example, John Caldwell's *South Asia Travel Guide*, they would still end up gazing at the sun-dappled white marble of the Taj Mahal.[31]

Tourism outside of Europe and America was easier than ever before. The hotels were even better in Asia and the Pacific than in Europe, Myra insisted. American chains, such as InterContinental and Hilton, offered a new first-class experience. There were 'fresh vistas and pleasures for American sightseers', but 'merely seeing the sights' was not enough. Food adventures, she advised, were the best way to get the 'feel' of a foreign land. Yet could tourists safely eat the food in local restaurants or from street stalls? Drink the water? What dishes should they eat and, just as importantly, which should they avoid?

Myra advised Americans on how to plan holidays that featured local foods. Begin with a visit to a Pan Am representative: 'it is the one airline that always keeps pressing for lower fares.'[32] Myra filled her guidebook with a list of 'hows', including how to pack. Pack 'wash-and-wear' fabrics and don't forget 'two folding *plastic hangers*'. Avoid the 'loud, splashy prints' that made tourists stand out ridiculously. Tourists would rarely need a white dinner jacket, the 'so-called "tropical" type of dinner clothes', and cholera belts were unnecessary. They now seemed little more than an invitation to prickly heat. The American army during the Second World War even skipped the cholera belts in its tropical kit.[33]

Eat out, Myra advised, but do so carefully and don't bother trying to sneak local foods like fruits or vegetables home past American customs. Instead, recipes made perfect souvenirs. Her guidebook advised travellers where to stay and, just as important, where to eat. Paid by Pan Am, she preferred InterContinental to Hilton. InterContinental, more than the Hilton, promoted local foods in its restaurants, but 'a Hilton hotel is the same all over the world', Myra warned. Even the Hilton's Tokyo branch offered only a hint of Japanese atmosphere and food. In Delhi, travellers could enjoy local tastes at the InterContinental. The Oberoi InterContinental offered six hundred opulent rooms – 'everything you'd expect in a luxury hotel'. Except a bar – the government hadn't yet decided whether alcohol would be permitted even 'for foreign tourists'.[34]

In some Pan Am destinations, Myra gently shoved her readers out of the hotel and into a select few local restaurants. Especially in modern, clean Japan, eat out, Myra advised. Sushi and sashimi were just like 'hot dogs of the Americans and fish and chips of the Britishers'. If you feel 'adventurous' and can overcome your 'prejudice against raw fish', then 'try *sushi* at Ozasa'. Sushi, though, was expensive, so sample just a few bites 'before you attempt a complete meal'.[35]

Myra urged more caution in India. The Western-style hotels where she advised tourists to sleep served 'just average' Western-style meals. After her visit with her husband to the Taj Mahal, Myra waited for lunch in a 'British' hotel. The waiters offered roasted leg of lamb and a clear consommé. 'My woebegone expression caused the Indian waiter to ask me if anything was wrong.' After some debate, he hesitantly offered the biryani that the waitstaff were enjoying for their lunch. She decided that the mixture of rice and spicy lamb, cooled with yoghurt, was 'to *memsahib's* taste, and yours too'. (She didn't explain what the staff ate for lunch after surrendering their food.)[36]

Indian foods might 'taste strange' at first bite. Be patient 'and give it a try'. Myra promised: 'within a day, you'll probably learn to like it.' Ingredients tasted different than at home. Lamb was actually 'heavily flavored mutton'. Pork was more fat than flesh. 'Forget beef', she advised; even if you can find it, it will be 'stringy and tough'. At least the chicken was 'familiar tasting', though stringy. If you like curry, however, you'll need 'an IBM computer to calculate the variations of curry dishes served throughout India'. Beware – 'mild to them may be hot to you!' The rice, a far cry from the American minute variety, was 'nutty' and the spices were pounded and ground fresh specially for each dish. 'The prepackaged curry powder you buy at home just doesn't exist here.' Still, tourists should sample those curries in more familiar 'Western-style' places. Calcutta 'jumps at night' and there are 'hundreds of Bengali restaurants', but tourists should stick to the tourist-friendly Skyroom or Trinca's.[37]

According to Myra, Jakarta, formerly Batavia, was a cramped, chaotic and noisy capital city. The old canals, a legacy of Dutch rule, were 'stagnant open ditches', she warned. There wasn't much to see but tourists could visit the Pasar Ikan fish market for its smells. Above all, in Jakarta, eat. The rijsttafel was the 'classic dish' and as exciting an attraction as you'll find in Indonesia. Myra said nothing about the troubled colonial history that journalist Rafael Steinberg recognized on his 1970 visit to Indonesia while drafting his book for the 'Time-Life' series. Myra's guide, instead, noted that a few hotels still served rijsttafel for tourists. Tempted by all the multicoloured curries and sweet, crunchy flavours of the 'forty or more different dishes', you'll take more than you can eat – 'but, then, who cares?' Leave room for the fruit, 'probably never again will you have the opportunity to sample so many different and fascinating luscious fresh fruits.' The durian's odour, however, is 'devastating': 'I wouldn't blame you if you didn't eat it.'[38]

There were travellers for whom 'nothing makes them happier on a trip' than chicken soup, roast beef and baked potatoes – even in Singapore. If you must eat at your hotel, the menu would be 'British', in other words, as Myra wrote, 'almost inedible food'. 'As for me,' Myra said, in the former British colony, 'I always have at least one Chinese meal a day.' She explained 'that part of traveling, part of having an open mind, and part of your sightseeing would consist of dining out, and seeing what the world eats'. However, avoid Singapore's street hawkers and their unclean foods, 'no matter how tempting they may seem'.

Myra's advice: dine local, eat cautiously, but drink from bottles. Tourists' hydrophobia – the deep and abiding belief that what locals drank would be poisonous to tourists – remained. Myra warned travellers to the tropics that they would undoubtedly experience a 'disturbance of the gastrointestinal tract'. Euphemistically, 'what it means, in plain language, is that you feel poorly, have various strange sensations in your stomach, complicated with a headache.' Myra insisted that germs, like food, were local. 'There are foreign organisms present in say Bangkok, for example, which are not present in Duluth.' She continued: 'in Bangkok, the local residents feel no effect from their own local bacteria.' The tourist suffered 'Hong Kong Belly', 'Bangkok Tummy' or 'fill in your own city and name'.[39]

On the one hand, Myra corrected older travel guides that condemned local people and their customs for tourists' illnesses, and chided tourists who upon waking up feeling unwell would declare it 'must be something I ate'. Sometimes tourists themselves were at fault when they ate too much and drank too much alcohol. Her politics of encouraging travel to unfamiliar places, to engage with local traditions and cuisines, led Myra to insist on waterborne germs as a fact of locality, not race or civilization.

On the other hand, tourists really did fall ill. Caught between her politics and her commercial goal of selling useful guides, she returned to familiar warnings to travellers in the tropics: avoid fresh fruit, except those like the mangosteen whose 'tangerine-like sections have an interesting taste'. She compiled a list of dangerous foods tourists must resist, no matter how tempting: 'no meringues, custards, ice cream, sherbets, butter, cottage cheese, raw fruit with thin skin, raw veggies, whipped cream, or unboiled milk.'[40]

When in Hong Kong, she warned, 'don't drink water from the taps under any circumstances.' In Thailand, 'it is best (to say the least!) to stay away from raw vegetables, raw seafood, etc., except in the first-class hotels and leading restaurants.' If you 'wander off the beaten path to small restaurants and coffee shops – stick to freshly cooked dishes and bottled soft drinks, Polaris water soda, or beer'. Iced drinks in Thailand were safe only in the 'best hotels'.

'India is going to require constant vigilance,' warned Myra. Despite 'colourful literature' courting tourists, the Indian government refused to admit that the food and drink just wasn't safe, and Myra was annoyed. 'India has a long, long (yes long) way to go before it becomes sanitary, at least to an American's way of thinking.' Sample the curries, but Myra's extensive list of rules ended up repeating the colonial-era distrust not just of Indian food and drink but of Indians. The water wasn't safe to drink and 'don't (please) ever forget it'. Even if the hotel management guarantees the tap-water, order instead a 'large bottle of mineral water, beer, etc.' Next, she turned to food: 'salad greens and raw vegetables are out – out – out.' Fresh fruit might be safe 'just so long as *you* personally cut them open, and providing you peel the skin yourself'. Throw away the tip of the banana. After reading those warnings, leave the hotel, eat local, but 'go easy at first with the spicy foods'.[41]

A previous generation of guides had recommended uncomfortable cholera belts, cumbersome medicine cases and largely ineffective water filters. Myra advocated taking Entero-Vioform pills once a day while in India. 'It tends to minimize your digestion (how's that for being delicate?),' said Myra. The brand name for the drug iodochlorhydroxyquin, Entero-Vioform was first introduced in 1934 as a cure-all for a wide range of travellers' ailments in the tropics. Myra recommended swallowing a dose three times a day to tourists suffering from 'Delhi Belly'.

The cure, though, was worse than the symptoms. Seven years after Myra published her guide, Entero-Vioform was banned in most of the world amid evidence that it could cause brain and nerve damage.[42]

How to Diet Round-the-World

After eighteen trips around the world, Myra admitted that food at home tasted dull. Even worse, if you were trying to diet, nothing could taste more 'boring' than a regimen of cottage cheese, shredded lettuce and skim milk.

In 1968 Myra published her *Round-the-World Diet Cookbook*. By then, Myra's celebrity had grown, and she now also served as a radio show host on New York's WCBS. By the 1960s Americans were increasingly concerned about weight gain, and diets, especially aimed at women, offered fast ways to slim.[43] In her diet cookbook, Myra questioned the superiority of how Americans typically ate. Too much food. Too many carbohydrates. Too much fat. Too boring. As a cookbook author – a tour guide across the world's tables – she removed strange ingredients and stranger tastes. She recast some of the foods that tourists encountered around the world as exciting and slimming. A few, like Korean kimchee, she encouraged her readers to taste and taste again until the spicy tang became pleasing. She ignored other dishes that were either too difficult to prepare or too alarming for American dieters, regardless of how important they might have been in local cuisines.

Exotic, edible and spicy foods from around the world would help Americans slim. Myra turned weight loss into a 'vicarious trip around the world'. With a healthy serving of portion control, margarine and sugar substitutes, the world's cuisines, she promised, could save bloated and bored Americans. Yet treating local food as a resource, an attraction and a diet didn't offer much in return to the postcolonial world. Rather, it reinforced many of the contradictions in the idea of around-the-world cuisine. While it invited diners to eat beyond their own traditions, it also seized local eats for the pleasures – and the diets – of American tourists, both real and virtual. Despite promises of liberal understanding, Myra often employed older stereotypes of Indians and colonial images of India to entice American eaters and dieters.

Myra praised 'Exotic, mysterious India', and warned not to be afraid of the food (only its safety, if you were travelling in person). The food was spicy, but not quite as spicy as one might think. Try a slimmed-down version of 'morgee korma', simply chicken and yoghurt. 'Simply' – she used that word a lot to render exotic foods accessible. In India, she advised the traveller, 'you are simply invited to dine at a certain hour.' Call it lunch or dinner, if you need to, 'but don't pass up the invitation'. For the dieter at home, she recommended curried fish. Sauté onions and celery in butter or margarine. Add yoghurt and three teaspoons of curry powder; the home dieter shouldn't worry about the specific spice mixtures of an Indian cook. Pour over strips of sole, flounder or haddock and bake – just 155 calories a serving.[44]

Continue your diet travelling across the Sea of Bengal from India to Malaysia – 'we're definitely in spice country!' To prepare 'dondeng', tamarind, garlic, onions and ginger spiced 'bits of steak'. 'It's all quite exotic' and 'highly spiced', like other 'warm climates'. Cross the Pacific all the way to Mexico where 'one of the high points of the cuisine' is the 'mole de guajolote (turkey in mole sauce)'. Mole, she explained, even included chocolate. Here was Myra's lesson for anything so exotic: 'Before you reject the thought, taste. Delicious.'[45]

How to Write an Encyclopedia

'Miss Waldo', admired the *Los Angeles Times*, 'literally travels as the Army does – on her stomach.' In 1967 Myra was on the road again, this time to promote her masterpiece: the two-volume *International Encyclopedia of Cooking*.[46] The first volume offered 4,000 recipes and the second, the glossary, included 20,000 terms. It remains a remarkably comprehensive reference guide to the foods of the world.

At each stop on her publicity tour, Myra, the home cook, wife, culinary tourist and 'food consultant for a globe-circling airline', prepared a dinner party from the *Encyclopedia*. The menu listed the courses alongside the page number of the recipe in her *Encyclopedia*. In San Francisco she cooked Chinese foods. In Phoenix a guest tasted hearts-of-palm salad. 'Delicious,' they declared, 'I wonder what it is.'[47] They could check the page number.

'Why go abroad to eat steak?' wondered Myra as she introduced her *Encyclopedia*. The core of the encyclopedia remained the '*haut* [*sic*] *cuisine* of France, and the tasty, homelike dishes of Italy'. The other dishes and vocabulary from 'eighty foreign countries' were, by contrast, souvenirs from her 'years of travel'. Readers, too, might recognize the dishes. 'Americans have thrown off their gastronomic inhibitions,' explained Myra, 'chiefly as a result of foreign travel.' Ever since she began collecting recipes for Pan Am, Myra – and a host of authors of other popular around-the-world cookbooks – insisted that tourists leave their hotels and that home cooks prepare something new. Amid the Cold War, in the era of decolonization, Myra urged American tourists to sample non-Western foods and not simply for the novel flavours.

Myra believed firmly that travel would produce understanding, if tourists were willing to taste some of what locals ate. The risks were minimal; there were always restaurants that toned down the spicing for Western palates and bottled water was available everywhere. But when cooking and tasting became food adventures on a whirlwind tour around the world, recipes became little more than mementos. Her cookbooks, especially her *Encyclopedia*, seem more like travel brochures or souvenir scrapbooks than genuine introductions into cultures and cuisines long dismissed by tourists as primitive and unclean. In the tailwinds of the Jet Age, Myra prioritized the knowledge she gathered through the experience of travel over the intricacies of non-Western cuisines. Her *Encyclopedia* represented a one-way guide, offering Western readers insights about non-Western foods (but hardly the other way around). Like a guidebook, this was a resource for curious visitors. The recipes she included were 'only those which are prepared with ingredients easily obtainable in our country'. The ability of the American home cook to prepare a dish at home was Myra's primary concern, as one newspaper noted: 'She writes her recipes first for practicality, second for authenticity.' The reviewer intended that observation as praise.[48]

Myra sifted through a career's worth of recipes and food notes. When she decided what to describe in her *Encyclopedia*, she highlighted those foods travellers might encounter because of their local importance. She also guided them to what they should taste and what they should avoid. Cook, taste and then travel. 'A try-out at home is a help to the prospective tourist,' suggested Myra. Be wary, though, of the durian and its 'repellant odor'. The fruit's local appreciation in independent Singapore, Malaysia or Indonesia as well as in wartime Vietnam was inconsequential.[49]

Through food, Myra had long blurred the boundaries between real and virtual travel, between the tourist and the cook. She published cookbooks and travel guides to help both real tourists and home cooks dine while circling the globe. Now, she began to write a guide to help diners travel all around the world without ever leaving her native New York.

How to Dine Out

For Myra, New York in 1971 offered a global buffet in which exoticism mattered more than French class. As she complained about the doyens of fine dining and enthused over cheaper, non-continental places, Myra politicized the choice for evenings out. She aligned herself with diners who craved nearby dining adventures and when she awarded her crowns, prices didn't matter; authenticity did.

A few of New York's French palaces earned four crowns. (She refused to award any restaurant five crowns, her highest ranking. No one achieved perfection.) La Côte Basque earned its four, but Myra had reservations. The service was 'competent and professional', but, if you weren't known to the restaurant, 'distant'. For its four crowns, you could expect 'generally quite good food' and a large bill.[50]

By contrast, she lavished praise on El Parador. The service was courteous, never distant. She particularly liked the 'chili bean soup'. La Côte Basque featured an extensive, expensive wine list; El Parador offered Mexican beers, 'the perfect accompaniment to this type of fiery food'. 'I have no hesitation', she decided, 'in recommending El Parador as a model restaurant.' Humble but authentic Chinese, Japanese and other non-Western restaurants bettered some of the city's Continental bastions. Màharlika earned three crowns. Its Philippine cuisine was interesting, the service welcoming and the atmosphere 'delightful'. Try the lechon.

Le Cirque, however 'handsome', earned only two crowns. Unless you were a regular, you were likely to be 'ignored'. Or you could save money and head cross-town to Tandoor, which served two-crown Indian delicacies like samosas, 'unsweetened pastries stuffed with meat or potatoes'. The eponymous tandoor chicken was excellent, even if the curries were 'toned down a bit for American tastes'.[51] At Tandoor, you didn't need to be a celebrity.

But that would help at Trader Vic's to improve the food and the service. On weekend nights, this Polynesian pioneer housed in the Hilton hotel was crowded, but Myra wondered why. Maybe it was the 'wildly expensive drinks'. She used the word 'Polynesian' with considerable caution. Trader Vic's food was, she scoffed, 'imitation Chinese' with 'imitation Malayan, imitation Hawaiian South Pacific, and so on'. The restaurant altered the dishes so dramatically that they no longer even resembled the authentic versions she had tasted on her own travels around the world. Trader Vic's was not even worth a single crown. You can have a 'much better and much cheaper Chinese meal' in Chinatown. Why not try my own family's favourite from the 1970s: Say Eng Look restaurant? Just like Myra, my family always ordered and enjoyed their green fish, 'strange looking but delicious'.[52] Myra gave it two crowns.

The Jet Age, of course, didn't last. By the time Myra published her encyclopedia and her dining guide to New York, the outlook for world travel had passed from giddy to gloomy. Amid the 1970s oil crisis and economic downturn, Pan Am announced losses and began trimming its schedule.

Even as oil shocks rattled the optimism of the post-war enthusiasm for mass tourism, Myra published the 22nd edition of *The Complete Round-the-World Cookbook*. In the revised edition, food promised virtual travel for couples stuck at home because of the added cost of travel. For those who could still afford to travel, her advice remained the same: 'Eat as much like the natives as possible.' For everyone else, 'in these times of higher-than-ever food prices', she offered new meanings for exotic foods. 'Because they're ethnic,' Myra explained in Pan Am's in-flight magazine in 1973, 'many of these recipes are moneysavers.'[53]

11

InterContinental

Meet Mr Big and Little Woman. Mr Big is a post-war American businessman. His business is now global and that demands travel. Once, it took 'a crisis as compelling as the Battle of the Bulge' to budge him from his swivel chair in an office tower in New York, Chicago or Houston. Today, Mr Big's secretary tells you that he is away in Colombia or Venezuela for a few weeks, combining business with pleasure.

Little Woman is also 'finally getting a break'. A businessman's wife, she once avoided travel to places where she confronted 'the rigors of a tropical climate'. Now exotic foods tempt her to travel. However, she remains reluctant to walk into a local restaurant to brave a confusing, strange-language menu, or to sip suspiciously murky water. Today, in 1954, the same year Myra Waldo published her *Around-the-World Cookbook*, Little Woman discovers that Caracas is only eight hours away in a comfortable Pan American plane. 'When do we start?' she asks.[1]

Mr Big and Little Woman were American, middle-class and imaginary. In 1954 the growing InterContinental hotel chain, a subsidiary of Pan American World Airways, dreamed up the couple as an embodiment of Americans on the move after the war. They were InterContinental's target tourists. The chain hoped to convince Americans like Mr Big to extend a quick business trip into a holiday and his wife to forsake home fires for tropical playgrounds. The chain's rooms were modern – comfortable, but not fancy. The trappings of the grand old colonial hotel disappeared. There were no servants or maid's rooms at the InterContinental, but there was a convenient shelf where tourists could rest their suitcases. The in-room telephone could call for room service or home to America. At the InterContinental, local water from the taps was purified, chilled and safe for Americans.

Restaurants were the centrepieces of the chain's business plan and marketing. Across the chain, hotel restaurants still served continental standards for squeamish travellers. Crucially, they also encouraged tourists to sample local flavours. InterContinental adapted recipes and transformed local food into an exotic tourist attraction. Little Woman could eat swiftly at a snack bar or more leisurely at an American-style grill. Even better, she could enjoy local foods prepared 'by a corps of international chefs'. Under the soft lights of the hotel night club, to the throbbing sounds of a Latin dance band, she might choose between 'lobster thermidor and marinated steak Argentine'. The chain spent as much energy planning the kitchen, bars and night-clubs, coffee shops and restaurants as it did the bedrooms where the first generation of post-war travellers would sleep.

Decades before open kitchens became today's domestic restaurant trends, they were an InterContinental innovation. They hinted at health and safety – each customer could act as a supervisor, watching and inspecting local cooks at work. The milk was pasteurized following 'standard u.s. procedures'. The kitchens were stainless steel. With safe water, but also flowing drinks, Mr Big and Little Woman asked the hotel only for 'aspirin'.

In the kitchen and at the restaurant table, InterContinental helped articulate one of the most enduring justifications of post-war development: tourism was good for everyone. In 1945, even as combat persisted across the world, Pan Am's Juan Trippe breakfasted with Franklin Roosevelt at the White House. The president asked the airline executive to 'aid international development' by opening hotels, beginning in Latin America. They shook hands. The next year, with the Second World War having ended only a few months prior, and with a $1 million investment, Pan Am launched the InterContinental Hotels Corporation.[2]

The chain began humbly with the renovation of a hotel in Belém, Brazil, an important stop for the airline's South American routes. InterContinental expanded, first throughout Latin America (Pan Am's original backyard) and later around the world, especially in those cities served by the airline's around-the-world flights. Through its restaurant and room service menus, InterContinental sparked tourism, especially by Americans, hungry and thirsty, to places new to the tourist trail. Everyone would win, the chain promised.

The chain spread, but it didn't fully own its hotels. Like Hilton International, its principal competitor, InterContinental depended on local partners. InterContinental designed the new buildings, managed the completed hotels and, with the support of American government development aid, augmented local investment. Spend dollars to earn dollars – InterContinental encouraged local entrepreneurs and governments to invest in hotels with sprawling restaurants and bars. The money could be raised in part from American loans. InterContinental and the Export-Import Bank, a key American source of development dollars, forged a partnership that endured from 1945 well into the 1970s. The bank, a government agency, invested on the premise that Mr Big and Little Woman would travel everywhere from Latin America to South Asia and spend their dollars. Their dollars would in turn flow back to the United States. As they became tourist destinations, countries would require manufactured goods, like air conditioners and stainless-steel kitchen equipment for modern, first-class hotels. This was a Cold War logic that assumed that tourist-led development – capitalism with cocktails – only had winners.

InterContinental imagined the hotel as mutual benefit for the diner and for the server. The hotel chain declared that it acted on behalf of American foreign policy but advertised its hotels as mini-United Nations. For Little Woman and Mr Big, this grand theory of tourism-based development meant cocktails served poolside by local waiters and hygienic, but exotic foods on offer in modern dining rooms. For those local waiters, though, this was logic that meant low wages after rounds of training about how to serve Americans. The inherent contradictions of hotel-led development politics unravelled when Mr Big and Little Woman checked in. The hotel promised them service and local food delivered with a smile. Behind the scenes, local governments often balked, and waiters and cooks resisted.

The Manila Hotel, 1949–54

'The hotel situation in Manila still leaves much to be desired, so far as service, food, etc. is concerned,' declared InterContinental's confidential report in autumn 1950. The sad condition was both an opportunity and a problem. Pan Am's around-the-world flight landed in Manila, but tourists had few choices of where to stay.

In the Philippines, the immediate post-war optimism had given way to Cold War slack, and the economy reeled. Japanese war reparations were scheduled to end the following year and government gold reserves had declined by more than 20 per cent in 1949 alone.[3] Rumours spread in the Philippine capital: the grand, ageing Manila Hotel might soon come up for sale. The landmark hotel was built in 1912, a monument to the American imperial vision for the capital city of their new colony. General Douglas MacArthur even kept a private suite there. When MacArthur and the Americans fled the islands, promising to return, the Japanese occupied the hotel. In 1945, as he toured the devastated city for the first time, MacArthur visited the hotel, partly burned in the Battle of Manila. In 1949 the Philippine government owned the hotel, which still showed the scars of its wartime damage.

InterContinental was expanding but was still perfecting its brand image. At the time, the chance to renovate a grand colonial hotel seemed sound business. Reopening the famed Manila Hotel as an InterContinental would mark a transition in world tourism, ushering in a postcolonial age of tourism-based development.

Mr Big and the Little Woman never would stay at the Manila Hotel. Instead, InterContinental spent almost five years fruitlessly pursuing a contract to rebuild and run the hotel. Initially, InterContinental believed that the Manila Hotel offered an enviable iconography. Its style reached back to an earlier era of grand colonial hotels, but American visitors would want air conditioning, a pool, beauty parlours, cocktail lounges, long-distance telephones and restaurants.

With national elections looming, the Philippine government seemed interested in divesting itself of the crumbling structure. 'In recent years,' the chain reported in 1950, 'the Hotel has become more and more polit-ical.'[4] Many in the Philippines resisted abandoning the iconic hotel. Selling or leasing this symbol of American colonial power back to an American chain seemed an affront to independence. Still, InterContinental rushed to submit its bid because, in a city awash in rumours, the chain learned that the Hilton International chain was also interested. InterContinental had the advantage of U.S. government connections. Visiting InterContinental staff could find a bed at the American consulate in Manila and the chain had easy access to government loans.

When InterContinental planned hotels, it aligned hotel financing with Cold War politics. American development policy discouraged the nationalization of assets like hotels in countries such as the Philippines. Nationalization hinted of socialism and communism. There were real dollars attached to anti-communism. Throughout Latin America and later in Asia and Africa, InterContinental depended on loans from the Export-Import Bank. Chartered with public funds in 1934 to facilitate trade with Latin America, the Export-Import Bank expanded after the war to facilitate loans that would allow non-communist governments to purchase American equipment and rebuild their infrastructure – including hotels fit for American tourists. The chain settled on a profitable finance plan for its hotels. One-third of the loans needed for new hotels would come from the Export-Import Bank. The local government or local investors would cover another third of the costs and InterContinental paid the remainder.[5]

InterContinental was building quickly around the world, solving the problem of space caused by the annihilation of distance. 'We need space for the flood of air passengers who wanted, and were able to see the world,' explained Peter Grimm, General Manager of Hotel Operations for InterContinental. Pan Am expected soon to trade slower, smaller piston-engine planes for jets. Grimm described 707s as the 'servants of all free peoples'. During the effort to acquire the Manila hotel, Grimm described InterContinental's vision to students training to be 'hotel men'. 'We must be leaders on the frontiers of cooperation among peoples,' he told the students. 'Peaceful armadas of jets are about to take to the skies, bringing our hotel industry – and our world – the greatest era it has ever known.'[6]

At InterContinental, at the dawn of the Jet Age, free enterprise and diplomacy merged. InterContinental reminded the Philippine Secretary of Finance: 'It has been the position of officials of our government that the development of tourism is highly desirable as a means of providing friendly countries with the u.s. dollars required for the purchase of American products.'[7] As the lines between Pan Am, InterContinental and the u.s. State Department effectively dissolved, the chain publicly promised universal benefits when nationalized hotels were privatized and began catering to American tourists. For wary Philippine politicians, InterContinental reassured that Philippine pesos invested in the hotel project would stay in the country to pay for local labour and materials. At the same time, to the Export-Import Bank, the hotel promised that every dollar loaned abroad would come home again 'for the purchase of u.s. materials and equipment'.[8]

The chain expected – and hoped – that the Philippine government would finally exit the hotel business. InterContinental's local agent leaked recommendations from 'reliable and informed sources' that a u.s. diplomatic mission led by Missouri congressman Jasper Bell would soon recommend the wholesale divestment of Philippine government assets, including the hotel. The Manila Hotel had become, according to the leaked report, a 'dumping ground' where the politically powerful could reward allies with jobs. InterContinental estimated that a stateside hotel hired one worker for each hotel room. By contrast, the Manila Hotel paid four hundred workers from the revenue generated by just 240 rooms.[9]

Publicly, InterContinental promised to retain current employees. Privately, the company officials planned a clean sweep of 'misfits, mostly employed for political considerations'. For almost four years, the hotel languished, and InterContinental waited impatiently for the government either to sell the hotel or open bidding for the hotel's lease. The problem for both the Philippine government and InterContinental was the gap between public promises of mutual benefit and private plans for firings. As a nationalized landmark, the Manila Hotel was 'run both as a hotel and as a government bureau', protested its manager, amid rumours of firings. The purpose was 'service, not profit'. InterContinental, though, expected both service and profit.

Finally, in spring 1954, the Philippine government at last sent a packet of photos advertising the grand hotel to possible investors. At the New York headquarters, InterContinental executives combed through the images. The empty, inviting lobby, lounges and bars suggested faded glamour and future first-class service. In the Continental Bar three servers, in white coats, stood ready by vacant tables. A bartender and a cook posed behind the bar in the deserted Bamboo Grill. The hotel was empty but prepared to serve. The government, quietly, promised the new managers a free hand 'to re-organize the personnel staff'.[10] In other words, the same waiters promising service in these publicity photos would soon be fired.

By the beginning of 1954, InterContinental submitted its bid but, by then, given the political tensions, had little hope of success or even of ulti-mate profit. 'We do not want to put any money into rehabilitation,' declared InterContinental and they suspected that Hilton, the other American

Winter Garden, Manila Hotel, 1954.

competitor, had the same reluctant approach. 'The local investors may do so,' and, ultimately, the government turned to 'local citizens' who owned the competing Bayview Hotel to rehabilitate and run the Manila Hotel. 'There the matter stands,' InterContinental admitted.[11]

InterContinental learned lessons in Manila that would guide its future development. InterContinental's staff on the ground were suspicious of local investors – even if those investors provided not only dollars up front but the crucial justification for a public relations strategy that cast hotels for American tourists as a benefit to locals. After the debacle in Manila, InterContinental came to believe that new was always better. Hotels like the Manila were too haunted by local histories of empire, war and independence struggles.

Lessons were learned in Manila. When InterContinental later planned hotels around the world, it started on empty ground, preferably the highest or most visible in town. The InterContinental style became globally recognized: towering buildings, balconies for every room and white, modernist architecture with hints of local crafts, all wrapped around swimming pools.

Victoria Plaza, 1949–56

'Latin America is busy building,' promised Pan Am in 1948, and in Montevideo, Uruguay, the InterContinental announced plans for the nearly $1 million Victoria Plaza InterContinental.[12] When it opened in December 1952, the luxury hotel was hard to miss, but easy for locals to resent. With 22 storeys it soared over the city, a metaphorical shadow of American power cast over Uruguayan independence and a very real shadow over the Plaza Independencia. Here in the capital city of a country that loved beef as much as Americans did, the Victoria Plaza was the perfect location to highlight the expanding chain's commitment to restaurants that provided safe tastes of something local. Customers could admire the sanitary, stainless-steel kitchen through a novel picture window. At the centre of its appeal to Mr Big and Little Woman, the Victoria Plaza promised steak – the best Uruguayan meat grilled to perfection on state-of-the-art American equipment.

Some 340 cases of hotel equipment and furnishings, imported from the United States, filled 358 air-conditioned rooms. A 'first-class' or 'international hotel' – and these two labels often meant the same thing to InterContinental – was different from colonial-era grand hotels. Even full room service was an InterContinental innovation. From any of the

Cocktail Lounge, Victoria Plaza.

Victoria Plaza's rooms, 'a guest will be able to call a waiter' with just the press of a button.[13]

At the Victoria Plaza, eat safe, but eat local. In the restaurant at the hotel, a mural by Uruguayan artists provided a local touch. Another wall was plate-glass, revealing the all-American kitchen. The InterContinental built modernity beginning with a 'complete stainless-steel' kitchen. Even when supplies remained scarce, so soon after the end of the Second World War, InterContinental spent $120,000 to buy 290 cases of stainless-steel kitchen equipment. However, a fire destroyed the valuable cases as they sat awaiting import clearance in Montevideo's custom house. If the chain sought to showcase local foods, local kitchen equipment was not an option. Hotel executives realized that a twice-built kitchen made good advertising copy. 'The Victoria Plaza is probably the only hotel in the world for which major equipment has been purchased twice,' boasted the hotel in its press releases.[14] American hygienic modernity would introduce exotic foods – that is, local (but utterly transformed) – to local waiters, foreign to diners.

Before the war, grand hotels allotted space to their kitchen, purchased standardized ingredients and only then planned the menu around warmed-over versions of continental classics. InterContinental 'reverses this procedure'. It surveyed likely customers: locals (with enough money to dine in a restaurant with prices pegged to dollars) and American tourists. Those surveys determined the weekly menus. 'No more buying a lot of pots and pans and making the trade like what it gets.' Hotel modernity meant more than towering white facades with shaded balconies that encouraged American visitors to gaze high across exotic cities, a tourist vantage point that reminded them of their privileges and American power. It also promised hygiene: clean kitchens and safe drinking water. Once assured that they were safe, Little Woman and Mr Big might then sample local flavours. InterContinental planned to offer 'native traditions of food and beverage but also to incorporate American know-how, efficiency in design, sanitation, construction and operation'.[15]

In the weeks before the hotel opened, the larders were stocked, the wine cellars were filled and the waiters were practising American serving techniques on each other. The 'native charm' was Uruguayan, but the manners and steel were American.[16] For tourists and many 'hotel men' who assumed that all South American food was chilli hot, the hotel chain produced startling new understandings of local foods through its questionnaires. On South America's west coast, 'the gourmet's taste ran to stews, ragouts, and fish'. Hotel kitchens there required 'storm-jacketed vessels' for boiling.

A Flair for Festivity

Every mealtime is an occasion at your IHC hotel where international delicacies, favorite American dishes and exotic foods of the native land provide an exciting choice of good things to eat. And every private party is an opportunity for the staff to win new laurels ▲ Beautiful public and private dining rooms, friendly bi-lingual service, superb cuisine served from immaculate kitchens and wine cellars stored with the fine liqueurs of many nations are characteristics of every IHC hotel.

The InterContinental brochure 'Ten Superb Hotels' advertised 'American dishes and exotic foods of the native lands' (*c.* 1950s–60s).

In Montevideo, and across the east coast, they craved roasted and grilled meats. InterContinental designed a charcoal grill 'of a type unknown in the United States'. Some 12 feet (3.7 m) long and divided into sections for low fires and for rotisserie, it sealed in the 'juices of chops and steaks'. The methods, meats and vegetables were Uruguayan; the technology was American; and the head chef was Swiss but trained in France.[17]

By the time he joined InterContinental and the Victoria Plaza as the executive chef, Gabriel Lugot had already forged a career in fine hotel dining. The 'austere Gabriel Lugot of the Waldorf', the gourmand Lucius Beebe once called him.[18] As the chef at New York's Waldorf Astoria, Lugot served saddle of spring lamb and some of the first Alsatian foie gras to arrive in the United States after the war. In Montevideo, he supervised local chefs as they grilled Uruguayan beef. 'In Montevideo,' reassured Lugot, 'never tell the waiter how you want your steak done. The South American chef has an uncanny ability to gauge the heat at which the steak will be at its peak best.'[19] The plate-glass picture window 'affords a complete view of Lugot's chefs at work' and of all that safe, sanitary steel.

For breakfast, if Mr Big and Little Woman craved a comfortable taste of home, the 'featured item' was waffles with fresh berries and cream.

Karachi InterContinental, 1956–64

InterContinental's director of public relations Max Hampton visited each new InterContinental branch long before Mr Big and Little Woman checked in. Like many who worked for the hotel chain and its parent airline, Hampton was a veteran. As an Air Force public relations officer during the Second World War, he learned to waterski in Guadalcanal and had his pocket picked in Cairo – good practice for work at InterContinental, a chain rooted in the military and aligned with foreign policy. 'I would like you to take care of our hotels,' noted his new boss at InterContinental, a retired Navy rear admiral. Like an officer planning a battle, the retired admiral, turned hotel executive, waved his hands across a map. 'We are building here.' His hands seemed to grasp the whole world, everywhere but the Arctic Circle and the Soviet Union. 'You will travel a bit,' he said.[20]

Karachi, a key stop on Pan Am's around-the-world flights, offered tourists few amenities when Hampton first visited. In the 'breathless heat of Pakistani night', the clerk at the hotel where Pan Am lodged its flight staff warned him to drink only from the bottled water the servant – his 'bearer'

– placed on the night table. 'My discipline was of steel,' and, necessarily so, 'I had been warned about Pakistani food and water.' At breakfast the next morning, hoping to avoid 'the germs which supposedly collected in teeming colonies', Hampton ordered only hot tea and toast.

'By noon,' said Hampton, 'I was writhing on my hotel bed.'

'Not awfully bright of you to put butter on the toast,' diagnosed the hotel doctor, unsympathetically.

When he had recovered enough to inspect the construction site for the new InterContinental Karachi, Hampton tripped over his bearer, asleep on the floor outside his room. Later, he witnessed his bearer 'carefully filling each' of the guests' water bottles from the tap.[21]

When InterContinental began construction, Pakistan had only recently won independence. In the midst of its second 'Six Year Development Plan', the Pakistani government, encouraged by the prospect of American loans, 'recognized the foreign exchange earning potential' of tourism.[22] Pan Am agreed: Mr Big and Little Woman might enjoy ancient historical attractions, deep-sea fishing and some of the best wild game hunting in the world. Pan Am projected jet air service to reach Karachi by 1960, so the Pakistani capital needed a 'first class hotel'.

In May 1956 the government paid InterContinental to begin planning. InterContinental envisioned a four-hundred-room hotel, a centrepiece of a vast, around-the-world expansion. Within a decade, InterContinental operated 33 hotels in 26 countries on six continents.[23] InterContinental typically employed military metaphors to describe its growth. When the company opened its Karachi branch, the chain insisted to reporters that tourism had entered its 'third strike phase' – the 'modern nuclear parlance' that the chain preferred. If the first strike featured visits to Paris and the second trips to slightly out-of-the-way places like Tokyo or Madrid, third-strike tourism sent Mr Big and Little Woman to countries such as Pakistan, 'backward regions where life is still splendidly picturesque', read a review of the new hotel. Outside, it was a 'baking' 95 degrees Fahrenheit (35 degrees Celsius). Inside, the hotel was air-conditioned. There were telephones in every room, private bathrooms and safe ice.[24]

The chain liked to remind local investors and American tourists alike that InterContinental began in the White House (rather than in the Pan Am board room). InterContinental 'really was the hotel arm of United States foreign policy'.[25] During the Cold War, the InterContinental offered profit as propaganda. 'InterCon both disseminates and displays the benefits of the capitalistic system,' it boasted. The chain banked heavily on

An InterContinental waiter serves drinks poolside, *c.* 1950s–60s.

ever-waxing floods of American travellers that Pan Am assumed would fly 707s. 'InterContinental is preparing for the Jet Age by making plans to extend its high standards of hotel operations as the revolutionary new method of transportation makes the world even smaller.'[26]

Once, a 'first class hotel' simply meant the 'best hotel in town'. Jets, though, could whisk tourists from Rome to Karachi in just five hours and, when they arrived, tourists expected 'the same standards of convenience, comfort, and cleanliness in all parts of world' – even in places like Karachi, where Hampton believed that germs lived everywhere 'but white-hot metal'. The chain declared: 'InterContinental was founded on the belief that the age of air transportation would break down the barriers of time and distance, which had prevented a free exchange of peoples of the world.' Yet InterContinental also promised to prevent the free exchange of germs. 'Even businessmen', the chain wrote, 'tend to shun outposts where the hot water runs cold, the cold water may be undrinkable, or the food too bacterial for tender Western stomachs.'[27]

A muddy pit when Hampton first visited, the Karachi Inter-Continental rose above the comfortably elite residential neighbourhood of Clifton. Its modern silhouette was visible even from downtown. From the hotel, guests in the lobby or the cocktail lounge could gaze over the pool to the Pakistani capital's buildings. A vertical garden, laced through a trellis, shaded the pool. Local fabrics inside and a giant white tile screen outside, pierced by windows and reminiscent of carved, Islamic room dividers, provided enough 'Moslem' elements to give a modern hotel 'an indigenous character'.

The chain expected as much profit from food and drink as lodging. 'It was not always safe to dine in some of the city's public restaurants – like all of them,' noted Hampton.[28] Reassuringly, as soon as guests arrived, they could look through glass partitions into the informal coffee shop and the more formal restaurants. In a city where InterContinental officials warned tourists against the restaurants, the hotel's offerings were impressively varied. The Nasreen Room, named for an 'exotic flower', featured an 'international menu'. For those interested in Pakistani food, try 'Cafe-O-Suroor', overlooking the pool. Behind the scenes, the staff dining room served 'the type of food preferred by local employees', spicier and a world apart from the other local food offered to tourists.[29]

Pan Am's around-the-world flights landed in Karachi after midnight and passengers walked into the air-conditioned lobby 'dying for drinks'. In Muslim Pakistan, guests could drink alcohol in the Chandi Lounge, the hotel's rooftop cocktail lounge, or the more intimate Meena Bar. Potable water flowed from every tap and machines offered shaved ice or ice cubes. The restaurant even manufactured its own ice cream.[30]

Tequendama InterContinental, 1953–63

'We have tried to design one of the truly fine hotels in the world,' proclaimed Wallace S. Whittaker, the InterContinental president when he inaugurated the Tequendama InterContinental in Bogotá. 'I think Colombians will be as proud of it as we are.' The lobby flowed elegantly into the dining rooms and lounge. The massive cocktail bar gazed through glass windows onto a profusion of orchids in the garden. The Tequendama InterContinental faced a park, with mountains looming behind.[31] For Mr Big and Little Woman, it might have felt like paradise. For InterContinental, the hotel was an achievement of engineering and planning. For its Colombian owners, the hotel became a scandal.

When InterContinental promoted the Tequendama, the chain recounted the struggle to open a first-class hotel in the landlocked, high-altitude Colombian capital. It advertised the hotel through a parable of American 'pioneers' armed with the power of dollars, triumphing over local conditions and corruption. Born from adversity, though, the hotel aged into open conflict. Given the advertising copy, antagonism between the Colombian owners and the American hotel chain seemed inevitable. The trouble began with cases of American whiskey.

The Tequendama was InterContinental's sixth Latin American hotel. Comprising four hundred rooms with reinforced concrete, it took a military-style campaign to build it. Berlin may have had its airlift (still on the public mind in 1953), but Bogotá had its 'furniture lift', declared InterContinental. The chain sent more than $1.5 million worth of American exports on 'the Road to Bogotá'. Riverboats hauled the largest pieces of mechanical equipment from sea level to the rail head at Puerto Salgar and then by train to Bogotá, 8,600 feet (2,621 m) up in the mountains. For one InterContinental executive who had served in Burma during the Second World War, lifting military equipment 'over the "Hump"' was a simple job compared to outfitting a first-class hotel in Bogotá. The shipments began with 660 tons of steel – InterContinental kept track of the amounts, not just for its accounting, but for its publicity. Then, water proofing, electrical equipment, pumps and a 'forest' of metal rods arrived. The hotel shipped $100,000 worth of radiators, and half that amount of ceiling tiles. 'The flood rolled on.' Pan Am Clippers flew 1,804 pieces of custom-built, American-made furniture to Colombia, enough to furnish the sixteen-floor hotel. It sent electrical clocks, fire alarms, pipe cutters and 40,000 square feet (3,716 sq. m) of plywood to make moulds for the modernist concrete walls.[32] Along the way, the chain suspected local thieves stole whatever they could grab.

Before the hotel could open, it required boilers to heat guest rooms to the perfect temperature for tourists. Forged in Pittsburgh, the boilers floated in freighters to the Colombian coast. Unfortunately, the river into the interior flowed shallow during the dry season. 'The Americans faced a desperate challenge.' Would the equipment – and the hotel opening – have to wait for the rains that would flood the rivers again? Would the South American jungle triumph over North American technology? The hotel's planners opted to haul the boilers on two flatbed trucks over mountains along winding roads. The first truck negotiated a hairpin turn. The second slipped on the edge of the cliff. The truck tilted. The boilers rolled off and down a 3,500-foot (1,067 m) mountainside. 'Again we faced the prospect of having to wait until Pittsburgh could send us another boiler,' reported InterContinental's engineers. Instead, in 'endless shifts', an army of Colombian labourers inched the boilers back onto the road and onwards to Bogotá. 'Today,' the hotel boasted, 'guests at the Hotel Tequendama enjoy hot water and heat in winter, air conditioning in summer.' Those two boilers 'symbolize some of the unknown difficulties that the pioneer hotel-builders had to overcome'.[33]

Orchids versus rebar steel – InterContinental's advertising narrative that contrasted American know-how with Colombian decor, American management with Colombian labour. At its peak, the hotel's construction employed five hundred Colombians. InterContinental promised to hire even more to serve the anticipated flow of tourists. The management, however, was an American import, just like the furniture and the boilers.

Following the now-standard InterContinental financing formula, the Bogotá branch depended on loans from the Export-Import bank – almost $3.5 million – and local investments. In Bogotá, the Colombian army's military pension plan was the local investor. The pension plan directors hoped to minimize costs and maximize profits, all the while negotiating Colombian nationalism and its suspicion of the United States. Antagonism was built into the very foundation of the hotel.

If Mr Big and Little Woman checked into the Hotel Tequendama in September 1963, they would have felt the tense atmosphere – especially if they ordered White Horse or King William American whiskey in the cocktail lounge. Earlier that year, the hotel purchased five hundred cases of each whiskey at the cost of 700 pesos per case. Between the order date and the delivery, however, the local price of whiskey dropped after Colombian customs authorities released confiscated alcohol for sale on the open market. The local investors demanded a rebate to reflect the new market price, accusing the InterContinental managers of profiting from inflated costs. 'There was no illicit dealing [in] the purchase of whiskey from U.S.,' declared the hotel manager, Gus Romea, defending himself not only to executives back in New York but to the hotel's local investors.[34]

Pension plan officials remained suspicious. The last-minute rebates, combined with above-market costs for American imports, seemed like kickbacks. By the end of September, the tension sparked by American whiskey imports exploded into accusations of misplaced funds. The American management and Colombian owners fought in court over 4 million pesos in 'material damages'. A dispute over the dollar cost of whiskey had metastasized into the 'Hotel Tequendama Affair'. 'Default at Hotel Tequendama

Denounced!' screamed the local newspapers and Romea begged the New York executives to respond.[35] They remained aloof. The chain's policy was to ignore accusations in local newspapers. This was, after all, an international chain, not a local hotel.

Inside the hotel, tensions were rising. 'Please bear in mind,' explained Romea to New York executives, 'we are dealing with a group of prejudiced, arbitrary men with no business experience, full of vanity and nationalism.' In October Robert J. Caverly, the vice president of Hilton International Hotels, quietly checked into the Tequendama. In New York, furious InterContinental executives wondered if the Colombian owners were attempting to play one American chain against the other. 'That would be a serious breach of an informal agreement which exists between Hilton and ourselves not to rock the boat while either one of us has troubles in a particular location,' they fumed. The Colombian investors, once dismissed by InterContinental for their nationalism and lack of business sense, had shrewdly injected competition into the quiet collusion between the two American companies.[36]

'This is a very dirty fight,' complained Romea to the New York office. 'I don't know how long I will be able to keep it away from another newspaper scandal.' Privately, InterContinental reminded the pension plan officials: 'Mr Trippe had been asked by President Roosevelt to undertake the establishment of a chain of hotels in Latin America.' Yet the pension plan's officers complained directly to the Colombian House of Representatives that Pan Am and InterContinental were 'taking out of the country the savings . . . of the Colombian armed forces.'[37]

In November, with the situation deteriorating, Romea complained that the hotel managers and department heads were 'insulted in public places by members of the Armed Forces or by guests who seemed to be directed to do so', he fumed. The pension plan, Romea protested, demanded details even for the cost of strawberries. Meanwhile, the emboldened hotel workers' union complained about conditions. 'Almost surely, they will obtain better salaries,' Romea fretted aloud to a meeting of American managers.[38]

Just ten years after the furniture airlift, the accord of dollars in exchange for service that lay at the very heart of the InterContinental model had broken down. The hotel 'is becoming shabby', management admitted. The restaurants and lounge 'look worn out'.[39] After a haphazard renovation, the once-open lobby now had a wall that blocked the view over the verdant garden and separated tourists from orchids and tropical splendour. Romea called it the 'wall of infamy'.

The building of the hotel recalled the Berlin Airlift. As it aged into conflict, managers thought about the Berlin Wall.

Ducor InterContinental, 1965–6

First opened in 1962, the gleaming white 209-room Ducor InterContinental towered 'majestically' – said the hotel – over the highest point in Monrovia, the Liberian capital.[40]

InterContinental designed the Ducor to become Monrovia's elite social centre. Films, dancing, nightclubs, cocktail lounges, restaurants and even the hotel's private beach were open to hotel guests and to nearby residents – at least those wealthy enough to pay its prices. In 1966 the hotel announced its Ducor Member Club. If they could afford it, the 'Liberian community' could enjoy the beach, pool and nightclubs.[41]

'The Ducor InterContinental hotel believes in serving its guests with some of the great dishes of the world,' the hotel boasted. Saturday luncheon featured Liberian dishes served poolside, and steak for dinner. A curry luncheon was poolside on Sunday. Wednesday advertised barbecue and every day (except Monday), the hotel promised 'exotic Chinese dishes'.[42] The inclusion of Liberian food, alongside other international cuisines, helped desegregate the Ducor – but that upper-class harmony still had to grapple with the reality that a first-class hotel required working-class service, and lots of it.

'We are particularly gratified to see more and more Liberians and our fellow Africans enjoying all the facilities of the Ducor,' said Ed Bouey, the hotel's public relations director. The new 'African Snack Bar', he hoped, would draw even more locals to the hotel alongside dollar-rich Americans. 'A related benefit', InterContinental claimed, 'is the mutual understanding of people of different races and nationalities promoted by intensified travel from abroad.'[43]

InterContinental was the hotel arm of American policy, but it also advertised its hotels as the mini-United Nations. The international press gathered at the Ducor and the Israeli ambassador hosted a party there to celebrate his nation's birthday, just one of many diplomatic gatherings at the hotel. The First Lady hosted a gala dinner. The Rotary Club met at the hotel; every Monday there was bingo. The beach was not just open, it was visually desegregated. 'A foundation has been laid for the development of tourism in Liberia,' declared the hotel as it snapped picture of 'these two young ladies', African women on the beach wearing bikinis. They posed

'What's on at the Ducor',
May 1966.

What's On
At the Ducor

FRIDAY	May 13, 1966
	ROTARY MEETS: at 7 p.m. DINNER:
	Chandelier Room Liberian Sea foods.
	LA PARISIENNE: Dancing to the "CESARES"
	Show PRINCESS AMINA
SATURDAY	May 14, 1966
	LUNCH: Liberian Dishes around the Pool
	STEAK NIGHT: Chandelier Room, $3.85
	LA PARISIENNE: Dancing to the "CESARES"
	Show PRINCESS AMINA
SUNDAY	May 15, 1966
	BUFFET DINNER: Chandelier Room
	CURRY LUNCH: around the Pool
	Dancing to the Cesares.
MONDAY	May 16, 1966
	BINGO: around the Pool, 8:30 p.m.
	TEENAGERS' JAZZ HOUR, 6 to 9 n.m. Dancing to the Heartbeats.
	Show PRINCESS AMINA
TUESDAY	May 17, 1966
	BRIDGE CLUB MEETS, Club Room, 7 n.m. Dancing to the Cesares.
	Show PRINCESS AMINA
WEDNESDAY	May 18, 1966
	BARBECUE: Around the Pool, 7:30 n.m. Dancing to the Cesares.
	Show PRINCESS AMINA
THURSDAY	May 19, 1966
	DINNER DANCE: Chandelier Room, Show PRINCESS AMINA
DAILY	**HAPPY HOUR:** 4:30 to 8:30 p.m.
	EXOTIC CHINESE DISHES: for Lunch, Dinner, except Monday
	COFFEE SHOP: 6 a.m. to Midnight.

HAPPY HOUR daily from 4:30/8.30 p.m.

next to a larger picture of Miss Yvonne Bryant, a Liberian employee at the Bureau of Immigration and Naturalization, wearing 'her native costume' at dinner. The hotel publicity also included a smaller photo of four white male tourists at the beach.[44]

Tourists from segregated America at the height of the American civil rights movement would have marvelled at the mixed-race world that gathered at the Ducor and across the world at the InterContinental. The Ducor had become, the chain boasted, a 'United Nations Palace'. Even the UN General Assembly with its boxy design and prominent waterside location might, at first glance, resemble the modernist InterContinental hotels.

In 1967, after the United Nations declared an 'international travel year', InterContinental promised that staying and dining at its hotel helped produce 'world peace'.[45]

The hotel's menus were crucial to the chain's plans to associate the hotel with the United Nations. Here in Africa, diverse foods also helped distance InterContinental from disturbing American domestic news, the violent attacks on African American protesters demanding desegregation and civil rights. The InterContinental served American barbecue (a food that, as many would recognize, had African American cultural links), Liberian specialities, Chinese menus and curry nights. Curry was certainly Indian, the hotel advertised, but still popular in Africa. The dish and the powder were exotic, yet practical. Add curry to mayonnaise, the hotel suggested in its free newspaper, which tourists and locals could read poolside. It even suggested how tourists and Liberians alike could become 'curry connoisseur[s]', authentically balancing the savoury tang with sweet and salty flavours. Placing Liberian food within the context of other exotic dishes like curry rendered it exotic, even in its homeland. Placed alongside American steak and barbecue, Liberian foods could be approachable for tourists.

Two bakers from Karachi InterContinental demonstrating baking at the Geneva InterContinental, 1966.

The hotel showcased Liberian dishes – 'native' food, the chain called them – and created expectations that tourists should eat them as part of their experience around the world.[46] 'I took a friend to dine at your luxurious Ducor Hotel,' wrote a guest in a letter that the hotel reprinted in its newspaper. His guest, an American businessman en route to Nigeria, was eager to sample an 'African delicacy'. Together, they feasted on 'dumboy with palm butter', pounded and fermented cassava warmed with melted palm oil. 'Dine at the Ducor' advertised the hotel to local elites, especially for 'Liberian Night Around the Pool', a buffet of Liberian specialities.[47]

The Ducor food service model reflected InterContinental's campaign to promote local foods as essential to the experience of a 'first-class hotel'. Across the chain, hotels promoted food festivals. Chefs travelled from east to west and west to east to 'feature national dishes and favourite foods of a particular country or locale'. The InterContinental Singapura hosted a week of French cooking, while the Hotel Tequendama advertised a 'Chinese Week'. The Frankfurt InterContinental sent chefs for 'German Food Week' to the Hotel Ivoire in Abidjan. The Geneva InterContinental hosted a Pakistani Week and its Michelin-starred 'Les Continents' featured a chef from Hyderabad for the 'Indian Culinary Week'. The Hotel Phoenicia in Beirut highlighted Danish food and Paris hosted chefs from the Phoenicia for 'Semaine Gastronomique Libanese' – Lebanese cuisine week. 'Culinary Festivals are becoming more popular in InterContinental hotels around the globe,' promoted the chain.[48]

Beginning in 1957, InterContinental also advertised its International Menus to celebrate United Nations Day. Across the chain's many hotels, tourists could choose 'Shish Kebab on a bed of Pilaff Rice, served with Tebuleeh Salad' from Lebanon or 'Kalbsgulyas with Noodles and Crisp Lettuce' from Austria. For dessert, why not try 'Pisang with Pineapple Goreng' from Indonesia and a 'Demi Tasse' of Kenyan coffee to follow?[49]

InterContinental's public relations department highlighted the local men – always men and always dressed in the clean, white chef uniforms normally associated with Continental cuisine – who produced 'native' foods and international menus. Freddy Yuppi, the Ducor's pastry chef, for example, posed with one of his extraordinary Christmas edible sculptures, an 'attractive artistic map of Liberia'. The hotel, however, focused, less on Yuppi's skill than on the sheer amount of material needed. His scale model used 5,345 sugar cubes, 39 pounds (17.7 kg) of granulated sugar and 7 gallons (32 l) of egg whites. The 126 hours of Yuppi's labour was just another jaw-dropping input. All that sugar and all that labour were part of a promise

Map of Liberia in candy, 1965.

of committed service. The Ducor's general manager offered a New Year's resolution for 1966: 'To encourage our staff to be conscientious workers.'[50]

In that encouragement, the model of the first-class hotel as United Nations crumbled. In the 'less developed lands of Africa and the Orient' InterContinental cast the training of waiters in ways that harkened back to an earlier, colonial-era language of civilizing. The 'help', the hotel wrote, 'had never worn shoes, much less seen the inside of a hotel, used knives or forks or had any exposure to Western customs, food or drink.'[51]

Behind the curry nights and publicity photos, the Ducor was a tense workplace and when the crisis finally erupted into the open, the Liberian government sided with the American managers against the local workers. The burden of development policy fell on the shoulders of cooks, waiters, bartenders and other hotel employees. They must 'make the Ducor not only an outstanding hotel in Libera, but in the entire West Coast of Africa'. Yet William C. Dennis, the hotel's American labour relations advisor, admitted that he sacked workers for lateness, rudeness, even sabotage. The Ducor, he discovered, had 'silent partners' – that is, workers who were pocketing bribes and tips from customers. The long hours of the night shift were especially plagued by 'absenteeism' and tourists complained that no one came to fix the air conditioning. On 1 May 1965 the hotel cried 'sabotage' when 250 workers simply walked out to attend an unauthorized labour meeting.[52]

Workers at the hotel, as they attempted to organize the Ducor Palace Hotel African Workers Union, threatened to take their grievances over worker dismissals directly to the Liberian president, William Tubman. The union elected officers in order 'to bring African employees of the Hotel together to discuss their common problems'. The InterContinental management, in response, complained about inconveniences to guests and claimed that the union was not 'legally organized' and, therefore, didn't even 'exist'.[53] Tubman proved unsympathetic to the hotel workers – on 17 May, in the midst of the labour conflict, he visited the hotel to attend a dinner in his honour hosted by the National Iron Ore Company.[54]

Tomorrow Night at Home

'Each job, no matter how seemingly insignificant' is a 'big one – world wide', wrote the chain's president Robert Huyot in 1967. The menu planner directed the food purchaser who turned to local businesses to supply frozen foods, packaged ingredients or imported bottled drinks, like American whiskey. The kitchen assistant cleaned, sanitized and prepared ingredients for the chef. The chef handed the completed 'savoury dish' to a waiter. 'No step can be left out and have a contented guest and a prosperous hotel.'[55] At stake was not just tourist pleasure but the development of a nation like Liberia and, maybe, even world peace.

Could a hotel really serve up world peace? InterContinental designed its hotels and restaurants for the heteronormative, middle-class couple like Mr Big and Little Woman. He played golf and worked for an oil company. She tended the home fires. They had enough money to travel but could neither afford nor desired the aristocratic snobbery that InterContinental associated with the bygone era of European empires and their grand hotels.

Instead, InterContinental offered them a modern American first-class hotel. At least as much as concrete facades, kitchens and restaurants made the hotel modern. InterContinental offered local foods as restaurant foods, the products of American, stainless-steel kitchens. It recast local food as an exciting attraction that liberal, post-war tourists, eager to realize the peaceful, prosperous potential of tourism, *should* eat. At the InterContinental, such foods were safe: gently spiced and free from bacteria and alarming ingredients. Eat local – and that was a historical departure in modern tourism – but eat at the hotel. Too squeamish still? Mr Big and Little Woman could still find American or continental favourites on the menu.

InterContinental invented, advertised and served the cuisine of foreign development. The InterContinental restaurant blended 'American know-how and conveniences' with 'local traditions and heritage'. Yet the model of local service to an American couple produced tensions and outright conflicts that not only threatened the magic formula of development politics but increased hostility to Americans themselves and to their local elite allies.

Myra Waldo and her husband visited the Ducor during its labour crisis. 'We sampled local specialties and many excellent ones.'[56] Waldo travelled around the world in the early 1960s, visiting each of the chain's hotels to sample its versions of local foods. She collected, revised and tested the recipes for home cooks. She distilled the labour needed to staff a hotel into the *Inter-Continental Gourmet Cookbook* (1967). Little Woman should expect service abroad, but could also cook exotic foods herself at home, Myra suggested.

The cookbook, a culinary brochure for the hotel chain, documented the transformation of the post-war hotel, its alignment with American development policy and its culinary evocation of the United Nations. She ignored its conflicts. The 'mid-century revolution' led by InterContinental discarded the 'great, ornate, palace-style buildings' of yesteryear, Myra explained. The 36 hotels in the chain were 'modern, efficient edifices' designed with air conditioning, potable water and visual and culinary reminders of wherever 'an ever-increasing group of travelers' found themselves.[57] Instead of vast 'hotel dining rooms', InterContinental offered restaurants that 'featured the very best of international cuisine highlighted by local dishes'. Tourist food had changed and with it, home cooking.

The American home cook – Little Woman – could use Myra's cookbook as a 'farflung menu' to select a dish she might soon taste on holiday at an InterContinental. Or she could 'whip it up for tomorrow night at home'.[58]

12

Hilton and Trader Vic's

Nina Khrushchev was visiting the United States in 1959 with her husband Nikita, the Soviet premier. Americans were curious about what the wife of the communist leader would purchase and eat. It was front-page news when she decided to lunch at Trader Vic's, the popular restaurant at Chicago's Palmer House Hilton hotel. Reporters smirked at the expense. The restaurant offered a taste of tropical Polynesian leisure to this visitor from the worker's paradise. She dined on hamburger Hawaiian (with a pineapple and fried egg) and papaya on ice.[1]

During their American tour, the Khrushchevs and their travelling party spent plenty of hard currency at various other Hilton hotels and their Trader Vic's restaurants as well. In Washington, the Soviet party dined at the Statler Hilton, where the hotel advertised a 'passport to Fine Dining'. The menu replicated a passport on its cover, with the Hilton crest replacing the American seal. Inside, it featured around-the-world dishes from across the Hilton chain. (The hotel had checked, to be sure: there was no law against 'simulating' a passport.) To complete the 'gimmick', as the hotel called it, the Statler offered an 'Around the World Festival of Drinks', one drink associated with each of the international hotels. The Havana Hilton had recently opened – just months before the Cuban Revolution began. In Washington, the Soviet visitors could sample the Havana Hilton El Trocadero, made from Cointreau, grenadine and Italian and French vermouths.[2]

Conrad Hilton, the chain's founder and president, hosted Khrushchev, his wife and their travelling party at his hotels; he also met the Soviet premier at a luncheon in San Diego. But he abhorred Soviet ideology. In fact, Hilton imagined his hotels and its restaurants as worldwide bastions of anti-communism. They provided jobs for locals, and by catering to tourists with American dollars to spend, he believed they could promote free markets and cultural exchange. He planned hotels around the world to welcome American tourists to some of the very countries on the frontlines of the Cold War and post-war conflict zones, from Tel Aviv to Addis Ababa. By 1964 the Hilton chain operated 34 domestic hotels and 26 international hotels, and about a quarter of the chain's 49,298 rooms were outside of the United States. Conrad boasted that Hilton chose its international locations because 'there is a job to do there.'[3]

In service of that aim, Hilton provided the air-conditioned rooms and Trader Vic's served up food and cocktails. Victor 'Vic' Bergeron, the former bootlegger and saloon keeper in Oakland who founded Trader Vic's, didn't outwardly share Hilton's anti-communist zeal, but he knew a good business deal when he saw it. The Hilton and Trader Vic's brands grew together, and massive tiki heads guarded the towering, white modernist facades of Hilton hotels everywhere from London to Puerto Rico. Together, Hilton and Bergeron built a worldwide hospitality empire made of concrete and palm fronds.

From the Second World War, when Vic began selling rum illegally to the armed services in the Pacific, until 1967, when Conrad sold his international hotels to Trans World Airlines, Hilton and Trader Vic's promoted the invented foods and drinks of Polynesia – fantasy cuisine evoking the exotic holiday and lush with tropical fruits and resplendent service. But tourists' endless demands for service and their engrained suspicion of local peoples and their foods meant that the 'free exchange' between 'free peoples' that Hilton promoted as an antidote to communism could devolve into hostility. Some of the hotel branches were swept up into geopolitical conflict even as the hotels – thanks to the success of Trader Vic's – delivered boozy parties.

The Little People

Before a September San Diego luncheon where Conrad met Khrushchev, he prayed that the Soviet leader would seem at least '1% phony'. Conrad later confessed to a conference of public relations professionals that Khrushchev 'frightened' him, and not because of his eloquence ('which was great') or his power ('which was greater'). Conrad realized, he said, that 'if we are to beat him, if we are to survive', the Soviets must be matched step for step. As he built hotels around the world at the height of the Cold War, Conrad found himself thinking about the fall of the Roman Empire. 'The time of the barbarian had come.'[4] Juan Trippe imagined his Pan Am Clippers in a race of tourist jets against bombers. Conrad thought of the competition between his hotels and communists.

Back in 1950, as Hilton plotted his chain's international expansion and planned the hotel menus, he was already reflecting on the fall of empires. 'After slumbering another eight centuries, the godless hordes are on the march again,' he wrote in the company magazine. 'Should there come a time when this communist flood overwhelms these free nations,' Conrad continued, 'we must be prepared to stand alone.' Two years later, he complained that while 'half-a-hundred nations of Asia and Africa have achieved self-government', somehow, the communists got the credit.

So Conrad called upon God for Cold War strength, including in a prayer that he transcribed and published in 1952: 'America on its knees: not beaten there by the hammer and sickle.' He transcribed and published his prayer. He imagined a gangly, kneeling Uncle Sam, top hat by his side, fingers clasped, beseeching the heavens for strength to combat communism. Hilton sent copies to anybody who wanted them. A church secretary in Chicago asked for copies; Conrad sent eight hundred.[5]

Conrad, a devout Catholic, was born in 1887 in the small town of San Antonio, New Mexico. He was drawn to conservative Republican politics at an early age. In his twenties, he served as a Republican representative in the New Mexico legislature, and later joined the army, serving in France during the First World War. During the Great Depression, he both purchased and opened a series of hotels in Texas, building a hotel chain that eventually expanded nationally. After the Second World War, Conrad bolstered the Hilton brand by purchasing the Statler Hotel chain, one of the nation's largest, as well as landmark domestic hotels, including the Palmer House in Chicago and the Waldorf Astoria in New York.

In 1948 Hilton launched its international brand, and opened its first location outside the continental United States the next year: the Caribe Hilton, in Puerto Rico.[6] During the 1950s and '60s, the chain went on to negotiate contracts for outposts in, for example, Tokyo, New Delhi, Bangkok, Cairo, Istanbul and Athens. He wanted to draw tourists to Cold War hotspots, using leisure travel to combat communism. In the fight against world communism, faith and hotels mattered.

For Conrad, international hotels were the business side of his anti-communist crusade: God's houses, but with beds instead of pews, and tropical-themed bars and restaurants instead of chapels. When opening the hotel in Istanbul in 1952, Hilton admitted that, however beautiful the city's sights, it might seem an unlikely choice for one of the first branches of a new international hotel chain. 'In Turkey', Conrad wrote, the government was committed to 'the absolute elimination of Communism'. So he built a hotel with the Turkish government as a partner. When communists took an 'Asian detour', Hilton followed, planning hotels for Djakarta, Bangkok, Colombo, India and Japan. In West Berlin, walled in by communists, he opened a Hilton. He joked that he might one day open a Hilton in Moscow as a capitalist oasis in the Soviet capital. However, he said, it will 'not be called the "Comrade" Hilton'.[7]

In 1963 Conrad planned to take an around-the-world tour of his hotels that would include thirteen hotel ground-breakings or openings on a route from London to Tehran to Tokyo. Then, he would cross the Pacific to Honolulu, where he invited journalists to sip drinks in the Hilton Hawaiian Village. The Dutch Prince Bernhard helped open the hotel in Rotterdam. All these hotels, all those drinks and luncheons, Conrad assured guests at the hotel openings, were politics through profit. His hotels would 'circulate good people everywhere around the world'. Ideally, tourists would meet locals, likely those serving them, and tourists and locals would share 'knowledge, wisdom and culture'. In Athens Conrad reminded reporters that Christianity, too, began in the stable of an inn.[8]

Many Americans could recognize Conrad Hilton on sight. As a business leader, he had become a celebrity. His energetic travels around the world seemed to capture the very essence of the post-war American zeal for both tourism and business. He lectured frequently to business groups about this new industry of first-class hotels. InterContinental, the other massive post-war American hotel chain, sold authenticity with a side of hygiene, promising safe tastes of local foods – all in keeping with its liberal politics of peace through tourist encounters. But Hilton presented his business pursuits as more zealously anti-communist.

'When we were children, the world was a great house', he told San Francisco's business elite gathered at the Commonwealth Club in 1956.[9] He used the metaphor of the house often. The house's owners were 'white men', he explained, this time to a national convention of public relations professionals. The 'servants' quarters were occupied by the yellow men, black men, even a handful of red men', Hilton told the Los Angeles Rotary Club. Post-war, he continued, the house walls had crumbled, and the 'little people' demanded recognition.

Conrad didn't much care for imperialism, but he believed that the 'little peoples of the earth' were not always ready for self-government and so their new countries became breeding grounds for communism. To counter the influence of 'communist gangsters' in the ruins of empire, Conrad announced a 'foreign policy for hotels'. He promoted tourism to bring money to local economies and foster support for the free market. Guns had their role, but hotels beckoned travellers with dollars.

Conrad frequently quoted a statistic: for countries and former colonies recovering from the Second World War, tourism was second only to coffee exports as the greatest dollar earner. In his business plan, the hotel was not 'colonialism' or even a refuge for 'big rich Americans' but a 'business fellowship'. He promised that while Hilton would supply managerial 'know how', only local labour and 'native supplies' would build his hotels.[10]

Hotels, Conrad believed, could be places of exchange where tourists could pleasurably experience local culture as well as national 'personality'. Yet Conrad's anti-communist politics met the imperatives of service. After all, 'the ultimate purpose of a true hotel is to serve' guests, Conrad admitted.

He liked to think of capitalism as 'fellowship' and race relations as hospitality offered by locals to Americans.[11] He envisioned Americans on their knees in prayer, but also at the bar, drinking and partying. Tourists would stay at Hilton hotels and in return for money they spent, they would expect hospitality. When Hilton partnered with Victor Bergeron to open Trader Vic's, they added party rooms to the imperial mansion, but the legacy of the servant's quarters remained.

Tiki Gods Stand Watch

Victor Bergeron's Polynesian dining empire began humbly. During the Great Depression he owned Hinky Dink's, a hunting-themed dive bar in working-class Oakland, California. The son of French immigrants, he suffered throughout his childhood from a recurring case of tuberculosis that eventually required amputating a leg. That kept him from being drafted during the Second World War, and later made him seem like a seasoned pirate to customers and restaurant reviewers: Vic blamed sharks for his losing a leg.[12]

He came up with the idea of Trader Vic's while on holiday. In the Caribbean, Vic sipped a daiquiri at Le Floride, then Havana's leading hotel, and dreamed of running something grander than his own ramshackle bar. Back in Oakland, he visited local tropical-themed bars and restaurants, most notably Don the Beachcomber, which later also developed into a massive tiki chain. For new food ideas, he turned to one of his cooks, Paul Wong, who acted as Vic's guide to Chinese American restaurants across the Bay Area, where Vic sampled dumplings and spareribs.[13] Vic recast that migrant food, which many white Americans still considered exotic but cheap, as an expensive tourist pleasure redolent of the faraway tropics. He sweetened Chinese American dishes, garnished them with pineapples, and rebranded them as 'Polynesian'. And he paired them with potent rum cocktails.

Vic discarded Hinky Dink's original hunting theme décor and replaced it with tropical souvenirs. He nicknamed himself 'Trader Vic', suggesting that he was one in a long genealogy of Pacific traders selling rum to Indigenous populations.

During the Second World War, Vic did sell booze that made its way across the ocean: as thousands of American men travelled to bases in the Caribbean and even more island-hopped across the Pacific, Vic worked with an officer on a nearby base in California as part of a Pacific bootlegging ring, shipping out crates of gin, bourbon, whiskey and, especially, rum. When he learned that their operations were well-enough known that officer's clubs across the Pacific were jokingly called 'Trader Vic's', Vic was thrilled. He was already scheming about a post-war Polynesia and booze-themed worldwide chain that would bring tourists to former battlefields and former colonies.[14] He was eager to expand. He briefly owned an outpost in Honolulu and, in 1949, he opened The Outrigger, a Polynesian-themed bar and restaurant in Seattle's Benjamin Franklin Hotel, a branch of the Western Hotel chain (later renamed Westin). His dreams of an around-the-world Trader Vic's chain, however, would have to wait for his partnership with Hilton.

Vic yearned to expand his business, but he didn't have the capital to do it himself. Hilton, though, had plenty. Conrad Hilton opened a Trader Vic's first in his flagship Beverly Hill's hotel in 1955. Soon he expanded the restaurant chain to the Palmer House in Chicago. In 1957 Conrad guaranteed Vic a yearly salary of $65,000 and paid $2 million to licence the brand name across the Hilton chain. In return, Vic promised to decorate and manage new restaurants and train the staff.[15] Together, they opened a worldwide chain of some of the most profitable hotel restaurants of the era.

The two men had a rocky working relationship. Privately, Conrad disliked Vic, who, in turn, posted Conrad a stream of complaints, especially when Hilton's other tropical-themed restaurants appeared too much like a Trader Vic's. Personal frustrations aside, Conrad knew that the Hilton brand was wrapped up with Trader Vic's. He understood that the Polynesian-themed restaurants generated more profits than the haute French cuisine that still dominated global fine dining. The restaurants helped his modernist hotels feel welcoming to any tourists with money, and they earned tidy profits to boot.[16] The food was plentiful – but not cheap – and the alcohol flowed in crowded rooms. In August 1960, King Wong, the manager at the Beverly Hilton's Trader Vic, reported a $105,033.31 monthly revenue. Overall, Trader Vic's earned Hilton about $5 million a year. For that money, Conrad was willing to be 'subjected to Vic's tirades'.[17]

'Napoleon said an army travels on its stomach,' and the 'tourist army', boasted Conrad Hilton, dined at Trader Vic's. At the Statler Hilton in Washington, at the base of the modern, white, boxy hotel, 20-foot-high (6 m) sculptures flanked the entrance to Trader Vic's. 'Tiki Gods stand watch,' advertised Hilton. The doorway itself was designed to match a thatched Polynesian hut. The windowless rooms inside mashed together decor from various Pacific and Asian cultures: Japanese fishing balls, shark jaws, spears and shields covered the walls. Twigs, matting and Chinese wood decorated the ceiling. Visitors could feast in the 'Captain's Deck' room or sip strong rum drinks in the Mai Tai and Puka cocktail lounges. Vic designed his restaurants as culinary rest-and-recreation, R&R for a Cold War generation, 'to help us relax and have fun'. Polynesia and its foods offered the 'abundance, laughter and joy' that a 'war-torn civilization' needed, said Vic.[18]

Reviewing another location, one reviewer praised the excess 'that the Polynesian restaurants do so well', and described her pineapple daiquiris.[19] Across the chain's locations, the fruit was tropical, the rum Caribbean and

Tiki gods stand watch, murals by Eduardo Castrillon, Statler Hilton, Washington, DC.

Zouzou and keeper arrive
for the opening of the
Caravan Tent, December
1962.

the decor was fantasy Polynesian. The menu completed the dash around
the world with updated Chinese American standards. The signature starter,
crab Rangoon, featured crab and cream cheese in a fried wonton. For a main
course, diners might order Cho Cho: flank steak marinated in soy sauce
and sugar, skewered and grilled.

During the Cold War, the Jet Age and in the headwinds of imperial
change in Asia and the Caribbean, Trader Vic's was a formula that worked.
Hilton opened outposts of the restaurants from Havana to London.
Even in Hilton hotels that, like the Cairo branch, didn't open Trader
Vic's, Polynesian foods, tiki drinks and the allure of the everlasting party
dominated the menus.

In 1962 two camels, Zouzou and Lucky, walked 15 miles (24 km) to the
Nile Hilton. When the Nile Hilton opened its Caravan Tent nightclub,
it enticed tourists by evoking Egypt's exotic appeal. The American hotel
recalled older and imperial fantasies about the Arab world, in particular
about the desert, nomads and harem women. Once inside the club, the two
camels calmly chewed their cud as the 'bread boy and coffee girl' circulated
around the tented room. A costumed waiter offered guests kharoub, 'an
Oriental drink' made from carob and traditional for Ramadan. Hilton
served it in 'a large oddly shaped container' as an exotic nightclub taste.

Human guests entered through a beaded screen and sat on camel saddles around low tables made from brass trays.

'The camel gimmick worked,' the hotel's manager delighted. He promised an 'authentic Oriental atmosphere', accented by bric-a-brac ripped from its original purpose. (The tent might have seemed 'typical' but would not have been intended for tipsy parties.)[20] During the day, the Caravan Tent served lunches to the tour groups before they departed for the pyramids. When they returned in the evening, the club offered Polynesian-style cocktails. The Nile Hilton Sphinx, the hotel's signature cocktail, mixed dry gin, orange juice and imported vermouth. Couples could try the Cleopatra's Love Cup made with Caribbean rum.

Polynesia at the Hilton became synonymous with boozy leisure and tourist food. Its cocktails blended easily with the Egyptian exoticism on offer at the Nile Hilton. At Gawharet El Nil restaurant, tourists could enjoy safe Continental classics, Trader Vic's-style Polynesian dishes and a few local tastes, washed down with rum drinks. Pigeon Fereek, the menu explained, featured cracked wheat; steak Diane, which was flambéed tableside, needed no explanation other than 'mignonettes of beef'.[21] The Nile Hilton offered a choice of places to drink. The Ibis Bar and Safari Bar gestured to Egypt and Africa. The Cabana Club turned to Polynesia and the Tropicana Club advertised live entertainment, Egyptian coffee and tropical mixed drinks.

Polynesian food spread across the Hilton. In fact, when Hilton opened other Polynesian restaurants under other names, Vic was annoyed, protesting that Conrad was using his successful formula without paying for it. Soon, there were plenty of Trader Vic's copycat and competitors, and not just at the Hilton. Sheraton, for example, which operated hotels throughout the United States and a handful in Canada, advertised its Ports o' Call and Kon-Tiki restaurants.[22]

When Hilton opened a West Berlin branch in 1958, the hotel's El Panorama rooftop club was another Trader Vic's lookalike, a tropical getaway from the Cold War. The opening came amid renewed threats from Khrushchev to seize the capitalist enclave in the centre of communist East Germany. Up on the roof, though, Hilton guests could indulge in drinks such as 'Pirate's Delight' or 'Tropical Itch', while sampling 'exotic delicacies' under palm fronds and banana bunches. The 'Suffering Bastard' could have been a riposte about life on the other side of the Berlin Wall.[23]

Four years later, the West Berlin Hilton hosted 250 American armed forces club managers for lessons on everything from menu covers to buffets.

They tasted 24 wines. Waiters learned how to serve meals to help 'create even better relations between American service personnel running and using these clubs' and the locals 'of the host country' who worked in them. On the other side of the world, the El Panama Hilton invited army officers of the Jungle Warfare Training Center in the Canal Zone to demonstrate to hotel guests how soldiers 'are taught to survive in the jungle terrain'. Tropical warfare became an exotic hotel party. In the nightclub, guests sampled 'jungle tidbits': monkey meat, boa constrictor and plenty of tropical fruits.[24] Tiki had gone to war.

Let the Drinker Beware

Hilton opened Polynesian-themed restaurants and bars in virtually all its hotels and, as often as possible, did so with an outpost of Trader Vic's. Hawai'i, though, was a problem. In 1950, early on in his expansion and before his contract with Hilton, Vic had opened a branch of his Polynesian bar in the middle of the Pacific. He soon sold it, and the Honolulu Trader Vic's remained a tumbledown independent. In 1960, as Hilton prepared to open Hawaiian Village, a sprawling tropical themed resort, he and Bergeron tried to buy back the extant Trader Vic's, but to no avail.

Yet tourists staying at the Hilton in Hawai'i still expected a Polynesian party with flower necklaces, rum drinks like the 'scorpion', roasted pig and, perhaps, like Edith James before them, a taste of poi. Hilton couldn't call what the hotel offered Trader Vic's, but the Hawaiian Village could – and did – offer a special, nightly, luau, as the highlight of the Polynesian menu. The luau was, in addition, an attraction across the entire Trader Vic's chain.

At the Hawaiian Village resort, the luau began with an hour-long cocktail party where guests nibbled barbecued shrimp, wontons and rumaki – Trader Vic's standard fare. They sipped the okolehao punch, which Hilton promised was 'authentic', and an 'island favorite'. In fact, it had been heavily modified for tourists: okolehao was traditionally made with fermented ti plant roots, but at the Hawaiian Village, just as at Trader Vic's, Caribbean rum substituted for the Indigenous drink.

Food and travel writer Clementine Paddleford described her luau at the Hilton Hawaiian Village. She ate with her fingers, as she was encouraged to do, but longed for a fork and knife to eat the filet mignon. The pig was roasted with hot lava stones in an underground oven. The poi – mashed taro, she explained – was traditional, but amid all the tropical flowers, Paddleford thought it looked like an unappealing grey, semi-liquid mass.

'You may not care too much for the food, but everyone loves the Hawaiian floor show,' Paddleford decided.[25]

At the Park Lane Trader Vic's in London, too, the music, palm fronds and alcoholic leisure all recalled the image of Polynesia as a primitive paradise of sensuous women, Indigenous hospitality, abundant fruits and foods and luxurious tropical warmth. 'Curl up in the shadowy depths of our Tonga Queen's chair and watch the gardenia floating in your cocktail,' Hilton and Trader Vic's invited. Filtered light danced through the rattan screens and soft music 'murmurs like the song of the Islands'. In the advertisement, a white woman relaxed in a cane chair and sipped her rum drink. 'Trader Vic knows how to pamper,' the ad read.[26]

In a cookbook, Vic claimed that he tried his first 'scorpion' cocktail at a luau in Manoa, Hawai'i. He described a prototypical scene of tropical

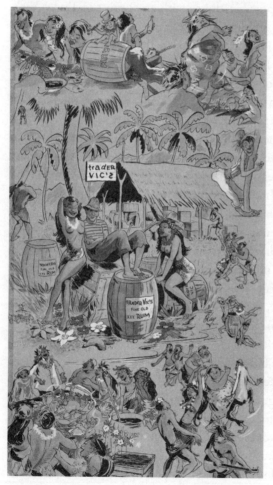

Hilton and Trader Vic's
menu, c. 1960s.

Conrad Hilton in front
of his new hotel in
Amsterdam, 1962.

paradise: a gentle rain fell to the tempo of soft Hawaiian music; exotic
flowers perfumed the air; and a Chinese punch bowl, in the centre of the
overflowing table, offered 'Honolulu's famous scorpion, a Caribbean rum
drink which does not shilly-shally or mess around in getting you under way.'
Vic presented the luau not as anything connected to Indigenous Hawaiian
culture, but as drunken excess hosted for the tourist relaxing in paradise.[27]

Trader Vic's was an invitation to inebriation. 'Let the drinker beware,'
the restaurant chuckled, the 'Samoan Fog Cutter' blended rums, fruits and
liqueurs. In this representation of the Polynesian way of life, hospitality
was naturally given, and happily taken by American tourists. Menu covers
pictured a Polynesian party. Roly-poly men danced with barely clothed
Polynesian women. The tourist, recognizable only by his fully clothed
outfit, perched on a wooden rum keg marked with the trader's 'xxx'. When
the London Trader Vic's promoted its Tahitian feast (a standard package throughout the chain), it returned Tahiti to an imagined state where
French colonialism simply never happened. In Trader Vic's interpretation,

Tahitians 'still cook and live in the old ways'. They may have – somehow – acquired 'a few of the white man's luxuries and an odd piece of clothing now and then', but they lived much as did their primitive ancestors.[28] For Vic, colonialism was just a form of administration, but 'it sure as hell' did not affect the local population or their hospitality, simplicity and love of a good party.

The notion of Polynesia as a primitive paradise, drunken or otherwise, had deep roots, first articulated in the seventeenth century and expanded in the eighteenth and nineteenth centuries by artists, botanists, writers, colonial officials and myriad other travellers. They returned to Europe with tales of abundant foliage, sweet fruits and beautiful women. Enough stories circulated that when Ida Pfeiffer arrived in Tahiti in 1847, she knew to anticipate eating roast pig cooked in an underground pit, and expected abundant hospitality from Polynesians.

Vic, for his part, assigned tourists the role not of explorers, but of pirates and beachcombers. 'Pirates, Buccaneers and Beachcombers never bandy with their drinking', said the Trader Vic's menu. Try the 'Kamaaina', an 'older timer' punch served in a souvenir ceramic coconut.[29] Here, Vic was drawing on a different set of stories that involved not only local hospitality, but the white men who, with a tinge of rebellion, enjoyed it.

For Harry Franck, beachcombers were white wastrels, often sailors, beached and waiting for the next boat. They were adrift in the tropics, taking advantage of the privileges empires afforded even to down-and-out white men. The life of the 'beachcomber' also seduced British author Alec Waugh in 1925, as he relaxed in the glow of his first literary success. He set off on a journey to the South Seas. 'Why, we asked ourselves, should man work himself in a cold inequitable climate towards an early grave?', the novelist wondered. 'Why avoid sunlight leisure?' When he sailed, he imagined the 'white man' emptying bottles of rum alongside the locals. By the time he arrived, Tahiti was already well visited by penniless beachcombers who, like him, expected 'native hospitality'. He joined them in easy living. The air was soft and warm. Soon, he wrote, you feel 'languid' and 'life is effortless and sweet.'[30]

Rum flowed. 'How many other exiles, wanderers and victims of mischance', Waugh later wondered, 'have not been consoled and fortified by this noble spirit?' Rum was, according to Waugh, 'the pirates' drink'.[31] Waugh's cocktail preferences – about which he went on to write a different book – presaged Vic's: a punch, for Waugh, was a 'noontime drink', to sip before lunch or be taken to the beach in a flask. He suggested light rum with lime juice and pineapple. On the Messageries Maritimes, he recalled, they added grated nutmeg. Trader Vic's would later sweeten and colour the same punch with grenadine and curaçao.[32]

Noted British travel writer Harry L. Foster followed a similar route, describing himself as a 'tramp' in the tropics. He was also, he wrote, a 'beachcomber in the Orient', a 'gringo in Mananaland' and, in Fiji, a 'vagabond'.[33] 'To a guest,' Foster wrote, 'the communistic generosity of Fiji was a source of delight.' In a small village in the heart of the island, the men dug pits to cook 'steaks and stews, eggs and chicken, and roast pig'. Women prepared 'Polynesian *poi*', kneading the sticky taro in a long wooden trough. The locals served a cornucopia of fruit and vegetables: breadfruit, kumala (a type of sweet potato) and dalo (with leaves like spinach and a root like a gummy potato). 'When the beverage appeared', he knew that 'we were in for another all-night *meke*' – a traditional dance. Rather than rum, they drank kava, the intoxicating root made from the chewed yangon root.

Amid the mountain breezes whispering through the palms, full of roasted pig, and reeling from kava and fatigue, Foster's mood soured. Suddenly, the shadows from the torches and feasting fires seemed 'barbaric'. The locals seemed less like genial hosts than savages. Like Pfeiffer long before him, he regarded Indigenous peoples as recently reformed cannibals. In his paranoid intoxication, the remains of the roasted pig reminded him of human carcasses – '*puaka balava,* or long pig'. When 'a hulking Fijian loomed out of the dark', Foster hit him in the pit of his stomach.[34]

When Vic recreated the South Seas, he omitted Indigenous peoples, and with them, any possibility for the type of relationships Foster described: with no threat, the customer could come out on top, and party on, assured that their expectations of privilege and service would be fulfilled. Besides, they weren't actually being welcomed with 'communistic generosity': they were paying customers.

The Pacific was also a battleground. Even before the World Wars, the German, American, French, British and Japanese empires all jostled for Pacific island colonies. Islands in Samoa, Tahiti and Hawai'i promised productive plantation economies and essential naval bases. Even smaller guano islands were valuable colonies.[35] Combat operations in the Second World War that stretched from Pearl Harbor to Guadalcanal actually reinforced – and popularized – notions of the Pacific as a tropical idyll. As the fighting receded from Pearl Harbor, American soldiers and sailors depended on Hawai'i as a place for rest and relaxation – complete with plenty of drinking. After the war, as the American military spread its influence everywhere from Guam to Okinawa, integrating colonial possessions into a network of military bases, popular cultural descriptions recast former South Pacific battlefields as tourist havens.

The restaurant drew on these associations when it promised a 'Polynesian paradise' ripped from 'a James Michener novel', the famous American novelist and navy veteran. His stories described love and war in Pacific paradise and were based on his own experiences and observations as a navy lieutenant during the Second World War.[36]

'The tropics never left you,' insisted Michener in *Tales of the South Pacific*, his 1947 bestselling collection of short stories, later adapted into the popular musical *South Pacific*. 'They were a vast relaxation.'[37] Michener led readers – veterans who might have fought in the Pacific and those who had read about its battles – to an imaginary island set near real-life Vanuatu. The island was an 'earthly paradise' whose residents believed that private property had no value until given away. The soldiers, guided by their chaplain, arrived on the island in time for a pig slaughter and the feast that followed. The women were alluringly naked, except for the thinnest strand of fibre around their waists and over their groins. The Pacific Islanders gave the soldiers hunks of roasted pork. 'Soon,' the chaplain explained to the soldiers, 'there would be dancing and feasting and love-making.'

Later, the soldiers departed on a mad island hop in search of alcohol, from officers' clubs to bootleggers' saloons. They were collecting for their own 'wine mess'. A 'wine mess', explained Michener, 'exists for the sole purpose of buying and selling beer, whiskey, rum, gin, brandy, bitters, cordials, and at rare intervals, champagne'. Along the way, the soldiers drank at a saloon run by a French planter and his beautiful mixed-race daughters. The alcohol flowed and the food was excellent, a mix of wild chickens from the jungle, seafood from the shore and steaks and corned beef that soldiers swiped from their canteens. One soldier, resting before battle, was overwhelmed by the beauty of the planter's daughters. The soldier wore dirty trousers and sneakers with a sun helmet perched on his head. Michener wrote: 'He looked like a beachcomber, a very special beachcomber,' in love, a little drunk and off to war.[38]

Trader Vic's was the stateside wine mess, with the mess of war omitted. Michener's soldiers collected the kinds of souvenirs that covered the walls at Trader Vic's. They bargained for wild pig tusks. They shipped home grass skirts. But, in all the bric-a-brac souvenirs that turned the restaurant into a South Seas paradise, Bergeron omitted shell casings. He mounted outrigger canoes and Japanese diving balls, not burned-out Japanese tanks. The party remained. 'Native life and fun in the South Pacific is pretty much the same on all islands,' said Vic. He designed food and drinks without attention to Indigenous cuisines. Vic collected souvenirs, not recipes. Instead, 'I have tried to capture the spirit of their feast and fun-making for you here on the mainland.' 'The Polynesians', he wrote, 'just know how to have fun in simple unaffected ways.' In his telling, a typical Tahitian party began with dumping wine, rum and every imaginable tropical fruit into an old wine barrel. To 'stir the mess', the host grabbed a canoe paddle. Somehow 'music appeared from the clouds', and the party magically began. Children were sent for food – shrimp, lobster, poi and chicken.[39]

In the Trader Vic's myth, which Vic perpetuated in his popular cookbooks, menus and advertisements, the Polynesian party, laced with rum, wasn't service demanded, but hospitality offered – and taken. In Tahiti, a good party doesn't need 'R.S.V.P.s' and Vic described his welcome at a local feast (invited or not). The chief selected pigs for the ovens and sent people into the jungle to fetch wild fruit. Vic didn't stop to listen to the chief's 'benediction' or even wonder at the reason for the feast. Assuming that he was the honoured guest, he was entranced by the rum punch and the evening's 'lovemaking'. Whether he had ever attended a Tahitian feast or simply spun a fictional yarn is immaterial. He was recycling and updating for the modern tourist an older fantasy of Polynesia: untouched, infinitely welcoming, unabashedly sensual and abundant in its food and – here was Trader Vic's touch – rum drinks. It was just what the mainland needed after a world war and during a Cold War. Trader Vic's tried 'to inject a little of their happy fun-making into our scheme of things'.[40]

In 1972 Vic set down another myth, adapting a Pacific folk tale into a children's storybook about the deeper origins of Polynesian hospitality. In his telling, a magical species of 'little people' called Menehunes arrived from a distant planet to a rocky Hawaiian archipelago, devoid of plants and people. They propagated plants, cultivated fruit and transformed it into a tropical paradise. Later, when the first humans landed on the Hawaiian beaches, they enjoyed feasts of fruits grown by the Menehunes. Trader Vic's featured the Menehunes and their parties in advertisements: 'They are jolly, happy little people and make other people happy too.' Vic seemed to equate real-life Polynesians with the mythical Menehunes. In places like Tahiti, they might have tossed out their colonial masters, but he depicted them as perpetually happy, accommodating hosts.[41] Vic liked the story as a parable of Polynesia and his restaurants. The feasts were copious and the drinks flowed. The labour needed to host the party, in addition, seemed magical. Everything was ready when the guests arrived.

Watery Drinks

Vic brought the party to the hotel but left behind the Polynesians. Instead, Trader Vic's mostly hired Americans of Chinese origin as cooks. White Americans travelled around the world to work as managers and, wherever the Hilton was located, locals and Chinese Americans played the role of Polynesians. They were waiters at the inebriated tourists' luau, and the work could be challenging.

Here's how Hilton's staff experienced the nightly luau, for example: the day began early, as they heated lava stones to the right temperature to slow roast a pig. Too hot, and the stones would sear the meat. Too cold, and the pig would not be ready when guests finished the cocktail hour. At 1.30 p.m. staff lowered the pig into a hot pit dug into the sand. They covered it with wet leaves to help keep the roasting pork moist and aromatic. Other cooks prepared the side dishes and the appetizers. For rumaki, for example, cooks had to laboriously wrap bacon around each centre of water chestnut and chicken liver. As evening approached, bartenders hurried to mix alcoholic punches to serve in tall ceramic cups that mimicked exotic South Seas head sculptures. Dancers and singers performed early and ended late. The next day, the party began all over again. When Hilton pictured the luau in its magazine, it inserted a cartoon of a broadly smiling Pacific Islander, wrapped only in a floral cloth, roasting his meat over an open fire with a tall drink nearby.[42]

Or consider the preparation that went into the opening of the Trader Vic's at the Caribe Hilton, where a faux palm frond gateway, flanked by tiki heads, jutted out of a white concrete facade of boxy balconies. Above the Trader Vic's doorway, a mural painted in faux-Polynesian style depicted scenes from Puerto Rican history. Inside, workers manufactured fake South Seas trinkets. Apart from a handful of genuine Chinese tiles, a Japanese fishing boat and a collection of spears, daggers and animal skins collected from 'wild spots', these locally produced objects would decorate the room. Other Puerto Rican artisans wove palm fronds into a thatched ceiling for this 'tribute to the South Pacific'.

Three weeks until opening, workers at last completed the restaurant's construction, but the labour of paradise had barely begun. The tables doubled as desks for the local waitstaff. Standing at blackboards, managers,

Employees at the Hilton Hawaiian Village prepare a pig for roasting at a luau.

drawn from other branches of the Trader Vic's chain, explained how to mix exotic drinks. Even the dishes, often flamed tableside with rum or brandy, needed mastering. Trader Vic's in Puerto Rico employed ninety people. Some were experienced waiters who had worked in other branches. Two head chefs supervised the kitchen staff. At the Caribe, most employees were Puerto Rican, and Conrad was delighted. Promoting local waitstaffs was propaganda for his chain.

Across the hotel chain, Hilton encouraged the hiring of locals. A Hilton newsletter described how an Iranian orphan, Ahmad Raman, became an apprentice cook at the Royal Tehran Hilton. 'To work and live in a Hilton Hotel, I cannot believe it,' enthused Raman. He was one of four orphans who would, as young men, spend two years working in the kitchens in Tehran followed by another year in a European branch. Hilton celebrated their story. During the day, they received practical training in food and drink service. In the evening, they took English classes.[43] Elsewhere, in Trinidad, Hilton launched a competition across the Caribbean for worthy men to work in the kitchens.

Not everything went smoothly. In 1958, on the eve of revolution in Cuba and during the visit by the Khrushchevs to the United States, Conrad began preparing for the grand opening of the Nile Hilton. Conrad loved hotel openings. He paid for celebrities to attend and flew in the press. The food was lavish. Drinks flowed (even in countries that officially or traditionally frowned on alcohol). Before the drinking began, he liked to remind his audience about the grave, Cold War responsibility of American hotels.

In Cairo, however, Warren Broglie, the hotel manager, worried. Gamal Abdel Nasser, the President of the United Arab Republic (the name, then, of Egypt), remained stubbornly neutral in the Cold War. He craved tourists, explained Broglie in a secret letter to the chain's home office in the United States, but he also appreciated abundant Soviet aid. Hard currency the government earned from taxing the tourist trade could, ironically enough, buy Soviet arms. 'The Communists so far have never let him down,' Broglie explained. Conrad's muscle-flexing anti-communism would find a weak reception in Egypt. Instead, Broglie advised Conrad to speak briefly. Stick to broad ideas that 'travel helps to break down the barrier of ignorance and gives people a wider horizon and makes them more tolerant'.[44]

'We have got to recapture that image of America as the hope of the little people in the world,' Conrad had once declared. 'Whether they look at us through the slanted eyes of Asia or the great round eyes of Africa, they must see a kind face.'[45] Such condescension aside, the eyes of local employees likely often saw demanding customers.

Customers were more interested in being served than in advancing free markets, and they were never entirely content, even when full and drunk. On the bedside table, Hilton hotels left a detailed customer service card, an opportunity for tourists to express their satisfaction or dissatisfaction. The card also reminded employees who delivered room service or cleaned the rooms that American tourists ultimately judged them. When James Lage and his wife visited the Nile Hilton, they were not impressed. The food tasted awful, the Lages complained on their card. The cleaning staff hardly cleaned and, during the night, the air conditioning was turned off.[46] (The local custom of enjoying the desert chill in the early morning clashed with the American love of air conditioning, the hotel management explained to the Lages.) The noise from the Polynesian-themed Tropicana Club kept the couple awake.

The same managers assured Marylin Nashashibi's tour that the drinking water was safe, but she witnessed local workers fill drinking glasses with used water from other tables. At the Ibis Café, Nashashibi ate a sandwich, drank a Coke and watched cockroaches parade across the counter. The 'pancakes tasted odd', complained Mrs D. R. Hillard, and when she and her family departed, the hotel waitstaff muttered 'good-bye to dirty American pigs'.[47]

Trader Vic's waiters, 1957.

In the Ibis Café, the waitstaff 'wandered around the room without appearing to know what to do to serve people', complained Mary Clemsha. A devoted birdwatcher, she also noticed that the birds painted on the café walls by local artisans were not actually ibises.[48]

Across the chain, Cold War promises of world peace through travel met the reality of tense relations in paradise between servers and the served. Walter W. Warren and his wife planned their tropical holiday for three years before arriving at the Virgin Isle Hilton in St Thomas. They 'were rewarded with indifference, rudeness, insolence, untruths, disrespect, miserable service, mediocre food, and faulty accommodations', Warren wrote directly to Conrad. Warren compared the hotel to 'a beautiful piece of tropical fruit, gone rotten inside'. D. J. Neale also grumbled in a personal letter to Conrad. 'The Colored help', he wrote, 'insult the guests.'[49]

The hotel manager himself admitted 'the many shortcomings of native labour'.[50] Conrad's promises of mutual exchange became mutual suspicion. 'We may be going down there to see how the natives live,' Evelyn Rosenthal wrote to Conrad after her visit to St Thomas, 'But we do not intend to live like the majority of them.'[51]

Even Polynesian cocktails could cause tension. 'They are serving there drinks at high prices so weak you cannot detect any liquor in them at all,' Ray Teal wrote to Conrad about the Panama Hilton. 'Someone is playing tricks in the Cocktail Bar.'[52]

The Dishwashers Wore Paper-bags

When Hilton planned a hotel and a Trader Vic's for Cuba, the local investor was the Caja de Retiro y Asistencia Social de los Trabajadores Gastronomicos – the 'Gastronomical Union', Conrad called it.[53]

Vic was nervous about opening a branch in Havana, but Conrad insisted. The hotel offered him a foothold in the booming Cuban tourist economy. Tourists flocked to Havana's famed casinos and brothels. The air of permissiveness especially around the sex trade signalled that Cuba's dictatorship valued tourists' dollars above all else.

The hotel opened its doors in 1958, just as the Cuban Revolution began. Conrad had always insisted on the political importance of tourism as the antidote to communism, and his modernist hotel and its Polynesian restaurant had an outsized political symbolism that matched its towering architecture. When Fidel Castro and his revolutionary followers occupied Havana, they stayed at the Hilton.

'We have Mr Castro in our hotel with five hundred of his soldiers,' complained Conrad in January 1959.[54] At first the hotel's managers remained warily sympathetic. 'Unfortunately, Dr Fidel Castro received some bad press,' reported the hotel's new manager to Conrad. Such kind words belied a desperate hope that the revolutionary Ministry of Labour and the emboldened unions wouldn't seek to damage the hotels and

Fidel Castro chatting with Havana Hilton employees, 1959.

the massive tourist business.[55] On 10 January 1959 Conrad circulated a memo from Castro himself. 'I wish to invite the American tourists and the American businessmen to come back to Cuba,' Castro typed on Hilton stationary.[56]

A month later, Conrad's public optimism lapsed into private pessimism as the reality of revolution settled over the Havana Hilton. 'The Communist element is particularly strong in the Gastronomical Union – our landlord,' Conrad worried. Tensions simmered between the American managers and the radicalizing union. When the hotel tried to save money by closing the main Supper Club, union members, refusing to sacrifice their jobs, removed food from the refrigerators and set up a buffet in the bar.[57] Without tourists, the food simply rotted.

Trader Vic's served only 75 guests a day. For Keith Hardman, the Trader Vic's manager in Havana, the situation was dire. In a microcosm of the souring relationship between the American government and Castro, someone (and he suspected it was a revolutionary) hotwired his car from the hotel's garage and Hilton refused to reimburse his loss. For good reason: by early 1959, Hilton was losing $100,000 a month on its Cuban investment. Hardman admitted: 'I often feel the desire to bundle up the restaurant, strap on the Trader Vic sign, and shove off looking for a happy home somewhere else in a location . . . where all the people are hungry millionaires.'[58]

The hotel frantically sought ways to save money. Yet as Hilton contemplated closing the hotel's restaurants, the revolutionary government, prodded by the hotel workers union, refused to allow firings. At a March 1959 meeting that lasted until the wee hours of the morning, the union insisted that Trader Vic's continue its full lunch service to a mostly empty room.[59]

The revolution had arrived at the Hilton and Trader Vic's, but the radicalized union didn't call a strike. After all, Hilton, more than anything, hoped for closures to save money. Instead, workers crashed the fantasy Polynesian party. In an affront to the myth of everlasting service, the union ordered Trader Vic's waiters not to wash or shave for three days. In place of the aroma of orchids or the wafting smoke of grilled meat, human sweat brought revolutionary politics into a make-believe South Pacific. Instead of Orientalist uniforms, workers wore 'guyaberas', Cuban shirts associated politically with Castro and the revolutionary movement. The kitchen crew wore paper bags.

'I know this all sounds like someone's D. T.'s but damn it, it's a fact,' bemoaned the Trader Vic's managers.[60]

The hotel had become a 'breeding ground for communism', Hardman fumed, and tourism suffered across Havana. The future of casinos was uncertain. Even pornographic movies were banned.[61] As it became clear that tourists were not returning, Vic quietly repatriated his American staff to stateside restaurants. In October 1960 the revolutionary government abruptly nationalized the hotel and Trader Vic's, leaving Conrad and Vic to squabble about unpaid bills.

Trader Vic's became the state-owned El Polinesio restaurant and, soon enough, a destination for Soviet advisors eager (like Khrushchev before them) for a taste of tropical paradise.

Conclusion

'This is one of those things that you just got to do, right?' Anthony Bourdain said, as he was about to eat a still-quivering cobra heart: 'It's one of those cocktail party stories that's sure to turn mom green.' The waitstaff at the restaurant in Vietnam were watching. Even other diners, all of whom appeared to be locals, paused their meal to observe the spectacle of a white tourist far off the tourist path and surrounded by camera operators. They were filming an episode of the television series *A Cook's Tour* (2002–3), and shots like these helped cement Bourdain's fame as the world's most fearless food adventurer. He looked into the camera, said 'Cheers, folks,' and swallowed. 'Maybe eating snakes and worms only seems more outrageous,' he wondered, 'because it's a different culture.'

By the time filming began, Bourdain was already a food celebrity. He'd been working as head chef of Les Halles, a French restaurant in New York, and his 2000 book about the seamy side of the culinary industry, *Kitchen Confidential*, was a bestseller. But he was worn out from work, his editor demanded a new book and the Food Network wanted a television show. So, like many travellers before him, Bourdain proposed a challenge: hunting out 'scary, exotic, wonderful food', he said, 'I'd eat my way around the world, right?'[1]

The repulsion viewers might have felt when Bourdain tucked into cobra heart suggests the enduring legacy of travellers like Edith James, as timid as Bourdain was adventurous. Tourists like James helped define the local food they encountered as fundamentally different, even dangerous. When viewers watched Bourdain sample his way through local markets, they marvelled at his willingness to eat everything, seemingly without fear of illness. He encouraged his audience to try everything at least once, but more for the taste than for the opportunity to build relationships. He made that point by eating whatever struck him as the most exotic, the strangest and the most likely to get the attention of viewers back home.

Bourdain, of course, was not the first to eat off the beaten path, or to sell his stories about it for profit. A century and a half earlier, Ida Pfeiffer had circled the globe on her own as a single woman, living off what the locals ate. Later, Harry Franck bet that he could vagabond all the way around without a penny, working or begging for his food along the way.[2] Myra Waldo, Conrad Hilton, Victor Bergeron and Juan Trippe offered to make people's culinary journeys a little easier: tourists could just dine at the hotel or, simpler still, eat around-the-world food from the comfort of their own kitchens.

Food is sustenance. It is produced often by hand, out of ingredients that typically mean a great deal emotionally and culturally to those doing the cooking. It is shared by families and friends; eaten at homes, on the street and in restaurants. It is also the source of many of the world's jobs and has become a tourist attraction.

After technologies of steamships and jet planes annihilated space and time, taste took their place as the measure of distance. While many tourists shrink from trying new foods, or try it only tentatively, others embrace it as an adventure. Both attitudes involve a belief that local food is markedly different from what tourists are accustomed to, and that while it may be something to share, it is, above all, exotic and potentially sickening.

However much Bourdain tried to escape the beaten tourist path, he still walked in the footsteps of imperial adventurers. Even the title of his television series and book recalled Thomas Cook – the British travel agency also called their packaged trips 'Cook's Tours'. Bourdain's show and books substituted a brave chef's eating adventure for the around-the-world package tour. He admitted his nostalgia for adventurers of earlier eras: 'I wanted to find – no, I wanted to be – one of those debauched heroes and villains out of Graham Greene, Joseph Conrad, Francis Coppola and Michael Cimino.' Bourdain even craved a 'dirty seersucker suit'. Bourdain's longings ensnared him in the histories of empire and its painful aftermath. In Vietnam, he preferred to stay at the Hotel Continental, a vintage hotel that dated to the French colonial era. It overlooked Givral's Pastry shop, another Ho Chi Minh City vestige of colonialism. At the market, he fingered Zippo cigarette lighters for sale that had been owned by long-dead American soldiers. Bourdain planned to spend New Year's Eve at a bar called Apocalypse Now where he was keen to find the seamy relics of empire: malarial French planters, international arms dealers and mercenaries. He was disappointed. At the buffet, he saw a cake that looked suspiciously like a Black Forest. It all seemed blandly touristy. He left.[3]

Around the World on a Nickel

Born in 1956 Bourdain grew up in the age of mass tourism. He was three years old when Hilton opened its branch in Cairo, four when the Hilton and Trader Vic's in Havana were nationalized and around ten when American soldiers sarcastically called their prison in Vietnam the Hanoi Hilton. He was eleven when Pan Am flew its 10,000th flight around the world and 35 when the airline declared bankruptcy. He came of age during the Cold War, during the Vietnam war; in the aftermath of the fall of Euro-American empires.

Bourdain's adventurer family tree stretches back to those who first sniffed at durian, feasted on rijsttafel and dreamed of fortunes in mangosteens. He swallowed a cobra heart on television because, more than 150 years before, tourists had come to believe that someone else's food was potentially dangerous, strange and the measure of difference. Food could also be hospitality and a welcome, but Juanita Harrison was the rare traveller who ate purely for flavour and friendship. Most travellers embellished stories of the very real hospitality they received with boasts about the exotic foods they tasted. What could have been narratives of encounters dissolved into bravura.

Jimmy Bedford, a journalism professor in Kansas who set off on an around-the-world trip in 1959, travelled in the midst of the era of decolonization. He decided that he could travel around the world and cross Africa on a Vespa scooter, eating whatever he was offered.[4] He set off with just a nickel, and financed the trip along the way by selling his stories to newspapers and magazines at home. Decolonization came painfully slowly and often violently in Africa.

In Algeria, Angola and Kenya, for example, colonial regimes fell only after wars of independence, and Bedford arrived in the Congo in the midst of an uprising against Belgian rule. Maybe, he wondered, 'black people in Africa are seeking vengeance on the white people'. For six months, he drove his scooter across the continent, enjoying foods offered freely by local peoples. 'I was greeted with unbelievable hospitality,' said Jimmy, before plunging into a familiar racist joke: 'The cannibals had me to dinner – but I was a guest instead of the main course.'[5]

Bedford came to Africa expecting exotic meals but encountered hospitality. After making his way across Africa to Tehran, he typed out a draft of an article: back home in Kansas, he'd weighed 265 pounds (120 kg). But thanks to 'adventure, travel, strange foods, and shortage of money', on the

Vespa ride across Africa, he now weighed '185 pounds [84 kg] and never felt better'.[6]

'Whenever anyone thinks of a trip, one of the first things he thinks about is eating,' he said. 'You dream of exotic foods served in special ways.'[7] To narrate both a food adventure and a story of the welcome extended to a white tourist in newly independent (or soon to be independent) Africa, he ate local. But that didn't mean that he didn't voice fears, especially of getting ill.

Fortunately, 'I was able to stay healthy *and* placate my hosts,' Jimmy boasted. He 'conditioned' his stomach to the 'simple foods of the African people'.[8] He ate local, less for its novel flavours than because he had resolved to travel frugally and because he knew instinctively that his narrative demanded it. In French Sudan, soon independent Mali, 'between NOWHERE and Timbuktu' his Vespa broke down. In the intense heat blowing off the Sahara, he was 'near collapse'. Locals led him to the shade of a tree, near a grass hut. They brought him water and food. They poured gravies of pounded peanut and of greens over the rice.

'It all tasted very good until the pepper hit me,' said Bedford. 'Then I thought my stomach was on fire.' The locals laughed at the teary, sweating, exhausted white man and offered him fresh yoghurt. Bedford was afraid that the yoghurt harboured germs, and nervous that the locals would be offended 'if I turned it down'.

'I ate it, thinking it wouldn't hurt me to eat it just once,' said Bedford.[9]

As vast colonies became independent African countries, Bedford boasted of the strange (to him) foods he sampled all the way from West Africa to the Nile in Egypt. He ate grilled warthog, roast gazelle, fried python, bush buck, buffalo, pheasant, hippo and, in Cameroon, villagers welcomed the 'weary vagabond' with shelter and 'fufu with fresh babboon [*sic*] stew'. He packed an expansive medicine chest and ate 'the "local" food in every country', he boasted.[10] 'African chop' was not a uniform but meagre diet, as many Americans might have imagined. He discovered that south of the Sahara, rice, peanuts and vegetables were staple ingredients and the foods lightly seasoned. In Guinea, Africans cooked meals for him using coconuts, bananas, yams and plantains. In Egypt, he enjoyed 'fool', the seasoned chickpeas consumed for breakfast.[11] Yet he didn't call any of it 'cuisine'.

Instead, as Bedford sat in front of his typewriter to describe the 'meals I've et', he focused on the strange meats, the abundant spicing and his own willingness to try them all. He boasted more than he savoured: 'You'll need a cast iron stomach or plenty of medicine – because what I've eaten would even put a goat off his feed.'[12]

In Ceylon, the Vespa reached the end of its road. Bedford traded it for a ticket on the Peninsular and Oriental's ss *Orontes* to Australia. On the ship, he was back on the tourist trail, the food was bountiful and it was comfortingly Western. He chose between roast pheasant and grilled lamb chops for the main course and selected just two of the three desserts. 'Life', he said, '*can* be beautiful.'[13] The food was familiar, he ate heartily and he no longer worried that what was on offer might be teeming with germs. By the time Bedford left Australia, he had travelled 39,000 miles (62,764 km), through 42 countries.[14] He'd also gained back 30 pounds (14 kg).[15]

'Twenty-Seven Cents'

Could food adventure travel really produce understanding – if travellers chose to describe the most exotic foods, most likely to prove their own bravery and disgust their audience at home? In 1960, just as Bedford was weighing himself again in Australia, Wendy Myers began her seven-year 'hitch hike round the world'. The eighteen-year-old British woman vowed to 'sleep anywhere, fight heat, cold, mosquitoes, and eat local food'. In the book she published upon her return, she included photos of eating with the locals. Here she was eating glutinous rice with a family in Laos. And here with a family in Aden.[16]

'Trust begets trust, respect begets respect,' she wrote. When she returned to England, people asked about the locals with whom she ate. 'Their colour?' She claimed not to have noticed their skin colour, and when asked about 'their smell', she – unlike the Comte de Beauvoir a century before – recognized that after rough travelling, she was the one who could use some cleaning up.

Yet she still described friendly meals as food adventures, writing that 'Readers with weak stomachs should stop here.' She ate 'chicken necks in Bethlehem, boiled dog in the Philippines', and pig's brain omelette in South Vietnam. Like Pfeiffer, she sampled parrot in Brazil.

By the 1960s and '70s, when Bourdain was a teenager, the road less travelled was becoming well worn, thanks to tourists from Europe, Britain and the United States. In 1972 the recently unemployed automobile engineer Tony Wheeler and his wife Maureen, a clerk for a wine merchant, decided to cross Europe and Asia in a beat-up minivan. They hoped to make their way all around the world. Douglas Brown's *Overland to Asia* was an inspiring guide, written for those 'staying in the cheapest hotels, taking local buses, and eating whatever is going'. And 'sharing dope'.[17]

The Wheelers followed Brown's 'hippie' trail all the way to Istanbul. The Turkish capital 'was our first taste of the exotic east', Tony recalled. A few days later, in Isfahan, Iran, Maureen snapped a picture of Tony posing with a large flatbread, their typical breakfast. The next day, he 'suffered our first case of "Delhi Belly"'. The trip across Asia to Australia featured 'assaults on your stomach'.[18]

In Afghanistan, they sold their van for a small profit, some of which they spent at a local Kabul café. On the bus over the Khyber Pass into Pakistan the next day, both were too ill to enjoy the view. It was a 'nightmare trip'.[19]

Next, Nepal. Kathmandu appealed to travellers such as the Wheelers with its cocktail of cheap lodging, spiritual aura and abundant drugs. They visited 'Pie Alley', named for the row of pie shops catering to Western tourists. The first pie shop, they explained, opened in the 1960s, turning recipes learned from a Peace Corps volunteer into tourist attractions. The shops also offered special menus, adding 'liberal' amounts of dope to Western-style baked goods.

Back in India, they lounged on the veranda of a Calcutta apartment owned by a friend of Tony's father. An Indian butler served them gin and tonic, a 'Raj-era tipple'.

Thailand offered a brief, comfortable respite at the Hotel Malaysia, a hotel built for rest and recreation for American soldiers fighting in Vietnam across the border. By 1972, the Americans were slowly withdrawing from the former French colony and the hotel owner had pivoted to serve a clientele of hippie tourists. By the time they reached Malaysia, their dwindling funds and Tony's growing hair provoked suspicion from border guards. Maureen was convinced that they stamped 'SHIT' in their passports: 'suspected hippies in transit'.

Australia welcomed white travellers, regardless of hair length. 'So, are you visitors or immigrants?' a customs official asked them on arrival. The Wheelers decided on immigration to receive three months free healthcare.[20] On Boxing Day 1972 they hitchhiked across the Harbour Bridge into downtown Sydney and counted their change: 'Twenty-seven cents', said Tony. Instead of continuing their around-the-world journey, they began writing the guide that launched Lonely Planet, the travel guidebook company that, more than any other, has come to define backpacking.

Their first book, *Across Asia on the Cheap*, was a homespun effort, 94 pages with a stapled cover. No matter how many shots you get, the

Wheelers cautioned, inevitably you'll fall prey to the 'Kabul Trots, Rangoon Runs and Bangkok Belly'. Best to accept it and go with the flow: 'Eat whatever you like, you are bound to get something that doesn't like you somewhere along the line so why worry about it.' But they did offer some advice: examine your potential food vendor. Does he look clean? Does he seem sick? If so, avoid his food, mixing adventurous engagement with mutual suspicion. Look at the state of the nation, too.

The state of the food, the Wheelers suggested, was edible evidence (or not) of the state of development. In 'less advanced countries', water was a particular problem. It was better to eat with the hands; utensils would be washed in unsafe water. Pack the antidiarrheal Lomotil and take two pills, three times a day.[21]

From the stapled guide to Asia, *Lonely Planet* became a guidebook empire, leading tourists, eager for adventure, around the world. In his 2007 book *No Reservations*, Anthony Bourdain noted: 'No matter where you go in the world,' he wrote, 'chances are someone from the Lonely Planet guide has been there before you.'[22] That same year, the Wheelers sold a 75 per cent stake in their company for £63 million.

Must Have Durian

Two episodes after sampling cobra heart, Bourdain was in Cambodia, on a food adventure with a long history. 'I want durian, must have durian, need durian,' narrated Bourdain. He bought a durian from a market vendor, reminded viewers that the durian wasn't welcome in hotels, and carried the 'dirty-diaper-smelling' fruit to a park bench to slice it open. (Local durian connoisseurs would have recognized that his inexpert cuts sliced into, rather than simply revealed, the tasty lobes of fruit.)

'Travel and food are inseparably intertwined,' reads the introduction to Lonely Planet's 2010 celebration of 'food adventures around the world'.[23] 'Where we go, we need to eat. As a result, when we travel, food inevitably becomes one of our prime fascinations.' Food can fascinate, it can nourish, but can it really unite? One person's adventure is someone else's labour. 'The proprietors of tourist restaurants have learned to make a deracinated, half-assed version of their own cuisine,' warned Bourdain. Go elsewhere, and 'you're an adventurer'.

But we should not dismiss the work of cooking just because of what tourists might want. The jobs of the millions on and off the tourist trail are not simply the physical work of cooking the food, serving the meals and cleaning up the dirtied plates and crumpled napkins. Restaurant staff might be the only locals tourists ever meet and, as such, they are often seen as representing their nations and their cultures. Their work involves emotional labour too: to stand calmly and respectfully with platters or menus even as tourists snap pictures, tell jokes and, in some cases, demean local fare. The tourist's imperative for service might be coupled with suspicion of local foods as too spicy, teeming with germs and made from strange ingredients – reflecting a belief that what some people can eat, others cannot. Bourdain himself refused to wash down his cobra heart with water: he judged beer safer. And, like the Wheelers before him, Bourdain hailed Lomotil as the 'traveling chef's best friend'. He snapped pictures of bathrooms wherever he travelled.[24] Those suspicions – or outright distaste – can be part of a tourist's pleasure, a way not of collapsing distance between themselves and others but affirming it.

'Scary-looking, huh?' As Bourdain talked into the camera and tentatively tasted the durian, the camera slowly panned right to reveal a curious Cambodian child watching Bourdain eat. Bourdain may have realized he was there, but this was the story of *his* taste – the Western food adventurer's, not the child's. Bourdain sampled but didn't share the fruit as he spoke to the camera, to viewers back home, and ignored the local child a few feet away: 'It's actually really good. Stinks to high heaven.'[25] Ensnared in his own image as the brave traveller, the bad-boy cook, Bourdain's choice about how to depict a beloved fruit placed him in a long line of food adventurers. Bourdain may have depicted empire as crumbling relics – ancient hotels and artefacts in street markets – but the imperialism that spurred mass tourism also wrote his script for tasting.

Bourdain decided that the lobes of durian pulp looked like foie gras, and he fantasized about taking durian back to New York. (No matter that the fruit was already accessible in East Asian supermarkets throughout the five boroughs, both fresh and frozen.) Even wrapped in layers of plastic, he opined, the noxious odours would escape. Perhaps, if it were treated 'like fissionable material' and 'segregated' from passengers, the durian could find its way to some New York chef who 'someday will harness durian's strange and terrible powers'.

Bourdain boasted that he would eat the durian, but 'probably alone'.[26]

REFERENCES

Introduction: Eating Apart

1 These statistics come from the World Travel and Tourism Council, a global industry organization. 'Where Does World Travel and Tourism Create the Most Jobs?', https://worldtraveltourismcouncil.medium.com, 28 March 2017.

2 '1st UNWTO World Forum on Food Tourism', www.unwto.org, 26 April 2015, and 'UNWTO/Basque Culinary Center Forum Highlights Gastronomy Tourism as Driver of Rural Development', www.unwto.org, 2 November 2021.

3 'Vaccines and Reopen Borders Driving Tourism's Recovery', www.unwto.org, 1 August 2022.

4 'World Food', www.staralliance.com; Josée Johnston and Shyon Baumann, *Foodies: Democracy and Distinction in the Gourmet Foodscape* (New York, 2010).

5 'Round the World', www.roundtheworld.staralliance.com.

6 *The Supreme Travel Adventure: Around the World in the 'Franconia'* (1929).

7 Carroll V. Glines, *Round-the-World Flights* (1983); 'Round-the-World Clippers – Then and Now', (1967), University of Miami Archives, Pan Am Papers, Series II Box 751, Folder 20, p. 2; Raymond Walter, Jr, 'Around the World', *New York Times* (28 June 1959), p. XXI.

8 Karl Marx, *Grundrisse* [1857–61], trans. Martin Nicolaus (New York, 1973), p. 538; 'Modern Annihilation of Space', *London Journal*, 23 (23 August 1856), p. 360; 'The Passion for Pace', *Saturday Review*, 104 (5 October 1907), p. 418; Clare Pettit, 'The Annihilation of Space and Time: Literature and Technology in the Nineteenth Century', in *The Cambridge History of Victorian Literature*, ed. Kate Flint (Cambridge, 2012), pp. 550–72.

9 *Cook's Tours Round the World, 1892–3*, Thomas Cook Archives, TCA, Box 'World 1893–93'.

10 Joyce E. Chaplin, *Round About the Earth: Circumnavigation from Magellan to Orbit* (New York, 2012), pp. 149–290.

11 'Travel Around the World', *Travel*, III (January 1884); *Around the World, 1913–14, Eastward and Westward* (Boston, MA, 1913), both in Warshaw Collection of Business Americana, Smithsonian Institution Archives, Series I, Box I.

12 'Nellie Bly's Story: The Obstacles Encountered on The Trip and How They Were Overcome', *Daily American* (27 January 1890), p. 8.

13 Nellie Bly, *Nellie Bly's Book: Around the World in 72 Days*, ed. Ira Peck (Brookfield, CT, 1998), p. 67.

14 *Over the Seven Seas* (New York, 1914), p. 5.
15 Round the Globe with Temple Tours – 1925–6, Warshaw Collection, Series I, Box 4, pp. 11–12.
16 *Round the Globe*, p. 12; John Urry, *The Tourist Gaze: Leisure and Travel in Contemporary Societies* (London, 1990), pp. 1–3; on the set itinerary tour, see Dean MacCannell, *The Tourist: A New Theory of the Leisure Class* [1976] (Berkeley, CA, 2013), pp. 91–108.
17 Lisa Heldke, *Exotic Appetites: Ruminations of a Food Adventurer* (New York, 2003), p. xxi; Lucy Long, ed., *Culinary Tourism* (Lexington, KY, 2004).
18 Wolfgang Schivelbusch, *The Railway Journey: The Industrialization of Time and Space in the Nineteenth Century* [1977] (Berkeley, CA, 2014), p. 23.
19 Pan American World Airways, *New Horizons World Guide* [1951] (New York, 1958), p. 6.
20 Ibid., pp. 454–6, 462.
21 bell hooks, 'Eating the Other: Desire and Resistance', in hooks, *Black Looks: Race and Representation* (Boston, MA, 1992), pp. 21–39.
22 Cynthia Enloe, *Bananas, Beaches, and Bases: Making Feminist Sense of International Politics* (Berkeley, MA, 2014), p. 38.

1 Ida Pfeiffer

1 Oscar Pfeiffer, 'A Biography of Ida Pfeiffer', in Ida Pfeiffer, *The Last Travels of Ida Pfeiffer: Inclusive of a Visit to Madagascar*, trans. H. W. Dulcken (New York, 1861), pp. xxxii–xxxiii.
2 'Ida Pfeiffer, The Great Female Traveler: Phrenological Character and Biography', *American Phrenological Journal*, 25 (May 1857), pp. 101–3. (The article appeared several years after her visit to the journal's offices.)
3 Ida Pfeiffer, *A Woman's Journey Round the World (An Unabridged Translation from the German)*, 2nd edn (London, 1852), p. 2.
4 Ibid., p. 7.
5 Ibid., pp. 10–12.
6 Ibid., pp. 116–18.
7 Ibid., pp. 27–8. On the demographics of the slave trade in Brazil, see Leslie Bethell, *The Abolition of the Brazilian Slave Trade* (Cambridge, 1970), p. 388; Angela Alonso, *The Last Abolition: The Brazilian Antislavery Movement, 1868–1888* (Cambridge, 2021).
8 Pfeiffer, *A Woman's Journey*, pp. 26, 33, 38.
9 Ibid., pp. 33–5; Hal Langfur, 'Moved by Terror: Frontier Violence as Cultural Exchange in Late-Colonial Brazil', *Ethnohistory*, LII/2 (April 2005), pp. 255–89.
10 Pfeiffer, *A Woman's Journey*, pp. 44–5.
11 Ibid., pp. 47–51.
12 Ibid., pp. 54, 58.
13 Ibid., p. 72.
14 Ibid., pp. 71–2.
15 Ibid., pp. 73, 78–80.
16 Ibid., pp. 74–5.
17 Ibid., p. 80.
18 Ibid., pp. 84–5.

19 Ibid., p. 139.
20 Ibid., pp. 143–4.
21 Ibid., pp. 140–41, 44–5.
22 Ibid., pp. 149–51.
23 Ibid., p. 170.
24 Ibid., pp. 170–71.
25 Ibid., pp. 200, 212.
26 Ibid., pp. 185, 192.
27 Ibid., p. 230.
28 Ibid., pp. 230, 233.
29 Ida Pfeiffer, *A Lady's Second Journey Round the World* (New York, 1856).
30 'Pfeiffer, The Great Female Traveler', p. 103.
31 Pfeiffer, *A Lady's Second Journey*, pp. 102–5.
32 T. J. Willer, 'Verzameling van Battahsche wetten en instellingen in
    Mandheling en Pertibi', *Tijdschrift voof Neêrland's Indië* (1846), Part II;
    Pfeiffer, *A Lady's Second Journey*, pp. 101–2.
33 Pfeiffer, *A Lady's Second Journey*, p. 107.
34 Ibid., pp. 111, 116–19.
35 Ibid., pp. 135–6.
36 Ibid., pp. 140–44.
37 Ibid., pp. 149–51.
38 Ibid., pp. 156–61.
39 Ibid., pp. 163–9.
40 Ibid., pp. 171–4.
41 Ibid., pp. 175–6.
42 Ibid., p. 177.
43 Ibid., pp. 181–4, 90.
44 Ibid., pp. 44–5.
45 Pfeiffer, *The Last Travels of Ida Pfeiffer*.
46 Ibid., pp. 207–8, 243–4.
47 Ibid., p. 253.
48 Ibid., pp. 269–70, 77–81.
49 'Death of Ida Pfeiffer', *Detroit Free Press* (19 November 1858), p. 1.

2 The Comte de Beauvoir

1 Marquis de Beauvoir, *A Voyage Round the World*, 3 vols (London, 1870),
   vol. I, p. 275; Comte de Beauvoir, *Voyage Autour du Monde*, 2 vols (Paris,
   1870). (All quotes are drawn from the English translation but checked against
   the French originals for clarity and accuracy.)
2 Beauvoir, *A Voyage Round the World*, vol. I, pp. 8–9.
3 Ibid., p. 18.
4 Ibid., pp. 19, 24, 26.
5 Ibid., p. 29.
6 Ibid., pp. 34–6.
7 Ibid., p. 134.
8 Ibid., p. 178.
9 Ibid., pp. 60–61.
10 Ibid., pp. 73–5.

11 Ibid., p. 175; Madeline Y. Hsu, 'On the Possibilities of Food Writing as a Bridge Between the Popular and the Political', *Journal of American History*, CIII/3 (December 2016), pp. 682–5; Madeline Y. Hsu, *The Good Immigrants: How the Yellow Peril Became the Model Minority* (Princeton, NJ, 2015).

12 Beauvoir, *A Voyage Round the World*, vol. I, p. 283.

13 Ibid., pp. 287–91.

14 Ibid., pp. 294, 307.

15 Marquis de Beauvoir, *A Voyage Round the World*, vol. II, p. 1.

16 Ibid., p. 2.

17 Ibid., pp. 3–9.

18 Milton James Lewis and Roy M. MacLeod, *Disease, Medicine, and Empire: Perspectives on Western Medicine and the Experience of European Expansion* (London, 1988); David Arnold, *Imperial Medicine and Indigenous Societies* (Manchester, 1988), pp. 1–26.

19 Beauvoir, *A Voyage Round the World*, vol. II, pp. 13, 15–16.

20 Ibid., pp. 30, 35–6, 39.

21 Ibid., pp. 72, 79.

22 Ibid., pp. 88–102, 118.

23 Ibid., pp. 137, 167.

24 Ibid., pp. 172, 181.

25 Ibid., pp. 199–200.

26 Ibid., p. 196.

27 Ibid., pp. 212–14.

28 Ibid., pp. 223–6; Jaclyn Rohel, 'Empire and the Reordering of Edibility: Deconstructing Betel Quid Through Metropolitan Discourses of Intoxication', *Global Food History*, III/2 (2017), pp. 150–70.

29 Beauvoir, *A Voyage Round the World*, vol. II, pp. 246–8.

30 Ibid., pp. 264–8, 291.

31 Ibid., pp. 282–4.

32 'Chinese Edible Dogs', *Illustrated London News* (12 July 1884), p. 37; R. G. Forman, 'Eating Out East: Representing Chinese Food in Victorian Travel Literature and Journalism', in *A Century of Travels in China: A Collection of Critical Essays on Travel Writing from the 1840s to the 1940s*, ed. Julia Kuehn and Douglas Kerr (Hong Kong, 2007), pp. 63–73.

33 Beauvoir, *A Voyage Round the World*, vol. II, pp. 308–12.

34 Ibid., pp. 358–9.

35 Ibid., p. 369.

36 Marquis de Beauvoir, *A Voyage Round the World*, vol. III (London, 1870), pp. 3–6, 38, 44.

37 Ibid., p. 221; Eric C. Rath, *Food and Fantasy in Early Modern Japan* (Berkeley, CA, 2010); Robert Hellyer and Harald Fuess, eds, *The Meiji Restoration: Japan as a Global Nation* (Cambridge, 2020).

38 Beauvoir, *A Voyage Round the World*, vol. III, pp. 128, 153.

39 Ibid., pp. 131–7.

40 Ibid., pp. 150, 205.

41 Ibid., pp. 184, 192, 196–8.

42 C. Mowbray Tate, *Transpacific Steam: The Story of Steam Navigation from the Pacific Coast of North America to the Far East and the Antipodes, 1867–1941* (New York, 1986), p. 41; Beauvoir, *A Voyage Round the World*, vol. III, p. 217.

43 Beauvoir, *A Voyage Round the World*, vol. III, pp. 206–8.
44 Ibid., pp. 236, 242.
45 'Local Intelligence', *New York Times* (2 August 1867).

Itinerary: ss Cleveland

1 'S. S. Cleveland, Hamburg Amerika Line, dinner menu' (14 December 1912),
   Culinary Institute of America Menu Collection (CIA), CIA 27-652.
2 'Girdling the Globe', 'Brochure and Replacement Insert for 3rd and 4th
   Round the World Cruises, Hamburg American Line, 1912', Hoboken
   Historical Museum, Hoboken Transportation Collection, 2008.012.0121.
3 'Grand Continental Hotel, dinner menu' (6 November 1912), CIA 27-641.
4 'S. S. Cleveland, Hamburg Amerika Line, dinner menu' (10 November 1912),
   CIA 27-643.
5 'Galle Face Hotel, tiffin menu' (24 November 1912), CIA 27-644.
6 'Queen's Hotel, lunch menu' (25 November 1912), CIA 27-646.
7 'Raffles Hotel, luncheon menu' (12 December 1912), CIA 27-651; 'Hotel Prinz
   Heinrich, luncheon menu' (31 December 1912), CIA 27-657.
8 'Hotel de Paris, Hamburg American Line, lunch menu' (2 December 1912),
   CIA 27-648.
9 'S.S. Cleveland, dinner menu' (3 November 1912), CIA 27-640.
10 'S.S. Cleveland's Departure', *Times of India* (27 April 1912), p. 5.
11 'S. S. Cleveland, HAPAG, farewell dinner menu' (29 January 1913), CIA 27-668.
12 'R.M.S. Franconia, menu' (2 September 1934). Author's collection.

3 Water

1 Deborah J. Neill, *Networks in Tropical Medicine: Internationalism,
   Colonialism, and the Rise of a Medical Specialty, 1890–1930* (Stanford, CA,
   2012).
2 'Colonial Medical Reports. No. 156. Asansol', *Journal of Tropical Medicine
   and Hygiene*, 26 (1 September 1923), p. 68; 'Notes on the Conditions
   Affecting the Health of the European Community in Assam', *Journal of
   Tropical Medicine and Hygiene*, 26 (15 November 1923), p. 346.
3 Bradley A. Connor, 'Traveler's Diarrhea', *CDC Yellow Book: Health
   Information for International Travel* (2020), ch. 2, www.nc.cdc.gov.
4 A. C. Mole, 'Round the World' (1939), National Maritime Museum,
   MSS/77/004.
5 Charlotte Ehrlicher, 'Around-the-World Letters', *American Journal of Nursing*,
   13 (December 1912), p. 215.
6 Edgar Allen Forbes, *Twice Around the World* (New York, 1912), pp. 43–4,
   110–11; William G. Frizell and George H. Greenfield, *Around the World on
   the Cleveland* (Dayton, OH, 1910), pp. 14, 44–5.
7 W. J. Simpson, 'Tropical Hygiene: Lecture I', *Journal of Tropical Medicine
   and Hygiene*, 6–7 (1 April 1903), pp. 101–4; ibid. (15 April 1903), pp. 117–19.
8 W. J. Simpson, 'Tropical Hygiene: Lecture II', *Journal of Tropical Medicine
   and Hygiene*, 6–7 (1 May 1903), pp. 133–8; W. J. Simpson, 'Tropical Hygiene:
   Lecture III, *Journal of Tropical Medicine and Hygiene*, 6–7 (15 May 1903),
   pp. 55–160.

9 'Le Domaine Colonial de La France, Guide du Voyageur et du Colon Dans Les Colonies Françaises' (Paris, 1893), p. 49.

10 *Guide Michelin Maroc, Algerie, Tunisie* (Paris, 1929), p. xxv.

11 'Le Domaine Colonial de La France', pp. 171–8.

12 Sir Edwin Arnold, 'Notes for a Tour Through India', *P&O Guide Book for Passengers* (1891), pp. 68–71; Mary Brodrick, ed., *A Handbook for Travellers in Lower and Upper Egypt* (London, 1900), pp. 9–10, 13–14.

13 *A Handbook for Travellers in India and Ceylon* (London, 1891), pp. xviii–xvix.

14 *A Handbook for Travellers in India, Burma and Ceylon* (London, 1919), pp. xxv–xcvi, cxxvi–cxxvii.

15 Edmund Hobhouse, ed., *Health Abroad: A Medical Handbook of Travel* (London, 1899), p. vi.

16 W. J. Simpson, 'India', in *Health Abroad*, ed. Hobhouse, pp. 306, 318–19, 343.

17 Delight Sweetser, *One Way Round the World* (Indianapolis, IN, 1898), pp. 160–62.

18 A.J.C. Skene, 'Health and Disease: Water as a Beverage', *Christian Advocate* (6 July 1882), p. 430; Robert Stuart Macarthur, *Around the World: Due West to the Far East* (Philadelphia, PA, 1900), p. 267.

19 Lucile Mann, 'Diary of East Indies Trip' (1937), William M. Mann and Lucile Quarry Mann Papers, circa 1885–1981, Record Unit 7293, Smithsonian Institution Archives, Box 23, pp. 19–20.

20 'Guide du Passager d'Extrême-Orient, 2e Edition Officielle' (Paris, 1902–3), p. 13.

21 'The Voyage to China', *Illustrated London News* (7 December 1872), pp. 532–4.

22 Forbes, *Twice Around the World*, pp. 43–4, 110–14.

23 Ernest William Gurney Masterman, *Cook's Handbook for Palestine and Syria* (London, 1907), p. v; Christopher Lumby, *Cook's Traveller's Handbook to Palestine, Syria and Iraq* (London, 1934), p. 11.

24 Harriet White Fisher, *A Woman's World Tour in a Motor* (Philadelphia, PA, 1911), p. 69.

25 Brodrick, ed., *A Handbook for Travellers in Lower and Upper Egypt*, p. 13.

26 'The Travellers' Bureau', *Gentlewoman and Modern Life*, XXXIII (10 November 1906), p. 670; Alice B. Conduct, '"Book-Khao" – India Fever', *Buffalo Medical and Surgical Journal*, XXXVIII (June 1889), pp. 665–6.

27 Walter Del Mar, *Around the World Through Japan* (New York, 1902), pp. 79, 420–28; Del Mar, *India of To-day* (London, 1905), pp. 260–65.

28 'The Surplice Shirt, Made to Measure by Sampson & Co. Complete India Outfit', *Bradshaw's Overland Guide to India, Egypt, and China* (1875–6), p. 438.

29 A.J.C. Skene, 'Health and Disease: Water as a Beverage', *Christian Advocate* (6 July 1882), p. 430.

30 'Risk of Travel', *The Sanitarian* (1 September 1888), p. 210.

31 Del Mar, *India of To-day*, p. 270.

32 'Le Domaine Colonial de La France', p. 181.

33 Charles Heaton, *Medical Hints for Hot Climates* (London, 1897), pp. 4–10, 21.

34 Frizell and Greenfield, *Around the World on the Cleveland*, pp. 14, 156, 203.

35 'Effect Is Marvellous, Classified Ad 13', *Times of India* (17 February 1898), p. 5.

36 'The Need Is Very Urgent, Classified Ad 16', *Times of India* (11 June 1927), p. 13.

37 Heaton, *Medical Hints for Hot Climates*, pp. xi–xiii, back matter.
38 'The Surplice Shirt, Made to Measure by Sampson & Co. Complete India Outfit', *Bradshaw's Overland Guide to India, Egypt, and China* (1875–6), p. vi.
39 'Cholera! Plague! Typhoid!' and 'Specialty in Whisky', *Times of India* (9 November 1897), p. 1.
40 Simpson, 'India', p. 319.
41 W. J. Simpson, 'Tropical Hygiene, Lecture III: Water Supplies', *Journal of Tropical Medicine and Hygiene* (15 June 1903), pp. 192–4.
42 J. Nield Cook, 'Pasteur Filtration at Darjeeling', *Public Health* (June 1899), pp. 620–23; Heaton, *Medical Hints for Hot Climates*, pp. 14–15 and back matter.
43 *Murray's Handbook Advertiser, 1902–3*, in Sir Lambert Playfair, *Handbook for Travellers in Algeria and Tunis*, revd edn (London, 1902), p. 11; *India, Burma, Ceylon, and South Africa: Information for Travellers and Residents* (London, 1904), pp. 205–40; Lumby, *Cook's Traveller's Handbook*, pp. 499–511; *The Malayan Traveller's Gazette*, I (July–September 1923), p. 36.
44 Sir Frederic Nicholson, 'Old Time Travel' (1936), P&O Company Records: Ports & Places: Ceylon, 1930–70 Date made 1930-01-01 - 1970-12-31 P&O/101/6; 'Diary of Cornelius B. Bradley' (1864), P&O/89/8.
45 'Life on Board, Food and Wine' (extract from *Saturday Review*, 15 December 1866) and 'Life on Board, Wines' (1871); 'P&O Handbooks of Information' (1873), P&O/101/6.
46 Thomas Cook, *Letters from the Sea and from Foreign Lands, Descriptive of A Tour Round the World* (London, *c.* 1872), Thomas Cook Archives, p. 67.
47 Ibid., p. 112; 'Programme of Cook's Twenty-First Annual Tour Round the World' (1892–3), Thomas Cook Archives.
48 '59,800 Bottles for Cruise: *Franconia* Returns from World Voyage with Liquor Stock Gone', *New York Times* (3 June 1927), p. 21.
49 Cecil Beaton, 'People and Ideas: Cairo Life', *Vogue* (15 August 1942), pp. 72–5, 109–10, 120.

4 Harry Franck

1 Harry Franck, 'Tales of a Vagabond' (n.d.), Harry Alverson Franck Papers, University of Michigan Special Collections (HAF), Box 5, Folder 18, p. 27.
2 Harry A. Franck, *A Vagabond Journey Around the World: A Narrative of Personal Experience* (Garden City, NJ, 1910), p. xv.
3 Walter Wyckoff, *The Workers: An Experiment in Reality* (New York, 1899); Seth Koven, *Slumming: Sexual and Social Politics in Victorian London* (Princeton, NJ, 2004); Daniel E. Bender, *American Abyss: Savagery and Civilization in the Age of Industry* (Ithaca, NY, 2009), pp. 132–61.
4 Harry A. Franck, 'Wandering Unskilled Laborers on the Edge of Trampdom, Thesis Written for Sociology 22, University of Michigan' (May 1903), HAF, Box 5, Folder 34; Joyce E. Chaplin, *Round about the Earth: Circumnavigation from Magellan to Orbit* (New York, 2012), pp. 274–5.
5 Franck, *A Vagabond Journey Around the World*, p. 19.
6 For the dates of his journey, see: 'Diary, 1905', HAF, Box 8, Folder 1.
7 Franck, *A Vagabond Journey Around the World*, pp. 54–5.
8 Ibid., pp. 27–8.

9 Ibid., p. 83.
10 Ibid., pp. 87–8.
11 Ibid., pp. 97–8.
12 Ibid., p. 102.
13 Ibid., pp. 102–4.
14 Ibid., pp. 115–16.
15 Ibid., p. 121.
16 Ibid., p. 128.
17 Ibid., pp. 155–6, 177.
18 Ibid., pp. 144–5.
19 Ibid., pp. 127–8.
20 Ibid., pp. 188–9, 194–6, 201–4.
21 Ibid., pp. 216–17.
22 Ibid., pp. 218–29.
23 Ibid., pp. 240, 248–9.
24 Franck, *A Vagabond Journey Around the World*, p. 251; 'Second Surviving V. J. Diary', HAF, Box 8, Folder 1.
25 Franck, *A Vagabond Journey Around the World*, pp. 252–3; 'Diary, 1905', HAF, Box 8, Folder 1.
26 Franck, *A Vagabond Journey Around the World*, pp. 254–5; René Alexander D. Orquiza Jr, *Taste of Control: Food and the Filipino Colonial Mentality Under American Rule* (New Brunswick, NJ, 2020).
27 Franck, *A Vagabond Journey Around the World*, p. 257.
28 Ibid., pp. 291, 294.
29 Ibid., p. 295.
30 'Diary, 1905', HAF, Box 8, Folder 1.
31 Franck, *A Vagabond Journey Around the World*, p. 298.
32 'Diary, 1905', HAF, Box 8, Folder 1.
33 Franck, *A Vagabond Journey Around the World*, p. 297; Noah Allison, Krishnendu Ray and Jaclyn Rohel, 'Mobilizing the Streets: The Role of Food Vendors in Urban Life', *Food, Culture and Society*, XXIV/1 (2021), pp. 2–15.
34 Franck, *A Vagabond Journey Around the World*, p. 303; Susan Bayly, *Caste, Society and Politics in India from the Eighteenth Century to the Modern Age* (Cambridge, 1999).
35 Franck, 'Tales of a Vagabond', pp. 206–7. Emphasis in original.
36 Franck, *A Vagabond Journey Around the World*, p. 298.
37 Ibid., pp. 296–8.
38 Ibid., p. 298.
39 Ibid., p. 303.
40 Ibid., p. 297.
41 Ibid., p. 306.
42 Ibid., pp. 318–20.
43 Ibid., p. 350.
44 Ibid., p. 361; 'Diary, 1905', HAF, Box 8, Folder 1.
45 Franck, *A Vagabond Journey Around the World*, pp. 393, 401–6.
46 Ibid., pp. 402–3.
47 Ibid., pp. 392–3.
48 Ibid., p. 412.
49 'Diary, 1905', HAF, Box 8, Folder 1.

50 Franck, *A Vagabond Journey Around the World*, p. 436.
51 'Diary, 1905', HAF, Box 8, Folder 1; Franck, *A Vagabond Journey Around the World*, pp. 456–7.
52 Franck, 'Tales of a Vagabond', HAF, Box 5, Folder 6, pp. 167–9.
53 Franck, *A Vagabond Journey Around the World*, p. 262.
54 'Diary 1922–24', (15 April 1922), HAF, Box 9, Folder 9; Harry A. Franck, *Vagabonding Through Changing Germany* (New York, 1920).
55 'Harry A. Franck to Dozier, Mary, and Billyus' (1 May 1922), HAF, Box 1, Folder 10; Rachel Latta Frank, *I Married a Vagabond, The Story of the Family of the Writing Vagabond* (New York, 1939), pp. 5, 35–7.
56 Franck, *I Married a Vagabond*, pp. 50–52.
57 'Rachel Latta Franck to Katherine Latta' (15 June–14 July 1922), HAF, Box 1, Folder 11.
58 'Diary 1922–24' (14 September 1922).
59 Franck, *I Married a Vagabond*, p. 86; 'Diary 1922–24' (2 October 1922).
60 'Rachel Latta Franck to Katherine Latta' (4 December 1922), HAF, Box 1, Folder 12.
61 'Diary 1922–24' (4 October 1922); Franck, *I Married a Vagabond*, pp. 104–5.
62 'Rachel Latta Franck to "Mother and Father" (May 1923), HAF, Box 1, Folder 11.
63 'Franck to 'Dozier, Mary, and Billyus'.
64 'Rachel Latta Franck to "Mother and Father".
65 Franck, *I Married a Vagabond*, p. 98.
66 'Rachel Latta Franck to "Mother and Father".
67 Franck, *I Married a Vagabond*, pp. 88–91.
68 'Rachel Latta Franck to "Margaret" (13 January 2923), HAF, Box 1, Folder 13; Franck, *I Married a Vagabond*, pp. 98–9; 'Diary 1922–24' (26 April 1923).
69 'Rachel Latta Franck to Katherine Latta' (4 December 1922).
70 'Harry A. Franck to "Katrinka" (27 December 1922), HAF, Box 1, Folder 11.
71 Franck, *I Married a Vagabond*, pp. 185–6.
72 Harry A. Franck, *Wandering in Northern China* (New York, 1923), pp. 183–6.
73 'Diary, 1922–24' (4 January 1923), HAF, Box 9, Folder 9.
74 Ibid. (28–30 May 1923).
75 Ibid. (1 June 1923).
76 Franck, *I Married a Vagabond*, pp. 123–5.

5 Durian

Parts of this chapter draw from my essay 'The Delectable and Dangerous: Durian and the Odors of Empire in Southeast Asia', published in *Global Food History*, III/2 (2017), pp. 111–32.

1 Paul S. Junkin, *A Cruise Around the World: A Series of Letters* (Creston, IA, c. 1910), pp. 7, 65–7.
2 Gary Y. Okihiro, *Pineapple Culture: A History of the Tropical and Temperate Zones* (Berkeley, CA, 2009); Lauren Janes, *Colonial Food in Interwar Paris: The Taste of Empire* (London, 2016).
3 'Sketches in the Malay Peninsula', *Littell's Living Age* (27 January 1883), p. 231.

4 F. W. Burbidge, *The Gardens of the Sun; or, A Naturalist's Journal on the Mountains and in the Forest and Swamps of Borneo and the Sulu Archipelago* (London, 1880), p. 304.

5 Florence Caddy, *To Siam and Malaya in the Duke of Sutherland's Yacht 'Sans Peur'* (London, 1889), p. 362.

6 W. Basil Worsfold, *A Visit to Java with an Account of the Founding of Singapore* (London, 1893), pp. 126–8.

7 'Early History of Buitenzorg Botanic Gardens', *Bulletin of Miscellaneous Information*, 79 (1893), pp. 173–5; J. J. Smith, *Guide to the Botanic Gardens, Buitenzorg* (Buitenzorg, 1929); Richard Harry Drayton, *Nature's Government: Science, Imperial Britain, and the 'Improvement' of the World* (New Haven, CT, 2000); Thomas Heyd, 'Thinking Through Botanic Gardens', *Environmental Values*, 15 (May 2006), pp. 197–212; John Merson, 'Bio-Prospecting or Bio-Piracy: Intellectual Property Rights and Biodiversity in a Colonial and Postcolonial Context', *Osiris*, 15 (2000), pp. 282–96; Donal P. McCraken, *Gardens of Empire: Botanical Institutions of the Victorian British Empire* (Leicester, 1997).

8 'Tropical Fruits', *Nature* (5 August 1886), p. 316.

9 Arnold Wright, ed., *Twentieth Century Impressions of British Malaya: Its History, People, Commerce, Industries and Resources* (London, 1908), p. 44.

10 Ibid., p. 657; James C. Jackson, *Planters and Speculators: Chinese and European Agricultural Enterprise in Malaya, 1786–1921* (Singapore, 1968).

11 John Soluri, *Banana Cultures: Agriculture, Consumption, and Environmental Change in Honduras and the United States* (Austin, TX, 2005).

12 David Fairchild, *Exploring for Plants* (New York, 1930), p. 6.

13 Ibid., pp. 6–7.

14 David Fairchild, *The World Was My Garden: Travels of a Plant Explorer* (New York, 1939), p. 73.

15 Ibid., p. 73.

16 Fairchild, *Exploring for Plants*, pp. 441–2.

17 Daniel Stone, *The Food Explorer: The True Adventures of the Globe-Trotting Botanist Who Transformed What America Eats* (New York, 2018).

18 Fairchild, *Exploring for Plants*, p. 444.

19 Stuart McCook, '"The World Was My Garden": Tropical Botany and Cosmopolitanism in American Science, 1898–1935', in *Colonial Crucible: Empire in the Making of the Modern American State*, ed. Alfred McCoy and Francisco Scarano (Madison, WI, 2009); Wilson Popenoe, *Manual of Tropical and Subtropical Fruits, Excluding the Banana, Cocoanut, Pineapple, Citrus Fruits, Olive and Fig* (New York, 1920); Peter Johnson Wester, *Plant Propagation and Fruit Culture in the Tropics* (Washington, DC, 1920).

20 Popenoe, *Manual of Tropical and Subtropical Fruits*, p. 421.

21 'Fruits and Flowers of Siam', *Southern Literary Messenger* (August 1857), p. 135.

22 Charlotte Cameron, *Wanderings in South-Eastern Seas* (Boston, MA, 1924), p. 72.

23 Poggio Bracciolini, *The Travels of Nicolo Conti in the East in the Early Part of the Fifteenth Century on India in the Fifteenth Century* (London, 1857), p. 9; Juan Gonzalez de Mendoza, *The History of the Great and Mighty Kingdom of China*, trans. Robert Parke (London, 1854), pp. 317–18; *The Voyage of John*

Huyghen van Linschoten to the East Indies (from the old English translation of 1598), trans. Arthur Coke Burnell and P. A. Tiele (London, 1885), pp. 51–3.

24 Thomas Forrest, 'Account of Atchenn, in the Island of Sumatra', *Literary Magazine and British Review*, 9 (August 1792), pp. 127–30.

25 Alfred Russel Wallace, *The Malay Archipelago* (London, 1869), p. 57; M. Henri Mouhot, *Travels in the Central Parts of Indo-China (Siam, Cambodia, and Laos)* (London, 1864), p. 165.

26 'Nature and Science', *Youth's Companion*, 78 (3 March 1904), p. 115; 'Sporting Reminiscences in the Malayan Peninsula', *New Sporting Magazine* (December 1868), p. 446; 'An Account of Batavia, from S. Parkinson's Journal', *The Monthly*, 1 (April 1773), pp. 178–87; O. W. Barrett quoted in 'A Malodorous Dainty', *Youth's Companion*, 87 (10 July 1913), p. 362.

27 'A Queer Fruit', *Youth's Companion*, 42 (1 July 1869), p. 205; Worsfold, *A Visit to Java*, pp. 198–9. This can also be metaphorically translated as 'Only the credulous believe it. Not I.'

28 Mark Twain, *Following the Equator: A Journey Around the World* (New York, 1924), pp. 478–9; John Carlos Rowe, 'Mark Twain's Critique of Globalization (Old and New) in Following the Equator, a Journey Around the World (1867)', *Arizona Quarterly*, LXI/1 (2005), pp. 109–35.

29 Lucile Mann, 'Diary of East Indies, National Geographic-Smithsonian Expedition' (1937), William M. Mann Papers: Smithsonian Institution, Box 7, Folder 1; Lucile Mann, 'Ark from Asia' (1937), William M. Mann Papers: Smithsonian Institution, Box 8, Folder 3G. See also G. B. Cerruti, *My Friends the Savages*, trans. I. Stone Sanpietro (Como, 1908); 'Villagers with Durian' (*c.* 1920s), Media – Image No: Slide No: S1647, Singapore National Archives.

30 Cameron, *Wanderings in South-Eastern Seas*, pp. 15–16, 72.

31 David Ker, *Among the Dark Mountains; or, Cast Away in Sumatra* (London, n.d.), pp. 206–7.

32 Burbidge, *The Gardens of the Sun*, p. 307.

33 Mann, 'Ark from Asia', p. 29; 'Perak and the Malays', *The Friend: A Religious and Literary Journal* (8 June 1878), p. 339.

34 Burbidge, *The Gardens of the Sun*, pp. 308–9.

35 'Durians', *Punch* (19 June 1929), p. 671.

36 [Charles Walter Kinloch], *De Zieke Reiziger; or, Rambles in Java and the Straits* (London, 1852), pp. 121–3.

37 'A Queer Fruit'; A. B. Morse, 'Garden Rambles in Siam', *Knickerbocker*, LVIII/4 (1861), p. 289; Popenoe, *Manual of Tropical and Subtropical Fruits*, p. 421.

38 'A Fruit in Bad Odor', *Youth's Companion*, 98 (24 January 1924), p. 66.

39 Twain, *Following the Equator*, p. 478.

40 E.J.H. Corner, 'The Durian Theory; or, the Origin of the Modern Tree', *Annals of Botany*, 23 (1949), pp. 367–414; Michael J. Brown, *Durio – A Bibliographic Review* (New Delhi, 1997), pp. 2–21; Popenoe, *Manual of Tropical and Subtropical Fruits*, p. 424.

41 Caspar Whitney, 'The Lost Seladang of Noa Anak', *Outing: An Illustrated Monthly Magazine of Recreation*, 46 (May 1905), p. 153; Rounsevelle Wildman, 'Amok! A Malayan Story', *Overland Monthly and Out West*, 138 (June 1894), p. 590; W. Gilmore Ellis, 'The Amok of the Malays', *British Journal of Psychiatry*, 39 (July 1893), pp. 325–38.

42 Arthur S. Walcott, *Java and Her Neighbours: A Traveller's Notes in Java, Celebes, the Moluccas and Sumatra* (New York, 1914), p. 71; Whitney, 'The Lost Seladang of Noa Anak', p. 153.

43 'Fruits and Flowers of Siam'. Emphasis in original. On disgust, see Carolyn Korsmeyer, *Savoring Disgust: The Foul and the Fair in Aesthetics* (Oxford, 2011); Paul Rozin and Jonathan Haidt, 'The Domains of Disgust and Their Origins: Contrasting Biological and Cultural Evolutionary Accounts', *Trends in Cognitive Sciences*, XVII/8 (2013), pp. 367–8; Sara Ahmed, *The Cultural Politics of Emotion* (New York, 2004).

44 Eliza Ruhamah Scidmore, *Java: The Garden of the East* (New York, 1922), pp. 21–3.

45 Walcott, *Java and Her Neighbours*, p. 68; 'Fruits and Flowers of Siam', p. 135; Cuthbert Woodville Harrison, *An Illustrated Guide to the Federated Malay States* (London, 1920), p. 161.

46 Harrison, *An Illustrated Guide to the Federated Malay States*, p. 176.

47 A. G. Plate, *A Cruise Through the Eastern Seas: Being a Travellers' Guide to the Principal Objects of Interest in the Far East* (Bremen, 1906), p. 64.

48 Harrison, *An Illustrated Guide to the Federated Malay States*, p. 155; Sydney M. English, 'Singapura', *The Academy and Literature* (29 April 1911), p. 527; Mann, 'Diary of East Indies', p. 19.

49 Cameron, *Wanderings in South-Eastern Seas*, p. 26.

50 Scidmore, *Java: The Garden of the East*, pp. 80–86.

51 [Alexander Hume Ford], 'My First Day in Java', *Mid-Pacific Magazine*, XII (July 1916), pp. 73–8.

52 Carveth Wells, *North of Singapore* (New York, 1940), pp. 128, 162–3.

53 Ibid.

54 A. Caboton, *Java, Sumatra and the Island of the Dutch East Indies* (New York, 1914), p. 180.

55 'Oriental Fruits', *Times of India* (2 May 1891), p. 6.

56 Harrison, *An Illustrated Guide to the Federated Malay States*, p. 4.

57 Scidmore, *Java: The Garden of the East*, p. 96; Harrison, *An Illustrated Guide to the Federated Malay States*, p. 178.

58 Fannie R. Feudge, 'Rambles Among the Fruits and Flowers of the Tropics', *Lippincott's Magazine of Popular Literature and Science*, 12 (August 1873), p. 197; Fabio Parasecoli and Paulo de Abreu e Lima, 'Eat Your Way Through Culture: Gastronomic Tourism as Performance and Bodily Experience', in *Slow Tourism: Experiences and Mobilities*, ed. Simone Fullager, Kevin Markwell and Erica Wilson (Bristol, 2012), pp. 69–72.

59 Feudge, 'Rambles Among the Fruits and Flowers', pp. 199–200.

60 Caddy, *To Siam and Malaya*, p. 273.

61 'The Natural History of the Eastern Archipelago', *Once a Week* (19 March 1870), p. 139.

6 Edith James

1 'Edith A. James World Tour, Vol. I' (1925–6), Royal Geographical Society Archives, 1–4; 'Franconia World Cruise', *South China Morning Post* (25 November 1925), p. 12.

2 Ibid., pp. 144, 237.

3 Ibid., p. 107.
4 Ibid., pp. 31–2; Douglas R. Burgess, *Engines of Empire: Steamships and the Victorian Imagination* (Stanford, CA, 2016).
5 'James, Vol. I', p. 30.
6 'A Feature of the New Cunard Liner Franconia', *Daily Telegraph* (19 May 1923), p. 11.
7 'The "Franconia" – A New Cunard Liner', *Sphere*, 19 (23 June 1923), p. vi.
8 'Cunard Steam Ship', *Financial Times* (8 April 1926), p. 2; Graham P. Gladden, 'Marketing Ocean Travel: Cunard and the White Star Line, 1910–1940', *Journal of Transport History*, XXXV/1 (June 2014), pp. 57–77.
9 'Cunard Steam Ship', p. 2.
10 'Second Around the World Cruise' (1923) of the American Express Travel Department.
11 'Thos. Cook & Son', *Vogue*, 65 (1 June 1925), p. 20; 'Thos. Cook & Son, Ltd', *Daily Telegraph* (14 October 1925), p. 12; 'Franconia', *Vogue*, 92 (1 November 1938), p. 37; 'Around the World – A Cruise', *Bankers' Magazine* (November 1925), p. 827; 'Thomas Cook & Son', *Vogue*, 69 (1 June 1927), p. 29; Fred Ingrid, *The Delicious History of the Holiday* (London, 2000), pp. 55–73.
12 'James, Vol. I', p. 47.
13 'Franconia Tourists: Cunard Liner Reaches Port Before Time', *South China Morning Post* (23 March 1926), p. 10.
14 'Franconia World Cruise', *South China Morning Post* (25 November 1925); 'James, Vol. I', p. 47.
15 'James, Vol. I', p. 84.
16 Ibid., pp. 47–54.
17 Ibid., pp. 58, 70, 90.
18 Ibid., p. 85.
19 Ibid., p. 104.
20 Ibid., pp. 232–3.
21 Ibid., pp. 71, 232–3.
22 Ibid., p. 96; Andrew Jon Rotter, *Empires of the Senses: Bodily Encounters in Imperial India and the Philippines* (Oxford, 2019).
23 'James, Vol. I', p. 164.
24 Ibid., pp. 232–3, 237, 278–80.
25 Ibid., p. 54.
26 Ibid., p. 108.
27 Ibid., p. 89.
28 Ibid., pp. 89–95; Eric G. E. Zuelow, *A History of Modern Tourism* (London, 2015), pp. 134–49.
29 'James, Vol. I', p. 77.
30 Ibid., pp. 91–5.
31 Ibid., pp. 115–17.
32 Ibid., pp. 148, 182, 223.
33 Ibid., p. 89.
34 Ibid., pp. 91–5, 152–3.
35 Ibid., pp. 155–6, 181, 193–4.
36 Ibid., p. 182.

37 Ibid., p. 163.
38 Ibid., p. 148.
39 Ibid., p. 98.
40 Ibid., p. 73.
41 Ibid., pp. 166–7, 195–201.
42 Ibid., pp. 96, 137.
43 Ibid., p. 121.
44 'Edith A. James World Tour, New Zealand–Fiji' (1928–9), Royal Geographical Society Archives.
45 'James, Vol. 1', pp. 89, 104, 115–17.
46 Ibid., pp. 73–5.
47 Ibid., pp. 91–5, 104, 144.
48 Ibid., pp. 115–17.
49 Ibid., p. 119.
50 Ibid., p. 135.
51 Ibid., p. 271.
52 Ibid., pp. 241–50, 252–3.
53 Ibid., pp. 252, 280, 297–8, 337.
54 Ibid., pp. 281–2.
55 Ibid., pp. 320–21.
56 Ibid., p. 348.
57 'Edith A. James World Tour, New Zealand–Fiji', p. 3.
58 Ibid., pp. 15–16, 26.
59 Ibid., pp. 35–47.
60 Ibid., pp. 83–8.
61 Ibid., pp. 97–9.
62 Ibid., pp. 105–8.
63 Ibid., p. 126.
64 Ibid., pp. 115, 130, 134; Hiʻilei Julia Hobart, 'A "Queer-Looking Compound": Race, Abjection, and the Politics of Hawaiian Poi', *Global Food History*, III/2 (2017), pp. 133–49.
65 'James, Vol. 1', p. 348.

7 Mangosteen

1 D. G. Fairchild, 'The Mangosteen', *Journal of Heredity*, 6 (August 1915), pp. 39–47.
2 Ida Pfeiffer, *A Woman's Journey Round the World*, 2nd edn (London, n.d.), p. 125; Michael Warboys, 'Germs, Malaria, and the Invention of Mansonian Tropical Medicine: From "Diseases in the Tropics" to "Tropical Diseases"', in *Warm Climates and Western Medicine: The Emergence of Tropical Medicine, 1500–1900*, ed. David Arnold (Amsterdam, 1996), pp. 181–207.
3 John Ellis, *Description of the Mangostan and the Breadfruit* (London, 1775), pp. 6–10.
4 Jean Baptiste Pallegoix, *Description du Royaume Thai ou Siam, Tome Premier* (Paris, 1854), pp. 130–32.
5 Frédéric Cuvier, *Atlas de zoologie* (Paris, 1816–30), p. 52.
6 'Guttiferae', *Natuur- en geneeskundig archief voor Neêrland's-Indië* (Batavia, 1847), p. 203.

7   Michel Étienne Descourtilz, *Flore médicale des Antilles; ou, Traité des plantes usuelles: des colonies Françaises, Anglaises, Espagnoles et Portugaises* (Paris, 1821–9), p. 118.

8   Charles Carleton Coffin, *Our New Way Round the World* (Boston, MA, 1869), pp. 231–6.

9   F. M. Huschart, *Eastward Around the World January to August 1906* (Cincinnati, OH, 1907), p. 151.

10 Isaac Newton Lewis, *Pleasant Hours in Sunny Lands in a Tour Around the World* (Boston, MA, 1888), pp. 5–10, 115; Rohan Deb Roy, *Malarial Subjects: Empire, Medicine and Nonhumans in British India, 1820–1909* (Cambridge, 2017).

11 Jules Verne, *Le Tour du monde en quatre-vingts jours* (Paris, 1874), pp. 91–2.

12 Mrs Howard Vincent, *Forty Thousand Miles over Land and Water: The Journal of a Tour Through the British Empire and America* (London, 1886), p. 224.

13 H. Allen Tupper Jr, *Around the World with Eyes Wide Open* (New York, 1898), pp. 144–5.

14 'Diary' (1927), Robert Casey Papers, Newberry Library, Box 7, Folder 113, p. 4

15 Sarah B. Adams, *Amy and Marion's Voyage Around the World* (Boston, MA, 1878), p. 230.

16 'The Notes of a Traveler: Netherlands India', *New York Times* (5 February 1878), p. 2.

17 Jules Leclercq, *Un Séjour dans L'Ile de Java* (Pairs, 1898), pp. 1–2; David Arnold, '"Illusory Riches": Representations of the Tropical World, 1840–1950', *Singapore Journal of Tropical Geography*, XXI/1 (2000), pp. 6–18; David Arnold, *The Tropics and the Traveling Gaze: India, Landscape, and Science, 1800–1856* (Delhi, 2005).

18 Thomas Stamford Raffles, *The History of Java*, 2 vols, 2nd edn (London, 1730), pp. 3, 5–41.

19 J. F. van Bemmelen and G. B. Hooyer, *Guide Through Netherlands India, Compiled by Order of the Koninklijke Paketvaart Maatschappij*, trans. J. Barrington (Amsterdam and London, 1903), p. 3.

20 Leclercq, *Un Séjour dans L'Ile de Java*, p. 15.

21 Ibid., pp. 41–3, 54–5.

22 Eliza Scidmore, *Java: The Garden of the East* (New York, 1897), pp. 9, 17, 335–6.

23 Ibid., pp. 30, 62–8, 79.

24 Ibid., p. 88.

25 Paul S. Junkin, *A Cruise Around the World* (Creston, IA, c. 1910), p. 67.

26 William Jennings Bryan, *The Old World and Its Ways* (St Louis, MO, 1907), preface and p. 211.

27 Ibid., p. 211.

28 Ibid., pp. 208–21.

29 Ibid., p. 225.

30 Ibid., pp. 204, 229.

31 James Macauley, 'Some Fruits of the East', *Leisure Hour* (30 October 1880), pp. 693–5.

32 J.E.C., 'The Queen of Fruits', *Christian Science Monitor* (27 March 1928).

33 David Fairchild, *The World Was My Garden: Travels of a Plant Explorer* (New York, 1939), pp. 71–4.

34 Ibid., p. 74.

35 Mary Hamilton Talbott, 'New Fruits and Vegetables', *Good Housekeeping Magazine*, 51 (August 1910), pp. 213–15; Frederick Boyle, 'New Fruits', *The Living Age* (27 June 1908), pp. 257, 3338.

36 David Fairchild, 'The Mangosteen', *Journal of Heredity*, 6 (August 1915), p. 343.

37 Fairchild, *The World Was My Garden*, pp. 106–52.

38 Fairchild, 'The Mangosteen', p. 341.

39 Fairchild, *The World Was My Garden*, p. 319.

40 'Queen Once Vainly Sought Rare Fruit U.S. Will Get', *New York Times* (23 August 1925), p. XX12.

41 'Foreign Fruits: The Durian', *Manchester Guardian* (20 March 1936), p. 8.

42 'Letter and list from J. Fisher to Sir Joseph Dalton Hooker; from Perseverance Estate, Singapore' (13 April 1869), folios 435–6, Library and Archives at Royal Botanic Gardens, Kew Directors' Correspondence; 'Letter from [Major John Frederick Adolphus] McNair to the Royal Botanic Gardens, Kew; from Penang, Straits Settlements' (6 April 1881), folio 516.

43 'Letter from R. [Robert] Derry to William Watson; from Botanic Gardens, Singapore' (19 July 1906), folio 45, Library and Archives at Royal Botanic Gardens, Kew Directors' Correspondence.

44 'Golden Apples', *Garden: An Illustrated Weekly Journal of Gardening in All Its Branches*, VII (10 April 1875), pp. 308–9.

45 Pen T. Johnson, 'How to Live in a Jungle – And Like It', *Leatherneck* (August 1944), pp. 9, 70.

46 Charles Morrow Wilson, *New Crops for the New World* (New York, 1945); R.K.S., 'New Fruits for American Dinner-Tables', *Christian Science Monitor* (6 September 1945), p. 18.

47 Kenneth O. Smith, 'What We Miss in Exotic Fruits', *Philadelphia Inquirer* (22 June 1947), p. 14; David Fairchild, *The World Grows Round My Door* (New York, 1947); J. H. Hart, 'The Mangosteen (Garcinia mangostana)', *Trinidad Cent. Agr. Bd. Agr. Rec.*, 5 (November 1891), pp. 176–7.

48 David Karp, 'Forbidden? Not the Mangosteen', *New York Times* (9 August 2006), p. F1; R. W. Apple Jr, 'Forbidden Fruit: Something About a Mangosteen', *New York Times* (24 September 2003), p. F1.

49 M. I. Ross, *Green Treasure* (New York, 1948), pp. 113–14.

50 Ibid., pp. 43–4; Y. Higgis, 'Fruits of the Mangosteen', *Gardeners' Chronicle*, 12 (30 July 1892), p. 136.

51 'The Mangosteen', *The Garden: An Illustrated Weekly Journal of Gardening in All Its Branches*, VII (15 May 1875), p. 413.

52 Letter from J. H. [John Hinchley] Hart to Sir William Thiselton-Dyer'; from Royal Botanic Gardens, [Trinidad]; 8 December 1891; folios 233–5, Library and Archives at Royal Botanic Gardens, Kew Directors' Correspondence, 213/233.

53 'Mangosteens from the West Indies', *Bulletin of Miscellaneous Information (Royal Botanic Gardens, Kew)* 133/134 (January–February 1898), pp. 26–7.

8 Juanita Harrison

1 Juanita Harrison, *My Great, Wide, Beautiful World* [1936] (New York, 1939), pp. 50–53.

2 Ibid., pp. 54–5; Cathryn Halverson, '"Betwixt and Between": Dismantling Race in My Great, Wide, Beautiful World', *Journal X*, IV/2 (2020), pp. 133–57.

3 Harrison, *My Great, Wide, Beautiful World*, p. 1.

4 Halverson claims, based on passport information, that Harrison was born, in fact, in 1887 and thus travelled when she was between 40 and 48 years old. Halverson, 'Betwixt and Between', p. 155. See also, Ellery Sedgwick, *Happy Profession* (Boston, MA, 1946), pp. 211–15.

5 Harrison, *My Great, Wide, Beautiful World*, p. x.

6 'Juanita Harrison to Alice Foster' (11 March 1931), Ann Cunningham Smith Collection of Letters from Juanita Harrison to Alice Foster, *c.* 1919–36, UCLA Library Special Collections, Charles E. Young Research Library, Collection Number 1846, Box 1, Folder 2.

7 Harrison, *My Great, Wide, Beautiful World*, pp. 265, 312.

8 Ibid., pp. 82, 85, 88.

9 Ibid., pp. 114–21.

10 Ibid., p. 116.

11 Ibid., pp. 32–9.

12 'Juanita Harrison to Alice Foster' (11 March 1931).

13 Harrison, *My Great, Wide, Beautiful World*, pp. 58, 69.

14 Ibid., pp. 62, 93, 286.

15 Ibid., p. 146.

16 Ibid., pp. 294–5; Marilyn Lake and Henry Reynolds, *Drawing the Global Colour Line: White Men's Countries and the International Challenge of Racial Equality* (Cambridge, 2008).

17 Harrison, *My Great, Wide, Beautiful World*, pp. 131–2, 308.

18 Ibid., pp. 75, 87; Peggy Pascoe, *What Comes Naturally: Miscegenation Law and the Making of Race in America* (New York, 2009).

19 Harrison, *My Great, Wide, Beautiful World*, p. 291.

20 Ibid., p. 96.

21 Allyson Hobbs, *A Chosen Exile: A History of Racial Passing in American Life* (Cambridge, 2014).

22 Juanita Harrison, 'My Great, Wide, Beautiful World', *Atlantic Monthly* (November 1935), pp. 601–12.

23 Harrison, *My Great, Wide, Beautiful World*, pp. 65, 81.

24 Ibid., pp. 111–12, 141.

25 Ibid., pp. 136–8, 293.

26 Ibid., p. 19.

27 Ibid., p. 148.

28 Ibid., p. 38.

29 'Juanita Harrison to Alice Foster' (11 March 1931); Harrison, *My Great, Wide, Beautiful World*, pp. 69, 94.

30 Harrison, *My Great, Wide, Beautiful World*, pp. 60, 100, 300.

31 Ibid., pp. 99, 101.

32 Ibid., p. 66.

33 Ibid., pp. 302–6.

34 Ibid., p. 296.
35 Ibid., pp. 102–3, 110.
36 Ibid., pp. 145–8, 158.
37 Ibid., pp. 156–7, 251.
38 Ibid., pp. 277–83.
39 Ibid., p. 310
40 Ibid., p. 311.
41 'Juanita Harrison to Alice Foster' (12 July c. 1936).
42 'A Cook's Tour', *St Louis Post-Dispatch* (3 May 1936), p. 4J.
43 'A Cook's Tour'; Betsy Smallwood, 'Safari on a Smile', *Washington Post* (7 June 1936), p. B8.
44 Wilbur Needham, 'Reviews of New Books Travel News and Notes: A Book to End Pessimism', *Los Angeles Times* (17 May 1936), p. C10.
45 'A Cook's Tour'; 'Very Engaging Travel Notes of Juanita Harrison', *Philadelphia Inquirer* (16 May 1936), p. 9.
46 'She Is Number One U.S. Servant', *Afro-American* (19 March 1938), p. 13.
47 Harrison, *My Great, Wide, Beautiful World*, pp. 312–18.

9 The Rice Table

1 Thomas H. Reid, *Across the Equator: A Holiday Trip in Java* (Singapore, 1908), p. 12; Elsbeth Locher-Scholten, *Women and the Colonial State: Essays on Gender and Modernity in the Netherlands Indies, 1900–1942* (Amsterdam, 2000).
2 Fadly Rahman, *Rijsttafel: Budaya Kuliner di Indonesia Masa Kolonial, 1870–1942* (Jakarta, 2011); Ann Laura Stoler, *Race and the Education of Desire* (Durham, NC, 1995); Jean Gelman Taylor, *The Social World of Batavia: European and Eurasian in Dutch Asia* (Madison, WI, 1983); Cecilia Leong-Salobir, *Food Culture in Colonial Asia: A Taste of Empire* (London, 2011).
3 Matthijs Kuipers, '"Makanlah Nasi! (Eat Rice!)": Colonial Cuisine and Popular Imperialism in The Netherlands During the Twentieth Century', *Global Food History*, III/1 (2017), pp. 4–23.
4 Aldous Huxley, *Jesting Pilate: An Intellectual Journey* (New York, 1926), pp. 184–6.
5 Marquis de Beauvoir, 'A Week at Batavia', *Appleton's Journal of Literature, Science and Art* (25 March 1871).
6 Arthur S. Walcott, *Java and Her Neighbours: A Traveller's Notes in Java, Celebes, the Moluccas and Sumatra* (New York, 1914), p. 28; Susie Protschky, 'Seductive Landscapes: Gender, Race and European Representations of Nature in the Dutch East Indies during the Late Colonial Period', *Gender and History*, 20 (August 2008), pp. 372–98.
7 J. F. van Bemmelen and G. B. Hooyer, *Guide to the Dutch East Indies, Composed by Invitation of the Koninklyke Paketvaart Maatschappij (Royal Steam Packet Company)* (Batavia, 1897), p. 3.
8 Koninklijke Paketvaart Maatschappij (KPM), *Guide Through Netherlands India* (Amsterdam, 1911), pp. 14–15.
9 Ibid., pp. 10–14.
10 Reid, *Across the Equator*, p. 2.

11 Augusta de Wit, *Facts and Fancies about Java*, 2nd edn (The Hague, 1900), pp. 15–19.
12 W. Basil Worsfold, *A Visit to Java* (London, 1893), pp. 34–6.
13 Wit, *Facts and Fancies*, p. 19.
14 Percy Stone, 'Rice Tafel in Java', *New York Herald Tribune* (21 August 1927), p. SM20; John Gunther, 'Dutch Treat', *Harper's Magazine* (1 June 1938), pp. 329–30.
15 M. F. Bridie, *Round the World Without a Pinprick* (Birmingham, 1932), p. 123.
16 Robert L. Ripley, 'The Seven Most Interesting Streets in the World', *Hearst's International-Cosmopolitan* (April 1932), p. 164.
17 Wit, *Facts and Fancies*, p. 21.
18 Ibid., pp. 19–23.
19 KPM, *Guide Through Netherlands India*, p. 11.
20 Stone, 'Rice Tafel in Java'; 'Mercury', 'The Traveller's Bureau', *Gentlewoman and Modern Life*, XXXIX/1002 (1909), p. 366.
21 Reid, *Across the Equator*, p. 91.
22 *Java the Wonderland* (Batavia, Official Tourist Bureau, c. 1900), p. 26.
23 'The Rice Table', *Hartford Courant* (25 April 1902), p. 9; Reid, *Across the Equator*, pp. 8–9.
24 Stone, 'Rice Tafel in Java'; Ripley, 'The Seven Most Interesting Streets in the World', p. 164.
25 Gunther, 'Dutch Treat'.
26 J. F. van Bemmelen and G. B. Hooyer, *Guide to the Dutch East Indies,* p. 14.
27 Worsfold, *A Visit to Java*, p. 36.
28 Lucile Mann, 'Diary of East Indies Trip' (1937), William M. Mann and Lucile Quarry Mann Papers, c. 1885–1981, Record Unit 7293, Smithsonian Institution Archives, Box 23, pp. 45–9.
29 Wit, *Facts and Fancies*, p. 24.
30 Eliza Scidmore, *Java: The Garden of the East* (New York, 1897), p. 29; Gunther, 'Dutch Treat'.
31 Huxley, *Jesting Pilate*, pp. 184–6, 195.
32 Reid, *Across the Equator*, p. 92.
33 George A. Dorsey, 'Finds Java a Land of Odd Mixtures', *Chicago Tribune* (12 September 1909), p. A3.
34 H. M. Tomlinson, 'Rice and Volcanoes', *Harper's Monthly Magazine* (1 December 1923), pp. 805–9.
35 KPM, *Guide Through Netherlands India*, pp. 240–45.
36 Huxley, *Jesting Pilate*, pp. 184–6; Worsfold, *A Visit to Java*, p. 34.
37 Wit, *Facts and Fancies*, p. 27.
38 Carrie Catt, 'Diaries, 1911–23', Papers of Carrie Chapman Catt, Library of Congress, pp. 5–15, 20–21.
39 Ibid., p. 5.
40 Mann, 'Diary of East Indies Trip', pp. 40, 69–70.
41 Tomlinson, 'Rice and Volcanoes', pp. 805–9.
42 Allen Raymond (by telephone), 'Picture Story of Java's Capital as It Waits for Japanese Attack', *New York Herald Tribune* (19 February 1942), p. 2.
43 Rafael Steinberg, *Foods of the World: Pacific and Southeast Asian Cooking* (New York, 1970), pp. 67–70.

Itinerary: Pan Am

1 'The Month', *New Horizons*, XII (January 1942), p. 9.
2 'Clipper's Detour from War in Pacific Brings it Home After 31,500 Miles', *Pittsburgh Press* (8 January 1942), p. 17.
3 'Epic', *New Horizons*, XII (January 1942), pp. 11–13.
4 Roland Nicholson, '4 Pilots Tell how President Followed Flight by Landmarks', *Washington Post* (4 February 1943), p. 1.
5 B. Candotti, 'Passenger Service Section Check List-Research' (December 1945–18 January 1946), Pan Am Papers (PA), Series I, University of Miami, Box 493, Folder 14; '28 PAAers Off on Flight Halfway Around the World', *Clipper* (13 December 1945), p. 1.
6 'The Clipper America Blazes the Trail!' *Pan American Clipper*, 6 (25 June 1947), pp. 1, 2, 4.
7 Clementine Paddleford, 'Globe-Girdling Clipper Plans Special Menus', *New York Herald-Tribune* (17 January 1947), p. 22.
8 'World-Wide Happenings, Too, Will Have a "Plus" or "Minus" Influence' (*c.* 1948), PA, Box 501, Folder 7.
9 'PAA Offers Air Travelers New Hotel Accommodations' (5 June 1947), PA, Series II, Box 383, Folder 4; 'Address, Impact of the Jet Age Upon the Hotel Industry, Delivered by Mr Peter Grimm at Cornell University', ('Extension of Remarks of Hon. Isidore Dollinger'), *Congressional Record, Proceedings and Debates of the 85th Congress, First Session* (15 May 1957), PA, Series I, Box 63, Folder 8.
10 'Round-the-World Clippers – Then and Now' (1967), PA, Series II, Box 751, Folder 20, p. 2.
11 Wayne W. Parrish, 'Five Days in Pakistan . . . Smiles Amid Hardship', *Airlift* (June 1963), PA, Series II, Box 318, Folder 11.
12 'Pan Am: Around the World by Clipper' (advertisement, 1956), John W. Hartman Center for Sales, Advertising and Marketing History, David M. Rubenstein Rare Book and Manuscript Library, Duke University, Pan Am Account Files.
13 'The Pan Am Story' (n.d.), PA, Series I, Box 403, Folder 35.
14 'Pan Am's 10,000th Round-the-World Flight Mirrors Air History' (July 1967), PA, Series II, Box 751, Folder 20, p. 3.
15 'Space Age View of 10,000 Round-the-World Flights' (July 1967), PA, Series II, Box 751, Folder 20.
16 'Card, Club, Pan Am First Moon Flights' (*c.* 1969–71), National Air and Space Museum Collection, Inventory Number A20180010000.

10 Myra Waldo

1 Myra Waldo, *The Complete Round-the-World Cookbook* (New York, 1954).
2 'For Release to Publications' (21 October 1954), Pan American World Airways Records, University of Miami Special Collections, Box 213, Folder 14; Jenifer Van Vleck, *Empire of the Air: Aviation and the American Ascendancy* (Cambridge, 2013).
3 Waldo, *The Complete Round-the-World Cookbook*, pp. 283–4.
4 Ibid., pp. 244–5.

5 Myra Waldo, *The Complete Book of Oriental Cooking* (New York, 1960).

6 Myra Waldo, *Complete Meals in One Dish* (Garden City, NY, 1965), p. 36.

7 Josée Johnston and Shyon Baumann, 'Democracy vs Distinction: A Study of Omnivorousness in Gourmet Food Writing', *American Journal of Sociology*, CXIII/1 (2007), pp. 165–204.

8 See, for example, Henry Smith, *Classical Recipes of the World, with Occasions for their Use, and Master Culinary Guide* (New York, 1954); Cyril Von Baumann and Beulah Phelps Harris, *The Four Winds Cookbook* (New York, 1954); Dorothy A. Stevens, *Table Talk and Tidbits: Stories and Recipes from Around the World* (Philadelphia, PA, 1953); Frank Dorn, *The Dorn Cookbook: A Treasury of Fine Recipes from All Around the World* (Chicago, IL, 1953); Ambrose Heath, *The International Cookery Book* (London, 1953).

9 Spice Islands Home Economics Staff, *International Dining with Spice Islands* (San Francisco, CA, 1963), pp. 25–31; Mary Collins (pseud.), *The McCormick Spices of the World Cookbook* (New York, 1964), p. 1; Lisa M. Heldke, *Exotic Appetites: Ruminations of a Food Adventurer* (New York, 2003), p. 70.

10 *Food for Thought . . . An International Cookbook* (New York, 1967); Mary Ann Zimmerman, *The Tupperware Book of Picnics, Parties and Snacks Around the World* (New York, 1967); Hilton Chefs, *Hilton International Cookbook* (Englewood Cliffs, NJ, 1960); Myra Waldo, *Inter-Continental Gourmet Cookbook* (New York, 1967); Charlotte Adams, *The SAS World-Wide Restaurant Cookbook* (New York, 1960); *Good Housekeeping: Around the World Cook Book* (Chicago, IL, 1958); *Woman's Day International Collector's Cook Book* (Greenwich, CT, 1967); Dorothy B. Marsh, ed., *The Good Housekeeping International Cookbook: Official World's Fair* (New York, 1964); Dorothy Krell, *Adventures in Food, by the Editorial Staffs of Sunset Books and Sunset Magazine* (Menlo Park, CA, 1964); Wendy Buehr, *The Horizon Cookbook: A Treasury of 600 Recipes from Many Centuries and Many Lands, by the Editors of Horizon Magazine* (New York, 1971).

11 William Irving Kaufman, *The Wonderful World of Cooking* (New York, 1964); Ruth Gilmour, *International Food Flair: The Gourmet Cook's Tour* (New York, 1967); Eileen Weppner, *The International Grandmothers' Cookbook: Favorite Recipes of Grandmothers from Around the World* (Boulder, CO, 1974). Within the 'Time-Life' series, all published in New York by Time-Life books, see Laurens Van der Post, *African Cooking* (1970) and Santha Rama Rau, *The Cooking of India* (1969).

12 Lesley Blanch, *Around the World in Eighty Dishes: The World through the Kitchen Window, Good Food from Other Lands and How to Cook It, Told to Young America* (New York, 1955), pp. vii–viii.

13 'Try Some Bengal Muchlee' (*c.* 1954), Pan Am Papers, Box 213, Folder 14.

14 Collins, *The McCormick Spices of the World Cookbook*, pp. 1–6.

15 NATO Cookbook Committee, *The Best of Taste: The Finest Food of Fifteen Nations* (Annapolis, MD, 1957); Army Language School Women's Club, *What's Cooking Around the World* (Monterey, CA, 1953).

16 United States Committee for the United Nations. *Favorite Recipes from the United Nations: 170 Authentic Dishes. Edited and Kitchen-Tested by the American Home Economics Association* (Washington, DC, 1951).

17 Carol A. Horton, *Race and the Making of American Liberalism* (New York, 2005); Michelle Brattain, 'Race, Racism, and Antiracism: UNESCO and the

Politics of Presenting Science to the Postwar Public', *American Historical Review*, CXII/5 (2007), pp. 1386–413.

18 United States Committee for the United Nations, *Favorite Recipes from the United Nations*, pp. 1–5.

19 'Gourmet Recipes', *Pan Am Clipper*, 29 (4 August 1969), p. 4.

20 Myra Waldo, *1001 Ways to Please a Husband* (New York, 1958).

21 Waldo, *The Complete Round-the-World Cookbook*, pp. 6, 8, 219–24.

22 Mary Louise Pratt, *Imperial Eyes: Travel Writing and Transculturation* (London, 1992).

23 Myra Waldo, 'How the World Cooks: A Basic Recipe – Plus Four Exotic Variations', *Baltimore Sun* (23 March 1969), p. 336; Myra Waldo, 'How the World Cooks: Cooking for the Nixons', *Baltimore Sun* (3 November 1968), p. TW12; bell hooks, *Black Looks: Race and Representation* (Boston, MA, 1992), pp. 21–39.

24 Waldo, *The Complete Round-the-World Cookbook*, pp. 270–71.

25 'Gourmet Recipes', p. 4.

26 'Press release: Doubleday' (*c.* 1954), PA, Box 213, Folder 14.

27 Waldo, *Complete Meals in One Dish*, pp. 1–3.

28 Waldo, *1001 Ways to Please a Husband*, pp. v–vi, 1–2, 22–33.

29 Ibid., pp. 107–8.

30 Myra Waldo, *Myra Waldo's Travel Guide to the Orient and the Pacific* (New York, 1965), pp. xxi–xxii, 21.

31 John C. Caldwell, *South Asia Travel Guide* (New York, 1960), p. 24.

32 Waldo, *Myra Waldo's Travel Guide to the Orient and the Pacific*, pp. xxi–xxii, 3–4, 21–2.

33 Ibid., pp. 41, 47–8; Lionel Everhard Napier, *The Principles and Practice of Tropical Medicine* (New York, 1946); E. T. Renbourn, 'The History of the Flannel Binder and Cholera Belt', *Medical History*, 1 (July 1957), pp. 211–25; S. Leigh Hunt and Alexander S. Kenny, *On Duty Under a Tropical Sun* (London, 1882).

34 Waldo, *Myra Waldo's Travel Guide to the Orient and the Pacific*, pp. 68, 112, 403.

35 Ibid., pp. 89, 118–22.

36 Waldo, *Complete Meals in One Dish*, pp. 178–9.

37 Waldo, *Myra Waldo's Travel Guide to the Orient and the Pacific*, pp. 386–8, 394–5.

38 Ibid., pp. 466–70.

39 Ibid., pp. 48, 445, 452–3.

40 Ibid., pp. 63–5, 342.

41 Ibid., pp. 281, 337, 381–2.

42 M. G. Schultz, 'Entero-Vioform for Preventing Travelers' Diarrhea', *JAMA*, CCXX/2 (10 April 1972), pp. 273–4.

43 Myra Waldo, *Myra Waldo's Round-the-World Diet Cookbook* (New York, 1968); Peter N. Stearns, *Fat History* (New York, 2002), pp. 71–97.

44 Waldo, *Myra Waldo's Round-the-World Diet Cookbook*, p. 43.

45 Ibid., pp. 44, 56.

46 'More Adventure in Eating', *Los Angeles Times* (16 November 1967), p. G24; Myra Waldo, *The International Encyclopedia of Cooking*, 2 vols (New York, 1967).

47 'An Atlas of Recipes from Aal to Zythum', *Arizona Republic* (15 November 1967), p. 22D.

48 'More Adventure in Eating'.

49 Waldo, *International Encyclopedia*, vol. II, p. 193.

50 Myra Waldo, *Myra Waldo's Restaurant Guide to New York City and Vicinity* [1971] (New York, 1976), pp. v–ix, 96–7; Krishnendu Ray, *The Ethnic Restaurateur* (London, 2016).

51 Waldo, *Myra Waldo's Restaurant Guide*, pp. 124, 242, 391–2.

52 Ibid., pp. 357, 404.

53 'Books that Make You Soar', *Pan Am* (December 1973), p. 38.

11 InterContinental

1 'The Little Woman Discovers South America' and 'Mr. Big Learns to Live' (1 April 1954), Pan Am Papers (PA), Series I, Box 383, Folder 4.

2 Oscar Schisgall, 'American Hotels: Cradle of Prosperity', PA, Series II, Box 314, Folder 32; 'Inter-Continental Hotels, A History of the Corporation' (*c.* 1967), PA, Series II, Box 578, Folder 18; and 'How Pan Am Launched and Operates Its Big Inter-Continental Hotel Chain', *Inter-Continental Hotels News*, 3 (May/June 1967), p. 1, PA, Series II; Box 314, Folder 2.

3 'W. I. Bond to Wallace S. Whittaker' (7 September 1950) and 'Notes on the Philippines' (3 September 1949), PA, Series II, Box 253, Folder 5.

4 'Vice President Bixby to President' (19 May 1950), PA, Series II, Box 253, Folder 5.

5 'A Plan to Meet Present Acute Worldwide Shortage of Modern Hotel Accommodations' (*c.* 1955), PA, Series I, Box 63, Folder 9.

6 'Address, Impact of the Jet Age Upon the Hotel Industry, Delivered by Mr Peter Grimm at Cornell University' ('Extension of Remarks of Hon. Isidore Dollinger'), *Congressional Record, Proceedings and Debates of the 85th Congress, First Session* (15 May 1957), PA, Series I, Box 63, Folder 8.

7 'Intercontinental Hotels Corporation to Hon. Pio Pedrosa, Secretary of Finance' (22 June 1949), PA, Series I, Box 253, Folder 5.

8 'H. Bixby to Eugene H. Clay, United States Embassy' (16 July 1949), PA, Series II, Box 253, Folder 5; 'A Plan to Meet Present Acute Worldwide Shortage of Modern Hotel Accommodations' (*c.* 1955), PA, Series I, Box 63, Folder 9.

9 'W. I. Bond to Wallace S. Whittaker' (7 September 1950); 'Lease Suggested as Manila Hotel Near Bankruptcy' (16 December 1953); and 'H. M. Bixby to Admiral Towers' (17 July 1949), PA, Series I, Box 253, Folder 6.

10 'Amos Hiatt to H. M. Bixby' (2 July 1953); 'J. Oppenheimer to H. M. Bixby' (7 December 1953); and 'J. Oppenheimer to H. M. Bixby' (24 February and 5 March 1954), PA, Series I, Box 253, Folder 6; 'Announce Terms of Lease', *Manila Bulletin* (5 March 1954), p. 2.

11 'Lease Suggested as Manila Hotel Near Bankruptcy' (16 December 1953); and 'H. M. Bixby to Roy W. Howard' (14 January 1954), PA, Series I, Box 253, Folder 6.

12 'PAA Brings New Clippers to Colombia; Hotel Planned' (10 September 1948), PA, Series I, Box 343, Folder 12.

13 'PAA Sponsors Hotels for Latin America' (14 March 1949), PA, Series I, Box 383, Folder 4, pp. 1–3.

14 'Intercontinental Hotels Goes into Dress Rehearsal for Opening of the New Victoria Plaza' (5 December 1952); 'Hotel Victoria Plaza, Montevideo' (*c.* 1950), PA, Series I, Box 343, Folder 12.

15 'InterContinental Hotels Public Relations' (26 April 1967), Series I, Box 342, Folder 8.

16 'Intercontinental Hotels Goes into Dress Rehearsal for Opening of the New Victoria Plaza'.

17 'Building a Kitchen' (December 1952), PA, Series I, Box 383, Folder 4.

18 Lucius Beebe, 'Along the Boulevards', *Gourmet* (July 1946).

19 'Intercontinental Hotels Goes into Dress Rehearsal for Opening of the New Victoria Plaza'.

20 Max Hampton, *Throw Away the Key* (Indianapolis, IN, 1966), pp. 13–15.

21 Ibid., pp. 190–93.

22 Intercontinental Hotels Corp., 'Proposed Hotel Karachi' (September 1956); and 'M. L. Dayton to Yousuf Haroon' (28 September 1956), PA, Series II, Box 12, Folder 15.

23 'Enterprise and Diplomacy', *Wall Street Journal* (14 April 1964), PA, Series II, Box 206, Folder 10.

24 John Crosby, 'Third-Strike Tourism', *New York Herald Tribune* (13 May 1964), PA, Series II, Box 206, Folder 10.

25 'Intercontinental Hotels Corporation, Origin and Background' (n.d.), PA, Series II, Box 383, Folder 4.

26 'InterContinental Hotels Public Relations' (26 April 1967), PA, Series I, Box 342, Folder 8; 'Intercontinental Hotels Corporation – A Brief Sketch' (June 1958), PA, Series 'I' Box 383, Folder 4.

27 Intercontinental Hotels Corp., 'Proposed Hotel Karachi' (September 1956), PA, Series II, Box 12, Folder 15; 'Inter-Continental Hotels, A History of the Corporation' (*c.* 1967), Series II, Box 578, Folder 18.

28 Hampton, *Throw Away the Key*, pp. 191–2.

29 'Hotel Karachi Intercontinental' (n.d.), PA, Series II, Box 578, Folder 20; 'Proposed Hotel Karachi'; 'Hotel Karachi Intercontinental Opens May 10' (*c.* 1964), Series I, Box 343, Folder 15.

30 Hampton, *Throw Away the Key*, p. 192.

31 'Intercontinental Hotels Corporation to Open New $8,750,000, 400-Room Hotel in Bogotá' (*c.* 1953), PA, Series I, Box 343, Folder 12; 'For Immediate Release' (*c.* 1950), PA, Series I, Box 343, Folder 12.

32 'Furniture Airlift Flown to Bogota' (24 February 1953), PA, Series I, Box 343, Folder 12.

33 Schisgall, 'American Hotels: Cradle of Prosperity'.

34 'Hotel Tequendama Affair' (24 September 1963), PA, Series II, Box 907, Folder 9.

35 'Damages for Four Million in the Hotel Tequendama Affair (Translation)' (24 September 1963); 'Default at Hotel Teequendama Denounced!', trans. *El Espectador* (14 September 1963); and 'Erwin Balluder to George Ellsworth' (30 September 1963), PA, Series II, Box 907, Folder 9.

36 'Tequendama – Renegotiation of Contract' (27 September 1963); 'Erwin Balluder to Hernando Castilla-Samper' (21 October 1963); and 'Re: Tequendama' (17 October 1963), PA, Series II, Box 907, Folder 9.

37 'Gus Romea to Robert Huyot' (30 October 1963); 'Erwin Balluder to John B. Gates' (30 September 1963); and 'Telegram, John B. Gates to Erwin Balluder' (30 October 1963), PA, Series II, Box 907, Folder 9.

38 'Minutes of Department Heads' (4 November 1963); 'Gus Romea to Robert Huyot' (8 November 1963); and 'Minutes of Department Heads' (4 November 1963), PA, Series II, Box 907, Folder 9.

39 'Gus Romea to Robert Huyot, Relations with Owners' (18 October 1963), PA, Series II, Box 907, Folder 9.

40 'A Message from the Gen. Manager', *Ducor Society Bulletin* (14 January 1966), p. 1, PA, Series II, Box 318, Folder 15.

41 'Ducor Club' (May 13, 1966), p. 1 and 'Resort-Hopping on African Hump', *New York Courier* (15 September 1962), PA, Series II, Box 318, Folder 16; 'In Operation' (*c.* 1965), PA, Series II, Box 318, Folder 15.

42 'What's On at the Ducor', *Ducor Society Bulletin* (13 May 1966), p. 2, PA, Series II, Box 318, Folder 15.

43 'Philippine Night at La Parisienne', *Ducor Society Bulletin* (24 May 1965), p. 2, PA, Series II, Box 318, Folder 16; and 'Enterprise and Diplomacy', PA, Series II, Box 206, Folder 10.

44 'Focus on Ducor', *Ducor Society Bulletin* (6 May 1966), PA, Series II, Box 318, Folder 15.

45 'InterContinental Hotels Public Relations' (26 April 1967), PA, Series I, Box 342, Folder 8; 'Mrs Opral Benson Picks a Winner', *Ducor Society Bulletin* (25 February 1966), PA, Series II, Box 318, Folder 15.

46 '28,500 Guests Lodged at the Ducor', *Ducor Society Bulletin* (14 January 1966), p. 2, PA, Series II, Box 318, Folder 15.

47 'Guest's Opinion' and 'Dine at the Ducor' (25 February 1966), p. 2, PA, Series II, Box 318, Folder 15.

48 'Culinary Showcases', *Intercontinental News*, 1 (July/August 1965), p. 5.

49 'Intercontinental Hotels Feature International Menus' (*c.* 1963), PA, Series II, Box 206, Folder 9.

50 'Map of Liberia in Candy', *Ducor Society Bulletin* (14 January 1966), p. 2, and 'A Message from the Gen. Manager', *Ducor Society Bulletin* (14 January 1966), p. 1, PA, Series II, Box 318, Folder 15.

51 'Enterprise and Diplomacy'.

52 'Workers Sacked for Rudeness and Absences', *Liberian Star* (6 May 1965), PA, Series II, Box 318, Folder 16.

53 'Ducor Workers' Union Illegal – Gilmore', *Daily Listener* (5 May 1965); 'Ducor African Workers Union Elects Officers', *Liberian Star* (6 May 1965), PA, Series II, Box 318, Folder 16.

54 'National Iron Ore Company Honours Chief Executive', *Liberian Star* (17 May 1965), PA, Series II, Box 318, Folder 16.

55 Robert Huyot, 'No Job is Unimportant', *Intercontinental News*, 3 (May/June 1967), p. 3.

56 'Monrovia', *Intercontinental News*, IV/3 (1968), p. 13.

57 'Inter-Continental Publishes Its Gourmet Cookbook', *Inter-Continental News*, 3 (May/June 1967), pp. 1, 3; Myra Waldo, *Inter-Continental Gourmet Cookbook* (New York, 1967).

58 'Globetrotter's Cookbook Lifts Lids of 36 Pots', *Pan American Clipper*, 27 (15 June 1967), p. 3.

12 Hilton and Trader Vic's

1 'Nikita's Wife Spends Happy Day: Shopping', *Chicago Daily Tribune* (22 September 1959), p. 4F.

2 'Passport to Fine Dining', *Hilton Items* (January 1960), p. 22.

3 Conrad N. Hilton, *Be My Guest, Autobiography of Conrad Hilton* (New York, 1958); 'Hilton Hotels Corporation, Statistics' (March 1964), Hilton Hotels International Papers (HHI), Box 6, Folder 8; 'President's Corner', *Hilton Items* (July 1956), p. 21.

4 'President's Corner', *Hilton Items* (January 1962), p. 20.

5 'The Battle for Freedom', *Hilton Items* (November 1950), pp. 8–9; 'The President's Corner', *Hilton Items* (January 1952), p. 2; Conrad Hilton, 'America on Its Knees' (7 May 1952), HHI, Box 7, Folder 7; 'James T. Meredith to Edward J. Bartus' (29 December 1961), HHI, Box 82, Folder 5.

6 'Hilton Hotels International, Inc, Comparative Summary of Profit and Logs by Operating Units' (*c.* 1958), HHI, Box 6, Folder 10; 'Hilton Hotels Corporation Statistics' (March 1964), HHI, Box 6, Folder 8.

7 'The President's Corner' (January 1952), p. 2; 'President's Corner', *Hilton Items* (July 1956), p. 2; 'President's Corner', *Hilton Items* (May 1958), pp. 2–3.

8 George Seddon, 'Keeping Up with the Hiltons' (*c.* 1963); 'Proposed Schedule of Openings and Other Ceremonies May 24 to July 1, 1963', Conrad N. Hilton Papers (CNH), Box 202, Folder 1.

9 'President's Corner' (July 1956), p. 2; 'President's Corner' (January 1962), p. 20; Conrad N. Hilton, 'Toward a Foreign Policy for Hotels, An Address Before the Los Angeles Rotary Club' (27 July 1956), HHI, Box 6, Folder 1.

10 'President's Corner', *Hilton Items* (June 1954), p. 4.

11 Bill Cunningham, 'Hilton Spreading Foreign Aid', *Boston Sunday Herald* (24 June 1956), HHI, Box 7, Folder 8.

12 'Hilton Hotels Corporation, Statistics' (March 1964), HHI, Box 6, Folder 8; 'Trader Vic's Menu' (*c.* 1950), Randall H. Greenlee Menu Collection, Box 1, Kroch Library, Division of Rare & Manuscript Collections, Cornell University.

13 'Starting a Bergeron Dynasty', *San Francisco Examiner* (6 January 1963) and 'Salty Czar of Cosmo Place', *San Francisco Examiner* (6 January 1963), CNH, Box 215, Folder 'Trader Vic'.

14 Edward J. Mayland, 'Dine in Tropical Splendor at the Traders', Cooking for Profit, 26 (July 1957), pp. 9–11, 18.

15 'Confidential' (20 June 1957), CNH, Legal Series, Box 22; 'Conrad Hilton to Robert Caverly' (22 February 1961), CNH, Box 159, Folder Trader Vic, 1959–62.

16 Victor Bergeron, *Trader Vic's Book of Food and Drink* (Garden City, NY, 1946), p. 91.

17 'King Wong to Victor Bergeron' (2 August 1960); 'Gregory R. Dillon to Conrad N. Hilton' (17 January 1959); 'Hilton Hotels Corporation – The Statler Hilton, Trader Vic's (1960), CNH, Box 159, Folder 'Trader Vic, 1959–62'.

18 'Tiki Gods Stand Watch', *Hilton Items* (September 1961), p. 21.

19 Kay Loring, 'Like Fresh Papaya? You'll Find it at Trader Vic's', *Chicago Tribune* (3 March 1968), p. 1.

20 'The Caravan Tent – A New Night Club at the Nile Hilton', *Hilton Items* (December 1962), pp. 1–2.

21 'Specialty Restaurants: "Gawharet El Nil"', *Hilton Items* (October 1959), p. 20.

22 'Ports O'Call' (menu, n.d.), Hilton Library and Archives; 'War of Exotic Restaurant Chains Comes to a Head in Portland' (26 December 1959); 'Conrad H. Hilton to Victor Bergeron' (11 May 1959); 'Robert J. Caverly to Gregory R. Dillon' (1 May 1959), CNH, Box 159, Folder 'Trader Vic, 1959–62'.

23 'El Panorama Opens at Berlin Hilton', *Hilton Items* (July–August 1959), p. 28.

24 'International Conducts Training Program for Armed Forces Club and Hotel Managers', *Hilton Items* (July–August 1962), pp. 24–5; 'A Night Club Zoo at El Panama Hilton', *Hilton Items* (November 1962), p. 4.

25 Clementine Paddleford, 'An Eating Travelogue: From Here to Hawaii', *New York Herald Tribune* (21 March 1962), p. 18.

26 'TRADER VIC'S', *London Life* (1966), p. 17.

27 Bergeron, *Trader Vic's Book of Food and Drink*, pp. 76–7.

28 Ibid., p. 135.

29 'Menu, Trader Vic's, Savoy Plaza, New York' (1958), Hilton Library and Archives.

30 Alec Waugh, *Hot Countries* (New York, 1930), pp. 2, 35–7, 129.

31 Alec Waugh, *In Praise of Wine and Certain Noble Spirits* (New York, 1959), p. 183.

32 Ibid., pp. 185–6.

33 Harry L. Foster, *A Vagabond in Fiji* (New York, 1927), pp. 144–6.

34 Ibid., pp. 286–90.

35 Teresia Teaiwa, 'Reading Gauguin's Noa Noa with Hau'ofa's Nederends: "Militourism," Feminism, and the "Polynesian" Body', in *Inside Out: Literature, Cultural Politics, and Identity in the New Pacific*, ed. Vilsoni Hereniko and Rob Wilson (Lanham, MD, 1999); Vernadette Vicuña Gonzalez, *Securing Paradise: Tourism and Militarism in Hawai'i and the Philippines* (Durham, NC, 2013).

36 'Tiki Gods Stand Watch', p. 21.

37 James Michener, *Tales of the South Pacific* (New York, 1950), p. 45.

38 Ibid., pp. 218–23, 259, 275.

39 Bergeron, *Trader Vic's Book of Food and Drink*, pp. 17, 75, 135–6.

40 Ibid., pp. 139–40.

41 Trader Vic, *The Menehunes* (Garden City, NY, 1972).

42 'It Happens Every Day', *Hilton Items* (July–August 1957), p. 2.

43 'The Royal Tehran Hilton: Home Sweet Home for Four Iranian Boys', *Hilton Items* (May–June 1964), p. 5.

44 'Warren R. Broglie to Arthur Forrestal' (1 October 1958), HHI, Box 12, Folder 7.

45 'President's Corner' (January 1962), p. 20.

46 'James R. Lage to Barron Hilton' (26 June 1969); 'Nile Hilton, Questionnaire' (June 1969), HHI, Box 12, Folder 12.

47 'Mrs D. R. Hillard to Conrad Hilton' (12 August 1963) and 'Marylin H. Hashashibi to Conrad Hilton' (5 September 1963), HHI, Box 12, Folder 14.

48 'Mary E. Clemsha to Conrad Hilton' (March 1962), HHI, Box 12, Folder 14.

49 'Walter W. Warren to Conrad Hilton' (29 March 1962); 'D. J. Neale to
   Conrad N. Hilton' (23 May 1962); 'John R. McTurk to Mervin Alembik'
   (7 September 1962), CNH, Box 132, Folder 1.

50 'D. J. Neale to Conrad N. Hilton' (23 May 1962); 'John R. McTurk to Mervin
   Alembik' (7 September 1962), CNH, Box 132, Folder 1.

51 'Evelyn Rosenthal to Conrad Hilton' (12 February 1962), CNH, Box 132,
   Folder 1.

52 'Ray Teal to Conrad Hilton' (12 April, n.d.), CNH, Box 203, Folder 3.

53 'Conrad N. Hilton Comments on Havana Hotel Situation' (15 June 1960),
   CNH, Box 16, Folder 8.

54 'Conrad Hilton to Bergeron' (21 January 1959), CNH, Box 159, Folder 'Trader
   Vic, 1959–62'; Annabel Jane Wharton, *Building the Cold War: Hilton
   International Hotels and Modern Architecture* (Chicago, IL, 2001); Robert A
   Davidson, *The Hotel: Occupied Space* (Toronto, 2018), pp. 7–46.

55 'José A. Menendez to Conrad Hilton' (29 January 1959), CNH, Box 159,
   Folder 'Trader Vic, 1959–62'.

56 'News Release: Castro Assures Welcome to American Tourists'
   (10–13 January 1959), CNH, Box 16, Folder 7.

57 'Robert J. Caverly to Conrad N. Hilton' (11 February 1959), CNH, Papers,
   Box 16, Folder 5; 'A Message from Trader Vic' (c. 1959), CNH, Box 159,
   Folder 'Trader Vic, 1959–62'.

58 'Keith Hardman to Chan Wong' (16 January 1959); 'Conrad N. Hilton to
   Victor Bergeron' (10 March 1959), CNH, Box 159, Folder 'Trader Vic, 1959–
   62'.

59 'Keith Hardman to Chan Wong' (7 March 1959), CNH, Box 159, Folder
   'Trader Vic, 1959–62'; Krista Thompson, *An Eye for the Tropics: Tourism,
   Photography, and Framing the Caribbean Picturesque* (Durham, NC, 2006).

60 'Keith Hardman to Chan Wong' (4 May 1959), CNH, Box 159, Folder 'Trader
   Vic, 1959–62'.

61 'Keith Hardman to Chan Wong' (23 May 1959), CNH, Box 159, Folder 'Trader
   Vic, 1959–62'.

Conclusion

1 Anthony Bourdain, *A Cook's Tour: In Search of the Perfect Meal* (New York,
   2002; Kindle edn, 2010); *A Cook's Tour* (TV series), 'Cobra Heart-Foods that
   Make You Manly' (Episode 3, 2002); Alison Hope Alkon and Rafi Grosglik,
   'Eating (with) the Other: Race in American Food Television', *Gastronomica*,
   XXI/2 (2021), pp. 1–12.

2 Joyce E. Chaplin, *Round About the Earth: Circumnavigation from Magellan to
   Orbit* (New York, 2012), pp. 378–82; Signe Rousseau, *Food Media: Celebrity
   Chefs and the Politics of Everyday Interference* (London, 2012).

3 Bourdain, *A Cook's Tour*, 'Very, Very Strong' (Kindle edn).

4 'Personal Data Sheet – Jimmy Bedford – January 1958', Jimmy Bedford
   Collection, University of Alaska Fairbanks (JB), Box 9.

5 'Jimmy Bedford to Gardner Cowles' (31 October 1959), JB, Box 3.

6 'Jimmy Bedford to Lewis W. Gillenson' (23 October 1959), JB, Box 3.

7 'Meals I've Et' (n.d.), JB, Box 3.

8 Jimmy Bedford, *Around the World on a Nickel* (New Delhi, 1967), pp. 111, 123.

9 'Sunday Dinner Around the World, Some Comical and Astronomical Gastronomical Tales of My Cast Iron Stomach' (*c.* 1959), JB, Box 3.
10 'Around the World on Sixpence' (n.d.), JB, Box 9; 'Photo Caption Material' (*c.* 1959), JB, Box 3; 'Gourmet's Diary' (n.d.), JB, Box 9; 'Circling the Globe on a Nickel', *Kansas City Star* (n.d., clipping), JB, Box 2; 'Meals I've Et'.
11 'Around the World on Sixpence'.
12 'Sunday Dinner Around the World'.
13 Bedford, *Around the World on a Nickel*, pp. 286, 291–3.
14 '50,000 Miles from Lawrence to Topeka' (*c.* 1959), JB, Box 3.
15 'Traveller' (*c.* 1959), JB, Box 3.
16 Wendy Myers, *Seven League Boots* (London, 1969), p. 232.
17 Douglas Brown, *Overland to Asia* (New York, 1971), pp. 1–2.
18 Tony Wheeler, *Across Asia on the Cheap* (Melbourne, 1975), p. 20.
19 Tony and Maureen Wheeler, *Unlikely Destinations: The Lonely Planet Story* (Singapore, 2005), pp. 10–18.
20 Ibid., pp. 1, 19–24, 30–31.
21 Wheeler, *Across Asia on the Cheap*, pp. 17–19.
22 Anthony Bourdain, *No Reservations: Around the World on an Empty Stomach* (New York, 2007), p. 277.
23 Don George, ed., *A Moveable Feast: Life-Changing Food Adventures Around the World* (Melbourne, 2010).
24 Bourdain, *No Reservations*, pp. 254, 278–9.
25 Bourdain, *A Cook's Tour*, 'Wild Delicacies' (Episode 5, 2002).
26 Bourdain, *A Cook's Tour*, 'Road to Pailin' (Kindle edn).

FURTHER READING

Arnold, David, *The Tropics and the Traveling Gaze: India, Landscape, and Science,*
  1800–1856 (Delhi, 2005)
Chaplin, Joyce E., *Round About the Earth: Circumnavigation from Magellan*
  to Orbit (New York, 2012)
Davidson, Robert A., *The Hotel: Occupied Space* (Toronto, 2018)
Drayton, Richard Harry, *Nature's Government: Science, Imperial Britain,*
  and the 'Improvement' of the World (New Haven, CT, 2000)
Enloe, Cynthia, *Bananas, Beaches, and Bases: Making Feminist Sense of*
  International Politics (Berkeley, CA, 2014)
Fullagar, Simone, Kevin Markwell and Erica Wilson, eds, *Slow Tourism:*
  Experiences and Mobilities (Bristol, 2012)
Gonzalez, Vernadette Vicuña, *Securing Paradise: Tourism and Militarism*
  in Hawai'i and the Philippines (Durham, NC, 2013)
Heldke, Lisa M., *Exotic Appetites: Ruminations of a Food Adventurer*
  (New York, 2003)
hooks, bell, *Black Looks: Race and Representation* (Boston, MA, 1992)
Horton, Carol A., *Race and the Making of American Liberalism*
  (Oxford, 2005)
Janes, Lauren, *Colonial Food in Interwar Paris: The Taste of Empire* (London, 2016)
Johnston, Josée, and Shyon Baumann, *Foodies: Democracy and Distinction in the*
  Gourmet Foodscape (New York, 2010)
Korsmeyer, Carolyn, *Savoring Disgust: The Foul and the Fair in Aesthetics*
  (Oxford, 2011)
Kuehn, Julia, and Douglas Kerr, eds, *A Century of Travels in China: A Collection*
  of Critical Essays on Travel Writing from the 1840s to the 1940s
  (Hong Kong, 2007)
Lake, Marilyn, and Henry Reynolds, *Drawing the Global Colour Line: White*
  Men's Countries and the International Challenge of Racial Equality
  (Cambridge, 2008)
Leong-Salobir, Cecilia, *Food Culture in Colonial Asia: A Taste of Empire*
  (London, 2011)
Locher-Scholten, Elsbeth, *Women and the Colonial State. Essays on Gender*
  and Modernity in the Netherlands Indies, 1900–1942 (Amsterdam, 2000)
Long, Lucy M., *Culinary Tourism* (Lexington, KY, 2004)
MacCannell, Dean, *The Tourist: A New Theory of the Leisure Class* [1976]
  (Berkeley, CA, 2013)

Okihiro, Gary Y., *Pineapple Culture: A History of the Tropical and Temperate Zones* (Berkeley, CA, 2009)

Orquiza, René Alexander D. Jr, *Taste of Control: Food and the Filipino Colonial Mentality Under American Rule* (New Brunswick, NJ, 2020)

Pratt, Mary Louise, *Imperial Eyes: Travel Writing and Transculturation* (London, 1992)

Rath, Eric C., *Food and Fantasy in Early Modern Japan* (Berkeley, CA, 2010)

Ray, Krishnendu, *The Ethnic Restaurateur* (London, 2016)

Rotter, Andrew Jon, *Empires of the Senses: Bodily Encounters in Imperial India and the Philippines* (Oxford, 2019)

Rousseau, Signe, *Food Media: Celebrity Chefs and the Politics of Everyday Interference* (London, 2012)

Roy, Rohan Deb, *Malarial Subjects: Empire, Medicine and Nonhumans in British India, 1820–1909* (Cambridge, 2017)

Schivelbusch, Wolfgang, *The Railway Journey: The Industrialization of Time and Space in the Nineteenth Century* [1977] (Berkeley, CA, 2014)

Stone, Daniel, *The Food Explorer: The True Adventures of the Globe-Trotting Botanist Who Transformed What America Eats* (New York, 2018)

Thompson, Krista, *An Eye for the Tropics: Tourism, Photography, and Framing the Caribbean Picturesque* (Durham, NC, 2006)

Urry, John, *The Tourist Gaze: Leisure and Travel in Contemporary Societies* (London, 1990)

Van Vleck, Jenifer, *Empire of the Air: Aviation and the American Ascendancy* (Cambridge, 2013)

Wharton, Annabel Jane, *Building the Cold War: Hilton International Hotels and Modern Architecture* (Chicago, IL, 2001)

Zuelow, Eric G. E., *A History of Modern Tourism* (London, 2015)

ACKNOWLEDGEMENTS

Writing food history is travel, and I'm deeply grateful to librarians and archivists all around the world. For this book, I traced my own itinerary with stops in London, Houston, Singapore, New York, Bologna, Turin, Pollenzo, Chicago, Amsterdam and Miami, following food adventurers. I am especially grateful to my friends, colleagues, students, former students, postdoctoral fellows and dinner companions at *Gastronomica: The Journal for Food Studies* and at the University of Toronto, Culinaria Research Centre. They have made this journey possible. Then I came home to my family: my parents Carl and Jessica and my brother Michael. And, to my wife and daughter, these are the happiest words I ever write in a book: 'To Jo and Piya with love.'

PHOTO ACKNOWLEDGEMENTS

The author and publishers wish to express their thanks to the below sources of illustrative material and/or permission to reproduce it:

From Comte de Beauvoir, *Java, Siam, Canton: Voyage autour du monde* (Paris, 1872), photo collection of the author: p. 53; collection of the author: pp. 11, 122, 129, 143, 161, 166, 175; courtesy of The Culinary Institute of America Menu Collection, Conrad N. Hilton Library, Hyde Park, NY: pp. 66, 69; from William G. Frizell and George H. Greenfield, *Around the World on the Cleveland* (Dayton, OH, 1910), photos collection of the author: pp. 67, 133; Leiden University Libraries (Special Collections Services, KITLV 182142): p. 214; Nationaal Archief, The Hague: p. 283; Nationaal Museum van Wereldculturen (TM-10013732): p. 211; National Museum of American History, Smithsonian Institution, Washington, DC (gift of University of Michigan Medical School, Department of Microbiology, acc. no. 253100): p. 86; The New York Public Library: p. 196; Österreichische Nationalbibliothek, Vienna (NB 504.188-B), photo ÖNB: p. 22; Royal Geographical Society, London (Edith A. James Collection): pp. 139, 153; from Eliza Ruhamah Scidmore, *Java, the Garden of the East* (New York, 1897), photos collection of the author: pp. 80, 171; Smithsonian Institution Archives, Washington, DC (William M. Mann and Lucile Quarry Mann Papers, SIA2016-008614): p. 125; from *The Supreme Travel Adventure: Around the World in the 'Franconia' 1929* (n.p., 1928), photo collection of the author: p. 9; courtesy of University of Houston, TX (Hilton Library and Archives): pp. 278, 279, 282, 289, 291, 292; courtesy of University of Miami Libraries, Coral Gables, FL (Special Collections): pp. 225, 229, 235, 237, 254, 256, 257, 260, 266, 267, 269; courtesy of University of Michigan Library, Ann Arbor (Harry Alverson Franck Photographs, Special Collections Research Center): pp. 103, 104, 108, 111.

INDEX

Page numbers in *italics* indicate illustrations